PC Technician Stree

A Real World Guide to CompTIA A+® Skills

Second Edition

PC Technician Street Smarts

A Real World Guide to CompTIA A+® Skills

Second Edition

James Pyles

WILEY

Wiley Publishing, Inc.

Acquisitions Editor: Jeff Kellum
Development Editor: Amy Breguet
Technical Editor: Neil Hester
Production Editor: Christine O'Connor
Copy Editor: Liz Welch
Editorial Manager: Pete Gaughan
Production Manager: Tim Tate
Vice President and Executive Group Publisher: Richard Swadley
Vice President and Publisher: Neil Edde
Book Designers: Judy Fung and Bill Gibson
Compositor: Jeff Lytle, Happenstance Type-O-Rama
Proofreader: Candace English
Indexer: Robert Swanson
Project Coordinator, Cover: Lynsey Stanford
Cover Designer: Ryan Sneed

Copyright © 2009 by Wiley Publishing, Inc., Indianapolis, Indiana

Published simultaneously in Canada

ISBN: 978-0-470-48651-1

For general information on our other products and services or to obtain technical support, please contact our Customer Care Department within the U.S. at (877) 762-2974, outside the U.S. at (317) 572-3993 or fax (317) 572-4002.

Wiley also publishes its books in a variety of electronic formats. Some content that appears in print may not be available in electronic books.

Library of Congress Cataloging-in-Publication Data

Pyles, James.

 PC technician street smarts : a real world guide to CompTIA A+ skills / James Pyles. — 2nd ed.
   p. cm.
 ISBN 978-0-470-48651-1 (pbk.)
 1. Electronic data processing personnel—Certification. 2. Computer technicians—Certification—Study guides. 3. Microcomputers—Maintenance and repair—Examinations—Study guides. 4. Computing Technology Industry Association—Examinations—Study guides. I. Title.
 QA76.3.P95 2009
 004.16--dc22
                              2009027778

10 9 8 7 6 5 4 3 2 1

Dear Reader,

Thank you for choosing *PC Technician Street Smarts: A Real World Guide to CompTIA A+ Skills, Second Edition*. This book is part of a family of premium-quality Sybex books, all of which are written by outstanding authors who combine practical experience with a gift for teaching.

Sybex was founded in 1976. More than 30 years later, we're still committed to producing consistently exceptional books. With each of our titles, we're working hard to set a new standard for the industry. From the paper we print on, to the authors we work with, our goal is to bring you the best books available.

I hope you see all that reflected in these pages. I'd be very interested to hear your comments and get your feedback on how we're doing. Feel free to let me know what you think about this or any other Sybex book by sending me an email at nedde@wiley.com. If you think you've found a technical error in this book, please visit http://sybex.custhelp.com. Customer feedback is critical to our efforts at Sybex.

Best regards,

Neil Edde
Vice President and Publisher
Sybex, an Imprint of Wiley

To my infant grandson Landon James, who is the newest light in my world.

Acknowledgments

No one writes a book alone. While my name may be on the cover as the author, a small army of people has been responsible for reviewing every word and image that appears in this book. Before I even knew that a second edition of PC Technician Street Smarts was being conceived, Jeff Kellum and the fine folks at Sybex were hard at work arranging for the book you now hold in your hands to come into existence. My special thanks go to everyone who has been involved in this book and has supported me in this endeavor.

My agent at Waterside Publications, Carole McClendon, who always finds the right projects for me at the right time.

Jeff Kellum, who first introduced me to the Street Smarts series and continues to put up with me by letting me write this book.

Kudos to development editor Amy Breguet for being able to see all of the little details in my writing that needed fixing. Thanks to Neil Hester, who was the technical reviewer on this book's first edition and continues to keep me on the straight and narrow. Also thanks to copy editor Liz Welch and production editor Christine O'Connor, who have toiled long hours in going over the pages of this book and making wise suggestions.

I have also depended again on the gang over at CertForums.co.uk for letting me bounce ideas off their collective heads and presenting some of the puzzles and solutions that added flavor to this book.

Finally, thanks to my wife, Lin, who graciously let me spend incalculable hours in my lair writing this second edition when I should have been mowing the lawn. Since she decided to take an Office 2007 class, I've also had ample opportunity to act as her personal help desk whenever Word or Excel didn't behave well.

About the Author

James Pyles, A+, Network+, has worked as a freelance consultant, technical writer, and editor. He has been involved in numerous Ethernet rollout projects, as well as many software and hardware installations. He has provided support services for a city-government IT department and a wireless-network vendor; supported a usability lab for Hewlett-Packard (HP); and served as a technical writer for EmergeCore Networks, Aquent Studios, and Sybase iAnywhere, and as a developmental editor for Global Support Content Operations at HP.

His most recent book is *MCTS: Microsoft Office SharePoint Server 2007 Configuration Study Guide: Exam 70-630* (Sybex, 2008). He has also authored *SharePoint 2007: The Definitive Guide* (O'Reilly, 2007) and *PC Technician Street Smarts, 1st ed.* (Sybex, 2006). Additionally, he was the technical editor for *SharePoint for Project Management* (O'Reilly, 2008) and *Essential SharePoint 2007, 2nd ed.* (O'Reilly, 2008).

James is a regular contributor to *Linux Magazine* and *Ubuntu User Magazine.* He has bachelor's degrees in psychology and computer network support and a master's degree in counseling. James currently works as a technical writer for Keynetics, Inc.

Contents at a Glance

Introduction   *xxix*

Phase 1   Installing Hardware and Software   1

Phase 2   Maintaining and Documenting Computer Systems   141

Phase 3   Networking Computer Systems   239

Phase 4   Troubleshooting and Restoring Computer Systems   309

Index   *409*

Contents

Introduction   *xxix*

Phase   1   Installing Hardware and Software   **1**

Task 1.1: Preventing ESD Damage   2
    Scenario   3
    Scope of Task   3
    Procedure   3
    Criteria for Completion   4
Task 1.2: Installing RAM   5
    Scenario   5
    Scope of Task   5
    Procedure   6
    Criteria for Completion   10
Task 1.3: Installing a PCI Card   10
    Scenario   11
    Scope of Task   11
    Procedure   12
    Criteria for Completion   13
Task 1.4: Installing a PCI Express Card   14
    Scenario   14
    Scope of Task   14
    Procedure   15
    Criteria for Completion   17
Task 1.5: Installing a CPU   17
    Scenario   17
    Scope of Task   18
    Procedure   19
    Criteria for Completion   21
Task 1.6: Installing a Power Supply   22
    Scenario   22
    Scope of Task   22
    Procedure   23
    Criteria for Completion   24
Task 1.7: Installing an IDE Hard Drive   25
    Scenario   25
    Scope of Task   25
    Procedure   26
    Criteria for Completion   28
Task 1.8: Installing a SATA Hard Drive   28
    Scenario   28

Scope of Task 29
Procedure 30
Criteria for Completion 32
Task 1.9: Installing a SCSI Drive 32
Scenario 32
Scope of Task 32
Procedure 33
Criteria for Completion 35
Task 1.10: Installing a CD Drive 35
Scenario 36
Scope of Task 36
Procedure 37
Criteria for Completion 41
Task 1.11: Installing a DVD Drive 41
Scenario 41
Scope of Task 42
Procedure 42
Criteria for Completion 45
Task 1.12: Installing a Motherboard 45
Scenario 46
Scope of Task 46
Procedure 47
Criteria for Completion 50
Task 1.13: Installing a Video Card 50
Scenario 50
Scope of Task 50
Procedure 51
Criteria for Completion 54
Task 1.14: Installing a Laptop Keyboard 54
Scenario 54
Scope of Task 55
Procedure 55
Criteria for Completion 58
Task 1.15: Installing SO-DIMM in a Laptop 58
Scenario 58
Scope of Task 59
Procedure 59
Criteria for Completion 61
Task 1.16: Installing a Laptop Hard Drive 62
Scenario 62
Scope of Task 62
Procedure 63
Criteria for Completion 64

Task 1.17: Installing a Laptop Optical Drive   64
  Scenario   64
  Scope of Task   65
  Procedure   65
  Criteria for Completion   67
Task 1.18: Installing a Docking Station   67
  Scenario   67
  Scope of Task   67
  Procedure   68
  Criteria for Completion   71
Task 1.19: Installing a KVM Switch   71
  Scenario   71
  Scope of Task   71
  Procedure   72
  Criteria for Completion   74
Task 1.20: Installing a Complete Workstation from the Box   74
  Scenario   75
  Scope of Task   75
  Procedure   76
  Criteria for Completion   79
Task 1.21: Installing Drivers from a Disc   80
  Scenario   80
  Scope of Task   80
  Procedure   80
  Criteria for Completion   82
Task 1.22: Installing Drivers from the Internet   82
  Scenario   83
  Scope of Task   83
  Procedure   83
  Criteria for Completion   85
Task 1.23: Reformatting a Hard Drive   85
  Scenario   85
  Scope of Task   86
  Procedure   86
  Criteria for Completion   88
Task 1.24: Installing Windows XP Professional
as a Fresh Install   89
  Scenario   89
  Scope of Task   89
  Procedure   90
  Criteria for Completion   97
Task 1.25: Installing Windows Vista as a Fresh Install   98
  Scenario   98

Scope of Task	98
Procedure	99
Criteria for Completion	103
Task 1.26: Uninstalling Software	103
Scenario	104
Scope of Task	104
Procedure	104
Criteria for Completion	105
Task 1.27: Installing Microsoft Applications	105
Scenario	105
Scope of Task	106
Procedure	106
Criteria for Completion	108
Task 1.28: Installing Non-Microsoft Applications	108
Scenario	108
Scope of Task	109
Procedure	109
Criteria for Completion	110
Task 1.29: Upgrading Windows 2000 to Windows XP	110
Scenario	111
Scope of Task	111
Procedure	112
Criteria for Completion	115
Task 1.30: Upgrading from Windows XP to Windows Vista	115
Scenario	116
Scope of Task	116
Procedure	117
Criteria for Completion	119
Task 1.31: Using Restore Points in Windows XP	119
Scenario	119
Scope of Task	119
Procedure	120
Criteria for Completion	122
Task 1.32: Shutting Down Programs	122
Scenario	122
Scope of Task	122
Procedure	123
Criteria for Completion	124
Task 1.33: Tweaking Windows XP	125
Scenario	125
Scope of Task	125
Procedure	126
Criteria for Completion	129

Task 1.34: Installing a Local Printer 129
    Scenario 130
    Procedure 130
    Criteria for Completion 134
Task 1.35: Installing Printer Drivers 134
    Scenario 134
    Procedure 135
    Criteria for Completion 136
Task 1.36: Installing a Bluetooth Device in Windows Vista 137
    Scenario 137
    Procedure 138
    Criteria for Completion 139

Phase 2   Maintaining and Documenting Computer Systems 141

Task 2.1: Identifying a Motherboard 142
    Scenario 142
    Scope of Task 143
    Procedure 143
    Criteria for Completion 146
Task 2.2: Identifying a Power Supply 146
    Scenario 146
    Scope of Task 147
    Procedure 147
    Criteria for Completion 148
Task 2.3: Testing and Replacing a Power Supply 148
    Scenario 148
    Scope of Task 149
    Procedure 149
    Criteria for Completion 153
Task 2.4: Managing a Swap File 153
    Scenario 154
    Scope of Task 154
    Procedure 154
    Criteria for Completion 157
Task 2.5: Imaging a Disk 157
    Scenario 157
    Scope of Task 157
    Procedure 158
    Criteria for Completion 160
Task 2.6: Searching for Drivers 160
    Scenario 160
    Scope of Task 161
    Procedure 161
    Criteria for Completion 163

Task 2.7: Searching for Windows Vista Drivers 163
Scenario 163
Scope of Task 164
Procedure 164
Criteria for Completion 165
Task 2.8: Listing All of the Drivers Installed
on a Windows Vista PC 165
Scenario 165
Scope of Task 165
Procedure 166
Criteria for Completion 166
Task 2.9: Cleaning Dust Bunnies out of Computers 167
Scenario 167
Scope of Task 167
Procedure 167
Criteria for Completion 169
Task 2.10: Cleaning out Fans 169
Scenario 169
Scope of Task 169
Procedure 169
Criteria for Completion 171
Task 2.11: Oiling Fans 171
Scenario 171
Scope of Task 171
Procedure 172
Criteria for Completion 174
Task 2.12: Cleaning and Degaussing CRT Monitors 174
Scenario 174
Scope of Task 174
Procedure 175
Criteria for Completion 176
Task 2.13: Cleaning Keyboards, Mice, and PCs 176
Scenario 176
Scope of Task 176
Procedure 177
Criteria for Completion 179
Task 2.14: Defragging a Hard Drive 179
Scenario 180
Scope of Task 180
Procedure 180
Criteria for Completion 182
Task 2.15: Scheduling Automatic Defragging in Windows Vista 182
Scenario 182
Scope of Task 182

Procedure   183
Criteria for Completion   184
Task 2.16: Defragmenting a Single File   184
Scenario   184
Scope of Task   184
Procedure   185
Criteria for Completion   186
Task 2.17: Upgrading a Graphics Card   186
Scenario   186
Scope of Task   187
Procedure   187
Criteria for Completion   189
Task 2.18: Checking and Reseating RAM   189
Scenario   189
Scope of Task   189
Procedure   190
Criteria for Completion   191
Task 2.19: Checking and Reseating PCI and PCI Express Cards   191
Scenario   192
Scope of Task   192
Procedure   192
Criteria for Completion   193
Task 2.20: Checking Internal Connectors   194
Scenario   194
Scope of Task   194
Procedure   194
Criteria for Completion   196
Task 2.21: Speeding Up Windows 2000 Professional   196
Scenario   196
Scope of Task   196
Procedure   197
Criteria for Completion   200
Task 2.22: Flashing the BIOS   200
Scenario   201
Scope of Task   201
Procedure   202
Criteria for Completion   205
Task 2.23: Changing the CMOS Battery to Correct a Slow
PC Clock   205
Scenario   205
Scope of Task   206
Procedure   206
Criteria for Completion   208

Task 2.24: Resetting Passwords   208
  Scenario   209
  Scope of Task   209
  Procedure   210
  Criteria for Completion   211
Task 2.25: Creating a New Local User in Windows Vista   212
  Scenario   212
  Scope of Task   212
  Procedure   213
  Criteria for Completion   213
Task 2.26: Testing Ports with an Online Scanner   214
  Scenario   214
  Scope of Task   214
  Procedure   214
  Criteria for Completion   216
Task 2.27: Changing Printer Toner   216
  Scenario   216
  Scope of Task   217
  Procedure   217
  Criteria for Completion   219
Task 2.28: Scanning a Document Using Windows Vista   219
  Scenario   219
  Scope of Task   220
  Procedure   220
  Criteria for Completion   221
Task 2.29: Managing Windows Startup and Recovery Behavior   222
  Scenario   222
  Scope of Task   222
  Procedure   222
  Criteria for Completion   223
Task 2.30: Performing Asset Management of PCs   223
  Scenario   224
  Scope of Task   224
  Procedure   224
  Criteria for Completion   227
Task 2.31: Performing Asset Management on Inventory   227
  Scenario   228
  Scope of Task   228
  Procedure   228
  Criteria for Completion   230
Task 2.32: Performing Asset Management of a PC's Hardware   230
  Scenario   230
  Scope of Task   230

Procedure   231
Criteria for Completion   234
Task 2.33: Performing Asset Management on a PC's Software   234
Scenario   234
Scope of Task   234
Procedure   235
Criteria for Completion   236
Task 2.34: Tracking Work Done on a PC   236
Scenario   236
Scope of Task   236
Procedure   237
Criteria for Completion   238

Phase   3   Networking Computer Systems   239

Task 3.1: Mapping Drives   240
Scenario   240
Scope of Task   240
Procedure   241
Criteria for Completion   243
Task 3.2: Creating File Shares   243
Scenario   243
Scope of Task   244
Procedure   244
Criteria for Completion   247
Task 3.3: Configuring PCs to Use Dynamic Addressing   247
Scenario   248
Scope of Task   248
Procedure   248
Criteria for Completion   251
Task 3.4: Renewing a Dynamic Address Assignment   251
Scenario   252
Scope of Task   252
Procedure   252
Criteria for Completion   253
Task 3.5: Installing a Network Printer   253
Scenario   254
Scope of Task   254
Procedure   254
Criteria for Completion   257
Task 3.6: Making a Straight-Through Cable   257
Scenario   257
Scope of Task   257
Procedure   258
Criteria for Completion   262

Task 3.7: Making a Crossover Cable 263
Scenario 263
Scope of Task 263
Procedure 263
Criteria for Completion 267
Task 3.8: Testing Network Cables 267
Scenario 267
Scope of Task 267
Procedure 268
Criteria for Completion 268
Task 3.9: Setting Up a Mail Account 269
Scenario 269
Scope of Task 269
Procedure 270
Criteria for Completion 272
Task 3.10: Joining a Computer to a Domain 272
Scenario 272
Scope of Task 272
Procedure 273
Criteria for Completion 276
Task 3.11: Creating a User in Active Directory 276
Scenario 276
Scope of Task 276
Procedure 277
Criteria for Completion 280
Task 3.12: Mapping Network Cables 280
Scenario 280
Scope of Task 280
Procedure 281
Criteria for Completion 284
Task 3.13: Setting Up a Local User ID 285
Scenario 285
Scope of Task 285
Procedure 286
Criteria for Completion 287
Task 3.14: Adding a Network Peripheral-Port Device to a PC 288
Scenario 288
Scope of Task 288
Procedure 289
Criteria for Completion 291
Task 3.15: Setting Up VPN on a PC 292
Scenario 292
Scope of Task 292

Procedure	293
Criteria for Completion	296
Task 3.16: Setting Up Dial-Up Networking	296
Scenario	296
Scope of Task	297
Procedure	297
Criteria for Completion	300
Task 3.17: Connecting a PC to a Network Printer	300
Scenario	300
Scope of Task	300
Procedure	301
Criteria for Completion	303
Task 3.18: Managing Windows Vista Outbound Firewall Settings	303
Scenario	303
Scope of Task	304
Procedure	304
Criteria for Completion	306
Task 3.19: Monitoring Network Activity with the Windows Vista Firewall	306
Scenario	306
Scope of Task	307
Procedure	307
Criteria for Completion	308

Phase   4   Troubleshooting and Restoring Computer Systems 309

Task 4.1: Scanning for and Removing Viruses	310
Scenario	311
Scope of Task	311
Procedure	312
Criteria for Completion	313
Task 4.2: Scanning for and Removing Malware	313
Scenario	313
Scope of Task	314
Procedure	314
Criteria for Completion	317
Task 4.3: Scanning for Rootkits	317
Scenario	317
Scope of Task	318
Procedure	318
Criteria for Completion	319
Task 4.4: Changing Backup Tapes on a Server	320
Scenario	320
Scope of Task	320

Procedure   321
Criteria for Completion   323
Task 4.5: Changing the Backup Schedule on a Server   323
Scenario   323
Scope of Task   323
Procedure   324
Criteria for Completion   325
Task 4.6: Backing Up Outlook   325
Scenario   325
Scope of Task   325
Procedure   326
Criteria for Completion   328
Task 4.7: Quickly Diagnosing Windows Vista Problems   328
Scenario   328
Scope of Task   328
Procedure   329
Criteria for Completion   329
Task 4.8: Troubleshooting a Randomly Rebooting PC   329
Scenario   330
Scope of Task   330
Procedure   330
Criteria for Completion   334
Task 4.9: Troubleshooting an Intermittent Boot Failure of a PC   334
Scenario   334
Scope of Task   334
Procedure   335
Criteria for Completion   337
Task 4.10: Troubleshooting a Failed RAM Upgrade   337
Scenario   337
Scope of Task   338
Procedure   338
Criteria for Completion   340
Task 4.11: Troubleshooting a PC That Can't Print
  to a Local Printer   340
Scenario   341
Scope of Task   341
Procedure   341
Criteria for Completion   344
Task 4.12: Troubleshooting a PC That Can't Print
  to a Network Printer   344
Scenario   344
Scope of Task   344
Procedure   345
Criteria for Completion   349

Task 4.13: Troubleshooting the Error Message
  "The Specified Domain Either Does Not Exist
  or Could Not Be Contacted"   350
    Scenario   350
    Scope of Task   350
    Procedure   351
    Criteria for Completion   356
Task 4.14: Troubleshooting Long Load and Print
  Times for Microsoft Word and Excel   356
    Scenario   356
    Scope of Task   357
    Procedure   357
    Criteria for Completion   359
Task 4.15: Troubleshooting a CD Player Not Recognizing
  Audio CDs   359
    Scenario   360
    Scope of Task   360
    Procedure   360
    Criteria for Completion   363
Task 4.16: Troubleshooting the Error Message
  "Print Processor Unknown"   364
    Scenario   364
    Scope of Task   364
    Procedure   365
    Criteria for Completion   368
Task 4.17: Troubleshooting a "New Hardware Found"
  Message Appearing Repeatedly After Installing a
  New Scanner   368
    Scenario   368
    Scope of Task   368
    Procedure   369
    Criteria for Completion   371
Task 4.18: Troubleshooting the Inability to Connect a
  USB Digital Camera to a PC   371
    Scenario   371
    Scope of Task   371
    Procedure   372
    Criteria for Completion   376
Task 4.19: Troubleshooting an Empty Outlook Contacts Folder   376
    Scenario   376
    Scope of Task   377
    Procedure   377
    Criteria for Completion   379

Task 4.20: Troubleshooting No Restart of UPS Device
  Service After Being Connected   379
    Scenario   380
    Scope of Task   380
    Procedure   380
    Criteria for Completion   384
Task 4.21: Troubleshooting a System Conflict with a
  Hidden Device   384
    Scenario   384
    Scope of Task   385
    Procedure   385
    Criteria for Completion   386
Task 4.22: Troubleshooting Excel Locking Up   386
    Scenario   387
    Scope of Task   387
    Procedure   387
    Criteria for Completion   389
Task 4.23: Troubleshooting No Monitor Image When
  the PC Is Powered Up   389
    Scenario   390
    Scope of Task   390
    Procedure   390
    Criteria for Completion   392
Task 4.24: Troubleshooting the Inability to Connect to
  a Mapped Drive   392
    Scenario   392
    Scope of Task   392
    Procedure   393
    Criteria for Completion   394
Task 4.25: Troubleshooting the Inability to Access a
  Shared Folder on a Remote Computer   394
    Scenario   394
    Scope of Task   394
    Procedure   395
    Criteria for Completion   397
Task 4.26: Troubleshooting the Inability to Connect to
  the Network   397
    Scenario   397
    Scope of Task   397
    Procedure   398
    Criteria for Completion   399
Task 4.27: Troubleshooting Connection Problems with
  an External USB Hard Drive   400
    Scenario   400

Scope of Task   400
Procedure   400
Criteria for Completion   401
Task 4.28: Troubleshooting a 691 Error Connection Problem   401
Scenario   402
Scope of Task   402
Procedure   402
Criteria for Completion   403
Task 4.29: Troubleshooting a Scanner Problem   403
Scenario   403
Scope of Task   404
Procedure   404
Criteria for Completion   405
Task 4.30: Troubleshooting a Persistent "Align
  Print Cartridges" Message After Cartridges Have
  Been Replaced and Aligned   405
Scenario   405
Scope of Task   406
Procedure   406
Criteria for Completion   407

Index   *409*

Introduction

The A+ certification was developed by the Computer Technology Industry Association (CompTIA) to provide an industry-wide means of certifying the competency of computer service technicians in the basics of PC support. According to CompTIA, the A+ certification "confirms a technician's ability to perform tasks such as installation, configuration, diagnosing, preventive maintenance, and basic networking."

Most books targeted toward certification candidates present material for you to memorize before the exam, but this book is different. It guides you through procedures and tasks that solidify related concepts, allowing you to devote your memorization efforts to more abstract theories because you've mastered the more practical topics through doing. Even if you do not aspire to become A+ certified, this book will be a valuable primer for your career as a PC technician.

What Is A+ Certification?

The A+ certification was created to offer an introductory step into the complex world of PC and laptop hardware and software support.

In 2006, CompTIA changed the format of the A+ exam to focus on various job roles, all of which can be rolled into the title of PC technician. A+ candidates must take two exams: the A+ Essentials exam (Exam #220-601)—which covers various concepts—and then one of three elective exams: IT Technician, Remote Support Technician, and Depot Technician (all of which can be referred to as "PC Technician"). Each elective exam maps to a particular specialty emphasis as a support technician.

NOTE The content areas for each exam are the same, but the weighting for each area is different depending on the elective.

For the 2009 certification, CompTIA dropped the job-specific electives, and instead only has two exams: A+ Essentials (Exam #220-701) and Practical Application (Exam #220-702), which focuses on how a technician applies the concepts tested on in the A+ Essentials exam.

Obtaining the A+ certification does not mean you can provide sufficient PC support services to a company. In fact, this is just the first step toward true technical knowledge and experience. Hopefully, by obtaining A+ certification you will be able to acquire more computer-support experience and gain an interest in hardware and software maintenance that will lead you to pursue more complex and in-depth knowledge and certifications.

For the latest pricing on the exam and updates to the registration procedures, call Prometric at (800) 776-4276. You can also go to either http://securereg3.prometric.com/ or www.prometric.com for additional information or to register online. If you have further questions about the scope of the exams or related CompTIA programs, refer to the CompTIA website at www.comptia.org.

Is This Book for You?

PC Technician Street Smarts is designed to give you insight into the world of a typical PC support technician by walking you through some of the daily tasks you can expect on the job. Some investment in equipment is advised to get the full effect from this book. However, much value can be derived from simply reading through the tasks without performing the steps on live equipment. Organized classes and study groups are the ideal structures for obtaining and practicing with the recommended equipment.

 The *CompTIA A+ Complete Study Guide (Exams 220-701 and 220-702)* or *CompTIA A+ Complete Deluxe Study Guide (Exams 220-701 and 220-702)* (Sybex, 2009) is a recommended companion to this book in your studies for the CompTIA A+ certification.

How This Book Is Organized

This book is organized into four phases. Each phase is separated into individual tasks. The phases represent broad categories under which related responsibilities are grouped. The tasks within each phase lead you step-by-step through the processes required for successful completion. When performed in order, the tasks in this book approximate those required by a PC technician over an extended period of time. The four phases and their descriptions follow:

- *Phase 1—Installing Hardware and Software* presents common tasks recommended for most projects involving the installation of hardware and software components on a PC or laptop.

- *Phase 2—Maintaining and Documenting Computer Systems* gives you tools to enable you to provide routine maintenance of computer hardware, operating systems, and peripherals as well as generate the required documentation.

- *Phase 3—Networking Computer Systems* shows you how to perform a series of basic networking tasks in a computing environment.

- *Phase 4—Troubleshooting and Restoring Computer Systems* provides real-world computer and network problems for you to solve. These tasks are derived from the trouble tickets acted upon by PC technicians in an actual production environment.

Each task in this book is organized into sections aimed at giving you what you need when you need it. The first section introduces you to the task and any key concepts that can assist you in understanding the underlying technology and the overall procedure. Descriptions of the remaining sections follow:

- *Scenario*—This section places you in the shoes of the PC support technician, describing a situation in which you will likely find yourself. The scenario is closely related to and often solved by the task at hand.

- *Scope of Task*—This section is all about preparing for the task. It gives you an idea of how much time is required to complete the task, what setup procedure is needed before beginning, and any concerns or issues to look out for.

- *Procedure*—This is the actual meat of the task itself. This section informs you of the equipment required to perform the task in a lab environment. It also gives you the ordered steps to complete the task.

- *Criteria for Completion*—This final section briefly explains the outcome you should expect after completing the task. Any deviation from the result described is an excellent reason to perform the task again and watch for sources of the variation.

How to Contact the Publisher

Sybex welcomes feedback on all of its titles. Visit the Sybex website at www.sybex.com for book updates and additional certification information. You'll also find forms you can use to submit comments or suggestions regarding this or any other Sybex title.

How to Contact the Author

James Pyles welcomes your questions and comments. You can reach him by email at james.pyles@gmail.com.

The A+ Exam Objectives

The A+ exams are made up of the A+ Essentials exam and the Practical Application exam. The following presents the detailed exam objectives of each test.

Exam objectives are subject to change at any time without prior notice and at CompTIA's sole discretion. Please visit the A+ Certification page of CompTIA's web site (www.comptia.org/certifications/listed/a.aspx) for the most current listing of exam objectives.

A+ Essentials 2009 Exam Objectives

The following table lists the domains measured by this examination and the extent to which they are represented on the exam:

Domain	Percentage of Exam
1.0 Hardware	27%
2.0 Troubleshooting, Repair and Maintenance	20%
3.0 Operating Systems and Software	20%
4.0 Networking	15%

Domain	Percentage of Exam
5.0 Security	8%
6.0 Operational Procedures	10%
Total	100%

1.0 Personal Computer Components

1.1 Categorize storage devices and backup media

- FDD
- HDD
  - Solid state vs. magnetic
- Optical drives
  - CD/DVD/RW/Blu-Ray
- Removable storage
  - Tape drive
  - Solid state (e.g. thumb drive, flash, SD cards, USB)
  - External CD-RW and hard drive
  - Hot swappable devices and non-hot swappable devices

1.2 Explain motherboard components, types and features

- Form Factor
  - ATX / BTX,
  - micro ATX
  - NLX
- I/O interfaces
  - Sound
  - Video
  - USB 1.1 and 2.0
  - Serial
  - IEEE 1394 / Firewire
  - Parallel

- NIC
- Modem
- PS/2
- Memory slots
  - RIMM
  - DIMM
  - SODIMM
  - SIMM
- Processor sockets
- Bus architecture
- Bus slots
  - PCI
  - AGP
  - PCIe
  - AMR
  - CNR
  - PCMCIA
- PATA
  - IDE
  - EIDE
- SATA, eSATA
- Contrast RAID (levels 0, 1, 5)
- Chipsets
- BIOS / CMOS / Firmware
  - POST
  - CMOS battery
- Riser card / daughterboard

1.3 Classify power supplies types and characteristics

- AC adapter
- ATX proprietary
- Voltage, wattage and capacity
- Voltage selector switch
- Pins (20, 24)

1.4 Explain the purpose and characteristics of CPUs and their features

- Identify CPU types
    - AMD
    - Intel
- Hyper threading
- Multi core
    - Dual core
    - Triple core
    - Quad core
- Onchip cache
    - L1
    - L2
- Speed (real vs. actual)
- 32bit vs. 64 bit

1.5 Explain cooling methods and devices

- Heat sinks
- CPU and case fans
- Liquid cooling systems
- Thermal compound

1.6 Compare and contrast memory types, characteristics and their purpose

- Types
    - DRAM
    - SRAM
    - SDRAM
    - DDR / DDR2 / DDR3
    - RAMBUS
- Parity vs. Non-parity
- ECC vs. non-ECC
- Single sided vs. double sided
- Single channel vs. dual channel
- Speed
    - PC100
    - PC133
    - PC2700

- PC3200
- DDR3-1600
- DDR2-667

1.7 Distinguish between the different display devices and their characteristics

- Projectors, CRT and LCD
- LCD technologies
  - Resolution (e.g. XGA, SXGA+, UXGA, WUXGA)
  - Contrast ratio
  - Native resolution
- Connector types
  - VGA
  - HDMi
  - S-Video
  - Component / RGB
  - DVI pin compatibility
- Settings
  - Refresh rate
  - Resolution
  - Multi-monitor
  - Degauss

1.8 Install and configure peripherals and input devices

- Mouse
- Keyboard
- Bar code reader
- Multimedia (e.g. web and digital cameras, MIDI, microphones)
- Biometric devices
- Touch screen
- KVM switch

1.9 Summarize the function and types of adapter cards

- Video
  - PCI
  - PCIe
  - AGP

- Multimedia
  - Sound card
  - TV tuner cards
  - Capture cards
- I/O
  - SCSI
  - Serial
  - USB
  - Parallel
- Communications
  - NIC
  - Modem

1.10 Install, configure and optimize laptop components and features

- Expansion devices
  - PCMCIA cards
  - Express bus
  - Docking station
- Communication connections
  - Bluetooth
  - Infrared
  - Cellular WAN
  - Ethernet
  - Modem
- Power and electrical input devices
  - Auto-switching
  - Fixed input power supplies
  - Batteries
- Input devices
  - Stylus / digitizer
  - Function keys
  - Point devices (e.g. touch pad, point stick / track point)

1.11 Install and configure printers

- Differentiate between printer types
  - Laser
  - Inkjet

- ▪ Thermal
- ▪ Impact
- ▪ Local vs. network printers
- ▪ Printer drivers (compatibility)
- ▪ Consumables

2.0 Troubleshooting, Repair and Maintenance

2.1 Given a scenario, explain the troubleshooting theory

- ▪ Identify the problem
  - ▪ Question user and identify user changes to computer and perform backups before making changes
- ▪ Establish a theory of probable cause (question the obvious)
- ▪ Test the theory to determine cause
  - ▪ Once theory is confirmed determine next steps to resolve problem
  - ▪ If theory is not confirmed re-establish new theory or escalate
- ▪ Establish a plan of action to resolve the problem and implement the solution
- ▪ Verify full system functionality and if applicable implement preventative measures
- ▪ Document findings, actions and outcomes

2.2 Given a scenario, explain and interpret common hardware and operating system symptoms and their causes

- ▪ OS related symptoms
  - ▪ Bluescreen
  - ▪ System lock-up
  - ▪ Input/output device
  - ▪ Application install
  - ▪ Start or load
  - ▪ Windows specific printing problems
    - ▪ Print spool stalled
    - ▪ Incorrect / incompatible driver
- ▪ Hardware related symptoms
  - ▪ Excessive heat
  - ▪ Noise
  - ▪ Odors
  - ▪ Status light indicators
  - ▪ Alerts
  - ▪ Visible damage (e.g. cable, plastic)

- Use documentation and resources
    - User / installation manuals
    - Internet / web based
    - Training materials

2.3 Given a scenario, determine the troubleshooting methods and tools for printers

- Manage print jobs
- Print spooler
- Printer properties and settings
- Print a test page

2.4 Given a scenario, explain and interpret common laptop issues and determine the appropriate basic troubleshooting method

- Issues
    - Power conditions
    - Video
    - Keyboard
    - Pointer
    - Stylus
    - Wireless card issues
- Methods
    - Verify power (e.g. LEDs, swap AC adapter)
    - Remove unneeded peripherals
    - Plug in external monitor
    - Toggle Fn keys or hardware switches
    - Check LCD cutoff switch
    - Verify backlight functionality and pixilation
    - Check switch for built-in WIFI antennas or external antennas

2.5 Given a scenario, integrate common preventative maintenance techniques

- Physical inspection
- Updates
    - Driver
    - Firmware
    - OS
    - Security

- Scheduling preventative maintenance
  - Defrag
  - Scandisk
  - Check disk
  - Startup programs
- Use of appropriate repair tools and cleaning materials
  - Compressed air
  - Lint free cloth
  - Computer vacuum and compressors
- Power devices
  - Appropriate source such as power strip, surge protector or UPS
- Ensuring proper environment
- Backup procedures

3.0 Operating Systems and Software

Unless otherwise noted, operating systems referred to within include Microsoft Windows 2000, Windows XP Professional, XP Home, XP MediaCenter, Windows Vista Home, Home Premium, Business and Ultimate.

3.1 Compare and contrast the different Windows Operating Systems and their features

- Windows 2000, Windows XP 32bit vs. 64bit, Windows Vista 32bit vs. 64bit
  - Sidebar, Aero, UAC, minimum system requirements, system limits
  - Windows 2000 and newer – upgrade paths and requirements
  - Terminology (32bit vs. 64bit – x86 vs. x64)
  - Application compatibility, installed program locations (32bit vs. 64bit), Windows compatibility mode
  - User interface, start bar layout

3.2 Given a scenario, demonstrate proper use of user interfaces

- Windows Explorer
- My Computer
- Control Panel
- Command prompt utilities
  - telnet
  - ping
  - ipconfig

- Run line utilities
  - Msconfig
  - Msinfo32
  - Dxdiag
  - Cmd
  - REGEDIT
- My Network Places
- Task bar / systray
- Administrative tools
  - Performance monitor, Event Viewer, Services, Computer Management
- MMC
- Task Manager
- Start Menu

3.3 Explain the process and steps to install and configure the Windows OS

- File systems
  - FAT32 vs. NTFS
- Directory structures
  - Create folders
  - Navigate directory structures
- Files
  - Creation
  - Extensions
  - Attributes
  - Permissions
- Verification of hardware compatibility and minimum requirements
- Installation methods
  - Boot media such as CD, floppy or USB
  - Network installation
  - Install from image
  - Recover CD
  - Factory recovery partition
- Operating system installation options
  - File system type
  - Network configuration
  - Repair install

- Disk preparation order
  - Format drive
  - Partition
  - Start installation
- Device Manager
  - Verify
  - Install and update devices drivers
  - Driver signing
- User data migration – User State Migration Tool (USMT)
- Virtual memory
- Configure power management
  - Suspend
  - Wake on LAN
  - Sleep timers
  - Hibernate
  - Standby
- Demonstrate safe removal of peripherals

3.4 Explain the basics of boot sequences, methods and startup utilities
- Disk boot order / device priority
  - Types of boot devices (disk, network, USB, other)
- Boot options
  - Safe mode
  - Boot to restore point
  - Recovery options
    - Automated System Recovery (ASR)
    - Emergency Repair Disk (ERD)
    - Recovery console

4.0 Networking

4.1 Summarize the basics of networking fundamentals, including technologies, devices and protocols
- Basics of configuring IP addressing and TCP/IP properties (DHCP, DNS)
- Bandwidth and latency
- Status indicators
- Protocols (TCP/IP, NETBIOS)

- Full-duplex, half-duplex
- Basics of workgroups and domains
- Common ports: HTTP, FTP, POP, SMTP, TELNET, HTTPS
- LAN / WAN
- Hub, switch and router
- Identify Virtual Private Networks (VPN)
- Basics class identification

4.2 Categorize network cables and connectors and their implementations

- Cables
  - Plenum / PVC
  - UTP (e.g. CAT3, CAT5 / 5e, CAT6)
  - STP
  - Fiber
  - Coaxial cable
- Connectors
  - RJ45
  - RJ11

4.3 Compare and contrast the different network types

- Broadband
  - DSL
  - Cable
  - Satellite
  - Fiber
- Dial-up
- Wireless
  - All 802.11 types
  - WEP
  - WPA
  - SSID
  - MAC filtering
  - DHCP settings
- Bluetooth
- Cellular

5.0 Security

5.1 Explain the basic principles of security concepts and technologies

- Encryption technologies
- Data wiping / hard drive destruction / hard drive recycling
- Software firewall
    - Port security
    - Exceptions
- Authentication technologies
    - User name
    - Password
    - Biometrics
    - Smart cards
- Basics of data sensitivity and data security
    - Compliance
    - Classifications
    - Social engineering

5.2 Summarize the following security features

- Wireless encryption
    - WEPx and WPAx
    - Client configuration (SSID)
- Malicious software protection
    - Viruses
    - Trojans
    - Worms
    - Spam
    - Spyware
    - Adware
    - Grayware
- BIOS Security
    - Drive lock
    - Passwords
    - Intrusion detection
    - TPM

- Password management / password complexity
- Locking workstation
  - Hardware
  - Operating system
- Biometrics
  - Fingerprint scanner

6.0 Operational Procedure

6.1 Outline the purpose of appropriate safety and environmental procedures and given a scenario apply them

- ESD
- EMI
  - Network interference
  - Magnets
- RFI
  - Cordless phone interference
  - Microwaves
- Electrical safety
  - CRT
  - Power supply
  - Inverter
  - Laser printers
  - Matching power requirements of equipment with power distribution and UPSs
- Material Safety Data Sheets (MSDS)
- Cable management
  - Avoiding trip hazards
- Physical safety
  - Heavy devices
  - Hot components
- Environmental – consider proper disposal procedures

6.2 Given a scenario, demonstrate the appropriate use of communication skills and professionalism in the workplace

- Use proper language – avoid jargon, acronyms, slang
- Maintain a positive attitude

- Listen and do not interrupt a customer
- Be culturally sensitive
- Be on time
  - If late contact the customer
- Avoid distractions
  - Personal calls
  - Talking to co-workers while interacting with customers
  - Personal interruptions
- Dealing with a difficult customer or situation
  - Avoid arguing with customers and/or being defensive
  - Do not minimize customers' problems
  - Avoid being judgmental
  - Clarify customer statements
  - Ask open-ended questions to narrow the scope of the problem
  - Restate the issue or question to verify understanding
- Set and meet expectations / timeline and communicate status with the customer
  - Offer different repair / replacement options if applicable
  - Provide proper documentation on the services provided
  - Follow up with customers / user at a later date to verify satisfaction
- Deal appropriately with customers confidential materials
  - Located on computer, desktop, printer, etc.

A+ Practical Application 2009 Exam Objectives

The following table lists the domains measured by this examination and the extent to which they are represented on the exam.

Domain	Percentage of Exam
1.0 Hardware	37%
2.0 Operating Systems	36%
3.0 Networking	15%
4.0 Security	12%
Total	100%

1.0 Hardware

1.1 Given a scenario, install, configure and maintain personal computer components

- Storage devices
    - HDD
        - SATA
        - PATA
        - Solid state
    - FDD
    - Optical drives
        - CD / DVD / RW / Blu-Ray
    - Removable
    - External
- Motherboards
    - Jumper settings
    - CMOS battery
    - Advanced BIOS settings
    - Bus speeds
    - Chipsets
    - Firmware updates
    - Socket types
    - Expansion slots
    - Memory slots
    - Front panel connectors
    - I/O ports
        - Sound, video, USB 1.1, USB 2.0, serial, IEEE 1394 / Firewire, parallel, NIC, modem, PS/2
- Power supplies
    - Wattages and capacity
    - Connector types and quantity
    - Output voltage
- Processors
    - Socket types
    - Speed
    - Number of cores
    - Power consumption

- Cache
- Front side bus
- 32bit vs. 64bit
- Memory
- Adapter cards
  - Graphics cards
  - Sound cards
  - Storage controllers
    - RAID cards (RAID array – levels 0,1,5)
    - eSATA cards
  - I/O cards
    - Firewire
    - USB
    - Parallel
    - Serial
  - Wired and wireless network cards
  - Capture cards (TV, video)
  - Media reader
- Cooling systems
  - Heat sinks
  - Thermal compound
  - CPU fans
  - Case fans

1.2 Given a scenario, detect problems, troubleshoot and repair/replace personal computer components

- Storage devices
  - HDD
    - SATA
    - PATA
    - Solid state
  - FDD
  - Optical drives
    - CD / DVD / RW / Blu-Ray
  - Removable
  - External

- Motherboards
  - Jumper settings
  - CMOS battery
  - Advanced BIOS settings
  - Bus speeds
  - Chipsets
  - Firmware updates
  - Socket types
  - Expansion slots
  - Memory slots
  - Front panel connectors
  - I/O ports
    - Sound, video, USB 1.1, USB 2.0, serial, IEEE 1394 / Firewire, parallel, NIC, modem, PS/2
- Power supplies
  - Wattages and capacity
  - Connector types and quantity
  - Output voltage
- Processors
  - Socket types
  - Speed
  - Number of cores
  - Power consumption
  - Cache
  - Front side bus
  - 32bit vs. 64bit
- Memory
- Adapter cards
  - Graphics cards
  - Sound cards
  - Storage controllers
    - RAID cards (RAID array – levels 0,1,5)
    - eSATA cards

- I/O cards
  - Firewire
  - USB
  - Parallel
  - Serial
- Wired and wireless network cards
- Capture cards (TV, video)
- Media reader
- Cooling systems
  - Heat sinks
  - Thermal compound
  - CPU fans
  - Case fans

1.3 Given a scenario, install, configure, detect problems, troubleshoot and repair/replace laptop components

- Components of the LCD including inverter, screen and video card
- Hard drive and memory
- Disassemble processes for proper re-assembly
  - Document and label cable and screw locations
  - Organize parts
  - Refer to manufacturer documentation
  - Use appropriate hand tools
- Recognize internal laptop expansion slot types
- Upgrade wireless cards and video card
- Replace keyboard, processor, plastics, pointer devices, heat sinks, fans, system board, CMOS battery, speakers

1.4 Given a scenario, select and use the following tools

- Multimeter
- Power supply tester
- Specialty hardware / tools
- Cable testers
- Loop back plugs
- Anti-static pad and wrist strap
- Extension magnet

1.5 Given a scenario, detect and resolve common printer issues

- Symptoms
  - Paper jams
  - Blank paper
  - Error codes
  - Out of memory error
  - Lines and smearing
  - Garbage printout
  - Ghosted image
  - No connectivity
- Issue resolution
  - Replace fuser
  - Replace drum
  - Clear paper jam
  - Power cycle
  - Install maintenance kit (reset page count)
  - Set IP on printer
  - Clean printer

2.0 Operating Systems

Unless otherwise noted, operating systems referred to within include Microsoft Windows 2000, Windows XP Professional, XP Home, XP MediaCenter, Windows Vista Home, Home Premium, Business and Ultimate.

2.1 Select the appropriate commands and options to troubleshoot and resolve problems

- MSCONFIG
- DIR
- CHKDSK (/f /r)
- EDIT
- COPY (/a /v /y)
- XCOPY
- FORMAT
- IPCONFIG (/all /release /renew)
- PING (-t –l)
- MD / CD / RD
- NET
- TRACERT

- NSLOOKUP
- [command name] /?
- SFC

2.2 Differentiate between Windows Operating System directory structures (Windows 2000, XP and Vista)

- User file locations
- System file locations
- Fonts
- Temporary files
- Program files
- Offline files and folders

2.3 Given a scenario, select and use system utilities / tools and evaluate the results

- Disk management tools
  - DEFRAG
  - NTBACKUP
  - Check Disk
  - Disk Manager
  - Active, primary, extended and logical partitions
  - Mount points
  - Mounting a drive
  - FAT32 and NTFS
  - Drive status
    - Foreign drive
    - Healthy
    - Formatting
    - Active unallocated
    - Failed
    - Dynamic
    - Offline
    - Online
- System monitor
- Administrative tools
  - Event Viewer
  - Computer Management
  - Services
  - Performance Monitor

- Devices Manager
  - Enable
  - Disable
  - Warnings
  - Indicators
- Task Manager
  - Process list
  - Resource usage
  - Process priority
  - Termination
- System Information
- System restore
- Remote Desktop Protocol (Remote Desktop / Remote Assistance)
- Task Scheduler
- Regional settings and language settings

2.4 Evaluate and resolve common issues

- Operational Problems
  - Windows specific printing problems
    - Print spool stalled
    - Incorrect / incompatible driver form print
  - Auto-restart errors
  - Bluescreen error
  - System lock-up
  - Device driver failure (input / output devices)
  - Application install, start or load failure
  - Service fails to start
- Error Messages and Conditions
  - Boot
    - Invalid boot disk
    - Inaccessible boot drive
    - Missing NTLDR
  - Startup
    - Device / service failed to start
    - Device / program in registry not found

- Event viewer (errors in the event log)
- System Performance and Optimization
    - Aero settings
    - Indexing settings
    - UAC
    - Sidebar settings
    - Startup file maintenance
    - Background processes

3.0 Networking

3.1 Troubleshoot client-side connectivity issues using appropriate tools

- TCP/IP settings
    - Gateway
    - Subnet mask
    - DNS
    - DHCP (dynamic vs.static)
    - NAT (private and public)
- Characteristics of TCP/IP
    - Loopback addresses
    - Automatic IP addressing
- Mail protocol settings
    - SMTP
    - IMAP
    - POP
- FTP settings
    - Ports
    - IP addresses
    - Exceptions
    - Programs
- Proxy settings
    - Ports
    - IP addresses
    - Exceptions
    - Programs

- Tools (use and interpret results)
  - Ping
  - Tracert
  - Nslookup
  - Netstat
  - Net use
  - Net /?
  - Ipconfig
  - telnet
  - SSH
- Secure connection protocols
  - SSH
  - HTTPS
- Firewall settings
  - Open and closed ports
  - Program filters

3.2 Install and configure a small office home office (SOHO) network

- Connection types
  - Dial-up
  - Broadband
    - DSL
    - Cable
    - Satellite
    - ISDN
  - Wireless
    - All 802.11
    - WEP
    - WPA
    - SSID
    - MAC filtering
    - DHCP settings
  - Routers / Access Points
    - Disable DHCP
    - Use static IP

- Change SSID from default
- Disable SSID broadcast
- MAC filtering
- Change default username and password
- Update firmware
- Firewall
- LAN (10/100/1000BaseT, Speeds)
- Bluetooth (1.0 vs. 2.0)
- Cellular
- Basic VoIP (consumer applications)
- Basics of hardware and software firewall configuration
  - Port assignment / setting up rules (exceptions)
  - Port forwarding / port triggering
- Physical installation
  - Wireless router placement
  - Cable length

4.0 Security

4.1 Given a scenario, prevent, troubleshoot and remove viruses and malware

- Use antivirus software
- Identify malware symptoms
- Quarantine infected systems
- Research malware types, symptoms and solutions (virus encyclopedias)
- Remediate infected systems
- Update antivirus software, educate end user
  - Signature and engine updates
  - Automatic vs. manual
- Schedule scans
- Repair boot blocks
- Scan and removal techniques
  - Safe mode
  - Boot environment

4.2 Implement security and troubleshoot common issues

- Operating systems
  - Local users and groups: Administrator, Power Users, Guest, Users
  - Vista User Access Control (UAC)

- NTFS vs. Share permissions
  - Allow vs. deny
  - Difference between moving and copying folders and files
  - File attributes
- Shared files and folders
  - Administrative shares vs. local shares
  - Permission propagation
  - Inheritance
- System files and folders
- Encryption (Bitlocker, EFS)
- User authentication
- System
  - BIOS security
    - Drive lock
    - Passwords
    - Intrusion detection
    - TPM

Phase

1

Installing Hardware and Software

Every common task that is performed by a PC technician is hands-on in some way. Although some of the work you do is performed at the keyboard, many of the tasks you will perform in this phase will be spent underneath a desk in someone's cubicle or at a workbench. These are the usual locations for opening up a computer case and installing or removing equipment. This phase of the book covers the most common installation tasks for hardware, such as RAM, hard drives, and power supplies. In this phase, you'll also learn how to install and uninstall various types of software, including operating systems, applications, and drivers. In general, you'll need at least one PC that you can open up and work with, as well as some common tools. Each task will list the specific requirements you'll need in order to complete the job. This is also true of the software portion of this phase. Now it's time to open the book to the first task, pick up a screwdriver, and get started.

The tasks in this phase map to Domains 1, 2, 3, 4, 7, and 8 for the CompTIA A+ Essentials (220-701) exam objectives and Domains 1, 2, 3, 4, and 8 for the CompTIA IT Practical Application (220-702) exam objectives.

Task 1.1: Preventing ESD Damage

It is amazingly easy to damage the delicate electrical circuitry inside a computer. As a child, you may have rubbed your feet back and forth on a carpet and then touched another person's hand to give them a static shock. What you probably don't realize is that your body carries some electrical potential all of the time. Most of the time, though, the discharge is insufficient to be perceived by the human nervous system. Unfortunately, it is more than enough to fry some components inside a PC. This type of damage can cause maddening intermittent faults in the computer that can seem to be impossible to diagnose.

Happily, there are precautions you can take to prevent such damage. The most common method (though not recommended as the only method) is to open the PC's access panel and touch the frame of the computer to equalize the electrical potential between you and the computer. This is the "quick and dirty" method of preventing electrostatic discharge (ESD). If you want to do this while working on your own computer, go for it. When you are working with other people's equipment, you'd better stick to safer procedures.

In the first edition of this book, I stuck this task at number 18 in the list, but this is something you really need to know before you stick your hands inside a computer case for the first time. Taking ESD precautions isn't the "sexy" part of PC repair and maintenance, but learning this first will save you one or more migraines as you progress through this book and your career.

Scenario

You have a PC on your workbench that needs to have its memory upgraded (see Task 1.2). You are about to remove the screws from the PC case's access panel and take off the panel. You have just been briefed by your supervisor on the proper method of preventing ESD damage to the inside of the computer. All of the necessary equipment has been provided, and you begin going through the necessary precautionary procedures.

Scope of Task

Duration

This should only take a few minutes.

Setup

You don't actually have to open the computer for this task; all you'll need to do is set up the ESD precautions.

Caveat

Although this is a single task, you would be wise to "perform" this task every time you open up a computer case. The few minutes it takes to implement these procedures could save you hours of trying to figure out some problem caused by a stray static shock.

Procedure

This lesson will show you how to implement proper ESD procedures.

Equipment Used

You'll need at least an ESD wrist strap, but you can also get an ESD cover for your workbench and a mat to stand on while working on the computer. Always have antistatic bags ready for any components you remove from the computer.

Use your favorite search engine and enter the search string "ESD equipment" to see the different tools available for taking ESD precautions.

Details

This exercise will show you the steps to take to prevent ESD damage while working on a computer.

Taking Steps to Prevent ESD Damage

1. Verify that your workbench is covered with an ESD mat before placing a computer on the bench.
2. Make sure there is an ESD mat where you will be standing while working on a computer.
3. Check to make sure whatever component you are installing is stored in an antistatic bag.

Try not to wear synthetic clothing while working on a computer.

Don't use Styrofoam while working on the computer. If you have to have a cup of coffee, use a ceramic cup (although drinking anything around an open computer is asking for trouble). Passing a piece of Styrofoam over electrical components can damage them.

4. Place an antistatic strap around one of your wrists.
5. Clip the other end of the cable attached to the strap to the frame of the computer.

Another activity that can cause ESD damage is vacuuming the interior of the PC case. (Use a can of compressed air instead.) To clean components, use antistatic sprays instead of detergents. Rubbing erasers inside the case also can build up static.

If compressed air seems too messy for you, there are special ESD vacuums available, such as the one at www.intertronics.co.uk/products/csmdvac.htm.

Criteria for Completion

You will have successfully completed this task when you have secured your work area and yourself with ESD equipment. You are now ready to open the computer case.

Task 1.2: Installing RAM

RAM, or random access memory, is the desktop of the computer. Anytime a PC user wants to open a program to read email, surf the Web, or play a game, that program is loaded into memory from the hard drive and will stay in memory for as long as it's active. How many programs a PC can run at the same time without a noticeable slowdown of performance depends on how much RAM is in the computer. Naturally, the more RAM a computer has, the better.

Installing RAM sticks is an extremely common task for a PC technician. You'll likely spend countless hours on the floor or at a workbench, installing or upgrading RAM. Although choosing the correct type of RAM is vitally important, it is fairly simple to research the computer you are working on to discover exactly which type it takes.

Once you have the correct stick of RAM for the computer, all that's left to do is to power down the PC, open it up, and install the stick. This task will guide you through the steps necessary to find the appropriate type of RAM for a particular computer and physically install it.

Scenario

One of the users in accounting has recently had installed on her PC new software that is required for a special project she is working on. She is using an older PC and complains that when she tries to open the application, computer performance slows to a crawl. Your supervisor has determined that the user's PC has insufficient RAM to run this piece of software and has assigned you to upgrade the amount of memory in her machine. You will need a computer with access to the Internet to research the type of RAM stick that is correct for the particular PC you'll be working on. You will also need to have a computer in which you can install a RAM stick and the appropriate RAM itself. Make sure you have a screwdriver to remove the side panel of the computer so you can access the interior. You'll need to take the appropriate steps to prevent electrostatic discharge (ESD) damage to the sensitive electrical components inside the PC as well as to the RAM stick you are about to install. See Task 1.1 for details about ESD precautions.

Scope of Task

Duration

This task should take about 15–30 minutes.

Setup

All you'll need for this task is a single computer with at least one empty RAM slot, an appropriate stick of RAM, and a screwdriver that will fit the screws holding the side access panel on the PC.

Caveat

Depending on the type of computer you are working on, how the PC's access panel is attached will vary, so the instructions in this task may not be quite the same for your PC. The memory slots can be located on different areas of the motherboard on different computers, so you will have to take a moment to locate them. Some RAM slots can be difficult to reach, making your task a bit harder. The occasional scraped knuckle is to be expected when working inside a PC. This example uses a computer running Windows XP Professional. If you are using a different operating system, the steps you use to test and verify that RAM has been added may not be identical to the steps in this task. When selecting the type of RAM, make sure that you use the correct memory frequency as well as the desired amount of RAM. Also, some motherboards care which memory slots you place the first and second sticks of RAM into, so you may have to switch sticks between slots in order to have the computer recognize all of the RAM installed.

Procedure

In this task, you will learn how to determine which type of memory is correct for a particular PC, open the PC, and install an additional stick of RAM on the motherboard, close the PC, and verify that the additional RAM is detected and being used by the computer. Part of locating the right type of RAM involves visiting the website of a commercial memory vendor. It will not be necessary to purchase RAM from this vendor; you will simply visit this site to find the type of RAM your computer uses.

Equipment Used

You should need only a single screwdriver to complete this task, although some PCs come with a latch system that lets you open the panel without any tools at all.

Details

The following sections walk you through determining the computer's manufacturer and model type, using that information to find out what kind of memory is correct for this machine, and installing and testing the additional RAM.

Determining the Correct Type of Memory for a Particular PC

DETERMINING THE MAKE AND MODEL OF A PC

1. Look at the front of the computer.
2. Locate the name of the computer manufacturer and the name and number of the model.

LOCATING THE CORRECT RAM TYPE FOR A COMPUTER

1. Open a web browser on a computer with an Internet connection.
2. In the URL field, type www.crucial.com.

3. On the Crucial website, under the Crucial Memory Advisor Tool, click the Select Mfgr drop-down arrow.

4. Select the name of the maker of the computer.

5. Click the Select Product Line drop-down arrow.
6. Select the model name of the computer.
7. Click the Select Model drop-down arrow.
8. Select the specific model of the computer.
9. Click the FIND IT button.
10. Locate the specific type and amount of RAM you need.

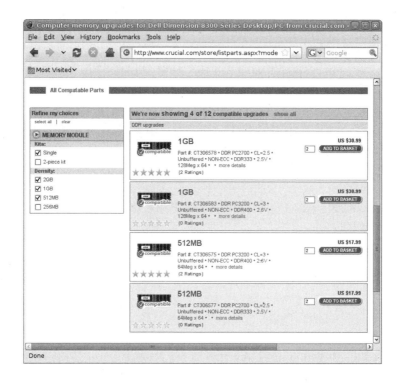

 You can also select the "Max It Out Recommendation" at the top of the results page to maximize the amount of RAM on your computer.

11. Click the picture of the RAM stick or the More Details link in the desired row.

12. Locate the memory-module details and, if necessary, scroll down and locate the product details.

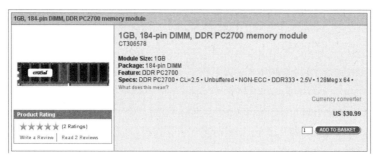

13. Write down the specific details about the stick of RAM you need.

14. Close the web browser.

Installing a Stick of RAM

OPENING THE CASE

1. Power down your computer and wait until it is completely off.

 Some technicians feel that to be completely safe, the power cord should be unplugged from the computer's power supply as well.

2. Use your screwdriver to remove the screws attaching the access panel to the computer case.

3. Remove the access panel.

INSTALLING A MEMORY STICK

1. Place the PC on its side or in a position that gives you access to the motherboard.

2. Locate the RAM slots.

3. Remove the RAM stick from its antistatic bag, being careful not to touch the pins.

4. Pull the latches back from the slot.

5. Position the stick of RAM so that the notch on the stick is appropriately aligned with the tab on the slot.

6. Slowly but firmly press down the stick of RAM until both latches on the slot click into position.

7. Replace the access panel.

8. Replace the screws so that the access panel is held firmly to the PC's frame.

9. Return the PC to its original position.

TESTING THE MEMORY

1. Power on the computer.

 If you unplugged the power cord, you will need to plug it back in first.

2. Listen for two beeps as the computer boots.

 Beep codes differ depending on the type of BIOS used in your motherboard. To learn more about different types of BIOS and their associated beep codes, visit www.pchell.com/hardware/beepcodes.shtml or go to your favorite search engine and search for "beep codes."

3. Look for a message on the monitor indicating that the amount of memory on the computer has changed.

4. Follow any instructions you see on the monitor.

5. Allow the computer to continue to boot and the operating system to load.

VERIFYING THE MEMORY

1. On the computer Desktop, click the Start button.

2. Right-click My Computer and select Properties.

 If My Computer isn't in your Start menu, it can most likely be found on the Desktop.

3. On the General tab of the System Properties box, locate the amount of RAM in the PC.

4. Click Cancel to close the System Properties box.

Criteria for Completion

You have completed this task when you have verified that the amount of RAM has increased to the correct amount. This amount will vary depending on how much RAM the computer originally had and how much you added.

Task 1.3: Installing a PCI Card

Despite the popularity and ease of use of USB devices and the growing popularity of PCI Express, many hardware features of a PC continue to be supported by PCI, or Peripheral Component Interconnect, cards. Actually, PCI is an industry standard that describes how data are managed on the PCI bus of a computer's motherboard in terms of clock speed and throughput rate. The PCI bus has replaced the older Industry Standard Architecture (ISA) expansion bus in modern computers. PCI cards are added to the main circuit board of a computer to add hardware functionality such as a modem, sound card, or network interface card (NIC).

 PCI Express is an up-and-coming standard and is replacing the aging PCI bus (see Task 1.4). You'll find an excellent overview of this technology here: www.directron.com/expressguide.html.

Installing or upgrading a PCI card in a computer is a common task for the PC technician; in most cases it is quite easy to do, thanks to Plug and Play (PnP) technology. Older expansion bus cards required the technician to manually configure the I/O and IRQ values for the new card to prevent it from attempting to use resources that were already allocated to another piece of equipment. Today, this configuration is done automatically for the most part (there are exceptions), and all you really need to do is install the card and expect it to work.

Scenario

Your company has just opened a small branch office nearby that requires several computers to be networked on a local LAN and to have Internet access. One of the computers is an older unit that had a failed NIC card. That card has been removed but a replacement was never installed. You have located an appropriate NIC that you can install in a PCI slot on the PC's motherboard. You must travel to the branch office to install the card. You will need to have a PCI card for this task as well as a screwdriver to remove the screws anchoring the side access panel to the computer's metal frame. Finally, you'll need to take the appropriate steps to prevent ESD damage to the sensitive electrical components inside the PC and the new NIC. See Task 1.1 for details.

Scope of Task

Duration

This task should take approximately 30 minutes.

Setup

All you'll need for this task is a single computer with at least one empty PCI slot, a PCI card, and a screwdriver that will fit the screws holding the side access panel on the PC. PCI-slot covers are also usually attached to the computer by screws. You may need an additional screwdriver if the screw types for the access panel and the PCI slots are different. Although the task scenario specifies a NIC, you can use any PCI card to perform the actual task on your computer. In the NIC scenario, the computer is already configured to accept an IP address dynamically, so a Dynamic Host Configuration Protocol (DHCP) server must be available on the network.

Caveat

The same caveats that applied to Task 1.2 apply here in terms of how to actually open the computer's access panel and where the PCI slots are located on your particular motherboard. The procedure for installing the new card is identical regardless of the operating system installed on the machine. The process of testing the card subsequently described uses Windows XP as an example.

Procedure

In this task, you will learn how to install a PCI card into the PCI slot on a computer's motherboard. You will also learn how to determine if the card is functioning correctly once it's installed.

Equipment Used

You may need one or two screwdrivers, depending on the types of screws holding the access panel and PCI-slot cover to the computer. As mentioned in Task 1.2, some computer access covers use a latch system that doesn't require the use of a screwdriver. Also, some PCI-slot covers are attached by latches that can be opened without a tool.

Details

The following sections guide you through the process of installing a PCI card on a PC and verifying that the card is functioning correctly.

Installing a PCI Card

OPENING THE CASE

1. Power down your computer and wait until it is completely off. For additional safety, unplug the power cord from the back of the computer.
2. Locate your screwdriver, and remove the screws attaching the access panel to the computer case.
3. Remove the access panel.

INSTALLING THE PCI CARD

1. Locate the PCI slots on the motherboard and select the one you will use.
2. Locate the appropriate screwdriver, and remove the screws attaching the PCI-slot cover from the PC's frame.
3. Remove the cover and put it aside.
4. Remove the PCI card from its antistatic container.

 All electronic components should be stored in an antistatic container to prevent ESD damage.

5. Orient the card so that the pins line up correctly with the PCI slot.
6. Orient the card so that the NIC's port lines up with the opening in the back of the PC.
7. Gently but firmly press the PCI card into the slot, making sure it is fully engaged.
8. Use the PCI-slot cover screw to secure the PCI card to the PC's frame.
9. Replace the access panel.

10. Replace the screws securing the access panel to the PC's frame.

11. Return the PC to its original location, and replace the PC's power cable.

TESTING THE PCI CARD

1. Power on the computer.

2. Wait for the PC to boot and load the operating system.

3. Plug the patch cable into the NIC's Ethernet port.

The link light on the NIC should go on if the NIC is active and if the other end of the cord is plugged into an active port on a hub or switch.

4. Click Start ➢ Run.

5. In the Run box, type **cmd** and click OK.

6. When the command emulator opens, type **ipconfig/all** and press Enter.

7. If the output displays the IP address and subnet mask of the PC and other network configuration settings, the PCI NIC is working and the computer successfully received an address dynamically.

The one exception is if the computer cannot connect to the DHCP server. Windows 2000, XP, and Vista are configured by default to use Automatic Private IP Addressing (APIPA) if the computer cannot acquire a dynamic address. If the address is returned in the 169.254.*x.x* range and the subnet mask is 255.255.0.0, the computer is using APIPA. Consult with your network administrator to find out what subnet mask and IP address range you should expect the computer to acquire. To learn more about APIPA, visit this site: http://msdn.microsoft.com/en-us/library/aa505918.aspx.

If the computer hasn't received addressing information, it doesn't necessarily mean that the installation didn't go well. You may have to type **ipconfig/release** and press Enter, then type **ipconfig/renew** and press Enter to acquire an IP address from the DHCP server.

Criteria for Completion

You have completed the task when the PCI NIC functions correctly, allowing network communications between the PC and the rest of the network. You may have installed a different type of PCI card, such as a video or sound card. If so, the criteria for completion would be the successful testing and operation of those cards based on their purpose.

Task 1.4: Installing a PCI Express Card

As mentioned in Task 1.3, the PCI is aging and is no longer capable of meeting the current needs for speed and performance, particularly in the arena of graphics cards. AGP (Accelerated Graphics Port) cards are also an aging technology having the same issues. The most common reason for an upgrade to a PCI Express (PCIe) graphics card is to let you run games faster and to add TV/DVI to your computer system.

Fortunately, installing a PCIe graphics card is a relatively simple task, akin to installing a PCI card. The processes are different enough to make creating a separate task worthwhile. To learn more about the PCIe standard, see the URL in the introduction to Task 1.3. Also, Wikipedia provides a good description of the PCIe standards and specifications: http://en.wikipedia.org/wiki/PCI_Express.

Scenario

You have a PC in your workshop with a customer request to install a PCIe graphics card. You have been provided with the necessary card and your only task is to install it and the drivers. The computer's motherboard is current and PCIe-capable. You will need to have available one or more screwdrivers to enable you to remove the PC's access panel and to remove the card-slot cover. After the card has been installed, you will need to use the accompanying CD to install the drivers. Be sure to follow ESD precautions to prevent damage to the PC's electronic components (see Task 1.1).

Scope of Task

Duration

This should take about 30 minutes.

Setup

You'll need a computer with at least one empty PCIe slot, a PCIe card, and a screwdriver that will fit the screws holding the side access panel on the PC. You may also need a second screwdriver for any screws attaching the PCIe-slot cover to the PC's frame. If you are unsure whether your motherboard supports the PCIe bus standard, check your motherboard manual.

The card may come with additional features such as a heat sink and cooling fan. The fan may need an external power source. Consult the card's documentation for any additional requirements before proceeding.

You will also need the driver CD for the PCIe graphics card. The driver CD should come with the card. Although the scenario specifies a PCIe graphics card, you can use any PCIe card you have available to complete this task, but make sure you have the drivers for the card. As always, follow ESD precautions while working inside the PC case.

 If you are interested in actually installing a PCIe graphics card suitable for gaming but are unsure how to select the right card, visit www.build-gaming-computers.com/gaming-video-card.html for more information.

Caveat

A PCIe card, unlike the older PCI or AGP cards, can fit into a slot its own size or larger on the motherboard, but cannot fit into a smaller-sized slot, so verify the size of the card and slot before proceeding. The PCIe bus uses pairs of point-to-point serial links called lanes, rather than a shared parallel bus. Depending on the lane speeds supported by the PCIe card and the motherboard, the number of pins on the card can be different. Make sure that the lane speeds for the card and motherboard are compatible by checking card and motherboard documentation.

Procedure

This lesson will show you how to install a PCIe graphics card and then install the card's drivers from CD.

Equipment Used

You'll need one or more screwdrivers to remove the screws from the PC access panel and from the PCIe-slot cover. Some covers however, are attached by tabs or latches that require no special tools. Although you may not consider a CD a tool, you'll need to have the card's driver CD handy.

Details

The following sections guide you through the process of installing a PCIe graphics card on a PC and installing the card's drivers from a CD.

Installing a PCIe Graphics Card

OPENING THE CASE

1. Power down your computer and wait until it is completely off. For additional safety, unplug the power cord from the back of the computer.

2. Locate your screwdriver and remove the screws attaching the access panel to the computer case.

3. Remove the access panel and position the PC on its side. Apply ESD precautions before proceeding.

INSTALLING THE PCIE CARD

1. Locate the PCIe slots on the motherboard and select the one you will use.

2. Locate the appropriate screwdriver and, if necessary, remove the screws from the PC's frame attaching the PCI-slot cover.

3. Remove the cover and put it aside. For some cards, you may need to remove more than one slot cover to accommodate the size of the heat sink and fan on the card.

4. Remove the PCIe card from its antistatic container, holding it by its edges.

5. Orient the card so that the pins are aligned correctly with the slot.

6. Gently but firmly, push the card into the slot until it is securely installed. If present, push the plastic slot latch to the up position to more securely seat the card.

7. Replace the PCIe-slot cover and, if required, secure the cover by replacing and tightening the screws.

8. If your card has a fan, verify that the fan is clear of any cables or other obstructions.

9. If your card's documentation states that it requires an external power connection, locate the necessary four-pin power cable that came with the card. Connect the correct ends of the cable to the motherboard and to the card.

10. Verify that the card is secure in the slot and that all connections are firm.

11. Replace the PC's access panel, securing it with the accompanying screws, upright the PC, and replace the PC's power cable.

INSTALLING THE PCIE GRAPHICS CARD DRIVERS

1. Power up the computer.

2. Wait for the computer to completely boot and for the operating system to load, verifying that no error messages occur.

3. Locate the CD containing the drivers for the graphics card.

4. Open the CD/DVD drive, insert the CD, and close the drive.

5. Follow the onscreen instructions for installing the drivers. The instructions will vary depending on the make and model of the graphics card. See Task 1.21 for more information about installing drivers from a disc.

6. When prompted, remove the CD and reboot the computer.

7. After the computer has rebooted and the operating system has loaded, open a web browser and locate the PCIe graphics card manufacturer's website.

8. Locate the current drivers for the card you installed and download and install the most current drivers from the website. The drivers on the CD will almost certainly be out-of-date. See Task 1.22 for more information on installing drivers from the Internet.

9. Reboot the computer again.

10. When the computer has rebooted and the operating system has loaded, verify the operation of the graphics card by right-clicking the desktop, clicking Properties, clicking Settings, and then configuring the screen resolution to the desired setting.

11. Close all dialog boxes when done.

Criteria for Completion

You will have successfully completed this task when you have installed the PCIe graphics card and the card's drivers, and have verified that the card and the PC are functioning correctly. If you installed a different type of PCIe card, the criteria for completion are the successful testing and operation of the card based on its purpose.

Task 1.5: Installing a CPU

All PCs require a central processing unit (CPU) to perform the calculations necessary to process all instructions provided by all of the programs running on the computer. You normally don't have to do this task very frequently because CPUs are pretty robust. The most common situations in which you will install a CPU are when you are building a computer from its component parts, when you are upgrading a PC to a faster CPU, and when (occasionally) the CPU fails and needs to be replaced.

The actual installation process is very simple, but it does require a bit of preparation. You must make absolutely sure that you have the right CPU for the processor slot on the motherboard. You must also verify that the motherboard supports the CPU's bus speed, voltage, multiplier, and other settings. Even if it is physically possible to install the processing unit, if the computer's BIOS doesn't support the CPU's specifications, the computer won't function.

Also, the process of installing a CPU actually consists of two installations—installing the CPU itself and installing the heat-sink fan on top. The temperature a CPU increases with the amount of work it is asked to do. CPUs in boxes used for heavy gaming take quite a beating. If the unit isn't kept within operational temperature limits, it may ignite and melt.

Beyond the actual installation, the BIOS must be specifically set for the CPU's parameters, so the job's not done until the BIOS recognizes the CPU and successfully boots. That said, let's move on and see how to install a processor.

Scenario

You have been assigned to upgrade the CPU on a computer. The old processor has been removed and all that needs to be done is to install the new one. Your supervisor wants you to install the CPU in the PC and then power it up, configure the BIOS, and confirm that it is operational. The computer is already open and sitting on the workbench. The correct processor, in an antistatic bag, is sitting next to the PC along with everything else you need.

If you didn't know which processors were supported by the motherboard, you could always go to the vendor's site on the Web and find out. This will be covered in Task 2.1, "Identifying a Motherboard." Also, your processor's documentation is a great help in telling you which motherboards support the CPU. Additionally, you can find this information on the CPU manufacturer's website or consult the motherboard manual.

From the following site, you can download a free utility that will tell you the manufacturer of your PC's motherboard. The tool is compatible with Windows XP, but use it with Windows Vista at your own risk: www.majorgeeks .com/download181.html.

   Your boss leaves and you go over to the workbench and start the installation. All you'll need is the CPU, the thermal compound, and the heat-sink fan. As always, take ESD precautions, as described in Task 1.1.

Scope of Task

Duration

This task should take about 30 minutes.

Setup

You'll need either a PC that doesn't have a CPU installed or one from which you can remove and reinstall the unit. If you are using the processor already installed in the computer, the heat-sink fan will be attached. You will need some fresh thermal compound for this task, though. You can buy a tube of the compound at any computer-hardware store. The task is worded as if you are installing the CPU on the motherboard for the first time, so your actual experience may vary a bit.

Caveat

There is a dizzying number of different CPUs and CPU slots and sockets. This means that there are nearly as many ways to install a CPU as there are different CPU slots or sockets on motherboards. This task will describe installing a CPU into a zero insertion force (ZIF) socket. You can open ZIF sockets by lifting a small lever on one side of the socket and then lock them by closing the lever again. ZIF sockets are very common, so if you are installing a CPU that uses a ZIF socket, this task should be very close, if not identical, to what you will actually be doing in the exercise.

Procedure

In this task, you will learn how to install a CPU onto a computer's motherboard, configure the BIOS, and verify that the computer is operational.

Equipment Used

In addition to the CPU itself, you'll need a tube of thermal compound to create a seal between the processor and the heat-sink fan. Although this scenario starts out with the computer case already open, you'll need a screwdriver at the end of the exercise to reattach the access panel. You will also need a piece of plastic wrap or a plastic bag to smooth the thermal compound onto the CPU.

Details

The following set of instructions will walk you step-by-step through the process of installing a CPU, configuring the BIOS setup, and testing to make sure the computer is operating after the installation.

Installing a CPU and Heat-Sink Fan

INSTALLING THE CPU

1. Locate the processor socket on the motherboard.
2. Lift the lever on the side to open the socket.
3. Carefully remove the CPU from the antistatic bag, holding it by its edges.
4. Turn the CPU until you can see the pins.
5. Verify that none of the pins are bent.

 Not all CPUs have pins. The Intel Socket 775 has only holes. The pins are mounted on the motherboard.

6. Locate the single diagonal corner on the CPU.
7. Line up the pins and the diagonal corner with their counterparts on the processor socket.
8. Gently lower the CPU onto the socket, keeping the pins aligned so that they insert into the holes in the socket.
9. Verify that the CPU is correctly aligned and positioned firmly in the socket.
10. Push the lever on the side of the socket back to the locked position.

 Some CPUs come with a cooling solution and protective plate that must be installed at this step of the process.

INSTALLING THE HEAT-SINK FAN

1. Locate the tube of thermal compound.

2. Open the tube and apply drops of the compound to the top of the CPU.

3. Cover your finger with a clean piece of plastic and rub the compound smoothly onto the CPU.

Depending on the installation kit you are using, you may also be applying paste as described in Step 3.

Do not use your bare finger or a cloth when smoothing the compound, to avoid introducing contaminants.

4. Locate the heat-sink fan.

5. Align the heat-sink fan so that the mounting clamps are lined up with the corresponding mount points on the CPU.

6. Place the aligned heat-sink fan directly on the CPU.

7. Lock the mounting clamps in place.

There is no one standard method of attaching a heat sink to a CPU. Some systems use clamps, whereas others require screws. Refer to the heat sink's documentation for details.

Be especially careful when locking the mounting clamps in place. Applying too much pressure or slipping with a clamp and damaging the motherboard could make all your efforts up to this point useless.

8. Locate the power wire on the heat-sink fan.

9. Locate the three-pin heat-sink fan header on the motherboard.

10. Connect the power wire to the fan header.

Initially Testing and Configuring the BIOS

INITIALLY TESTING THE INSTALLATION

1. Leave the access panel off the PC.

2. Place the PC in an upright position.

3. Verify that a monitor, keyboard, and mouse are attached to the PC.

4. Plug the power cord into the PC's power supply.

5. Plug the power cord into an electrical socket or powered surge protector.

6. Power up the computer.

7. Verify that the heat-sink fan is spinning up.

8. Allow the machine to boot while you are looking at the monitor.

CONFIGURING THE BIOS FOR THE CPU

1. Verify that the BIOS setup screen is displayed on the monitor.

 The BIOS setup should appear automatically, but if you are using the same model of processor that was originally installed on the PC, it may not. If it doesn't, you can manually get into the BIOS. Different computers have different ways of entering the BIOS setup, including pressing the F7 key or pressing the Esc key.

2. Select the menu item for the CPU.

 Because BIOS setups vary, there is no standard method for locating specific menus and submenus.

3. Locate the settings for CPU multiplier, voltage, and memory timing speeds (there may be other entries as well).

4. Set them to Auto if the option exists for each setting. For those settings without an Auto option, set the values for those matching your CPU. For example, if your CPU's bus speed is 133MHz, you may need to set that value in the BIOS.

5. When you have completed the configuration, navigate to the BIOS main menu.

6. Select the Save and Exit option.

7. The PC should now continue the boot process and load the operating system.

8. Once the system is running, reattach the access panel.

9. Secure the access panel by screwing it to the frame of the PC.

Criteria for Completion

You have completed the task when the PC has successfully booted, loaded the operating system, and is running normally.

Task 1.6: Installing a Power Supply

The term *power supply* is a bit misleading. A PC's power-supply unit takes the AC current from an electrical wall socket (actually, from the wall socket and through a surge protector if you're smart) and converts it to DC current that the computer can use. Should the power supply fail, however, the PC and its components are about as useful as a box of rocks.

Installing a power supply is pretty straightforward. However, you do need to make sure that the voltage and wattage match the computer's requirements. Unless you buy a "bare-bones" PC kit, any PC you purchase will have the power supply already installed. You are likely to need to install a power supply only if you're building a computer from scratch. It is more common that you'll replace a power supply that has failed. The original power supply will have the necessary specifications recorded on its case, telling you what you need to know to order a suitable replacement.

If you truly don't know what power supply you need, you can look up the computer's requirements on the manufacturer's website or go to the motherboard maker's site and search there.

Replacing a power supply may seem like a daunting task, but it's one of the easiest jobs you'll face as a PC technician.

Scenario

You receive a trouble ticket stating that the power supply in the HR manager's computer has failed. You have removed the PC from the manager's office and now have it on your workbench. You looked up the computer make and model on the Web and found out the specifications for the appropriate replacement. You pulled the replacement unit from the supply closet and have it on the bench with the computer. You are ready to open the case, remove the old power supply, and install the new one.

Scope of Task

Duration

This task should take about 15 minutes.

Setup

Ideally, you'll need a PC and an appropriate replacement power supply for the computer. If your power supply doesn't need to be replaced and you want to save yourself the cost of buying a new one, you can just remove the power supply unit from your PC and then reinstall it. You will follow the same steps in either case. As always, take ESD precautions (discussed in Task 1.1) to avoid accidentally damaging electrical components on the motherboard.

Caveat

You can upgrade a PC to use a more robust power supply, especially if you have installed newer components in the computer that are electricity-hungry. Just make sure that the specifications of the power-supply upgrade match the computer's requirements. Check the motherboard's and power-supply's documentation to determine whether you need additional adapters or other equipment to correctly perform the upgrade. It should also go without saying that you will need to completely unplug the power supply from its power source before beginning this exercise.

Procedure

In this task, you will learn how to replace a PC's power supply and verify that the new unit is operational.

Equipment Used

Other than the new power supply, all you'll need is a screwdriver to remove the PC's access panel and the old power supply. To verify that the replacement is successful, you'll need a monitor, keyboard, and mouse attached to the PC when you power it up.

Details

The following exercise will walk you through the process of removing a failed power supply and replacing it with a new unit.

Before attempting this exercise, make sure you have powered down the computer and unplugged the power cord from the back of the PC!

Removing and Replacing a Power Supply

REMOVING THE POWER SUPPLY

1. Locate the screwdriver and remove the screws from the PC's access panel and put them aside.
2. Remove the access panel.
3. Locate the power supply.

It's virtually impossible to not be able to find a computer's power supply. The back of the power supply contains a large fan and the connector for the power cord, and is easily seen on the back of the PC.

4. Make note of how the unit is mounted and how the wires are connected to the motherboard.

 Not all power supplies have the same number or type of power connectors. Three is a common number, but your unit may be different. See this site for an example: www.atxpowersupplies.com/atx-power-supply-powmax-ag-480-watt.htm. Note in the example that, depending on the requirements of the replacement unit and your motherboard, you may need additional pin adapters, extensions, or an IDE-to-SATA drive adapter.

5. Disconnect the power supply's wires from the motherboard.
6. Unscrew the power supply from the PC's frame.
7. Lift the old power supply out of the computer.

INSTALLING THE POWER SUPPLY

1. Locate the replacement power supply.
2. Mount the new unit in the PC frame in the same way the old unit was mounted.
3. Screw the new unit to the computer frame, making sure it is secure.
4. Connect the power supply's wires to the motherboard in the same pattern as the old unit was attached.
5. Make sure the connections are firm.
6. Replace the PC's access panel.
7. Secure the access panel to the PC by replacing the screws.

TESTING THE POWER SUPPLY

1. Verify that a monitor, keyboard, and mouse are attached to the PC.
2. Plug the power cord into the socket on the back of the power supply.
3. Verify that the power cord is plugged into a surge protector that is receiving AC current.
4. Power up the computer and watch the boot process.

Criteria for Completion

You have successfully completed this task when the PC powers up normally and the operating system loads.

Task 1.7: Installing an IDE Hard Drive

Periodically, hard drives fail (which is why you always back up your computers and servers…right?). If your data is backed up, it's an inconvenience but not a total disaster. You can simply replace the failed unit with a new comparable drive (while you're at it, you might as well put in a hard drive with more capacity). You might also end up installing a second hard drive in a computer, but that's pretty unusual in a production environment.

There are a few details that you'll need to know to successfully install a hard drive, but it's a fairly routine task. The time-consuming part is reinstalling the operating system and the application software and then restoring the data from your backup tape or external drive.

 Installing an operating system is covered in Tasks 1.24 and 1.25, and installing application software is addressed in Tasks 1.27 and 1.28. The actual restoration of data from backups is usually handled by an experienced tech in an IT department, so that task is beyond the scope of this book.

Scenario

You have been directed to install a hard drive in a new computer. The hard drive already has an operating system and application software installed via ghosting.

 It's typical in production environments to configure a hard drive on a master machine and then ghost it to other drives and install those drives in PCs. This saves a lot of time in deploying PCs with identical configurations in the company.

The computer is on your workbench, with the hard drive and IDE ribbon cable sitting next to it.

Scope of Task

Duration

This task should take 15 to 30 minutes.

Setup

For this task, you'll need a hard drive and a PC. If you are not in a position to install a new hard drive, you can remove the hard-disk drive (HDD) from the computer and then replace it. As always, take ESD precautions to avoid damaging electrical components in the computer.

Caveat

In this exercise, you will be installing an integrated drive electronics (IDE) hard drive. An IDE drive is also referred to as ATA or PATA (Parallel ATA) drive. As of 2009, most PCs ship with SATA drives onboard, all but replacing PATA drives. Installing a serial drive is only slightly different from installing an IDE drive; however there are enough differences to require that the process have a task dedicated to such an installation.

Installing a SATA drive is described in Task 1.8.

Procedure

In this task, you'll learn how to install an IDE hard drive in a computer.

Equipment Used

You'll need an IDE hard drive and a parallel ribbon cable to connect the hard drive to the motherboard. Besides a screwdriver, you'll also need a pair of needle-nose pliers or a pair of strong tweezers.

Details

The following steps will guide you through the process of installing an IDE hard drive into a PC.

Installing a Hard Drive

INSTALLING THE HARD DRIVE IN A PC

1. Verify that the PC is powered down and unplugged.
2. Locate a screwdriver and remove the screws from the PC's access panel.
3. Remove the access panel.
4. Locate the IDE connectors on the PC's motherboard.

A motherboard usually has two IDE connectors. One is used for the primary hard drive, which you are installing now. The other is typically used to attach a CD or DVD drive or can be used for a second hard drive.

5. Locate the power cord for the hard drive; it will be coming out of the power supply.
6. Locate the holes in the hard drive's bay in the computer; this is where you will use screws to attach the hard drive to the bay.
7. Locate the drive jumpers or switches.

Hard drives need to be set to function as a master, slave, or only drive or cable select. This is controlled by a set of either jumpers or switches on the hard drive. They are usually located on the part of the drive containing the ribbon and power connectors. A diagram on the hard drive will show you the position for the jumpers or switches for each role. Your drive is most likely set up to function as the only drive in the PC.

8. Locate the jumper or switch diagram on the drive.

9. If the jumpers or switches are set for the only hard drive or master role, move on.

10. If the jumpers or switches are not configured correctly, move them to the correct position with your needle-nose pliers or your tweezers.

You can use your fingernails if you are fairly dexterous, but the chances of dropping a tiny jumper into the bowels of your PC are high.

11. Connect the ribbon cable to the ribbon connector on the hard drive.

12. Connect the hard drive power cable to the power connector.

Both of these connectors can fit only one way. Be especially careful connecting the ribbon cable to the hard drive and motherboard, because the pins are thin and easily bent.

13. Place the hard drive in its bay but do not attach it.

Putting one or both hands inside a PC case is difficult; often there isn't very much room for you to work. Make sure all your connections are in place before you mount the hard drive to the PC bay.

Some hard drives mount more like floppy or CD drives. Instead of installing them from the inside, you must remove the face plate from the front of the PC and slide the hard drive in from the front. However, if this is the case, you will not be able to connect the cables to the drive until after it is mounted in the front loading bay.

14. Connect the ribbon cable to the IDE connector on the motherboard.

15. Use the screws that came with the hard drive to mount the drive into the bay securely.

You could probably leave the hard drive sitting loosely in the bay and finish the installation. PCs don't move around much once they are installed in an office or cubicle, but there is still a risk that the hard drive will fall out of the bay and damage the motherboard if the PC is subsequently kicked or moved.

16. Replace the access panel.

17. Secure the access panel to the PC by replacing the screws.

TESTING THE HARD-DRIVE INSTALLATION

1. Verify that a monitor, keyboard, and mouse are connected to the PC.

2. Make sure the power cord is connected and that the computer is receiving power.

3. Power up the unit and watch the boot process.

Because a ghosted hard drive is used in this scenario, there shouldn't be any issues with hard-drive formatting or loading of software.

Criteria for Completion

You will have successfully completed the task when the computer boots normally and the operating system loads.

Task 1.8: Installing a SATA Hard Drive

Now that you've experienced the installation of an IDE drive, it's time to move on to some more recent technology. The most common reason to install a SATA drive is to enjoy the increased performance benefits over IDE. As previously mentioned, the installation process isn't very much different than installing an IDE drive, but there are enough dissimilarities to warrant a separate task in this book.

While Task 1.7 didn't require you to install an operating system, application software, or data onto the IDE drive once it was physically installed, this task is constructed to end at the point where you would normally begin installing an operating system. Tasks 1.24 and 1.25 describe installing Windows XP and Windows Vista respectively, so for additional details, you can skip ahead to those tasks. This task does require that you set the BIOS to recognize the new SATA drive, which isn't always a straightforward process.

Scenario

Your company is in the process of conducting a long-term upgrade of the PCs in each department from IDE to SATA drives. The operating systems, applications, and data are to be reinstalled on the new drives once they are physically upgraded in each computer. You have been tasked to install the SATA drive and then reinstall Windows XP on a PC. The PC is sitting on your workbench and you are ready to begin work.

Scope of Task

Duration

This task should take about 30 minutes

Setup

For this task, you'll need a SATA hard drive and a PC, including any peripheral equipment necessary to complete the installation process. If you don't have a new SATA hard drive, assuming your computer already has such a drive installed, you can uninstall the drive and reinstall it in the PC. As always, take ESD precautions to avoid damaging electrical components in the computer.

You can install a SATA drive in a computer that already has an IDE drive installed, as long as your motherboard supports both standards. This lets you enjoy the performance advantages of using SATA for your data-storage partition while continuing to use the IDE drive for the operating system.

Caveat

Installing a serial drive is only slightly different from installing an IDE drive; however, there are enough differences to require that the process have a task dedicated to such an installation. The major variation is the type of cables and connectors used; however, SATA drives may have no jumpers because SATA supports only one drive per controller. This means that you don't have to set drives as master and slave or cable select.

There is a jumper block next to the SATA interface connector on SATA 150Mbps drives, but it is for factory use only. On the SATA 300Mbps drives, the jumper block next to the SATA connector can be used to force the drive to use 150Mbps mode. You would use this option only if the motherboard came equipped with an older SATA controller that could accommodate only SATA 150Mbps drives.

If your motherboard does not have a SATA host adapter present, you can add an adapter as a PCI card into the PC.

Before proceeding, refer to your motherboard manual to make sure your motherboard supports a SATA drive installation.

Procedure

In this task, you'll follow the steps required to install a SATA drive in a computer and set the BIOS to recognize the drive.

Equipment Used

You'll need a SATA hard drive and separate SATA interface cables and power cables or adapters, which are usually sold separately. You will also need an appropriate screwdriver for removing the PC's access panel as well as for attaching the SATA drive to the PC's frame. Although this task does not require you to install Windows XP, if you wish to do so, you'll need an authentic Windows XP installation CD.

Details

The following steps walk you through the process of installing a SATA drive into a computer and setting the BIOS.

Installing a SATA Hard Drive

INSTALLING THE SATA HARD DRIVE IN A PC

1. Verify that the PC is powered down and unplugged.
2. Locate a screwdriver and remove the screws from the PC's access panel.
3. Remove the access panel.
4. Locate the SATA connector on the PC's motherboard.
5. Locate the SATA drive interface cable.
6. Attach one end of the drive interface cable to the SATA connector on the motherboard and the other end to the cable connector on the drive.

 The connectors on the interface cable can be attached only in one way, preventing attaching the cable incorrectly.

7. Locate the drive power cable.
8. Attach one end of the cable to the power supply and the other end to the SATA drive.

 The PC's power supply may already have a power cable attached that is SATA-compatible. If the power cable is for IDE, you will need an IDE-to-SATA drive power cable adapter.

9. Place the drive into the drive bay.

10. Locate the mounting screws for the drive and the appropriate screwdriver, and secure the drive to the bay.

11. Locate the mounting screws for the PC's access panel and the appropriate screwdriver, and replace the access panel.

12. Reconnect the power cable to the PC's power supply.

CONFIGURING THE BIOS

1. Verify that a monitor, keyboard, and mouse are connected to the PC.

2. Make sure the power cord is connected and that the computer is receiving power.

3. Power up the unit.

4. When the system begins its start-up routine, enter the BIOS setup.

The BIOS setup should appear automatically, but if it doesn't, you can manually get into the BIOS. Different computers have different ways of entering the BIOS setup, including pressing the F7 key or pressing the Esc key.

5. Select the menu item for the SATA drive and set it to Auto.

Because BIOS setups vary, there is no standard method for locating specific menus and submenus.

If you used a PCI SATA host adapter, your BIOS may not recognize the new SATA drive because the PCI card uses its own BIOS. Consult the documentation for the PCI adapter. This issue will not affect the SATA drive's functioning or storage capacity. If you have your drive connected to the SATA adapter on the motherboard and your BIOS does not recognize the drive or identifies it as a SCSI drive, install the drivers for the SATA drive and reboot. Consult the drive's documentation for instructions on how to install the drivers.

6. Verify that your computer is set to look first at your CD drive when booting.

7. Save the settings and exit the BIOS.

8. Locate the Windows XP installation CD and place it in the computer's CD or DVD drive.

9. Reboot the computer.

Continue to Task 1.24 for instructions on how to install Windows XP onto the new SATA drive or Task 1.25 to perform the same task using Windows Vista.

Criteria for Completion

You will have successfully completed the task when the computer boots normally and it is ready to install an operating system.

Task 1.9: Installing a SCSI Drive

Installing a SCSI drive can be a challenge. It is definitely not a Plug and Play technology. As you know, SCSI chains need to be terminated at both ends. Either the motherboard of the computer must have an onboard SCSI controller or you need to install an expansion card with a controller before doing anything else.

 In Task 1.8, you may have had to install an expansion card with a SATA controller in order to complete the task.

Not all devices on a SCSI chain have to be drives. A wide variety of SCSI devices can be linked, although for the sake of this exercise, we will be dealing with only SCSI drives on the chain.

Improperly terminating a SCSI chain is probably the most common problem with an installation. If either end of the chain isn't properly terminated, electrical signals hitting an "unterminated" point will be reflected back along the cable, interfering with normal electrical signals.

Each SCSI device must have a unique ID number in the chain. On some occasions, a specific device needs a particular ID number. Check the manufacturer's documentation before attempting the installation to avoid any pitfalls. Sometimes you'll run into a SCSI device that has a built-in terminator, meaning that it must be installed at the end of the chain.

Installing a SCSI device is not for the faint of heart, but with proper preparation, it is an accomplishable task.

Scenario

You are assigned to install a SCSI drive in a small server. The server has four SCSI drives and one of them has failed. The failed drive has already been removed and all you are expected to do is configure, install, and terminate the replacement drive. The high-level formatting and all subsequent tasks will be handled by the supervising technician.

Scope of Task

Duration

Due to the level of difficulty in successfully installing a SCSI drive, this task could take from 15 to 30 minutes.

Setup

The ideal setup would be to use an older server with SCSI drives installed. You can sometimes "rescue" old servers as they are being decommissioned. More than one starving student has retrieved an ancient server from the trash heap. Although installing a SCSI drive is quite similar to installing an IDE or SATA drive, there are enough differences to require that you have "the real thing" on hand. As always, take ESD precautions to avoid damaging electrical components in the computer.

Caveat

The task includes only the physical installation. Formatting a drive and installing an operating system are separate tasks and not within the scope of this exercise.

 Reformatting a hard drive is covered in Task 1.23, and installing an operating system is discussed in Tasks 1.24 and 1.25.

Procedure

In this task, you will learn how to install and terminate a SCSI drive.

Equipment Used

You will need a screwdriver or screwdrivers to open the access panel of the server and mount the SCSI drive in its bay. SCSI drives are linked in chains, so the connector and power cables are already inside the server. The drive is to be connected to the end of the chain, so it must be terminated. In this scenario, the terminator is the last connector on the linking cable. You will need a small pair of needle-nose pliers or tweezers to adjust the jumpers or switches on the drive.

Details

In this exercise, you will learn each step of the process of installing and terminating a SCSI drive in a server.

 Remember, only the ends of the chain need to be terminated. If you were installing the drive somewhere in the middle, the termination portion of this task would be unnecessary.

Installing a SCSI Drive

SETTING THE JUMPERS OR SWITCHES

1. Locate the jumpers or switches on the SCSI drive.
2. Locate the diagram on the drive describing what each jumper setting means.

This part of the task walks you through an example of the default settings on a particular SCSI drive. The drive you are using may require different settings.

3. Set the SCSI ID to an unused number in the chain.

Narrow SCSI IDs are 0 through 7, with the host adapter usually set to 7. You must select an ID for your drive that is not being used by the adapter or any other devices on the chain. Also, some drives are configured to receive an ID number from the host adapter over the I/O channel.

Some SCSI devices must be set for a particular ID number. Consult the documentation that came with the drive to see if this is true for your device.

4. Set Motor Start to Disable.
5. Set Delay Motor Start to Disable.
6. Set Write Protect to Disable.
7. Set Parity Check to Enable.
8. Set Terminator Power to Other.

The Other setting in step 8 means that another device will provide power to the terminator, even though your drive will be terminated. The host adapter typically provides the terminator power.

INSTALLING THE SCSI DRIVE INTO A SERVER

1. If necessary, power down the server.
2. Remove the power cord from the server's power supply.
3. Use your screwdriver to remove the screws securing the access panel.
4. Remove the access panel.
5. Locate the vacant drive bay in the server.
6. Locate an unused power cable from the power supply.
7. Locate the vacant connector and terminator on the end of the SCSI cable.
8. Insert the SCSI drive into the bay but do not secure it.
9. Attach the power cable to the power socket on the drive.

10. Attach the SCSI cable connector to the connector socket on the drive.

11. Attach the terminator to the terminator socket on the drive.

12. Locate the screws that are to be used to secure the drive to the bay.

13. Locate the holes for the screws in the bay and drive.

 Sometimes the holes for the screws can be at awkward angles or in tight spaces, making this part of the procedure difficult.

14. Secure the drive to the bay with the screws.

15. Replace the access panel.

16. Secure the access panel by replacing the screws.

TESTING THE SCSI-DRIVE INSTALLATION

1. Verify that a mouse, keyboard, and monitor are attached to the server.

2. Plug the power cord into the power supply socket.

3. Verify that the other end of the power cord is plugged into a power source.

4. Power up the server.

5. Listen as each SCSI drive spins up in sequence and verify that the newly installed drive is spinning up.

Criteria for Completion

You will have successfully completed this task when you can hear the newly installed SCSI drive spinning up in the server.

Task 1.10: Installing a CD Drive

As you can see in Tasks 1.7, 1.8, and 1.9, installing different types of drives in a computer requires a very similar process with just a few important differences. Although installing a SCSI drive involves a few different steps compared to installing IDE and SATA drives, in the end you still use the same tools and connect the drive to the motherboard and the power supply.

Installing a CD drive in a PC involves many of the same steps but does present a difference or two. Most PCs come with some type of optical drive, so you won't often be installing the first CD drive in a PC. It is more likely that you'll either be upgrading the optical drive in a computer or adding a second one. For example, a user could have a basic CD drive in their computer but want a CD burner added.

Most new computers come with a DVD drive installed by default, so when installing or repairing CD drives, you will likely be working with older computers.

In any event, the procedures involved are practically the same. Installing a DVD drive is also similar but there are enough differences of substance to require this to be a separate task.

Task 1.11 will go through the details of installing a DVD drive.

Scenario

One of the users at a small branch office has purchased an accounting tutorial on a set of audio CDs. He uses an older computer that does not have a CD drive installed. You have been assigned to go over to the branch office and install a compatible drive. You have been provided with a suitable CD drive kit and tools, have traveled to the branch office, and intend to install the drive in the user's computer while he is away at lunch.

Although it's ideal to be able to take the computer back to your office and perform the installation at your workbench, it's faster to work on the computer where it is. You'll find that you spend a great deal of time under people's desks in their office or cubicle.

Scope of Task

Duration

This task should take no longer than 30 minutes.

Setup

The ideal setup would be to have one PC with no CD drive installed and to possess a suitable CD drive to install in the computer. With just a slight bit of tweaking, you could install a second drive in a computer that already has a CD drive installed. As always, take ESD precautions to avoid damaging electrical components in the computer.

Caveat

You may or may not have to install the drivers for the CD-ROM drive. Windows 2000 Professional, Windows XP, and Windows Vista most likely already have the drivers on board (although Vista has become notorious for having insufficient drivers available). If not, you can use the drivers on the disc accompanying the drive or download them from the manufacturer's site. Also, you will need to attach the three-wire audio cable to either the sound card or the audio circuitry connector on the motherboard.

 I continue to mention Windows 2000 Professional, even though it is an aging operating system, because you will likely encounter it from time to time. Many companies keep using older operating systems to perform "workhorse" tasks based on the principle, "If it ain't broke, don't fix it."

Procedure

In this task, you will learn how to install a basic CD-ROM drive.

Equipment Used

You should need only a flat-head and/or Phillips-head screwdriver to open up the access panel and attach the CD drive securely to the drive bay. You will need a pair of needle-nose pliers or tweezers to set the jumpers or switches. You might also need a flat-head screwdriver if you must pry the face off the computer to get at the selected drive-bay cover. To test the installation, you'll need an audio CD with content on it.

Details

This exercise will guide you through the specific steps necessary to install a CD-ROM drive in a PC and test the installation.

Installing a CD Drive

OPENING THE COMPUTER AND CONFIGURING THE CD DRIVE

1. Power down the PC.
2. Unplug the power cord from the power supply.

 Remember to take ESD precautions before opening the computer case. See Task 1.1 to learn the specific details of preventing ESD damage.

3. Using your screwdriver, remove the screws attaching the access panel to the PC's frame.
4. Remove the access panel.
5. Locate the desired drive bay.
6. Locate the desired drive-bay cover on the front of the PC.
7. Remove the drive-bay cover.

There are usually two tabs on the drive bay cover that attach inside the computer. You need to reach inside the bay, feel for the tabs, depress them, and push the cover out. Some older PCs will require that you pry off the face of the computer before you can access the drive covers.

Some drive bays come with rails installed. If the drive you are installing does not have corresponding drive rails attached, the rails may come with a kit that has the parts necessary for you to screw the rails into the drive bay. From there, it is just a matter of sliding the drive in on the rails.

8. Remove the CD drive from the antistatic bag.

9. Locate the jumpers or switches on the drive.

10. Locate the jumper diagram on the drive.

11. Locate your needle-nose pliers or tweezers and set the jumpers or switches to the master or only drive position.

Step 11 assumes that your CD drive will be on a separate controller from the computer's hard drive and that it will be either the first or only CD drive in the PC. If you are installing this unit as a second CD drive, you must set the jumpers or switches to the slave position and attach it to the connector at the middle of the ribbon cable rather than the end.

For much older drives, do not connect an IDE and a CD drive to the same disk-drive controller. IDE and CD drives operate at different read and write speeds, and having them on the same ribbon attached to the same controller will reduce data transfer to the level of the slowest drive. This is true only of older drives, however. Drives made since about 2000 use independent device timing, which has eliminated this issue. To read an article on this subject, visit www.pcguide.com/ref/hdd/if/ide/confTiming-c.html.

Also, older 40-pin ribbon cables either do not support cable select as in the previous note or, if they do, they use the middle connector for the master and the end connector for the slave. See this site for more: www.pcguide.com/ref/hdd/if/ide/confCS-c.html.

INSTALLING THE CD DRIVE

1. Slide the CD drive into the drive bay from the front.

The front of the CD drive should fit flush against the face of the computer.

2. Locate the ribbon cable that came with the CD drive.

3. Locate the unoccupied disk-drive connector on the motherboard.

The second disk-drive connector is usually labeled as IDE 2.

4. Locate the red or blue edge on one end of the ribbon cable.

The red or blue edge on the connector indicates the location of pin 1.

5. Locate pin 1 on the motherboard disk-drive connector.

6. Carefully match the holes in the ribbon connector to the pins on IDE 2, including pin 1.

7. Gently and firmly push the connector down, attaching it to the motherboard.

8. Match the other end of the ribbon-cable connector to the pins on the CD drive.

9. Gently and firmly push the connector onto the pins.

In step 9, since you haven't yet attached the CD drive to the drive bay, you will need to hold the drive in place with your other hand.

10. Locate a vacant power cable coming from the power supply.

11. Connect the power cable to the power socket on the back of the CD drive.

12. Locate the audio cable coming from the back of the CD drive.

13. Locate the three-pin audio connector on either the sound card or the motherboard audio connector.

14. Match the pins on the audio cable to the audio connector.

15. Gently and firmly attach the cable to the connector.

16. Attach the CD drive to the drive bay with the screws that came with the drive.

17. Replace the access panel.

18. Replace the screws, securing the access panel to the PC's frame.

If necessary, replace the face on the PC after you've completed step 18.

INSTALLING DEVICE DRIVERS AND OTHER SOFTWARE FOR THE CD DRIVE

1. Verify that a standard monitor, keyboard, mouse, and speakers are attached to the PC.

2. Plug the power cable into the PC's power supply.

3. Power up the PC.

4. Locate the driver disc that came with the CD drive.

 In the past, the drivers would be on a floppy diskette if the newly installed device was the only CD drive on the PC. Today, it's unlikely that a computer will not have an optical drive installed by the manufacturer at the factory. If you are installing a CD drive on an older computer, you will likely need to download the latest drivers from the drive manufacturer's website. They are unlikely to still be available on a floppy diskette.

 When working on a user's computer, you will need to be able to log on to the device without knowing the user's password. Make sure there is a separate user account on company computers that allows you to log in for testing purposes. Otherwise, the user must be present to log in to the computer.

5. When the PC is fully booted, insert the driver disc into the appropriate drive or download the drivers from the manufacturer's website onto the desktop.

6. Locate and start the executable file on the disc or the desktop (e.g., Setup.exe) and follow the onscreen instructions.

 The onscreen instructions vary widely depending on the make and model of the CD drive, but they should guide you in how to correctly load the device drivers and other required software.

7. Reboot the PC if necessary.

TESTING THE CD-DRIVE INSTALLATION

1. Verify that speakers are attached to the audio connector on the PC.

2. Verify that the speakers are receiving power and turned on. (Make sure the volume is adjusted to a suitable level.)

3. Locate a test CD that has audio content.

4. Open the CD drive.

5. Place the CD in the drive.

6. Close the drive.

7. Click Start ➢ My Computer.

8. Locate the CD drive in the My Computer window.

> Usually, the first CD drive in a Windows computer is drive D.

9. Look for a change in the CD-ROM icon indicating the contents of the CD.

> If Autoplay is set up, the disc will start to play automatically. Otherwise, a dialog box will open asking which program you want to select to play the disc. If necessary, right-click the CD-ROM icon and select Play.

Criteria for Completion

You will have successfully completed this task when the CD begins to play and you can hear the content.

Task 1.11: Installing a DVD Drive

Although, in principle, installing a DVD drive is similar to installing a CD drive (see Task 1.10), there are quite a few more cables and connectors involved. Specifications vary for DVD drives made by different vendors, so it is prudent to completely read the instructions that came with your new DVD unit before beginning the installation.

This task will cover a basic DVD installation; however, the details of installing the DVD you are using may be different. You may have to divert from some of the steps presented here to successfully install your particular drive.

Most PCs come standard with a DVD drive, so it won't be as common for you to install the first DVD drive into a modern computer as it once was. That said, you may likely install the first DVD drive into older PC hardware. A computer that is a few years old will already have a CD drive, so you will be installing the second optical device in the computer. DVD drives are most commonly used to play movies, although they are also used for mobile data storage.

Scenario

One of your company's managers wants a DVD drive installed in her computer so she can watch video tutorials. She has an older PC with a CD-RW as the only optical drive. You have brought the PC to your workbench and laid out the appropriate tools. Your supervisor has provided you with the DVD-drive installation kit and you are ready to install the drive.

Scope of Task

Duration

This task should take between 30 and 45 minutes.

Setup

Ideally, you will have one PC and one DVD-drive installation kit available for this exercise. You will need to verify that the DVD unit is supported on your PC. You can get this information from the store where you purchased the unit or from the manufacturer's website. The kit should contain all of the cables and other parts necessary for you to install the DVD drive, as well as the driver disc. For this task, it is assumed that the computer already has a CD drive and that the DVD drive will be the second optical drive on board. As always, take ESD precautions to avoid damaging electrical components in the computer.

Caveat

As previously mentioned, there is no one standard method of installing a DVD drive, so the steps you need to take to install your drive may differ from those in this exercise. Also, because of the different features provided by DVD drives, the installation process is somewhat more complex than for a CD or IDE drive. Another consideration is how compressed video data will be managed. DVDs use MPEG-2 compression, so you'll need a method of decompression. Many high-end graphics cards support hardware decompression, but it is still possible that some computers will need an MPEG expansion card installed.

For this task, there should be an appropriate graphics card or MPEG PCI card already installed and working in the PC. If necessary, consult the steps for installing a PCI card in Task 1.3.

Procedure

In this exercise, you will learn to install a generic DVD drive in a computer.

Equipment Used

You may need a flat-head screwdriver, Phillips-head screwdriver, or both to open the access panel and attach the DVD drive securely to the drive bay. You will need a pair of needle-nose pliers or tweezers to set the jumpers or switches. You might also need a flat-head screwdriver if you must pry the face off the computer to get at the selected drive-bay cover. To test the installation, you'll need a DVD disc with content on it. You will also need to have a standard monitor, mouse, keyboard, and pair of speakers available for testing.

Details

This lesson will walk you through the step-by-step process of installing and testing a DVD drive in a computer.

Installing a DVD Drive

OPENING THE COMPUTER AND CONFIGURING THE DVD DRIVE

1. Verify that the power cord is unplugged from the power supply.
2. Use your screwdriver to remove the screws from the access panel.
3. Remove the access panel.
4. Locate the desired drive bay.
5. Locate the desired drive-bay cover on the front of the PC.
6. Remove the drive-bay cover.
7. Remove the DVD drive from the antistatic bag.
8. Locate the jumpers or switches on the drive.
9. Locate the jumper diagram on the drive.
10. Locate your needle-nose pliers or tweezers.
11. Set the jumpers or switches to the slave position.

 Since the PC already has a CD drive installed on the second IDE controller, it is configured as the master drive.

INSTALLING THE DVD DRIVE

1. Slide the DVD drive into the drive bay from the front.
2. Locate the ribbon cable that is attaching the CD-ROM drive to the disk-drive controller.
3. Locate the connector at the midpoint of the ribbon cable.
4. Locate the red or blue edge on the midpoint connector of the ribbon cable.
5. Match pin 1 in the connector with pin 1 on the DVD drive.
6. Gently and firmly connect the ribbon to the drive.
7. Locate an unused power cable from the power supply.
8. Attach the cable to the power connector on the drive.
9. Locate the audio cable that came with the DVD drive.
10. Locate the audio connector on the DVD drive.
11. Attach one end of the cable to the drive.
12. Locate the audio-in connectors on the MPEG card.

13. Connect the audio cable from the DVD drive to the first audio-in connector on the card.

14. Locate the audio cable on the CD-ROM drive.

15. Disconnect the cable from the sound card or motherboard.

16. Connect the cable to the second audio-in connector on the MPEG card.

17. Locate the audio-out connector on the MPEG card.

18. Locate the sound card's three-pin connector.

19. Locate an audio cable in the DVD-drive installation kit.

20. Connect one end to the MPEG card's audio-out connector.

21. Connect the other end to the sound card's connector.

22. Locate the monitor's connection to the video card.

23. Locate the monitor connector on the back of the MPEG card.

24. Disconnect the monitor connector from the video card.

25. Connect the monitor connector to the MPEG card.

 You will need to have a pair of speakers on hand when you begin testing.

26. Locate the video loopback cable included with the DVD-drive installation kit.

27. Connect one end to the output connector on the video card.

28. Connect the other end of the connector to the MPEG card.

29. Use the screws that came with the drive to attach it securely to the drive bay.

30. Replace the access panel.

31. Replace the screws securing the access panel to the PC frame.

INSTALLING DRIVERS AND SOFTWARE FOR THE DVD-DRIVE

1. Verify that a standard monitor, keyboard, mouse, and speakers are attached to the PC.

2. Plug the power cable into the PC's power supply.

3. Power up the PC.

4. Locate the driver disc that came with the DVD drive.

5. When the PC is fully booted, insert the driver disc into the appropriate drive.

6. Navigate to the executable file on the disc and launch it. Then, follow the onscreen instructions.

 The onscreen instructions vary widely depending on the make and model of the DVD drive, but they should guide you in how to correctly load the device drivers and other required software.

7. Reboot the PC if necessary.

TESTING THE DVD-DRIVE INSTALLATION

1. Locate the test DVD disc.

2. Open the DVD drive.

3. Place the disc in the drive.

4. Close the drive.

5. If Autoplay is engaged, the disc will begin playing automatically.

 The program used by the DVD drive may prompt you to answer some questions before playing the disc.

 You can also use a CD audio disc for testing, since the DVD drive should play standard CDs as well; however, this will not test the video playback.

Criteria for Completion

You will have successfully completed this task when you can play a DVD in the drive, view the video, and hear the audio output.

Task 1.12: Installing a Motherboard

A motherboard is also called a system board or mobo, and is the main circuit board of a computer. As a PC technician, you would be installing a motherboard if one were to fail in a PC or if you were building a custom computer from its component parts.

If you are making a PC from scratch, your first step would be to install the power supply in the computer case (see Task 1.6), although it could be installed just prior to physically attaching the motherboard to the PC case. Next, you would install sticks of RAM and the CPU on the motherboard before actually installing the motherboard in the case (see Tasks 1.2 and 1.5, respectively). You might also decide to install the hard drive, optical drives, and other components before the motherboard is secured in the case (as illustrated in Tasks 1.7, 1.8, and 1.11).

Older motherboards required that jumpers and switches be configured, setting the CPU voltage and speed as well as bus speed. On modern motherboards, these settings are configured by the complementary metal oxide semiconductor (CMOS). This makes motherboard installation pretty much a straightforward affair.

Scenario

One of the engineering staff needs a custom-made computer workstation. Your supervisor has assigned you to assist in making the device by installing the motherboard. You have been provided with all the materials, have opened the new case, and have already installed the power supply, the CPU, and the required RAM. Your next step is to begin the motherboard installation itself.

 See Task 1.2 for how to install RAM, Task 1.5 for how to install a CPU, and Task 1.4 for how to install a power supply.

 For practical purposes, you can install the power supply, RAM, and CPU as part of the motherboard installation process, rather than doing so beforehand. The steps in this exercise will prompt you as to when they can be installed. Also, check your motherboard's documentation for further suggestions.

Scope of Task

Duration

This task should take about 30 to 45 minutes.

Setup

You'll need an empty PC case with the power supply already installed. You will also need a motherboard with the CPU and RAM sticks installed. Usually new PC cases and motherboards come with the necessary screws, washers, and riser pins you'll need. As always, take ESD precautions to avoid damaging electrical components on the motherboard.

Caveat

You'll need to consider the form factors of the motherboard and the case so they will match. There is a wide variety of motherboard makes and models, so read the motherboard manual prior to beginning the installation to see if you need to make any other preparations in the installation of your particular motherboard. Do not assume anything regarding the materials that come with your motherboard. Verify the use of all materials prior to beginning work.

For instance, positioning the motherboard in the case is critically important, so before installing anything on the motherboard itself, make sure you practice lining up the holes on the motherboard with the holes on the computer case's metal plate. Also, verify where and how the numerous screw nuts, screws, and washers are to fit before beginning the installation. Some holes on the motherboard are metallic, which means they are meant to have metal screws directly inserted, and other holes are non-metallic, meaning that you must place one or two washers between the screw and the hole. Consult the motherboard documentation for specific details.

Procedure

In this exercise, you will learn how to prepare a PC case for a motherboard installation and how to install a motherboard.

Equipment Used

You will need one or more screwdrivers to fit the different screws used in attaching the motherboard to the case. You will also need a screwdriver and a pair of needle-nose pliers to remove the PCI covers and any other items in the case prior to the installation. Have a marker handy so you can use it to indicate where the riser pins will go.

> Some screws used to attach the motherboard to the case are now able to be inserted and tightened by hand, so a screwdriver for that specific task might not be necessary.

Details

This lesson will guide you through each step in the installation of a motherboard into a PC case.

Installing a Motherboard

PREPARING THE PC CASE

1. Locate a screwdriver and a pair of needle-nose pliers.
2. Locate the PCI covers and any other I/O panels or slots in the case.
3. Use the tools to remove the metal faceplates covering the external drive bays and pop out the tabs covering the portholes in the I/O shield for the motherboard ports.
4. Pull any loose power-supply cables out of the case.

> The types of PC case parts and how they are removed are different depending on the make of the case. You will have to look at your particular case carefully to determine how to remove these elements.

> PC cases can contain sharp metal corners and edges, so take care not to injure yourself.

5. Locate your marker.

6. Locate the screw holes for the riser pins in the PC case.

7. Use the marker to mark the screw holes in the case that line up with the holes in the motherboard.

Sometimes it's helpful to position the motherboard in the case and use the motherboard holes as a guide to mark the holes in the case.

8. Locate the riser pins.

9. Screw each riser pin into the indicated screw holes.

Riser pins are installed just like ordinary screws, turning in a clockwise direction. Screw each pin in completely so when the board is mounted, it will lie flat.

Riser pins are used to keep the motherboard from having direct contact with the metal PC case.

CONNECTING THE FRONT PANEL WIRES

1. Position the motherboard in the case with the holes and riser pins correctly lined up, but do not use the screws to attach the motherboard to the case.

Do not attempt this part of the task without using ESD precautions. See Task 1.1 for details.

To make things easy on yourself, if you haven't done so already, you'll want to install the RAM and CPU before inserting the motherboard into the case, since the relevant slots will be easier to reach right now.

2. Locate the computer case's front panel wires, including the following:

   ▪ HDD LED

   ▪ Power LED

   ▪ Power switch

   ▪ Reset switch

   ▪ Speaker

3. Locate the front panel connectors for each of these wires on the motherboard.

4. Connect each of the front panel wires to their corresponding motherboard connector, matching the positive and negative polarity pins on the wires to the motherboard connectors.

This is usually the point in the process where you would install the PC's power supply into the case if it isn't already present. If you choose to install the hard drive, optical drive, and other units now, you will need to attach the cables from the drives to the motherboard and from the power supply to the drives before proceeding. See Tasks 1.7, 1.8, and 1.11 for details.

INSTALLING THE MOTHERBOARD

1. Locate the screw holes on the motherboard.

2. Locate the screws and washers to be used in securing the motherboard to the riser pins.

Remember to pay attention to which holes are metallic and non-metallic and use the available washers accordingly.

3. Lift the motherboard and align it so that the screw holes and riser pins are matched. Also, move the motherboard toward the back of the case so that the ports that stick out from the motherboard are matched up with the corresponding holes in the case.

4. Place the motherboard on the riser pins, being careful with the handling of any attached cables, the processor, RAM, and so forth.

5. Locate a screwdriver.

6. Attach the motherboard to the riser pins using the appropriate washers and screws.

7. Locate the motherboard power cable on the power supply.

8. Locate the motherboard's power connector.

Consult the motherboard manual if you have difficulty locating the power connector.

9. Carefully align the cable connector to the motherboard connector.

10. Attach the cable to the motherboard connector.

11. Verify that all cables and other connections have been made and are secure.

12. Prior to closing the case, position the cables inside to make sure that good air flow will be maintained once the computer goes into operation.

You will not apply power to the motherboard until the entire computer is assembled and ready for testing.

Criteria for Completion

You will have successfully completed this task when the motherboard is attached to the riser pins in the PC case, the front panel wires are connected, and the power supply and other cables are connected to the motherboard. The motherboard will not be tested until all of the components are installed and the completed unit is powered up.

Task 1.13: Installing a Video Card

Unless you are building a system from scratch, all PCs come with some sort of video capacity—either an integrated video card or a PCI, PCI Express, or accelerated graphics port (AGP) card. Most video expansion cards today are installed in the motherboard's AGP slot. There is only one AGP slot on a motherboard, so it's pretty easy to find.

The most common reason for you to install a video card is to upgrade the system to display high-level graphics. Gamers especially need high-end video cards; however, web and graphic designers also require high-quality video displays.

The process isn't very different from installing a PCI or PCI Express card (see Tasks 1.3 and 1.4 for details), but there are a few extra steps, especially if you are upgrading a video card.

Scenario

Your company has just hired a new graphic designer. A suitable PC has been located for the new employee but the video card needs to be upgraded to run the design programs the company uses. The PC is already on your workbench, as are the video card and everything else you need to do the upgrade.

Scope of Task

Duration

This task should take about 30 minutes.

Setup

Ideally, you will have a PC with a video card already installed and another video card available so you can use it to replace the original. The driver disc for the new card should be in the installation kit with the video card. As always, before the installation begins, take ESD precautions so you don't damage electrical components in the PC.

Caveat

Make sure to completely read any documentation that comes with the new video card prior to doing this exercise. Your card may require specific procedures that are not included in this set of instructions. Also, for this task it is assumed you are using Windows XP.

Procedure

In this exercise, you will learn how to upgrade a video card in a computer and install the video card's drivers.

Equipment Used

You should need only a screwdriver(s) to open the access case, remove the old card, and install the new card in the AGP slot.

Details

This exercise will take you through the motions of uninstalling an old video card and its drivers and installing a new card.

Uninstalling an Old Video Card

UNINSTALLING THE VIDEO-CARD DRIVERS

1. With the system powered up, click Start ➢ Control Panel.

 Control Panel should be set to Classic view to follow along with this task.

2. Double-click Add/Remove Programs.

 The Add/Remove Programs list may take a few moments to populate.

3. Scroll down the list and locate the display drivers for your current video card.
4. Click on the name of the drivers.

5. Click the Change/Remove button.

6. Follow the instructions to remove the video drivers.

7. Close Control Panel.

8. Power down the computer.

 If you are using a Windows 9x/Me computer, you must go to the Display Drivers tab on the Video Card Properties box and select Standard Display Adapter and click OK before powering down the PC.

UNINSTALLING THE OLD VIDEO CARD

1. Unplug the power cable from the power supply.

2. Lay the PC on its side.

3. Locate your screwdriver and remove the screws attaching the access panel to the PC frame.

4. Remove the access panel.

5. Locate the video card.

6. Unscrew the video card from the frame of the computer.

7. Gently pull the old card out of the AGP socket.

 You may have to gently rock the card end to end to loosen it. This prevents putting pressure on the card connector or the AGP port. Also, many video cards have a retention mechanism that must be released prior to removing the card. For a description of this, see http://news.thomasnet.com/fullstory/457886.

8. Remove the card and put it in an antistatic bag.

Installing a Video Card

INSTALLING THE VIDEO CARD IN THE AGP SLOT

1. Locate the new video card.

2. Remove it from the antistatic bag.

3. Line it up with the AGP slot.

4. Gently but firmly press the card into place.

5. Screw the card onto the PC frame.

WARNING   If the video card has an onboard fan, make sure that no cables are at risk of interfering with the fan's operation. Also make sure to follow any special instructions that are required for the proper installation and operation of the fan.

6. Replace the access panel.

7. Replace the screws, securing the access panel to the PC frame.

8. Set the PC upright.

9. Plug the power cord into the power supply's socket.

10. Power up the PC.

INSTALLING THE NEW VIDEO CARD DRIVERS

1. Locate the CD containing the video card drivers.

2. After the PC powers up insert the CD into the optical player, launch the CD, and follow the onscreen instructions to install the drivers.

NOTE   The onscreen instructions may be slightly different depending on the make and model of card you've installed. You will usually be offered the option of searching for drivers or installing from media. It is usually advisable to download the install the latest drivers from the manufacturer's site, if available.

3. When prompted, remove the driver disc and restart the PC.

4. After the PC reboots, right-click anywhere on the Desktop.

5. Click Properties.

6. Click the Settings tab.

7. In the Screen Resolution box, configure the setting for the desired resolution.

8. In the Color Quality box, use the drop-down list to select the desired color quality in bits.

WARNING   Before performing this portion of the task, read the monitor and video-card documentation and make sure the hardware and software support the desired settings.

9. Click the Advanced button.

10. Under DPI Setting, use the drop-down list to select the desired refresh rate.

11. In the Compatibility box, click the Apply the New Display Settings Without Restarting radio button.

12. Click OK to close the Advanced dialog box.

13. Click OK to close the Display Settings box.

Criteria for Completion

You will have successfully completed this task when the card and drivers are installed, you have set the display to the desired settings, and the monitor is correctly displaying the desktop.

Task 1.14: Installing a Laptop Keyboard

Swapping out a keyboard on a PC is just a matter of unplugging the keyboard's PS/2 or USB connector from the back of the computer and plugging in the new one. On a laptop, the procedure is quite a bit more involved. New PC techs sometimes shy away from working on laptops because it seems so much more difficult to access the various components. Also, depending on the make and model of laptop, the process of performing repair tasks is highly variable.

All this is true; however, sooner or later you'll have to face laptop repair and maintenance as part of your job. With a bit of practice, you'll become more comfortable working on laptops.

Users can be particularly hard on laptop computers. If a user travels a lot with the laptop, it probably gets a great deal of use and sometimes abuse. Keyboards are vulnerable to having all manner of substances dropped or spilled in and on them. Keys can get stuck and even come off. If the keyboard can't be repaired by a good cleaning, it will need to be removed and a suitable replacement installed.

Scenario

One of the sales associates has just come back from a trip and brings you her laptop. She complains that one of the keys has fallen off and several others are stuck or nonfunctioning. After a careful examination, you explain that the keyboard will need to be replaced. You put in an order to the manufacturer for a replacement keyboard. The sales associate has already uploaded her data to the file server and will be working on her PC at her desk for the next few weeks. She leaves the laptop with you. The keyboard arrives within a few days. You take the laptop and new keyboard to your workbench and prepare to replace the broken keyboard.

It is becoming very common for a laptop to be the only computer a user has access to, even if the user isn't a "road warrior." Often, people need to attend multiple meetings and conferences throughout the work week, and find it necessary to take notes and access virtual meeting rooms via their networked laptops. When working at their desk, the user places the laptop in a docking station, where he or she is able to use a standard keyboard, mouse, and monitor. In this eventuality, you won't have the luxury of waiting days or weeks for the laptop's replacement part to arrive before you repair the device.

Scope of Task

Duration

This task should take from 30 to 45 minutes.

Setup

Ideally, you should have a laptop and replacement laptop keyboard on hand to perform this task. You can also simply remove the keyboard and install it again to perform the same set of actions. Of course, you will absolutely need a laptop of some type to do this exercise. As always, use ESD precautions to avoid damaging electrical components in the laptop.

Caveat

There seem to be as many types of laptops as there are stars in the sky. This translates into as many different ways of replacing a keyboard on a laptop. In this task, a Dell Inspiron 8200 laptop is used; however, the actual process of doing the same exercise on your laptop could be quite different. Always consult the documentation for your machine or the manufacturer's website for instructions relevant to the laptop you are using.

Procedure

In this exercise, you will learn how to remove and replace a keyboard on a Dell laptop.

Equipment Used

You will need a screwdriver to remove a number of screws on the bottom of the keyboard. You will also need a plastic scribe or similar object to pry the keyboard up from the laptop once it's unsecured.

Details

This task will walk you through the steps of removing a laptop keyboard and installing a new one.

Replacing a Laptop Keyboard

PREPARING TO WORK ON THE LAPTOP KEYBOARD

1. Power down the laptop.
2. Unplug the power cord and external mouse cable, if present.
3. Remove any PC cards, if present.
4. Close the display lid.
5. Remove the battery.

 On an Inspiron 8200, the battery is usually located on the front edge of the laptop on the right. To remove it, locate the triangular latch on the bottom of the laptop just under the battery. Depress the latch and pull the battery forward. It should just slide out.

 The preceding instructions should be followed when you are planning on repairing or replacing any component in the laptop.

REMOVING THE LAPTOP KEYBOARD

1. Turn the laptop over and place it so the front is facing you.
2. Locate three screws labeled with a *K* in a circle.
3. Locate one screw labeled with a *K/M* in a circle.
4. Locate your screwdriver and remove each of these screws.

 The screws in a laptop can be quite long and it can be somewhat time-consuming to remove them.

5. Turn the laptop over with the front facing you.
6. Open the display.
7. Locate your plastic scribe.
8. Locate the "blank" key on the keyboard.

The blank key is located just above the right arrow key on the lower-right side of the keyboard on the Inspiron 8200.

9. Place the scribe under the right side of the blank key.

10. Apply pressure from left to right, pushing the keyboard to disengage the tabs on the left side.

11. Gently lift the right side of the keyboard and balance it on its left side on the laptop.

12. Locate the keyboard ribbon cable.

13. Disconnect the cable from the bottom of the keyboard.

14. Lay the keyboard aside.

INSTALLING THE NEW KEYBOARD

1. Locate the new keyboard.

2. Remove it from the antistatic bag.

3. Rest it on its left side on the laptop.

4. Connect the keyboard ribbon cable to the bottom of the keyboard.

Make sure that the cable does not get crimped when you install the keyboard.

5. Locate the two tabs on the left side of the keyboard.

6. Insert the tabs under the edge of the keyboard housing.

7. Slowly place the keyboard in the housing.

8. Verify that the keyboard is lying flush in the housing.

9. Close the display.

10. Turn the laptop over with the front facing you.

11. Locate the screws removed from the bottom of the laptop.

12. Locate your screwdriver and replace the screws.

13. Turn the laptop over so its bottom is on the workbench and the front is facing you.

TESTING THE KEYBOARD INSTALLATION

1. Replace the battery.

The battery should just slide back in and click into place.

2. Replace the power cord.

3. Lift the display.

4. Power up the laptop.

5. After the laptop has completely booted, open a blank document.

6. Type in the document, verifying that all the keys function properly.

7. Replace any PC cards and other equipment that were attached to the laptop when you received it.

Criteria for Completion

You will have successfully completed this task when the keyboard is installed, the laptop is completely reassembled, and you can use the keyboard normally with all of the keys functioning.

Task 1.15: Installing SO-DIMM in a Laptop

In some ways, installing memory in a laptop is easier than performing the same action in a PC. There seems to be a universal law that says whatever component you need to reach in a PC will be in the most inconvenient and hard-to-reach place. On a laptop, this isn't necessarily so...at least for memory.

The trade-off is that laptop components are smaller and sometimes more delicate (read "easier to break"). SO-DIMM (which stands for small-outline dual inline memory-module) sticks are quite a bit smaller than DRAM (dynamic random access memory), and the clips that hold them into the SO-DIMM sockets are tiny. That's the only real hang-up, though. The actual installation is uncomplicated. You can upgrade a laptop's memory in no time.

Scenario

You have received a trouble ticket stating that one of the testing engineers needs a memory upgrade for his laptop. You receive the specifics regarding the make and model of the laptop and look up the appropriate SO-DIMM module.

See Task 1.2, "Installing RAM," to learn how to research which type of memory is right for a particular computer.

You order the appropriate module, and when it arrives, you take it and your tools to the user's cubicle. The user is about to take a break, leaving you free to upgrade his laptop's memory.

Scope of Task

Duration

This task will take about 10 minutes.

Setup

You'll need a laptop and an appropriate stick of SO-DIMM to upgrade its memory. In a pinch, you can simply remove an existing memory module in your laptop and replace it to simulate the task. As always, take ESD precautions to keep from damaging any electronic components.

Caveat

This task is based on upgrading memory in a Dell Inspiron 8200. The exact method of upgrading memory in your laptop may vary. Consult the documentation for your laptop or search the manufacturer's website for specific instructions. The operating system used in this exercise is Windows XP.

Procedure

This exercise will teach you how to upgrade the memory of a laptop.

Equipment Used

You should only need a screwdriver to open the memory-module cover on the bottom of the laptop.

Details

In this task, you will learn the procedures necessary to upgrade the memory in a laptop.

Installing SO-DIMM in a Laptop

PREPARING TO WORK ON THE LAPTOP

1. Power down the laptop.
2. Unplug the power cord and external mouse cable, if present.
3. Remove any PC cards, if present.

4. Close the display lid.

5. Remove the battery.

Find the procedure for removing a battery in the section "Preparing to Work on the Laptop Keyboard" in Task 1.14.

UPGRADING SO-DIMM IN THE LAPTOP

1. Turn the laptop over with the front facing you.

2. Locate the memory-module cover.

The memory-module cover on an Inspiron 8200 is a small panel located on the left-hand side of the laptop (when it is upside down) and attached by a single screw. Consult the documentation for your laptop to locate the module cover on your device.

3. Locate your screwdriver and remove the screw securing the module cover.

4. Release the two metal tabs holding the cover in place.

5. Lift out the cover.

6. Locate an empty SO-DIMM module slot.

The Inspiron 8200 typically has two slots. The original SO-DIMM module should be in the slot labeled DIMM A.

7. Locate the slot labeled DIMM B.

8. Locate the SO-DIMM module you brought with you.

9. Remove it from the antistatic bag, holding it by its side edges.

10. Align the module to the slot in the correct direction.

The module is made to fit in the slot in only one direction.

11. Slide the module into the slot.

The latches on either side will move aside slightly to allow the module to be placed in the slot.

12. Push the module down into the slot until the two latches on either side click into place.

If the latches don't click and engage, the module may be misaligned. Remove the module and replace it again.

13. Replace the module cover, inserting the side with the metal tabs first.
14. Replace the screw securing the module cover.
15. Place the laptop right side up with the front facing you.
16. Replace the power cord and any other cords and cards you previously removed.
17. Replace the battery.

TESTING THE MEMORY

1. Open the display lid.
2. Power on the laptop.
3. Listen for two beeps as the computer boots.
4. Look for a message on the display screen indicating that the amount of memory on the computer has changed.
5. Follow any instructions you see on the screen.
6. Allow the laptop to continue to boot and the operating system to load.

VERIFYING THE MEMORY

1. On the computer's Desktop, click the Start button.
2. Right-click My Computer and select Properties.
3. On the General tab of the System Properties box, locate the amount of SO-DIMM in the laptop.
4. Click Cancel to close the System Properties box.

The steps to test and verify the memory upgrade are identical to those found in Task 1.2.

Criteria for Completion

You will have successfully completed this task when you have verified that the amount of memory has increased to the correct amount. This amount will vary depending on how much memory the computer originally had and how much you added.

Task 1.16: Installing a Laptop Hard Drive

As you learned in Task 1.7, "Installing an IDE Hard Drive," hard-disk drives periodically fail for a number of reasons. The same can be said for laptop hard drives; however, the procedure to replace a laptop's hard drive is quite a bit different and, in many cases, easier than replacing a drive in a PC.

This task is about as common as replacing an IDE drive in a PC. As always, replacing the drive is easy. Recovering the lost data is harder. Make sure you periodically back up any data you can't live without.

Scenario

You have received a trouble ticket stating that a marketing associate's hard drive appears to have locked up. You call the associate and she agrees to bring the laptop to the IT department.

When she arrives, she explains that while she was out of town and using her laptop, she started hearing clicking noises coming from the computer. The noises increased in frequency until they abruptly stopped. At that point, she got a blue screen displaying error messages she couldn't understand. She turned off the power by pressing and holding the power button down. When she tried to power the device back up, power was applied but the screen remained blank.

You verify that the problem is the hard drive, agree to replace it, reload the operating system and application software, and upload her data from the most recent backup on the file server.

You order a new hard drive, and when it arrives you take it and the laptop to your workbench and begin to work.

This task will cover only the physical replacement of the hard drive. Tasks 1.24 and 1.25 cover installing an operating system, and Tasks 1.27 and 1.28 describe installing Microsoft and non-Microsoft application software.

Scope of Task

Duration

Physically replacing the drive should take about 15 minutes.

Setup

The ideal setup is to have a laptop and a compatible spare hard-drive unit to use in this task. If a spare unit is not available, you can remove the existing hard drive and then replace it. As always, use ESD precautions to prevent damaging the electrical components in your laptop.

Caveat

As with all laptop tasks, there are many different ways to do this exercise, depending on the make and model of your computer. Read the documentation for your laptop, either the hard copy or online at the vendor's site. In this task, a Dell Inspiron 8200 is used.

Procedure

This exercise will teach you how to replace a hard drive in a laptop.

Equipment Used

You'll only need a screwdriver to remove the screw securing the hard drive to the laptop.

Details

This lesson will take you through the steps of removing a hard drive from a laptop and replacing it with a new unit.

Replacing a Laptop Hard Drive

PREPARING TO WORK ON THE LAPTOP

1. Power down the laptop.

2. Unplug the power cord and external mouse cable, if present.

3. Remove any PC cards, if present.

4. Close the display lid.

5. Remove the battery.

REMOVING THE LAPTOP HARD DRIVE

1. Locate the hard drive.

The hard drive on an Inspiron 8200 is located on the left side of the laptop (when it's upside down) at about the midsection.

2. Locate the screw securing the hard drive.

3. Locate your screwdriver and remove the hard drive's restraining screw.

4. Grasp the hard drive and slide it out of its bay.

5. Put the unit aside.

INSTALLING THE LAPTOP HARD DRIVE

1. Locate the new hard drive.

2. Remove it from the antistatic bag.

3. Orient it correctly at the opening of the bay.

4.   Slide the hard drive into the bay until it snaps into place.

5.   Replace the restraining screw.

6.   Turn the laptop right side up with its front facing you.

7.   Plug the power cable back in.

8.   Replace the battery.

VERIFYING THE INSTALLATION

1.   Once the laptop is completely reassembled and connected to a power supply, power it up.

2.   When the drive boots, you should receive a message indicating that there is no operating system installed.

   The hard drive is now ready to have an OS installed.

Criteria for Completion

You will have successfully completed this task when your laptop successfully boots. In the task scenario, a complete recovery would require the installation of the operating system, applications, and backed-up data.

Task 1.17: Installing a Laptop Optical Drive

As you saw in Tasks 1.10 and 1.11, there is quite a bit of difference between installing a CD drive and a DVD drive in a PC. In a laptop, however, the process is exactly the same. Part of what makes it more simple is that laptops support only one optical drive and one hard drive, so there's no need to set jumpers or switches to master and slave position. Also, the units are modular, so there are no cables to deal with.

The drawbacks are size, capacity, and heat. All of the laptop components are literally on top of each other, so dispelling excess heat remains a problem. However, the process of installing a laptop CD or DVD drive is about the same as installing a laptop hard drive (see Task 1.16).

Scenario

You receive a trouble ticket stating that one of the sales reps is complaining that the DVD player on his laptop is broken. You arrange a time to meet the rep at his cubicle. Once there, he explains that he was placing a DVD into the open drive two days ago and he slipped and fell forward, cracking the unit. You examine the drive and confirm that it is damaged.

You take the laptop back to the IT department and place it on your workbench. You locate a suitable replacement unit in the stock room and place it next to the laptop. You lay out your tools and begin your work.

Scope of Task

Duration

This task should take about 15 minutes.

Setup

The setup is virtually identical to the one in Task 1.16. If you don't have a spare optical drive, just remove and replace the existing optical drive on your laptop.

Caveat

As with all laptop tasks, before you begin, check the documentation for your particular laptop and determine if the procedure to perform this exercise differs from the instructions you are reading here. The laptop used in this task is a Dell Inspiron 8200.

Procedure

This exercise will show you how to replace the optical drive in a laptop.

Equipment Used

All you should need is a screwdriver to remove the screw holding the optical drive in place. Have a DVD handy for testing purposes.

Details

This lesson will walk you through the steps of removing an optical drive from a laptop and replacing it with another unit.

Replacing a Laptop Optical Drive

PREPARING TO WORK ON THE LAPTOP

1. Power down the laptop.
2. Unplug the power cord and external mouse cable, if present.
3. Remove any PC cards, if present.
4. Close the display lid.
5. Remove the battery.

REMOVING THE OPTICAL DRIVE FROM A LAPTOP

1. Locate the optical drive.

On an Inspiron 8200, the optical drive is located on the right-hand side (when the laptop's upside down) of the computer.

2. Locate the drive's restraining screw.

You should find the screw on the bottom of the laptop, directly below the drive. Verify the location of the screw for your laptop in its documentation.

3. Locate your screwdriver and remove the restraining screw.
4. Locate the tab on the optical drive.
5. Pull the tab, sliding the drive out of the bay.
6. Put the drive aside.

INSTALLING THE NEW OPTICAL DRIVE IN A LAPTOP

1. Locate the replacement optical drive.
2. Remove it from the antistatic bag.
3. Correctly orient the drive to the bay.
4. Slide the drive into the bay until it clicks into place.
5. Replace the restraining screw.
6. Turn the laptop to its upright position.

TESTING THE OPTICAL DRIVE INSTALLATION

1. Plug the power cable back in.
2. Replace the battery.
3. Lift the display lid.
4. Power on the laptop.
5. After the laptop boots, open the DVD door.
6. Locate your test DVD and place it into the drive.
7. Close the drive door.

You should hear the optical drive spin up as it prepares to play the DVD.

8. If Autoplay is functioning, the DVD's display program will open and the disc will start to play.

In this scenario, the unit that was replaced was identical to the original, so the appropriate drivers and software were already loaded on the laptop.

Criteria for Completion

You will have successfully completed this task when the new optical unit is installed and it correctly plays the test media.

Task 1.18: Installing a Docking Station

As I mentioned in Task 1.14, it is becoming increasingly common for a laptop to be the only computer that users are issued in the work environment. This doesn't just include excessively mobile users, but all workers. This allows a user to perform standard computing tasks at their desks and still take a mobile computer with them to meeting rooms and other remote locations.

Of course, no one ever said that a laptop monitor and keyboard were as easy to use as the desktop counterparts. That's where the docking station (otherwise known as a port replicator) comes in. As you are likely aware, the docking station is a hardware interface that allows the user to "plug in" the laptop to a piece of machinery that then allows connections to a desktop mouse, keyboard, and monitor, as well as network, power, and other cables. The worker experience using the docking station is as if they had a PC under their desk rather than a laptop sitting on their desk.

Installing a docking station isn't a very complex task, but in today's enterprise computing environment, it is a job you'll find yourself doing often.

Scenario

Your company has just hired a new analyst. She has been issued her laptop and has a flat-screen monitor, keyboard, and mouse available to her. You have been informed that her docking station, which was ordered last week, has arrived and is at the analyst's desk, waiting to be installed. You arrange a time at the beginning of the work day to visit her cubicle so you can install and test the docking station. After arriving at the analyst's desk and unpacking the docking station, you're ready to get to work.

Scope of Task

Duration

This task should take 30 minutes or less.

Setup

You'll need a laptop that is docking station–capable. That is, the laptop must have an interface located traditionally on the bottom or back of the laptop that will allow it to attach to the docking-station interface. In the work environment, a standard laptop and corresponding docking station are ordered together, but you may have to do some shopping to gather the correct units if you intend to perform this task. You'll also need a standard monitor, keyboard, and mouse to attach to the docking station. Ideally, you'll have a network cable ready to connect. The power cable will come with the docking-station kit.

Caveat

As you might have guessed, unless you already own a laptop that is made to be used with a docking station, you won't be able to perform this task, even if you purchase a docking station. Most individual laptop owners don't buy such a setup, so performing this task can be accomplished only if you work for an organization that has such equipment available or if you decide to purchase the hardware yourself. Also, the make and models of the laptop and docking station to be used must be compatible. There are a wide variety of units to choose from, so check the documentation before proceeding.

Procedure

This scenario will show you the steps to install a docking station, attach a laptop and other devices, and test the laptop performance while docked.

Equipment Used

You won't need any tools to install the docking station and to connect the laptop and other equipment. All of the connections you'll need to make can be done by hand.

Details

You will be taken through the steps of setting up a docking station and attaching all the necessary equipment to allow a person to use a laptop as if it were a desktop computer.

Installing a Docking Station

SETTING UP THE DOCKING STATION

1. At the user's desk, verify that the laptop and the docking station are compatible by checking the make and model numbers or other available documentation.

2. Verify that the laptop, monitor, keyboard, and mouse are present as well as a network cable.

3. Open the docking-station packaging if you have not already done so and remove the contents.

4. Verify that the correct docking station and all necessary peripherals, such as a power cable, are present.

5. Position the docking station in a location that the user has requested and verify that the location will be within reach of power and network outlets and cables.

6. Locate the power connector on the docking station.

7. Locate the power cable and power supply for the docking station.

8. Plug in one end of the power cable to a power outlet or power strip and plug in the other end to the docking station.

NOTE   Most business desks in cubicles have openings in various areas on the desk surface to allow cabling to pass from the top of the desk to underneath the desk. You will most likely be feeding cables through such an opening as you progress through this exercise.

9. Press the power button on the docking station to verify that it is receiving power, and then press the power button again to turn off the unit.

TIP   Most docking stations have a power light so you can see power is reaching the unit, even when a laptop or other equipment is not attached.

ATTACHING PERIPHERALS TO THE DOCKING STATION

1. Locate the connectors for the peripherals on the docking station, such as the monitor, keyboard, and so on.

2. Position the monitor where the user has requested, verifying it is within reasonable distance from the docking station.

3. Connect the monitor I/O cable to the monitor port on the docking station.

4. Locate the monitor's power cable and connect one end to a power outlet or power strip, and the other end to the monitor.

5. Press the monitor's power button to verify that it is receiving power and then turn it off.

6. Locate the keyboard and place it in front of the monitor or where the user has requested.

7. Connect the keyboard cable to the corresponding port on the docking station.

8. Locate the mouse and place it where the user has requested.

9. Connect the mouse cable to the corresponding port on the docking station.

10. Locate the Ethernet cable and verify it is connected to an available LAN port.

It is typical for business environments to have all cubicles and other work spaces wired for LAN connections, so finding a network connection and cable available should be no problem.

11. Connect the other end of the cable to the corresponding port on the docking station.

12. If any other equipment needs to be attached, such as a local printer, locate and connect the equipment using the proper cables and ports.

ATTACHING THE LAPTOP AND TESTING THE DOCKING STATION

1. Consult the docking station and laptop documentation to verify the proper method of attaching the laptop to the docking station.

There are a wide variety of procedures, so make sure you are familiar with how your equipment connects before proceeding.

2. Attach the laptop to the docking station.

3. Press the power button on the monitor.

4. Press the power button on the docking station to power up both the docking station and the laptop.

5. Watch the monitor to verify that you can see the boot or splash screen as the operating system loads.

6. Either have the user log on to the laptop or log on using a test account for the computer.

This effectively tests the keyboard connection.

7. After the operating system has finished loading, test the functioning of the mouse, keyboard, network connection, and so forth to verify that the computer can be used normally while attached to the docking station.

8. Power down the computer and disconnect the laptop, then power it up without being connected to the docking station to verify that it operates correctly.

9. Power down the laptop, reconnect it to the docking station, then power up the docking station to verify that the user can interact with the laptop normally while using the docking station.

Don't assume that just because the connection initially works, the laptop and docking station will work correctly with repeated connections and disconnections. Disconnect and reconnect the laptop at least once to make sure it works in both modes.

Criteria for Completion

You will have successfully completed this task when you can connect, disconnect, and reconnect the laptop to the docking station and be able to use the computer normally, both disconnected and connected to the docking station.

Task 1.19: Installing a KVM Switch

The idea of a keyboard-video-mouse (KVM) switch is that it allows you to use a single keyboard, monitor, and mouse on two or more computers or servers. KVMs are traditionally used to attach several servers so you can switch the use of your keyboard, monitor, and mouse between them. After all, this equipment takes up a lot of space, and space is usually at a premium in a server room. Chances are you don't need to see the display of more than one of your servers at any given time.

 With the current popularity of running numerous virtual machines on a single piece of hardware, KVMs are used less, but you will no doubt still be required to install and maintain such equipment.

If you have two computers connected through a KVM device, you can switch to unit A and work on the first server and then switch to unit B and access the second server. Although junior PC techs don't do a large amount of work with server maintenance (the more typical role is in desktop support), occasionally you'll be asked to install a KVM switch and verify that it works.

Scenario

A second server has just been installed at one of your company's branch offices. Both servers have been configured but are currently shut down. You've been assigned to install a KVM switch so that a single keyboard, monitor, and mouse setup in the server room can be used to work with both servers.

The senior tech provides you with a KVM installation kit and explains the setup. You take the kit and your tools and drive to the branch office. You introduce yourself to the supervisor on duty and she takes you to their small server room. You set the KVM unit and toolkit on the table next to the monitor, mouse, and keyboard and start the job.

Scope of Task

Duration

This task should take about 20 minutes.

Setup

You will need to have two PCs, one KVM unit, and one monitor, keyboard, and mouse. Have both PCs powered down before starting this exercise. You will also need the appropriate cabling to connect both computers to the KVM device. Those cables should come with the KVM switch. ESD procedures are not necessary because you won't be coming in direct contact with delicate electrical components.

Caveat

There are a number of different makes and models of KVM switches on the market, so the procedure for installing yours may differ slightly.

Procedure

This lesson will teach you how to connect two computers to a single KVM switch and, using a single monitor, keyboard, and mouse, be able to switch back and forth between the two computers.

Equipment Used

No tools are needed to complete this task besides what is described in the "Scope of Task" section. The only thing you might need is a set of plastic ties for cable management.

Details

You will be guided through the steps necessary to connect two computers to a KVM switch; attach a single monitor, keyboard, and mouse to the switch; and use the switch to toggle back and forth between the two computers.

Installing a Two-Port KVM Switch

CONNECTING THE PERIPHERALS TO THE KVM SWITCH

1. Place the switch in its permanent location in proximity to the servers, monitor, keyboard, and mouse.
2. Verify that both servers have power cords plugged into their power supplies.
3. Verify that both servers are powered down.
4. Locate the output ports for the monitor, keyboard, and mouse on the back of the KVM switch.
5. Attach the monitor connector to the video output port on the switch.
6. Attach the keyboard connector (PS/2 or USB) to the keyboard output port on the switch.
7. Attach the mouse connector (PS/2 or USB) to the mouse output port on the switch.

CONNECTING COMPUTERS TO THE KVM SWITCH

1. Locate the input ports for the monitor, keyboard, and mouse connections for position A.

2. Locate the input ports for the monitor, keyboard, and mouse connections for position B.

3. Locate the two sets of KVM cables to be used to connect the KVM switch to the two servers.

4. Attach the monitor, keyboard, and mouse connectors on one end of the first cable to the input ports for the monitor, keyboard, and mouse connectors for position A on the switch.

5. Locate the monitor, keyboard, and mouse connectors on the first server.

6. Locate the loose end of the cable you just attached to the switch.

7. Attach the monitor, keyboard, and mouse connectors on the cable to the appropriate ports on the first server.

Connecting individual cables from the switch to server A and then from the switch to server B will help avoid confusion as to which cable goes with which server.

8. Attach the monitor, keyboard, and mouse connectors on the second cable to the appropriate input ports for position B on the KVM switch.

9. Locate the loose end of the second cable.

10. Attach the monitor, keyboard, and mouse connectors on the cable to the appropriate ports on the back of the second server.

11. Locate the power cord for the KVM switch.

12. Plug it into the power socket of the switch.

13. Locate a vacant plug on the power strip or UPS unit.

14. Plug the other end of the KVM power cord into the power device.

15. Locate your plastic ties in your toolkit.

16. Organize the different sets of cables and contain each bundle with a set of ties.

Although you don't need to practice good cable management for the sake of this exercise, in the real world you are expected to be not only technically proficient, but also tidy. Nobody wants to deal with a nest of snakes... or cables.

TESTING THE KVM INSTALLATION

1. Power up the KVM device.

2. Power up the first server.

3. Power up the second server.

4. When all devices are fully powered and booted, press the A button.

 You should see the desktop of the first server with the login dialog box.

 It is assumed that you have login credentials for these servers.

5. Log in to server A.

6. Set the background color or some other obvious visual indicator to a nondefault configuration.

7. Press the B button to switch to the other server.

8. Log in to server B.

9. Repeat switching back and forth between A and B to test the installation.

10. Practice using the keyboard and mouse on both servers A and B to test them.

11. When done, log off both servers.

Criteria for Completion

You will have successfully completed this task when you are able to freely switch back and forth between both computers and use the monitor, keyboard, and mouse normally on both machines.

Task 1.20: Installing a Complete Workstation from the Box

When you think of working as a PC technician, especially from the hardware point of view, you probably imagine either repairing or replacing bits and pieces of an overall computer. However, there is something called a workstation rollout that you will occasionally partici-pate in. This is when a company is opening a new department or expanding a department and needs to have 80 new workstations up and running in two days. You can also have a rollout when PC hardware and the OS are being upgraded in an existing office.

What you can face as a tech is 80 boxes sitting beside 80 desks in different offices and cubicles waiting for you (and the rest of your team) to unbox them, assemble the different parts, hook them up to the network and power, and boot them. If you are operating on a much smaller scale, you could be solely responsible for the rollout.

Then the fun begins because they all have to be set up to a specific set of configurations, which means either you'll be carrying around a CD to load that information on the computer, or the computer's hard drive is ghosted and you'll need to go through a setup wizard. It's not all a drag, though. If you have to work long hours on a large rollout over the weekend, the team lead usually springs for pizza.

Scenario

One of your company's branch offices is still using Windows 2000 Professional on its PCs. You have been assigned to perform a complete hardware and operating-system upgrade for the office's six PCs. You will need to physically replace the computers and configure the new PCs to connect to a local server and run proprietary software. You will also be responsible for boxing up the old equipment and using the provided labels to prepare them for shipping back to the corporate office.

You've been provided with instructions that will walk you through the procedure of performing the hardware and OS rollout. You have been assigned to start on a Friday morning so you'll be working around the employees at the branch office. You have arrived at the branch office and introduced yourself to the manager. She has shown you where all the boxes containing the new machines are placed as well as the tape and packing labels you'll need later. You go to the first workstation, lay out your instructions, and begin to follow them.

Scope of Task

Duration

Realistically, rolling out six desktops and testing them should take four to five hours, depending on how much configuration is needed and how smoothly the job goes. Performing this task with a single computer should take about an hour.

Setup

The setup for this exercise can only be approximated in a home or small lab environment. The best you could do would be to have access to a completely boxed computer that needs to be unboxed, have all of the physical cabling connected, have a connection to the network, and be set up to communicate with the other computers in the network.

Caveat

This is a very common task for a PC tech at a company that is budgeted to slowly upgrade its PC hardware and operating-system platforms. However, it is a difficult task to replicate in terms of practicing because the PCs involved in a rollout have already been configured to run through a setup routine when booted. Your job is to follow instructions, call the IT department if something doesn't go as planned, and clean up after yourself. Part of your job in this case is to empty the garbage, or at least take the empty boxes to the nearest dumpster.

Even if you aren't in a position to follow every step of this task, just going through it will provide you with an inside glimpse into one of the ordinary activities done by technicians. Although it is typical for your instructions to include all six PCs, this task will cover only the first one; it is assumed that the setup for the other five is identical.

For the purpose of this exercise, assume the new operating system being rolled out is Windows XP Professional.

Procedure

This lesson will show you how to perform a small hardware and OS rollout.

Equipment Used

You won't be opening up any of the PC cases, so you won't need much in the way of tools. In a scenario such as this, you will need a box cutter to open the boxes, tape to seal them once you put the old units inside and ready them for shipping, and probably some plastic ties to tidy up the cabling.

Details

This exercise will take you through the whole process of a hardware and OS rollout, including unboxing the new computer, physically setting up the computer, running the configuration wizard, and verifying that the PC can communicate with the network, including the server.

Preparing to Roll Out the First Computer

INVENTORYING THE NEW EQUIPMENT

1. Locate your box cutter.
2. Carefully cut the tape on the top of the box.
3. Open the box.
4. Remove the invoice from inside the box.
5. Read the invoice, taking note of what you should find in the box.
6. Remove all of the equipment from the box, including the new PC.
7. Compare the equipment to the invoice, making sure they match.
8. Write on the invoice that everything listed was delivered.

 You will be expected to keep track of all of the paperwork and transport it to the main IT department when the work is done.

DECOMMISSIONING THE FIRST WINDOWS 2000 PROFESSIONAL WORKSTATION

1. Locate the first computer you are going to replace.

2. Ask the user to log off the computer.

3. After the user logs off, sit at the workstation and perform a graceful power down.

As part of your introduction to the workers at the office, you are usually instructed to tell them what to expect and that you will try to disrupt their work as little as possible. They have typically received this information before your arrival, but you need to be polite and remember that you are a guest in their office.

4. Get under the desk and access the old unit.

5. Unplug the keyboard, mouse, and monitor connectors.

6. Unplug the Ethernet connector and the power cord.

7. Lift the old PC out from under the desk.

PCs can be situated either on or under the user's desk, depending on the size of the unit and the user's personal preferences.

8. Place the old PC in the box the newer unit arrived in.

9. Replace the packing material (such as Styrofoam) to protect the older unit.

10. Seal the box securely with packing tape.

11. Attach the preaddressed shipping label to the box.

12. Set the box in a preselected area in the office, out of the way of the users.

Rolling Out the First Computer

PHYSICALLY INSTALLING THE FIRST COMPUTER

1. Locate the first new PC.

2. Place it under the user's desk in the same position the old PC occupied.

3. Locate the power cord used by the old PC.

In this scenario, you'll be using all of the old cables and peripherals for the rollout. Only the PC will be new.

4. Plug the cord into the new computer's power supply. The power supply is inside the PC. A connection for it is located on the back of the computer. See Task 1.6 for the definition of a computer's power supply.

5. Locate the Ethernet cable you removed from the old PC.

6. Plug the Ethernet cable into the new computer's NIC port.

7. Locate the keyboard, mouse, and monitor connectors from the old PC.

8. Connect them to the appropriate ports on the new PC.

PERFORMING THE INITIAL CONFIGURATION

1. Sitting at the keyboard, power up the PC and let it boot.

> Usually once the operating system loads, a proprietary login screen appears. Your instructions will include login credentials. The credentials used in the subsequent steps, including the IP address of the local server, are bogus and just used as examples.

2. Type the username **tech01** in the Username field.

3. Type the password **csicsic** in the Password field.

4. Click Start.

5. Click Run.

6. In the Run box, type **cmd** and press Enter.

7. At the command prompt, type **ipconfig/all**.

8. Verify that the PC has received a dynamic IP address from the DHCP server at the branch.

> It seems prudent to mention again that Windows XP and Vista are configured by default to use Automatic Private IP Addressing (APIPA) in the event that the computer cannot acquire a dynamic address. If the address is returned in the 169.254.*x.x* range and the subnet mask is 255.255.0.0, the computer is using APIPA. Consult with your network administrator to find out what subnet mask and IP address range you would expect the computer to acquire.

9. Type **ping 192.168.0.1** at the prompt and verify that there is a connection to the server.

10. Type **ping www.google.com** at the prompt and verify that there is a connection to the Internet.

11. Close the command-line interface (CLI).

At this point, you usually run through a routine to configure the new PC for the office. The following is an example. This part of the process can be highly variable.

CONFIGURING THE NEW PC FOR ITS ENVIRONMENT

1. Double-click the CSIC icon on the Desktop.
2. In the Available Servers list, click on server CSIC-1701 to select it.
3. Click OK.
4. When the Configuration Status box appears, watch the green progress indicator until it moves completely across the box and flashes green.
5. Click Done.
6. Log out of the workstation.
7. Repeat the entire process for the other five computers.

Completing the Rollout

1. Verify that you have completed the rollout for all six new machines.
2. Verify that you have boxed and sealed all six of the old workstations in their boxes.
3. Verify that you have correctly labeled all six boxes for shipping and moved them to an out-of-the-way area.

On the next business day, the office will arrange for its selected shipping company to come, take the boxes, and transport them to their destination.

4. Clean up any excess packing material or other waste that was created during the roll-out and dispose of it in a nearby dumpster.
5. Verify that all six users can log in to the network and perform their jobs.
6. Complete and sign all documentation and have the manager countersign.
7. Call the IT department and advise them that the job is completed and you'll be bringing in the paperwork.

Criteria for Completion

In the scenario, you will have successfully completed the task when all six new workstations are fully operational and networked. If you have been simulating the exercise by assembling and networking a PC, you will have successfully completed the task when you have attached all peripherals to the PC, connected it physically to the rest of the network, powered up the machine, and are able to perform typical tasks and have network connectivity.

Task 1.21: Installing Drivers from a Disc

Long gone are the days when a computer could contain by default all of the hardware drivers necessary to work and play well with every device and component on the market. Chances are, if you install a piece of hardware or a peripheral, you'll also have to install the drivers.

Most of the time, this isn't much of a chore, especially if you are installing a new device and have the driver disk that came with the hardware. Windows makes it pretty easy, but you do have to go through a few steps. Get used to them. As a PC tech, you'll be installing or updating drivers almost all the time.

Scenario

A user has turned in a trouble ticket stating that he is having difficulty playing audio tutorials on his PC. You've investigated and determined that the problem is his sound card. You install a replacement PCI sound card (see Task 1.3) and now you need to install the drivers. You have the driver disc that came with the sound card and are ready to do the installation.

The sound-card scenario is only an example. You'll end up installing drivers for a wide variety of components.

Scope of Task

Duration

This task should take about 10 minutes.

Setup

Ideally, you will have just installed a new device or component and have the driver disc for the new piece of hardware handy.

Caveat

In this lesson, you'll be using Windows to do the installation, but often the vendor's driver disc has its own interface and installation procedure. In the vast majority of cases, you just need to follow the onscreen instructions and the drivers will be successfully installed.

Procedure

This lesson will teach you how to install device drivers from a CD.

Equipment Used

The only thing you'll need after the device is installed is the driver disc.

Details

This task will walk you through the steps of using Windows to install a device driver from a CD.

Installing Device Drivers from a Disc

GETTING READY TO INSTALL DRIVERS FROM THE DISC

 For this task, you should have already installed the sound card and powered up the Windows XP computer.

 Some devices require that you install the drivers before you power up the new equipment. Consult the device's documentation before continuing.

1. Locate the driver disc.
2. Locate the driver installation instructions.
3. Verify that the correct procedure is to use Windows to install the drivers.

 You may fail to correctly install the device drivers if you don't follow the recommended method of installing them from the driver disc.

INSTALLING FROM THE DEVICE DRIVER DISC USING WINDOWS

1. Sitting at the keyboard, click Start.
2. Right-click My Computer.
3. Click Properties.
4. Click the Hardware tab.
5. Click the Device Manager button.
6. Locate the new device in the Device Manager list.

 A yellow exclamation point may appear next to the device, indicating that it is not functional at this time.

7. Expand the Sound Card notation in the list.

8. Right-click the name of the sound card.

9. Click Properties.

10. Click the Update Drivers button.

11. In the Hardware Update Wizard, click the Install from a List or Specific Location (Advanced) radio button.

12. Click Next.

13. Insert the driver disc in the PC's CD or DVD drive.

14. Click the Search for the Best Driver in These Locations radio button.

15. Verify that the Search Removable Media (Floppy, CD-ROM) box is checked.

16. Click Next.

17. When the search of the disk locates the driver, select it and click OK.

 A dialog box may appear indicating that the driver isn't digitally signed. This is not a serious situation; it only means that Microsoft has not specifically tested the driver with Windows XP. Click the Continue Anyway button.

18. After the driver installs, click Finish.

19. If prompted, click the Restart button to reboot the PC.

20. Remove the driver disc.

Criteria for Completion

You will have successfully completed this task when the computer reboots and you can use the new device normally.

Task 1.22: Installing Drivers from the Internet

Probably the most difficult task in installing drivers from the Internet is finding them. Although it makes sense to go to the manufacturer's site first, depending on how the company's site is set up, it may not be easy to locate the right drivers. Also, if you are looking for drivers for a legacy device, the vendor may have gone out of business. Task 2.6 will focus on how to find drivers online. For this task, it is assumed that you've located the right driver page to find the needed driver, download it, and install it.

Scenario

You are installing an HP All-in-One device as a local printer/fax/scanner on a user's computer. You don't have the driver disc that originally came with the device but can find the drivers online. The computer has an Internet connection and you can go to HP's site and find the drivers page for the product.

Scope of Task

Duration

This task should take about 15 minutes.

Setup

You'll need a computer with an Internet connection and, ideally, a device that's connected to the PC and needs updated drivers. You can also download the drivers for just about any device but not install them.

Caveat

If you wanted to update the drivers of a device already installed on your computer, you could just use the Device Manager to search for drivers online. (Task 1.21 used the Device Manager to install drivers from a CD.) This task focuses on a situation in which you are installing a new device and must locate and download drivers from the Internet. In this example, you are downloading an HP device driver, but this task is applicable for any manufacturer or device.

Procedure

This task will show you how to download and install device drivers from an Internet site.

Equipment Used

You only need a computer with an Internet connection to complete this task.

Details

This task will show you the steps necessary to download and install device drivers from a manufacturer's site.

Downloading and Installing Device Drivers

SELECTING AND DOWNLOADING DRIVERS

1. With the www.hp.com site open in your browser, select Support and Drivers.
2. On the Support page, select the Download Drivers and Software radio button.

3. In the For Product field, enter the name and model number of the device, such as **officejet 6110**.

4. Click the Go button.

 Your product make and model may have several submodel numbers, and you may have to enter or select the one that most closely matches your device.

5. On the Product Search Results page, select the model number that most closely matches the device you are installing.

6. Click the name of your operating system.

7. Find the specific driver you need and click the link.

8. Review the information on this page to make sure it is the correct driver.

9. Click the Download Only button.

10. Browse to the folder on your hard drive where you want to place the driver.

 When downloading drivers or any file from the Internet, prepare a folder in your directory system ahead of time so you can find the file later. For example, you could create a folder named Drivers off your C drive and download all your drivers to one folder. This makes it easy to find them later.

11. Click OK to download the driver to the selected folder.

 The amount of time it takes for the drivers to download depends on your connection speed and the size of the software package.

INSTALLING DEVICE DRIVERS

1. Browse to the folder where you downloaded the driver package.

2. Double-click the driver package.

3. In the installation wizard, accept the default location for the installation.

4. Click Next to extract the drivers.

 This part of the task may take a few minutes. After the drivers are extracted, the process is largely automatic, with the installation software checking your system, preparing for the installation, conducting the installation, and configuring the product.

5. After the installation is complete, restart the computer.

Depending on the device involved, you may have to complete the configuration wizard before being able to use the device.

Criteria for Completion

You will have successfully completed the task when the drivers are installed, the device is configured, and you are able to use the device normally.

Task 1.23: Reformatting a Hard Drive

Reformatting a hard drive is no fun. It usually means that there is something seriously wrong with the computer that cannot be repaired in any other way. Reformatting means erasing everything on the hard drive and then reinstalling the OS, drivers, application software, and data. If possible, back up all of the data on the drive before reformatting.

Reformatting a hard drive will erase everything on it and all of your data will be lost.

Sometimes a computer will become so overrun with malware that it becomes impossible to recover it through normal means. The solution of last resort is to wipe the drive and reinstall everything. The Windows XP Recovery Console provides an ideal tool for doing this.

There are a number of other methods you should use to attempt to recover a compromised computer before reformatting the hard drive. Proceed with all of those methods prior to resorting to this option.

Scenario

You receive a trouble ticket from a user that his Windows XP laptop seems to go out of control when powered up and connected to the network. You investigate and determine that the laptop has been severely overrun by malware during a business trip taken by the user. Antivirus and antimalware removal solutions have been unsuccessful. Other methods such as System Restore and Last Known Good Configuration have also proved unsuccessful. Your supervisor advises you to reformat the hard drive of the laptop. Fortunately, most of the data on the laptop can be recovered from the last backup, prior to the computer being compromised.

You take the laptop to your workbench and locate the Windows XP installation disc that you'll need for the reformatting. You know that the file system on the XP machine is NTFS.

Scope of Task

Duration

This task should take about 20 minutes

Setup

You'll need to have a computer running Windows XP that must be able to boot from a CD drive. You'll also need to have the recovery disc. Most important, the computer must not contain data and software that you will need.

Caveat

Be very sure you have any data you want backed up before proceeding with this task. Once you're done, any data on the drive will be gone forever. If your computer doesn't check the optical drive before the hard drive when it starts booting, you'll have to change the boot order in the BIOS. Once this process is done, make sure you have all of the application installation discs if you want to reinstall the operating system and all the apps.

To reinstall the operating system and all the apps, see Task 1.24, "Installing Windows XP Professional as a Fresh Install," Task 1.27, "Installing Microsoft Applications," and Task 1.28, "Installing Non-Microsoft Applications."

Procedure

This task will show you how to reformat a hard drive using the Recovery Console in Windows XP.

Equipment Used

You won't need any tools for this task, just the Windows XP computer itself and the recovery or installation CD.

Depending on where you bought your computer, you were given either the full installation disc with the computer when you received it or a recovery disc that contains all the XP repair tools but not the operating-system installer. If at all possible, when you buy a computer, make sure the full installation disc comes with it.

Computer manufacturers such as HP now create a separate directory on the hard drive that contains all of the recovery-disc tools. The user is required to create the disc themselves. I highly recommend that you do so as soon as you buy the computer. If you don't, and subsequently suffer a severe hardware or software failure, you'll most likely be without a method of recovery.

Details

This task will show you all of the information regarding changing the boot order of a computer and using Windows XP Recovery Console to reformat the hard drive.

Changing the Boot Order of a Computer

GETTING INTO THE BIOS AND CHANGING THE BOOT ORDER

1. Verify that the laptop is connected to a power source.

2. Open the CD or DVD drive.

3. Insert the recovery disc.

4. Boot the computer.

5. As the boot sequence begins, scan the bottom of the screen for the key or key combination that will let you enter the setup.

The key or key combination depends on the computer manufacturer and the type of BIOS the computer uses. Some of the more common are F1, F2, Del, Esc, or Ctrl+Alt+Del.

6. When the setup screen appears, look for an area or list referencing the boot order.

Exactly how the setup screen is configured varies widely. This task takes you through a basic procedure, but how your BIOS is set up may differ.

7. Follow the onscreen notes to enter the boot order menu.

8. View the listing of the boot order.

9. If necessary, change the boot order to make the CD or DVD drive the first in the list.

10. Press the key that will save your changes and restart the computer.

Reformatting a Hard Disk

USING WINDOWS XP RECOVERY CONSOLE TO REFORMAT THE HARD DISK

1. As the computer boots from the CD, look for the Welcome to Windows Setup screen.

2. Press either the F10 function key or the R (for repair) key.

3. When the Recovery Console opens, select the Windows installation from the list.

 Windows will most likely be at the top of the list and be called C:\WINDOWS.

4. Press Enter.

5. At the login screen, use your administrator name and password to log in.

 On home Windows systems, the primary user is usually the administrator. In a work setting, admin usernames and passwords are set by the IT-department staff. Your supervisor will have provided you with this information.

6. Press Enter.

7. In the command-line emulator, type **map** at the prompt.

 Typing **map** will provide a list of drive letters with the associated file system, size, and device name of each drive.

8. Press Enter.

9. Type **format C: /fs:ntfs**.

 Step 9 assumes that the drive you want to reformat is the primary or C drive. If the drive you are reformatting uses a different drive letter, use that one instead.

10. Press Enter.

11. Type **y** and then press Enter.

12. After the reformatting process finishes, type **exit**.

13. Press Enter to restart the computer.

Criteria for Completion

You will have successfully completed the task when the computer reboots and the hard drive has been reformatted with the operating system, application software, and data deleted.

Task 1.24: Installing Windows XP Professional as a Fresh Install

As you saw in Task 1.23, there are times when even good PCs go bad and there's nothing left to do but reformat the hard drive. Of course, this is only part of the rehabilitative therapy for your ailing computer. To fix the original problem, you had to throw out the good software with the bad. Although you have guaranteed that all viruses and other malware have been removed from the hard drive, you also deleted the operating system, application software, and all your data.

Hopefully you backed up your data and located software installation discs. You're going to need them if you ever want to use your computer for more than a paperweight. Assuming you took all of the appropriate steps to find your software discs; you'll soon be tapping away at the keyboard and clicking the mouse once again.

Scenario

You have just completed reformatting the hard drive of a laptop that had been corrupted with various forms of malware (see Task 1.23). You have located a Windows XP Professional installation disk and are ready to reinstall the operating system. You will be performing a fresh install, so it will be as if you were installing Windows XP on a brand-new hard drive.

You can use a Windows XP Home edition install disk for this task because the installation process is virtually identical.

Scope of Task

Duration

This task should take about 30 to 45 minutes, depending on the capacity of your computer's CPU and memory.

Setup

You'll need a computer with a newly reformatted hard drive. You will also need a genuine Windows XP Professional installation disc and the accompanying product key.

Caveat

This task will take you only as far as the installation of the operating system. Tasks 1.27 and 1.28 will continue the recovery process by teaching you how to install Microsoft and non-Microsoft application software. You can complete this task only by reinstalling Windows XP on a reformatted drive.

Procedure

This task will instruct you on how to reinstall Windows XP on the reformatted hard drive of a computer.

Equipment Used

You will need only a computer with a reformatted hard drive and a valid Windows XP installation disc with the accompanying product key.

Do not use pirated software for this or any other task you perform in this book!

Details

This lesson will walk you step-by-step through the procedure of performing a fresh install of Windows XP on a reformatted hard drive.

Reinstalling Windows XP

REINSTALLING WINDOWS XP ON A REFORMATTED COMPUTER

1. Verify that your computer is hooked up to a power supply.
2. Locate the Windows XP install disc.
3. Insert the disc into the CD or DVD drive of the computer.
4. Reboot the computer.

In Task 1.23, you made sure that the computer would look to the optical drive first to boot. Watch carefully for the message "Press any key to boot from CD." It will appear for only a few seconds, so quickly press any key on the keyboard to initiate a boot from the CD.

You may be asked to activate the product (operating system) at this time or at some point in the installation process. Skip this part of the setup since you will need an Internet connection to complete product activation.

5. When the Welcome to Microsoft Windows XP window appears, click the arrow in the green box next to Install Windows XP.

You can also press Enter at this step.

6. The initial Windows Setup window appears. At this point, Setup will format the partition.

7. When the Welcome to Setup window appears, press Enter.

8. When the End-User License Agreement appears, press F8 to agree.

```
Windows XP Licensing Agreement

 Microsoft Windows XP Professional
 END-USER LICENSE AGREEMENT
 IMPORTANT-READ CAREFULLY: This End-User
 License Agreement ("EULA") is a legal agreement between you
 (either an individual or a single entity) and Microsoft
 Corporation for the Microsoft software product identified above,
 which includes computer software and may include associated
 media, printed materials, "online" or electronic documentation,
 and Internet-based services ("Product").   An amendment or
 addendum to this EULA may accompany the Product.  YOU AGREE TO BE
 BOUND BY THE TERMS OF THIS EULA BY
 INSTALLING, COPYING, OR OTHERWISE USING THE
 PRODUCT. IF YOU DO NOT AGREE, DO NOT INSTALL
 OR USE THE PRODUCT; YOU MAY RETURN IT TO YOUR
 PLACE OF PURCHASE FOR A FULL REFUND.

   1. GRANT OF LICENSE. Microsoft grants you the following rights
      provided that you comply with all terms and conditions of
      this EULA:

       * Installation and use.  You may install, use, access,
         display and run one copy of the Product on a single
         computer, such as a workstation, terminal or other device
         ("Workstation Computer").  The Product may not be used
         by more than two (2) processors at  any one time on any

 F8=I agree   ESC=I do not agree   PAGE DOWN=Next Page
```

9. When the partition window appears, verify that the desired partition is selected and the press Enter to install Windows XP on that partition.

You can also create a new partition by pressing C. To toggle through a list of partitions in the partition window, use the up and down arrow keys.

```
Windows XP Professional Setup

 The following list shows the existing partitions and
 unpartitioned space on this computer.

 Use the UP and DOWN ARROW keys to select an item in the list.

   •  To set up Windows XP on the selected item, press ENTER.

   •  To create a partition in the unpartitioned space, press C.

   •  To delete the selected partition, press D.

 8190 MB Disk 0 at Id 0 on bus 0 on atapi [MBR]
     Unpartitioned space                    8189 MB

 ENTER=Install   C=Create Partition   F3=Quit
```

10. When the file-system window appears, use the up and down arrow keys to select Format the Partition Using the NTFS File System, and then press Enter.

11. Setup will format the partition and then copy files to the Windows installation folders. When it finishes copying files, Windows will reboot.

After Windows reboots, the GUI installation screen appears, informing you of the current stage of the installation and about how long it will take. Notice the flashing green lights at the lower-right side of the screen. The moving lights indicate that the installation is proceeding.

If those lights stop moving or are moving extremely slowly, it probably indicates a problem with the install. The most common cause is a smudge or dirt on the disc. You will need to stop the installation, remove the disc, and examine it for smudges or damage. If possible, clean the disc and make another attempt to do the installation.

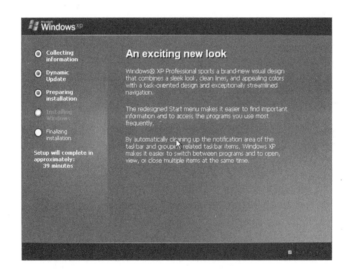

12. When the Regional and Language Options box appears, click Next.

If you live someplace besides the United States, you will want to click the Customize and Details buttons to adjust the Regional and Language Options settings so they are appropriate to your location. After these settings are adjusted, you can click Next to proceed.

13. When the Personalize Your Software box appears, enter your name or the name of the end user in the Name field. You can optionally enter a company name in the Organization field.

14. Click Next.

15. When the Your Product Key box appears, enter the 25-character product key that came with the installation disc.

 You can usually find the product key on a label attached to the disc case.

16. After you've entered the key, click Next.

17. When the Computer Name and Administrator Password box appears, type the hostname of the computer in the Computer Name field.

18. Type the password for the local computer administrator account in the Administrator Password field and repeat this step in the Confirm Password field.

 This is the password for the administrator account on the local machine, not the domain administrator password.

19. Click Next.

20. When the Date and Time Settings box appears, adjust the Date, Time, and Time Zone settings using the drop-down lists and arrow keys.

 Usually, the Date and Time are correct and you will only have to adjust the Time Zone setting.

21. If desired, verify that the Automatically Adjust Clock for Daylight Saving Changes check box is checked, and click Next.

![Windows XP Professional Setup screen showing Date and Time Settings with the date Sunday, July 30, 2006, time 11:00:58 AM, and Time Zone set to (GMT-07:00) Mountain Time (US & Canada), with "Automatically adjust clock for daylight saving changes" checked.]

After you click Next in the Date and Time Settings window, you will be returned to the GUI installation window. Allow the installation process to continue until your input is required.

22. When the Networking Settings box appears, select Typical Settings and click Next.

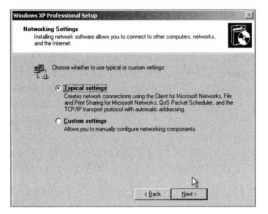

23. When the Workgroup or Computer Domain box appears, select the No, This Computer Is Not on a Network radio button and accept the default workgroup name of WORKGROUP.

24. Click Next.

If you are installing Windows XP Home edition, the default name of the workgroup is MSHOME.

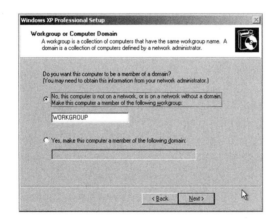

> You will join this computer to the domain after the installation is complete. See Task 3.10 for details.

> After you click Next in the Workgroup or Computer Domain window, you will be returned to the GUI installation window. The installation will proceed to its conclusion after about 30 minutes and the computer will reboot at that time.

25. When the computer reboots and the Display Settings box appears asking to adjust the screen resolution, click OK.

26. When the screen resolution is adjusted, if you can read the message in the Monitor Settings box, click OK.

> After you click OK in the Monitor Settings box, Windows XP will load.

CONFIGURING A NEWLY INSTALLED WINDOWS XP PROFESSIONAL COMPUTER

1. When the Welcome to Microsoft Windows screen appears, click Next.

> If you have speakers attached to the computer, turn them on and turn up the volume. If the sound card and speakers are operating correctly, you will hear a test "song."

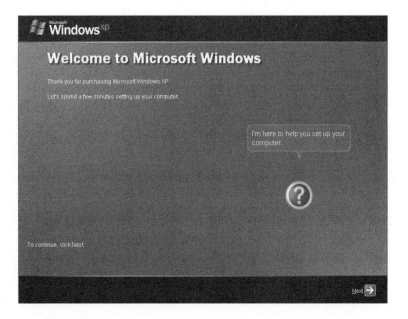

2. When the Internet Connection screen appears, select the Yes, This Computer Will Connect Through a Local Area Network or Home Network radio button and click Next.

> **NOTE** You also have the option to skip the screen in step 2 by clicking Skip.

3. When the Ready to Register with Microsoft? screen appears, select the No, Not at This Time radio button and click Next.

4. When the Who Will Use This Computer? screen appears, type the name of the primary user in the Your Name field.

5. If other users need to have their own local computer accounts on this PC, use the additional fields to enter their names.

6. Click Next.

![Windows XP setup screen titled "Who will use this computer?" with text fields for Your name, 2nd User, 3rd User, 4th User, and 5th User, and Back and Next navigation buttons.]

7. When the Thank You! screen appears, indicating that Windows XP Professional has been successfully configured, click Finish.

Windows will reboot and the operating system will complete loading. The Desktop will then appear and you will be ready to start using Windows XP Professional. You can remove the installation CD at this time.

Criteria for Completion

You will have successfully installed and configured Windows XP on a computer when the operating system loads and you can use the computer normally.

Under normal circumstances, your next steps are to activate the onboard firewall, configure the network connection, connect to the Internet, and go to the Windows Update site. You will need to install all the service packs and security patches before you resume any other activity on the computer.

Task 1.25: Installing Windows Vista as a Fresh Install

This exercise will build on Task 1.23, just as Task 1.24, "Installing Windows XP Professional as a Fresh Install," did. In this case, you will be performing a fresh install, but using Windows Vista instead of XP. While many people continue to have concerns about Vista, and are considering postponing upgrading from Windows XP until Microsoft Windows 7 is formally released in 2010, Vista has taken hold in the home and workplace and, as a technician, you'll be expected to perform this sort of job.

Scenario

You have just completed reformatting the hard drive of a laptop that had been corrupted with various forms of malware (see Task 1.23). In this scenario, the laptop previously ran Windows Vista and you have been tasked with installing Vista on the notebook device. You have located a Windows Vista DVD and are ready to reinstall the operating system. You will be performing a fresh install, so it will be as if you were installing Windows Vista on a brand-new hard drive.

Scope of Task

Duration

This task should take about 30 to 45 minutes, depending on the capacity of your computer's CPU and memory.

To check on the system requirements of the computer you want to use to install Windows Vista, including CPU and memory, visit http://support .microsoft.com/kb/918884.

Setup

You'll need a computer with a newly reformatted hard drive. You will also need a genuine Windows Vista installation DVD and the accompanying product key. The laptop or other computer used for this exercise must be set to boot from the DVD drive.

Caveat

This task will take you only as far as the installation of the operating system. Tasks 1.27 and 1.28 will continue the recovery process by teaching you how to install Microsoft and non-Microsoft application software. You can complete this task only by reinstalling Windows Vista on a reformatted drive.

You are most likely aware of the plethora of varieties of Vista available. For the sake of this exercise, the Windows Vista installation will not favor any particular edition of Vista. Since the laptop we are using for this example previously ran Vista adequately, this exercise will not include the steps for checking system requirements or hardware and software compatibility.

Procedure

This task will instruct you on how to reinstall Windows Vista on the reformatted hard drive of a computer using the Windows Vista installation DVD.

Equipment Used

You will need only a computer with a reformatted hard drive and a valid Windows Vista installation DVD with the accompanying product key.

 WARNING   Do not use pirated software for this or any other task you perform in this book!

Details

This lesson will walk you step-by-step through the procedure of performing a fresh install of Windows Vista on a reformatted hard drive.

Reinstalling Windows Vista

REINSTALLING WINDOWS VISTA ON A REFORMATTED COMPUTER

1. Verify that your computer is hooked up to a power supply.
2. Locate the Windows Vista install DVD.
3. Insert the disc into the DVD drive of the computer.
4. Reboot the computer.

5. When the GUI setup launches, make whatever regional settings changes you desire and then click Next.

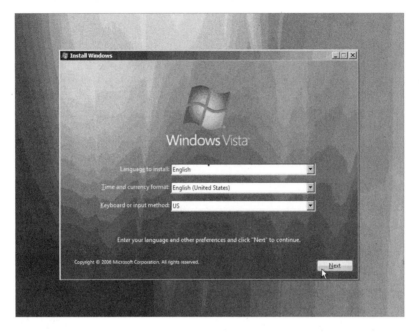

6. When the next screen appears, click Install Now.

7. When the Type Your Product Key for Activation screen appears, enter the product key in the available field and click Next.

The Automatically Activate Windows When I'm Online check box is selected by default.

8. On the license agreement screen, select the I Accept the License Terms check box and then click Next.

9. On the Which Type of Installation Do You Want? screen, select Custom (Advanced).

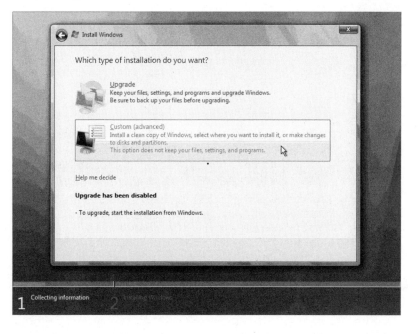

The Upgrade button is disabled because this is a fresh install. This button would only be active if you were installing Vista on a computer that had an operating system present.

10. On the Where Do You Want to Install Windows? screen, select the partition where you want Vista installed, click Apply, and then click Next. In this case, there should be only one partition available: Disk 0.

11. The Installing Windows process will launch, which will take some time to complete, as Windows is performing tasks such as copying files, installing features, and installing updates from the Internet.

12. After the Windows Vista updates are downloaded and installed from the Internet, Vista will automatically reboot the computer.

13. When rebooted, Vista will continue to perform necessary tasks. This may take some time.

14. When the necessary tasks are complete, Vista will reboot the computer again.

SETTING UP WINDOWS VISTA

1. After the computer reboots, the Set Up Windows screen launches. When you are prompted, enter the username and password for the first user on the computer, and then click Next.

> You will either need the laptop user's name and password, or you can enter the administrative credentials here and have the user enter their logon information at a later time.

2. On the next screen, enter the hostname for the computer, select the desktop background, and then click Next.

3. On the Help protect Windows automatically screen, select the desired setting that fits your company's security requirements.

> If you are performing this task on a computer in a home or small lab setting, the best option is to select Use Recommended Settings.

4. On the Review Your Time and Date Settings screen, confirm that the time zone, date, and time settings match your location and then click Next.

5. When the Thank You screen appears, click Start.

6. The computer will display a series of promotional screens while Windows Vista performs the final configuration tasks.

Criteria for Completion

You will have successfully completed this task when the Welcome screen appears showing the Vista version information and the Get Started with Windows screen.

Task 1.26: Uninstalling Software

Sometimes it's necessary to uninstall software on a computer. Usually you do this when a program is no longer used by the company because it has become obsolete or the firm has decided to go with another vendor for that type of software. Although there is quite a variety of programs out there, Windows uses the same process to uninstall a program and all its components. It's really a piece of cake.

Scenario

The payroll department has decided to discontinue the use of its current accounting software and has purchased similar software from a different vendor. You have been assigned to go to the payroll office and uninstall the relevant program from the computers there. It is just past regular business hours, so none of the users will be present. You are free to log on to each PC using your administrator credentials and remove the programs.

Scope of Task

Duration

This task will take 10 to 15 minutes.

Setup

You will need one computer with a program you can uninstall. It can be any sort of software.

Caveat

This is a fairly benign task, so there shouldn't be any particular issues.

Procedure

This task will teach you how to remove a program from a Windows XP computer.

Equipment Used

You will only need a computer and a program on that computer you are willing to remove.

Details

This task will show you the process of removing a program from a Windows XP computer.

Uninstalling a Program

 For this task, it is assumed that you are at a computer that is powered up and you are logged on with an account that has administrator privileges.

1. Click Start ➢ Control Panel.

If your Control Panel is currently in Category view, switch it to Classic view.

2. Double-click the Add or Remove Programs icon.

3. When the list populates, click the name of the program you want to remove.

4. Click the Change/Remove button.

5. When the dialog box opens asking if you are sure you want to remove the program, click Yes.

 You may be asked to remove multiple components. In this event, click Delete All.

Criteria for Completion

You will have successfully completed the task when you return to the Add or Remove Programs list and the program you selected is no longer present.

Task 1.27: Installing Microsoft Applications

Although most computers you will purchase come with all the necessary application software already installed, you may occasionally have to install some piece of Microsoft application software. Like installing a Microsoft operating system, the process is heavily scripted and doesn't leave much to chance. In the vast majority of cases, you'll need the product key to install the software and you'll need to activate it within 30 days of the installation.

IT departments tend to keep their software discs, including the product keys, under lock and key, and they will be keeping track of the number of licenses they have available. Before doing an install, always verify the number of licenses your company has for the software. Installing a Microsoft application is as simple as popping the install DVD in the optical drive and following the instructions.

Scenario

You have just finished installing Windows XP on a laptop that had to have its hard drive reformatted (see Tasks 1.23 and 1.24). You have configured a network connection and restored all of the service packs and security updates. Your next step is to install all of the Microsoft application software. You will start by installing Microsoft Office 2003 Professional.

 Microsoft Office 2003 is used as an example for this task, but if you're installing Office 2007 or any other Microsoft application software, the process should be quite similar.

You have located the DVD and product key and are ready to begin.

Scope of Task

Duration

Depending on the software package, this task will take about 15 to 20 minutes.

Setup

You'll need access to a computer and an installation DVD containing a Microsoft application.

Caveat

As you must be aware, Microsoft products are not inexpensive, so you may not want to go out and buy a Microsoft Office suite. In a pinch, you can uninstall and reinstall a Microsoft application on your computer. Make sure you have the appropriate install discs available before you begin. Also, if you have installed a Microsoft product on one computer and you attempt to install and activate the product on a second computer, this may violate the licensing agreement.

Procedure

This task will show you how to install a piece of Microsoft application software.

Equipment Used

All you'll need is a computer and a Microsoft application installation CD or DVD.

Details

This lesson will guide you through the process of installing a Microsoft application.

Installing a Microsoft Application

1. Verify that the computer is powered up.

2. Log on as Administrator.

3. Locate the Microsoft Office 2003 installation disk.

4. Insert the CD into the computer's optical drive.

The disk should autoplay; if it doesn't, you'll need to open My Computer, right-click the CD or DVD icon, and click Open. Look for a launch or startup file and double-click to execute it. The installation program should launch.

5. When the Product Key screen appears, input the product key that accompanied your installation disc and click Next.

The product key is usually found on a label attached to the disc case.

6. When the user-information dialog box opens, type the name of the user and the organization in the appropriate fields and then click Next.

7. When the licensing-agreement dialog opens, check the I Accept the Terms in the Licensing Agreement check box, and then click Next.

8. In the Type of Installation area, verify that the default location (path) is present.

The path for Microsoft Office will look like this: `C:\Program Files\Microsoft Office\`.

9. Click Complete Install.

10. Click Next.

11. In the Summary box, click the Install button.

The installation process will begin when you click the Install button in the Summary box.

12. When the Setup Completed box appears, select the Check the Web for Updates and Additional Downloads check box.

13. Click Finish.

14. Internet Explorer will launch; when the Windows Update page displays, click the Check for Updates button and then download and install all Microsoft Office updates.

 For this task, you should have already established a network connection and downloaded and installed all service packs and security patches for Windows XP or Windows Vista.

15. When prompted, reboot the computer.

16. When the computer reboots, log on as Administrator and verify that Microsoft Office 2003 Professional was installed.

Criteria for Completion

You will have successfully completed this task when you can verify that the Microsoft Office suite has been installed on the computer.

Task 1.28: Installing Non-Microsoft Applications

It is said that man does not live by bread alone, and neither does he (or she) work with just Microsoft applications. Beyond using a wide variety of well-known commercial software packages, organizations also can use proprietary software and packages that are written just for certain types of businesses or business functions. You will find that one of your common tasks is installing both Microsoft and other vendor software.

This task uses a specific piece of software for demonstration purposes, so the exact installation procedure may be different from what you experience. That being said, most software installs use some sort of "wizard-like" framework, so it's usually a matter of following the instructions and clicking Next.

Scenario

You have reinstalled Windows XP and all the Microsoft applications on a recently reformatted laptop (see Tasks 1.23, 1.24, and 1.27 for details). Now you need to restore the non-Microsoft applications. You have the different installation discs available and are ready to begin.

Scope of Task

Duration

This task should take about 15 to 20 minutes.

Setup

You will need a computer and access to the installation disc of a non-Microsoft application. Alternatively, you can download software from the Internet and install it on your computer.

You can find and download plenty of freeware at www.freewarehome.com/; however, I can't guarantee the results, so make your selections wisely.

Caveat

If you are going to download and install freeware, make sure you are using a trusted source. There are plenty of dodgy websites that advertise free software just to get you to download and install some vicious variety of malware that hangs onto your PC worse than a third-degree burn.

Procedure

This lesson will show you how to install non-Microsoft applications.

Equipment Used

All you'll need is a computer and a software-installation disc. Alternately, you'll need an Internet connection so you can download and install freeware from the Internet.

Details

This task will walk you through the procedure for installing a non-Microsoft application.

For the sake of this task, a freeware program called HTML Tidy will be installed. The exact steps you use to install your software may differ.

Installing a Non-Microsoft Application

1. Verify that the computer is powered up.
2. Verify that you are logged on with an account that has administrator privileges.
3. Locate the application's installation disc.
4. Insert the disk into the optical drive.

 The disc should autoplay; if it doesn't, see Task 1.27 for details regarding launching the installation program manually.

5. When the install wizard launches, click Next.
6. Use the default location (path) to install the program.

 The path for the default location will look something like C:\Program Files\HTML Tidy\.

7. Click Next.
8. If the program offers you the option of putting an icon on the Desktop, accept it.
9. Click Next.
10. Review your selections in the Ready to Install dialog box to make sure they are correct.
11. Click Install.
12. When the program installs, click Finish.
13. If necessary, reboot the computer.

Criteria for Completion

You will have successfully completed this task when the computer reboots (assuming this was required) and you click Start ➤ All Programs and see the new program displayed in the list.

Task 1.29: Upgrading Windows 2000 to Windows XP

Usually, most companies maintain an upgrade schedule for their equipment based on their budget and the usability of devices and utilities. Although Windows 2000 is getting a little long in the tooth, there's still plenty of life in the OS. However, many companies believe the time has come for their Windows 2000 computers to be upgraded to Windows XP. Task 1.30 will demonstrate how to upgrade a Windows XP computer to Windows Vista.

> **NOTE** The probability that you'll be required to perform this particular job is rapidly declining; however, there are still sufficient computers in the business world that run Windows 2000 Professional for a variety of reasons. With many companies reluctant to roll out Windows Vista, an upgrade from Windows 2000 to the still-reliable Windows XP remains a likely technician task.

Operating-system upgrades can be managed in two ways:

1. Both the hardware and operating systems can be upgraded at the same time.
2. The operating system on an existing piece of hardware can be upgraded via installation or upgrade disc.

This task presents the latter solution. (See Task 1.20 for an example of the former solution.) Assuming the hardware is robust enough to run XP reasonably well, your CIO could save quite a chunk of change by not having to pop for 50 or 100 new PCs as well as the software licenses.

Scenario

You've been assigned to upgrade the four PCs in your company's shipping department from Windows 2000 to Windows XP. You have come in on the weekend so that you'll have free access to the computers and won't have to interrupt the users. You have been provided with the necessary installation disc and product key to accomplish your task.

Scope of Task

Duration

This task should take about an hour.

Setup

You'll need a computer running Windows 2000 Professional and a Windows XP Professional installation or upgrade disc.

Caveat

On most occasions, the upgrade from 2000 to XP is fairly routine, but always plan for the unexpected. Make sure you've backed up your data in case the upgrade goes wrong. There is no viable upgrade path from Windows 2000 to Windows XP Home Edition. You must upgrade to Windows XP Professional.

Procedure

You will learn how to upgrade a computer's operating system from Windows 2000 Professional to Windows XP.

Equipment Used

You will need only a computer running Windows 2000, and a Windows XP upgrade disc.

Details

This task will conduct you through the procedure of upgrading a Windows 2000 Pro computer to a Windows XP computer.

Upgrading a Windows 2000 Computer to Windows XP

PREPARING THE COMPUTER FOR UPGRADE

1. Defragment the hard drive of the computer before beginning the upgrade.

    Task 2.14 will cover how to defragment a hard drive.

2. Close any applications that may be running, especially the antivirus program.
3. Make sure you have the original Windows 2000 installation disc as a precaution in the event that the upgrade fails.
4. Locate the Windows XP upgrade disc.
5. Insert the disc in the computer's optical drive.
6. When the Welcome to Windows XP Upgrade screen appears, choose Check System Compatibility.

RUNNING THE WINDOWS XP UPGRADE ADVISOR

1. When the Windows XP Upgrade Advisor Welcome screen appears, click Next.
2. When the program asks if you want to download the latest files, click Yes.

    Step 2 is optional but advisable.

3. When the informational screen appears telling you that most computers will support Windows XP, click Next.
4. When the upgrade-advisor screen appears, click Next.

The upgrade-advisor screen will list any issues that might affect the upgrade in Blocking and Compatibility. A blocking issue would be a condition that would prevent Windows XP from being run on the computer (which is exceedingly rare). A compatibility issue is when some piece of hardware or software on the computer may not run with Windows XP. Usually, these sorts of issues are resolved by driver updates.

Most of what happens after step 4 is automatic. The option to download the latest files you selected in step 2 will now cause these files to download. Next, the Upgrade Advisor examines the system and generates a report listing any issues that will affect the upgrade. There are bound to be at least some issues. Take note of them because you will be required to take steps to resolve these issues once Windows XP is installed.

5. After the Upgrade Advisor report appears, click Finish.

In this example, there won't be any significant issues affecting the upgrade. When the Advisor finishes, leave the Windows CD in the computer.

UPGRADING TO WINDOWS XP

1. When the Welcome to Windows XP screen appears, select Install Windows XP.

2. When the Choose an Installation Type screen appears, select the Upgrade option.

3. Click Next.

4. When the License Agreement page appears, press F8 to agree to the terms of the license.

5. When the Product Key page appears, enter the key that came with the Windows XP disc.

6. When prompted, choose to update the computer over the Internet from the Windows Update site.

For this task, it is assumed that the computer has an Internet connection.

7. Click Next.

The Update Advisor may show you a report again on software and hardware compatibility issues. You should already have made notes from this report in the section "Running the Windows XP Upgrade Advisor" earlier in this task. Verify that the report is the same.

After the necessary files are downloaded and installed, the computer will automatically reboot.

If you see a message saying to press "any key" to boot from the CD, do not do so. To complete the installation, you must boot from the hard drive.

The next part of the process is the actual installation of Windows XP. This is pretty automated, so there won't be a lot for you to do until the installation is complete.

POSTINSTALLATION TASKS

1. Once the installation is complete, open Internet Explorer.
2. Select Tools ➢ Windows Upgrade.

Windows Update will check your computer for any needed security updates, hotfixes, and drivers.

3. When prompted, select Express Upgrade.
4. Select all the update options offered.

Windows Update will download and install the necessary software.

5. When prompted, reboot the computer.
6. After the computer has rebooted, defrag the hard drive again.

During the Windows Upgrade process, the data on the drive becomes significantly fragmented, slowing performance.

7. Verify that the computer seems to be operating normally.

 Your supervisor usually will give you a list of tasks to perform to test the computer. This includes playing a music CD to test sound, doing a test print, connecting to mapped drives, and any other activity the user will need to perform as a normal part of their work.

8. Reactivate the antivirus program and any other security measures you turned off during the upgrade.

9. Log off the computer.

Criteria for Completion

You will have successfully completed this task when the computer displays as a Windows XP computer and you are able to perform tasks on the PC normally.

Task 1.30: Upgrading from Windows XP to Windows Vista

Task 1.29 demonstrated the process of upgrading a Windows 2000 Professional computer to Windows XP Professional. While this skill may still be useful from time to time, you are more likely going to find yourself upgrading a Windows XP Home or Professional computer to Windows Vista. Since Vista is known to be rather demanding in its need for resources, an essential task is to determine if the computer running Windows XP is capable of supporting Vista.

As with all upgrades, you should back up any data on the computer beforehand, in case the upgrade results in data loss. Also have handy all of the installation discs for your application software.

 You will need to access both the Hardware Compatibility List (HCL) for Vista and Vista's hardware requirements. The HCL resource can be found at www.microsoft.com/whdc/hcl/default.mspx and the requirements list can be found at www.microsoft.com/windows/windows-vista/get/system-requirements.aspx.

Scenario

You've received a request to upgrade the finance manager's PC from Windows XP to Windows Vista as part of a project to upgrade the managerial-staff computers over the next month. You have come in on the weekend so that you'll have free access to the computer, and you have the required administrator logon information for the PC.

You have been provided with the necessary installation disc and product key to accomplish your task. You have also previously consulted the HCL and system requirements for Vista, compared that information to the subject computer, and determined that it will support the Vista upgrade. You have defragmented the hard drive as a necessary preparation step.

You have logged on to the Windows XP computer, visited the Windows update site, and updated all of the hardware drivers and other software to the most current versions for XP. You have the Vista upgrade DVD and product key and are ready to proceed.

Scope of Task

Duration

This task should take about an hour to an hour and a half depending on the speed of the PC's CPU, the amount of RAM present, and how much hardware and software Vista must detect during the upgrade.

Setup

You'll need a computer running Windows XP Home or Professional and a Windows Vista installation or upgrade disc. This exercise does not specify a particular edition of Windows Vista for the upgrade.

Caveat

Before performing the upgrade, it is essential that you go to the Windows Update site and download and install the most current hardware drivers for the computer. The operating-system upgrade may fail if you do not perform this task, even though you are directed to update drivers and other software during the upgrade process.

You can decide to remove any devices and peripherals that are not absolutely necessary for the running of the computer, including sound cards, printers, scanners, and the like, to improve the success of the upgrade.

To play it safe, you can also uninstall all unnecessary software applications and particularly programs that you seldom or never use. You should also (temporarily) uninstall your antivirus software but immediately reinstall it after the upgrade is complete. Make sure the antivirus software you use is Vista-compatible. If not, you will need to purchase a software package that will work with Vista.

You can run the compatibility check after you insert the upgrade DVD by clicking Check Compatibility Online on the Windows Vista upgrade splash screen before clicking Install Now.

Procedure

You will learn how to upgrade a computer's operating system from Windows XP to Windows Vista.

Equipment Used

You will need only a computer running Windows XP Home or Professional and a Windows Vista upgrade DVD.

Details

This task will take you through the steps of upgrading a Windows XP computer to Windows Vista.

Upgrading a Windows XP Computer to Windows Vista

1. Open the optical drive on the computer, insert the Windows Vista DVD, and close the drive.

2. If Autorun does not begin the process, open My Computer, select the DVD drive, browse to the root folder, and double-click setup.exe.

3. When the Windows Vista Setup screen appears, click Install Now.

4. On the subsequent screen, click Next.

5. Click Go Online to Get the Latest Updates (Recommended) to download and install the latest updates for the Windows XP computers. If updates are found and installed, the computer will automatically reboot before continuing with the upgrade procedure.

Although you already completed this task before beginning the upgrade, it is recommended, though optional, that you take this step to verify that all required updates have been installed. If you have uninstalled the computer's antivirus software, it is vital that you connect to only the authentic Windows upgrade site. You do not want to introduce malicious software during the upgrade.

6. Enter the Windows Vista product key in the available fields and then click Next.

7. Click I Accept the License Terms (required to use Windows), and then click Next.

8. On the Which Type of Installation Do You Want? screen, click Upgrade (Recommended) to start the upgrade process.

9. The Vista upgrade will perform necessary tasks, including copying windows files, gathering files, detecting hardware, installing drivers, and so on. This may take some time.

10. When the necessary tasks are complete, Vista will reboot the computer.

SETTING UP WINDOWS VISTA

1. After the computer reboots, the Set Up Windows screen launches. When you are prompted, enter the username and password for the first user on the computer; then click Next.

> You will either need the computer user's name and password, or you can enter your administrative credentials here and have the user enter their logon information at a later time.

2. On the next screen, enter the hostname for the computer, select the desktop background, and then click Next.

3. On the Help Protect Windows Automatically screen, select the desired setting that fits your company's security requirements.

> If you are performing this task on a computer in a home or small lab setting, the best option is to select Use Recommended Settings. Otherwise, use the option required by your company's IT security policy.

4. On the Review Your Time and Date Settings screen, confirm that the time zone, date, and time settings match your location and then click Next.

5. If you are prompted to install Windows Vista updates, you can either choose to do so now, or select Ask Me Later to install updates after the upgrade is complete and you have reinstalled the PC's antivirus software.

6. If prompted for the computer's current location, select Home if you are working at home or in a small lab, or Work if you are performing the upgrade in a business environment.

7. The computer will reboot again.

8. After the computer reboots and Windows Vista is finished loading, a list of compatibility issues (if any exist) will be displayed for anything that has loaded on startup that Windows Vista is unable to run.

9. Reinstall a Vista-compatible antivirus program and update the virus definitions.

10. Now it is safe (or as safe as possible) to update any drivers and other software required by Vista to run the hardware and software that Vista detected.

Criteria for Completion

You will have successfully completed this task when Windows Vista loads as the computer's software and any hardware and software issues have been resolved.

For the sake of completing this exercise, it is not necessary to have 100 percent of all potential compatibility issues resolved, since it may take some time to track down every single issue. This is especially true if you have uninstalled your application software, and intend to reinstall it at this point. See Tasks 1.27 and 1.28 for more information.

Task 1.31: Using Restore Points in Windows XP

Windows XP comes with a handy little tool called System Restore. Sometimes making a change on a computer, such as downloading a program or updating a device driver, will cause some unforeseen damage. System Restore automatically creates restore points every time a major change is made to the computer. If something goes wrong with a change, you can literally turn back the clock and restore the computer's configuration settings to a previous point in time. You can also manually create a restore point if necessary. System Restore can solve a multitude of problems by taking the computer to a point when it was functioning well, and at the same time preserving all of your documents, emails, and any other settings and data.

Windows Vista has the same utility and you could probably use this exercise with a Vista computer, but the task was written specifically for Windows XP.

Scenario

You receive a trouble ticket stating that a user is unable to open Windows Explorer and Internet Explorer on her Windows XP computer. After an investigation, your supervisor determines that a number of system files have been corrupted within the past few days. You are instructed to use System Restore to take the computer's configuration back to a restore point created a week ago. You are at the user's computer in her cubicle and ready to perform the task.

Scope of Task

Duration

The task should take about 10 minutes.

Setup

All you'll need is a computer running Windows XP.

Caveat

System Restore is a useful and benign program and there should be no issues in restoring the computer to a particular restore point. If you restore a computer to a previous point and the problem is still not corrected, you can run System Restore again and take the computer further back in time.

 Restore Points aren't the ultimate cure-all for Windows XP and Vista computer problems. I encountered a situation where I was unable to restore a computer to any previous restore point. The computer had become infected with a virus that had been written to, among other things, disable the ability to use restore points. My only option in that case was to use the recovery disc that came with the computer (which, fortunately, worked).

Procedure

In this task, you will learn how to use the Windows XP System Restore utility to undo a harmful change to a computer.

Equipment Used

You will need no equipment for this task.

Details

This task will take you through the process of restoring a Windows XP computer's settings to a previous point in time.

Using the Restore Point System on Windows XP

VERIFYING THAT THERE IS SUFFICIENT SPACE FOR RESTORE POINT STORAGE

 By default, System Restore allocates a maximum of 12 percent of hard-drive space to store restore points. After this space becomes full, the system overwrites the stored data from the oldest restore points to the newest.

1. Click Start ➤ Control Panel.

In this example, Control Panel is in Classic view.

2. Double-click the System applet.

3. Click the System Restore tab on the System Properties box.

4. Confirm the Disk Space to Use bar is set at 12%.

5. Click OK.

System Restore might be turned off on your computer. Verify that the Turn Off System Restore check box is unchecked.

6. Close Control Panel.

SETTING A WINDOWS XP COMPUTER TO A RESTORE POINT

1. Click Start ➤ All Programs ➤ Accessories ➤ System Tools ➤ System Restore.

2. When the Welcome to System Restore box opens, click Restore My Computer to an Earlier Time.

3. Click Next.

4. In the Select a Restore Point box, click on the day on the calendar where you want the computer restored.

You may have to click on the left-pointing arrow at the top of the calendar to go to the previous month.

5. Select the specific restore point you want to use, and then click Next.

6. On the Confirm Restore Point Selection page, verify that the correct restore point has been selected.

7. Click Next.

The computer will automatically reboot.

8. Log on to the computer after it reboots.

9. On the Restoration Complete page, click OK.

10. Test the computer to see if it is functioning normally and perform the tasks the user said she was not able to do.

Criteria for Completion

You will have successfully completed this task when the Restoration Complete message displays and you can use the computer normally.

Task 1.32: Shutting Down Programs

Every so often, a program in Windows will hang and refuse to close. Worse, it might be a program that has a memory leak, sucking up more and more of your available RAM and giving nothing back. When an average user wants to close Microsoft Word or Internet Explorer, they click the little red box with the white X inside in the upper-right corner of the document or window. The vast majority of the time this works quite well, but when it doesn't, an end user could wind up both frustrated and unproductive. There is actually a very simple way to shut down a stubborn program.

Scenario

You are walking past the accounting department when one of the users motions you over to her desk. She has been working extensively in Microsoft Excel for most of the morning but complains that the application has now locked up on her. She asks if you'd mind helping fix the problem. You take a look at the Excel header bar and see the message "Not Responding." You realize this could be a pretty easy fix, and since you have a few minutes, you agree to help her.

In a larger business with an in-house IT department, requesting help for a computer problem requires the end user to call the help desk and file a trouble ticket before a tech is assigned to respond. Smaller businesses are less formal, but if you drop whatever you're doing all the time to help out just because you're handy, you'll never get any of your assigned work finished. Word to the wise.

Scope of Task

Duration

This task should take less than 5 minutes.

Setup

All you'll need is a Windows XP computer running some application. The easiest way to set up the task is to start a program you'll recognize as it's listed in the Processes tab in Task Manager. You'll easily be able to recognize the program and shut it down.

Sometimes, the offending process is not a normal application like Excel. You may have a rogue process running that was planted there by a virus or other malware. If you don't recognize some of the listings on the Processes tab, you can do an Internet search for the names of the processes to see what results you get. Alternately, you can go to a site such as www.neuber .com/taskmanager/process/ and search there for the definitions of Windows processes.

Even when you have no application software running (look in Task Manager's Applications tab), the Processes tab will still show numerous programs running. The vast majority of those processes are necessary to provide various services. Occasionally, one is an indication of a problem.

Caveat

Every once in a while, closing a program in this manner causes unusual results in the computer. You'll receive a warning dialog box when you attempt to close the program later on in the task. However, it is considered a safe method of shutting down stalled processes.

Procedure

In this task, you'll learn how to shut down stalled processes, including background processes in Windows XP.

This method also works on Windows 2000 and Windows Vista computers and is similar but not the same on Windows 98.

Equipment Used

You won't need any equipment to complete this task.

Details

This task will take you through the steps of shutting down a running process in Windows XP.

Shutting Down a Process in Windows XP

1. While sitting in front of the keyboard, press Ctrl+Alt+Del.
2. When the Windows Task Manager opens, click the Processes tab.
3. In the Image Name column, locate EXCEL.EXE.

> For the purpose of this task, you can choose to stop another program by selecting its name.

4. Select EXCEL.EXE by clicking on it.
5. Click the End Process button in the lower-right corner of the Task Manager box.

> You'll receive a Task Manager warning stating that "terminating a process can cause undesired results" and explaining what some of those results could be. The message asks if you still want to terminate the process.

6. When the Task Manager Warning box appears, click Yes.

> You'll be tempted to use the Applications tab in Task Manager to kill Excel, but keep in mind that only application software is listed there. Many other running processes in Windows won't appear in this display, so it's better to use the Processes tab in the vast majority of cases.

Criteria for Completion

You will have successfully completed this task when the selected process disappears from the list in the Processes window. In this example, Excel should close immediately.

> Sometimes applications hang for unknown reasons and the next time you go to use them, they work fine. This task is an example of that situation. Keep in mind that there are other circumstances where this symptom could indicate a larger problem that's not so easily solved.

Task 1.33: Tweaking Windows XP

Tweaking or hacking a computer is a method or series of methods designed to improve hardware and software performance beyond their default settings.

> The title of this task could have just as easily been "Hacking Windows XP," but the word *hacking* is sometimes taken the wrong way.

There is no one procedure for tweaking a computer, so this task will actually be a series of "mini-tasks" written to show you different ways to improve the performance of a Windows XP computer. The list is by no means exhaustive; entire books can be (and have been) written on hacking operating systems and software.

> Of course, there is a large list of Windows Vista hacks that exists as well, but this exercise will address Windows XP tweaks specifically.

Scenario

You've received a trouble ticket from a user stating that his computer is running slowly but not complaining of a specific set of symptoms. After looking into the matter, your supervisor suggests that you perform a "tune-up" on the user's computer, optimizing various settings for faster and more efficient performance.

Scope of Task

Duration

This task could take anywhere from 15 minutes to an hour depending on the extent of the "tweaking."

Setup

All you'll need to do for this task is to sit at a Windows XP computer and follow the task instructions. You'll need to use Windows XP Professional to complete this task successfully.

Caveat

The results of this task on your computer may vary from the "ideal," depending on a number of factors such as the age of the computer and how well it has been maintained.

The tasks presented in this exercise are meant to be used on a computer that runs a large amount of resource-intensive applications on a regular basis or one that is at least somewhat underpowered. If you are running PCs that are no more than a few years old and are being used "normally," you shouldn't run into this situation too often.

Procedure

You'll learn a number of techniques that will result in improved performance of your Windows XP computer.

Equipment Used

No special equipment will be needed.

Details

This task will show you the specific activities to go through that will result in a general improvement of computer performance.

Free System Resources

CUSTOMIZING HOW VISUAL EFFECTS ARE DISPLAYED

1. Click Start.
2. Right-click My Computer.
3. Click Properties.
4. When the System Properties box opens, click the Advanced tab.
5. Under Performance, click the Settings button.
6. Click the Visual Effects tab if it doesn't display by default.
7. Click the Customize radio button.

 Most of the boxes in the display window will be checked.

8. Uncheck the checked boxes.
9. Click OK.

 You may notice a change in how objects display visually as a result of shutting down all of these effects. You'll most likely have to re-enable some of them until you get your system displaying as you desire.

DISABLING A HARD DRIVE'S INDEXING SERVICE

1. Click Start ≻ My Computer.

2. Right-click the hard drive of your choice and click Properties.

3. Verify that the General tab is selected in the Local Disk properties box.

4. Uncheck the Allow Indexing Service to Index This Disk for Fast File Searching check box.

> The disk-indexing service uses an executable named Cidaeamon.exe to create and update the indexing catalog on the disk drive. Although this does make searching for files and folders faster, the process also consumes a great deal of CPU processing and page file space. (See "Customizing Virtual Memory" later in this task to learn more about page files.)

5. In the box that pops up, check Apply Change to (*drive letter*):\ Subfolders and Files.

6. Click OK.

7. Close the My Computer box.

8. Reboot the computer.

CUSTOMIZING THE START MENU

1. Right-click Start.

2. Click Properties.

3. Click the Classic Start Menu radio button.

4. Click the Customize button.

5. In the Advanced Start menu options window, scroll up and down checking or unchecking the features you want to appear in the menu.

6. Click the Add button.

7. Click OK.

> The Start menu will change to an older version that takes up less space on the Desktop and uses fewer resources to open and display.

DISABLING WALLPAPER

1. Right-click any empty area on the Desktop.

2. Click Properties.

3. Select the Desktop tab.

4. Scroll to the top of the Background window.

5. Click None.

6. Click OK.

> This saves some memory and will make your boot time a bit faster. Of course, the desktop will be completely impersonal.

> In large enterprise settings using Active Directory domains, end-user desktops and a variety of other services and features are configured automatically on all user computers by Active Directory Group Policy objects (GPOs).

CUSTOMIZING VIRTUAL MEMORY

> Virtual memory uses hard-drive space to supplement the RAM in a computer. When a PC has insufficient RAM, some open services and data requiring memory are temporarily switched to a page file on the hard drive. This frees up memory; however, excessive "paging" (switching of data and services back and forth between RAM and the hard drive) results in performance slowdowns.

> This exercise requires that you have more than one partition on the computer's hard drive.

1. Click Start.

2. Right-click My Computer.

3. Click Properties.

4. In the System Properties box, click the Advanced tab.

5. In the Performance box, click Settings.

6. In the Performance Options box, click the Advanced tab.

7. Click the Programs radio buttons under both Processor Scheduling and Memory Usage.

8. Under Virtual Memory, click the Change button.

9. Select a drive partition other than C:\.

10. Set the initial size and the maximum size of the page file to 1½ times the amount of RAM in your computer.

11. Click Set.

12. Click OK.

You can achieve the best performance by placing virtual memory on a separate physical drive, if available. According to Microsoft, to optimize your virtual memory space, divide virtual memory space among as many different physical hard drives as possible. For more details, see http://support.microsoft.com/kb/308417. You can also create a second page file on a partition using FAT32 rather than NTFS, but this is used only when a separate, very small partition is created for the sole purpose of "hosing" the paging file.

DISABLING SYSTEM SOUNDS

1. Click Start ➤ Control Panel.
2. Double-click Sounds and Audio Devices.
3. On the Volume tab, uncheck the Place Volume Icon in the Taskbar check box.
4. Click the Sounds tab.
5. On the Sounds tab, click the Save As button.
6. Save your current sound scheme under a name such as Normal.
7. Click the Sound Scheme drop-down list.
8. Select No Sounds.
9. Click OK.

Criteria for Completion

You will have successfully completed this set of tasks when you've customized all of the settings as described. Performance on the computer should be improved; however, your mileage may vary.

There are literally hundreds of tweaks you can perform on XP to improve system performance and stability. The ones presented in this set of tasks are only a sample of the more common methods.

Task 1.34: Installing a Local Printer

In most business settings, users print to one or more network printers. This allows printer resources to be shared among a large number of users, avoiding the need to rely on one user sharing their printer with the rest of the workgroup. A print server performs the queuing and is always (hopefully) available to the network.

There are occasions when one or more users will require a local printer to be attached to their PC. Some businesses still use old dot-matrix printers to print multicopy No Carbon

Required (NCR) documents such as invoices. Department heads may want to print confidential documents in their offices rather than risk sensitive material being printed on a network printer shared by the rest of the staff. You will occasionally find it necessary to install a local printer on a computer.

Scenario

You receive the assignment of installing a local printer on a new sales executive's PC. You are provided with the new printer and installation kit on a cart, and you take the equipment to the appropriate office and get ready to install it.

Duration

This task should take about 15 to 20 minutes at most.

Setup

You'll need a PC, a printer, the USB cable, and the driver disc that came with the printer. If you already have a printer installed, you can uninstall the printer drivers and disconnect the printer from your computer. Then follow the instructions in this task to reinstall the printer. In most cases, you probably don't even need to have the driver disc since XP contains an extensive list of drivers for common print devices. Of course, having the disc doesn't hurt, just in case.

Caveat

Installing a printer on Windows XP should be a snap. Just make sure you have the right driver disc in the event that Windows doesn't have the drivers on board (a remote possibility). Also, some printers require that you use their installation software to do the setup rather than using the Add Printer Wizard. Read the instructions that come with your printer completely before beginning this exercise.

 It is unlikely that you'll use a printer cable for this task, since current printers come almost exclusively with USB cables, but if you are performing this task with an older setup, using a printer cable won't appreciably change the installation process.

Procedure

This task will take you through the process of installing a local printer on a PC.

Equipment Used

The only piece of equipment you might need is a small screwdriver if you are using an older setup requiring a standard printer cable. Even then, some of the connectors are screwed in while others can be tightened by hand. If you are unpacking a brand-new printer from a box, you may need a box cutter to cut through the tape and any other restraints used to secure the printer for shipping.

Details

This exercise shows you the steps necessary to connect a local printer to a PC and verify that it's working.

Installing a Local Printer

CONNECTING THE PRINTER

1. Power up the computer.

2. Log on as the local administrator.

3. Unpack the printer.

4. Place the printer at a desired location near the computer.

5. Verify that all packing equipment and tape have been removed from the printer.

6. Locate the USB cable used to attach the printer to the PC, as well as the printer's power cable.

7. Locate the installation kit, which should include a driver disc, installation manual, and any other equipment or materials that came with the printer.

8. Read the installation manual completely before proceeding.

9. Attach the power cable to the printer and plug the other end into a power socket or surge protector.

10. Attach one end of the USB cable to the printer's USB port and attach the other end to the PC's USB port.

 The connectors at each end of the USB cable will be different. The connector for the printer will be more of a square while the connector for the computer will look like a thin rectangle.

11. Following the instructions that came with the printer, open the printer and find the printer head(s).

12. Locate the printer cartridge(s) that came with the printer.

 If cartridges did not come with the printer, your supervisor should provide you with the appropriate cartridges for this device.

13. Install the cartridge(s) in the printer following the instruction guide.

There's no one method of installing printer cartridges, so we won't go into detail on this part of the task.

14. Close the printer.

15. Power up the printer.

The printer should go through a self-check routine and perform the alignment of the printer head(s) at this point, or it may perform some parts of this process after it is fully installed. There can be a special process associated with printer alignment, depending on the make and model of printer you are installing. Check the printer's documentation for details.

INSTALLING THE PRINTER

1. Click Start ➢ Printers and Faxes.

You can also click Start ➢ Settings ➢ Control Panel ➢ Printers and Faxes if the Printers and Faxes option isn't available in the Start menu.

If Windows autodetects the printer as a new USB device or the Add Hardware Wizard launches, close the wizard and proceed with the instructions in this task.

2. In the upper-left corner of the Printers and Faxes page, click Add a Printer.

3. When the Add Printer Wizard launches, click Next.

4. On the Local or Network Printer page, click the Local Printer Attached to This Computer radio button and check the Automatically Detect and Install My Plug and Play Printer check box.

5. Click Next.

6. Under Select a Printer Port, use the drop-down list to select USB.

If you are using an older standard printer cable, select LPT1: [Recommended Printer Port].

7. Click Next.

8. On the Install Printer Software page, in the Manufacturer window, scroll down and select the manufacturer of the printer (HP, Brother, etc.).

9. In the Printers window, scroll down and select the specific model of printer you have.

In the vast majority of cases, your computer manufacturer and model will be included in these lists.

10. Click Next.

11. On the Name Your Printer page, give a name to the printer.

Use a name that clearly identifies the printer.

12. Click Next.

13. On the Printer Sharing page, verify that the Do Not Share This Printer radio button is selected.

14. Click Next.

15. On the Location and Comment page, you can add the location of the printer and a brief description. This step is completely optional, especially for an unshared local printer.

16. Click Next.

TESTING THE PRINTER

1. When the Print a Test Page window appears, click Yes.

A box will appear asking if the test page printed properly. The page should print after a few seconds.

2. When the test page prints, click OK.

If the test page doesn't print or if it doesn't print properly, instead of clicking OK in step 2, click Troubleshoot. The Help and Support Center page will open and you can work your way through a wizard process to diagnose the problem. You can also consult the Troubleshooting section of the printer's documentation for information about the error.

3. Click Next.

4. When the Completing the Add Printer Wizard page appears, click Finish.

5. Once the wizard closes, open the application or applications the user will normally print from.

The user will probably print from Word and Excel, but find out in advance which applications will be used to print. Occasionally the test page will print fine but a particular application will refuse to share and play well with the printer.

6. Systematically open each application, create a small document, and then print it.

7. When you have successfully printed from each application, close it.

8. When the test is completed, verify that all application software is closed.

9. Log off the PC.

10. Make sure that the user has plenty of printer paper and extra print cartridges.

Criteria for Completion

You will have successfully completed this task when you have printed a test page from the Add Printer Wizard and from each application you will be printing from.

Task 1.35: Installing Printer Drivers

You may think this task is a subset of Task 1.34. Although the steps are similar, the situation is different. Besides, there's more than one way to install printer drivers.

Occasionally drivers (or any kind of software) will become corrupted or newer drivers will become available. Sometimes the print device begins to act strangely and the solution is to update or reinstall the drivers. In any event, there are various reasons why you will be asked to perform this task.

Scenario

One of the marketing executive's local printers has started printing "garbage." Your supervisor believes the printer drivers have been corrupted and provides you with the driver disc appropriate for the user's device. You have been assigned to reinstall the printer drivers and correct the problem.

Duration

This task should take about 10 minutes.

Setup

You will need a driver disc for your local print device.

Caveat

You can also attempt to install drivers from Windows Update if they are available or from the printer manufacturer's website.

Procedure

You will learn the steps necessary to install printer drivers on a computer.

Equipment Used

You will need no special equipment to complete this task besides the driver disc.

Details

This task will walk you through the procedure of installing new printer drivers on a computer from a disc.

Installing Printer Drivers

INSTALLING PRINTER DRIVERS USING THE ADD A PRINTER DRIVER WIZARD

1. Click Start ➤ Printers and Faxes.

> You can also click Start ➤ Settings ➤ Control Panel ➤ Printers and Faxes if the Printers and Faxes option is unavailable in the Start menu.

2. Right-click the desired printer.
3. Click Properties.
4. Click the Advanced tab.
5. Click the New Driver button.
6. Click Next.

> After you click the New Driver button and click Next, the Welcome to the Add a Printer Driver Wizard page will launch.

7. In the Printer Driver Selection page, in the Manufacturer window, scroll down and select the manufacturer of your printer.
8. In the Printers window, scroll down and select the specific model of your printer.
9. Click the Have Disk button.
10. Insert the driver disc in the computer's optical drive.
11. In the Install from Disk box, use the drop-down list to select the drive letter of the optical drive.

Instead of using the drop-down list to select a drive letter, you can click the Browse button and use Windows Explorer to browse to the correct drive.

12. Click OK.

13. Click Next.

14. When the Completing the Add Printer Driver Wizard page appears, click Finish.

 The drivers should install at this point of the process.

TESTING THE PRINTER DRIVER INSTALLATION

1. In the Printers and Faxes box, right-click the printer.

2. Click Properties.

3. On the General tab, click Print Test Page.

 After you click Print Test Page, a box will appear asking if the test page printed properly. The page should print after a few seconds.

4. When the test page prints, click OK.

 If the test page doesn't print or if it doesn't print properly, instead of clicking OK in step 4, click Troubleshoot. The Help and Support Center page will open and you can work your way through a wizard process to diagnose the problem. You can also consult either the printed documentation for the printer or the printer's documentation on the manufacturer's website.

5. Click OK to close the Printer Properties box.

6. Open the applications the user will use to print.

7. Create a test document in each application and print it.

8. When done, close all applications.

Criteria for Completion

You will have successfully completed this task when you have installed the drivers and the printer operates normally.

Task 1.36: Installing a Bluetooth Device in Windows Vista

As you likely know, Bluetooth is a wireless protocol used to connect devices over a very short distance to construct personal wireless networks, or PANs. A Bluetooth device can be almost anything, from a keyboard or mouse to a PDA. Bluetooth uses the same frequencies as Wi-Fi devices but at higher power levels. This renders Bluetooth incompatible with Wi-Fi, since the Bluetooth signals will literally "overpower" the Wi-Fi radio transmissions.

As a support technician, you won't need to know a great amount of detail about the specifications associated with Bluetooth, but you will need to know how to install a Bluetooth device on a PC. This task will show you the basics.

Scenario

The chief operations officer at your company wants a Bluetooth keyboard installed for his Windows Vista computer. He has just left for lunch and expects the keyboard to be up and running when he gets back.

Your supervisor has already installed the necessary Bluetooth technology onto the computer, so all you have to do is physically install the device and set it up. You have already unplugged and laid aside the old USB keyboard. You have been provided with the Bluetooth keyboard and adapter. You have been shown how to turn on the Bluetooth device and make it discoverable.

Duration

This task should take about 10 minutes.

Setup

You will need a Bluetooth device and adapter. It would be ideal if your computer has Bluetooth technology installed, but it's not absolutely necessary, because you can also install the device directly from the device's control panel. You can use any Bluetooth device, but the steps for the installation may differ somewhat from this exercise. Also, although it is common to use a passkey with Bluetooth devices, since this is just a keyboard, a passkey won't be necessary for this task.

NOTE A passkey, or passcode, is a number used to associate a Bluetooth device with a computer. Passkeys are used to provide security so that your device cannot be accessed using another computer. Low-security devices such as keyboards and mice typically don't use passkeys.

Caveat

If you use Wi-Fi at or near the PC you plan to use for this exercise, you will need to turn off your wireless network so that this task will succeed. The process of activating the Bluetooth device and making it discoverable will vary depending on the device, so consult the device's documentation for details. You will also need to refer to the device's documentation if you will be installing it from the device's control panel, rather than using Windows Vista.

> Recent developments with Bluetooth have addressed the 802.11b and 802.11g conflict, particularly with Bluetooth 1.2 (2003), with the use of adaptive frequency hopping spread (AFH) spectrum signaling. See the following for more information: http://bluetooth.com/Bluetooth/Press/SIG/Bluetooth_SIG_Adopts_Version_12_of_Wireless_Technology_Specification.htm.

> Making a wireless or Bluetooth device "discoverable" is the process of configuring the device to transmit so it can be detected by a receiving unit, such as an access point in the case of Wi-Fi, or the computer in the case of installing the Bluetooth keyboard. It may mean that you will temporarily need to disable the Windows onboard firewall and other security measures.

Procedure

You will learn the steps needed to install a Bluetooth keyboard on a Windows Vista computer.

Equipment Used

You will need the Bluetooth device and a Bluetooth adapter, unless the computer has a built-in adapter. The adapter plugs into any USB port, so installation is straightforward.

Details

This exercise will show you how to install a Bluetooth device.

Installing a Bluetooth Device

SETTING UP THE BLUETOOTH DEVICE

1. Make sure you are logged on to the computer with an account that has administrator privileges.
2. Locate the Bluetooth adapter and remove it from its packaging.
3. Insert the adapter in an available USB port on the computer.
4. Locate the Bluetooth keyboard and remove it from its packaging.

5. Verify that the keyboard has a power source and turn it on.

6. Place or hold the keyboard in the proximity of the computer.

7. Verify that the keyboard is discoverable (consult the keyboard's documentation for the specific steps needed).

SETTING UP BLUETOOTH IN WINDOWS VISTA

1. Click the Windows Vista Start button.

2. Click Control Panel.

3. Click Hardware and Sound, and then click Bluetooth Devices.

4. Click Add.

 Follow the instructions in the screens that follow. The instructions may vary depending on the device being installed.

5. After the installation process is completed, attempt to use the keyboard normally, such as opening up Notepad and typing some characters. Make sure all of the keys work as expected.

Criteria for Completion

You will have successfully completed this exercise when the Bluetooth device is installed and behaving as expected.

Phase
2

Maintaining and Documenting Computer Systems

A large part of your day-to-day duties as a PC tech will involve maintaining computer and server systems and documenting your work. Many people don't think a great deal about the paperwork side of IT, but despite the promise of a "paperless society" at the advent of the information age, documentation is still a large part of nearly everyone's workday.

That being said, you will still find plenty of hands-on work to do with computer systems. In this phase of the book, you will build on the basic skills you learned in Phase 1, "Installing Hardware and Software." You will discover how to leverage those elementary exercises and learn how to perform regular maintenance tasks on computers.

Among other tasks, you'll learn how to identify a motherboard, how to clean and oil cooling fans, and how to flash BIOS. So take the book over to your lab computer and get ready for the next step.

The tasks in this phase map to Domains 1, 2, 3, 5, and 6 for the CompTIA A+ Essentials (220-701) exam objectives, and to Domains 1, 2, and 4 for the CompTIA Practical Application (220-702) exam objectives.

Task 2.1: Identifying a Motherboard

On occasion, you may have to replace a computer's motherboard. Most of the time the type of motherboard is easily identified by the documentation that came with the computer. Sometimes, though, you won't be able to locate any relevant information about the motherboard. In this case, you can use one of a number of handy (and free) utilities that have the ability to extract that information from the system BIOS and other sources on the device.

Scenario

You have been assigned to replace the motherboard of an older server that has been providing print services to one of your company's branch offices. You attempt to locate the computer's documentation but it can't be found. You open up the server's case and examine the motherboard but can't determine the make and model. You close the server, power it up, and log on. Then you open up a web browser to begin the process of identifying the motherboard.

Scope of Task

Duration

This task should take about 10 to 15 minutes, including download and installation time.

Setup

You'll need a computer with an Internet connection. This task also requires that you download and install software that can query your computer and gather relevant information.

Caveat

This method isn't practical if you are trying to identify the motherboard of a computer that is nonfunctional. Also, this task was performed on a Windows XP computer, but is applicable to other Windows PCs.

Procedure

This task will teach you the steps to take in identifying a motherboard.

Equipment Used

You won't need any special equipment for this task, but you will have to download and install a piece of software on your computer to query the motherboard's BIOS and other resources.

Details

This task will take you through the process of searching for a motherboard's make and model.

Using the Internet to Find, Download, and Install a System-Querying Utility

1. At a computer with an Internet connection, open a web browser.
2. Type in the following URL: www.majorgeeks.com/download181.html.

I found the site mentioned in step 2 by using the search string "find out motherboard type." Since the Internet is very changeable, if the URL is not available when you attempt this task, use the same string in any search engine and locate a site with the same or a similar tool. That said, I found this utility in the same location when writing this second edition as I did when I was writing the first.

3. Read the instructions on the web page that appears, and determine which download mirror is closest to you.

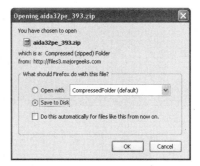

4. Click the appropriate link. The download page will open and the download will begin a few moments later.

5. When the download dialog box opens, make sure the Save to Disk radio button is selected and click OK.

6. Browse to a folder where you want to place the zip file.

7. Click Save.

Depending on your Internet connection speed, the zip file should download in a few seconds.

8. Navigate to the folder where the zip file is saved.

9. Right-click the zip file.

10. Click Extract All.
11. At this point, the Welcome to the Compressed (Zipped) Folders Extraction Wizard will launch. Click Next.

> In step 11, you can choose to extract the files in the current directory or browse to another folder.

12. When you are ready, click Next.
13. Verify that the Show Extracted Files box is checked.
14. Click Finish.
15. Double-click on the `aida32.exe` file to begin the installation.
16. When the installation is complete, double-click the Motherboard icon in the large pane on the right-hand side of the display window.
17. When the next window appears, double-click the Motherboard icon.

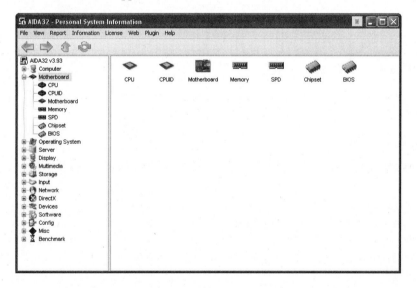

> When you double-click the Motherboard icon, all of the information regarding the motherboard will display, including the manufacturer. You'll notice that this utility displays much more information about the computer than just the motherboard. Feel free to explore the rest of this information. It can often be helpful when you're trying to collect a detailed list of information about a device.

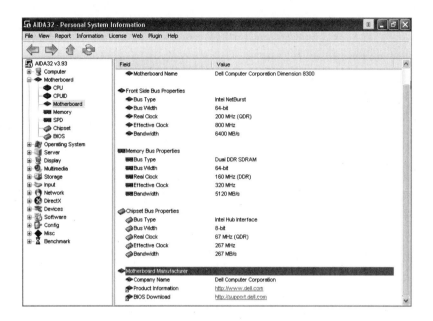

Criteria for Completion

You will have successfully completed this assignment when you have located all of the information to identify your computer's motherboard.

Task 2.2: Identifying a Power Supply

While the utility used in Task 2.1 has the ability to present a report on almost every system that makes up your PC, it can't do everything. One device it does not identify is the power supply attached to the computer. As you might imagine, if you should ever need to replace the power supply on the PC, you would need to know the make and model required by your computer.

Scenario

You have recently replaced the motherboard on a computer that functions as a print server for one of your company's branch offices. You receive another trouble ticket for the same device stating that the PC is subject to intermittent reboots. You investigate and determine that the power supply may be failing. You will still need to test the power supply to be sure, but you want to identify the proper replacement unit, should it become necessary.

You are unable to locate any documentation identifying the power supply and there are no identifying markings in the unit itself. You will need to determine the correct power supply to use as a replacement based on the make and model of the computer.

Scope of Task

Duration

This task should take about 10 minutes.

Setup

All you'll need is a computer with an Internet connection. You will only be identifying the correct power supply to be used for your computer.

Task 2.3 will show you how to test a potentially failing power supply and how to replace the unit in a computer.

Caveat

All you will need to know is the manufacturer, make, and model number of the computer that may require the new power supply.

Procedure

This task will teach you how to determine the correct power supply required by your computer.

Equipment Used

You will need no special equipment for this task.

Details

This task will take you through the process of searching for the correct power supply for a computer.

Locating the Correct Power Supply for your PC

1. Verify that you have the specifications for your computer available.

2. Open a web browser and go to www.pcpower.com/products/power_supplies/selector/.

3. On the PSU Selector page, under Select Motherboard type, click on the name of the manufacturer of your computer's motherboard.

4. On the Systems Brands page, click on the series name for your computer.

> You can also click on the specific series and model number for your computer under the Most Popular Series section.

5. Click on the series and model number for your computer.

6. Review the results of your search and, if there is more than one power supply recommended, review the specifications and determine which unit is best suited to your computer's requirements.

7. Click the Details button for more information on the desired power supply and write down all of the identifying information for your selection.

Criteria for Completion

You will have successfully completed this task when you have identified the power supply most suited to your computer.

Task 2.3: Testing and Replacing a Power Supply

Now that you have determined the correct model of power supply required for your computer, you will need to know how to verify that the power supply is actually failing and, if it is, how to replace it.

> See Task 2.2 for more details on the current scenario.

    While you are reasonably convinced that the power supply of the computer is failing, you will need to test it to be sure, prior to installing a replacement unit.

Scenario

You previously received a trouble ticket (Task 2.2) stating that the computer used for print services at one of your company's branch offices has been spontaneously rebooting. This is a likely symptom of a failing power supply. You have determined the type of power supply required if the unit needs replacing. You have a replacement unit in your department's inventory, so you take the replacement unit, along with your tools, to the branch office to test and, if necessary, to replace the power supply.

Scope of Task

Duration

This task should take 30 minutes or longer, depending on your familiarity with using a multimeter for testing, and the complexity of removing and replacing the power supply for the computer you are using for this task.

Setup

You will need a multimeter for the testing phase of the task and the proper replacement unit for the power supply. Chances are, your lab computer doesn't need a new power supply, so you can just remove and replace the same unit in your computer.

Caveat

Basic instructions for how to use a multimeter are beyond the scope of this book. To view a tutorial on how to use a multimeter, go to www.youtube.com/watch?v=KzjMIcER4EU. You can also search for "how to use a multimeter" on the Internet.

   While the process of removing and replacing a power supply isn't complex, it can be cumbersome. Also, the power supply is the largest and heaviest single component in a computer's case. Proceed slowly and carefully with all the steps in this task.

Procedure

Equipment Used

You will need to have a multimeter, which can be purchased at almost any electronics store. You will also need to have the type or types of screwdrivers needed to remove the screws attaching the access panel to your PC's case and to remove the attachment screws holding the power supply in place. You should have a small notepad and pencil to write down the multimeter test results for each connection.

Details

This task shows you how to test a potentially failing power supply and then how to replace the power supply with a new unit.

Testing and Replacing a Power Supply

TESTING A POWER-SUPPLY CONNECTION TO A DRIVE WITH A MULTIMETER

1. Arrange your tools, including the multimeter, next to the PC case.

2. Power down the computer, but do not unplug the unit.

3. Use ESD precautions before opening the PC case.

4. Remove the screws attaching the access panel to the PC case.

5. Remove the access panel and set it aside.

6. Check the connections between the power supply and the motherboard, hard-disk drive and other units, to make sure the connections are secure.

7. Locate your multimeter and set it to DC volts in the next range higher than 12 volts.

8. Disconnect a power connection, such as the one from the power supply to the CD or DVD drive, and keep the connector from the power supply available.

9. Power on the PC.

10. Locate the power connector from the power supply you disconnected from the CD or DVD drive.

11. Insert the black probe into one of the black-wire sockets on the connector.

If the connector is for a SATA power cable, which is commonly an extension from a Molex power supply, you can test "upstream" of the extension. For details, see www.satacables.com/html/molex-to-sata-power-15-pin-ada.html.

12. Touch the red probe to a yellow-wire socket on the connector.

13. Write down the reading.

14. Touch the red probe to the red-wire socket on the connector.

15. Write down the reading.

When you inserted the black probe into the socket for the black wire, and then touched the red probe to the yellow-wire socket, the multimeter should have read +12 volts. When you touched the red probe to the red-wire socket, the multimeter should have read +5 volts. If you got no readings or the readings were significantly different, skip to the steps in this task that tell you how to replace the power supply. If the readings were correct, go to the next set of steps.

TESTING A POWER-SUPPLY CONNECTION TO THE MOTHERBOARD WITH A MULTIMETER

1. Locate the connections between the power supply and the motherboard.

The connections should be labeled P8 and P9 but may alternately be called P4 and P5. For the purpose of this task, we will use P8 and P9.

These instructions are valid for the AT form factor; however, this form factor is not part of the current CompTIA A+ objectives. The ATX, BTX, NLX, and micro ATX form factors are included in the current objectives, and they all use the P1 connector to the motherboard, rather than the P8 and P9 connectors.

2. With the PC still powered, insert the black probe into the P8 connector for one of the black wires.

3. Insert the red probe into the P8 connector for a red wire.

4. Write down the readings.

5. Insert the red probe into the P8 connector for a yellow wire.

6. Write down the readings.

7. Insert the red probe into the P8 connector for a blue wire.

8. Write down the readings.

9. Remove the black probe from the P8 connector and insert it in the black-wire socket for the P9 connector.

10. Insert the red probe into the P9 connector for a white wire.

11. Write down the readings.

12. Insert the red probe into the P9 connector for each red wire.

13. Write down the readings.

14. Remove the multimeter probes from all connectors and turn off the multimeter.

15. Replace all connectors from the power supply to the drive units and motherboard as necessary.

For the P8 connector, the reading for the red wire should be +5 volts, and the reading for the yellow wire should be +12 volts. The reading for the blue wire should be –12 volts.

For the P9 connector, the reading for the white wire should be –5 volts, and for each of the red wires, it should be +5 volts.

The readings may not be precise, but if the variance is something like 5.02, the unit is most likely functioning properly. If the variance is much more, the power supply will need to be replaced.

REPLACING A POWER SUPPLY IN A COMPUTER

1. Power down the PC.

2. Continuing to use ESD precautions, remove all of the connections between the power supply and the computer's motherboard, drive units, and any other components.

 To remove the connectors on the motherboard, you may have to press down on a latch on the connector to release it, and then gently pull the connector away from the motherboard.

3. Remove the power cable from the power supply at the back of the PC case.

4. Locate the screwdriver that is appropriate for removing the screws attaching the power supply to the PC case (most likely a Phillips screwdriver).

5. Remove the screws holding the power supply to the PC case, while supporting the power supply inside the case with your other hand.

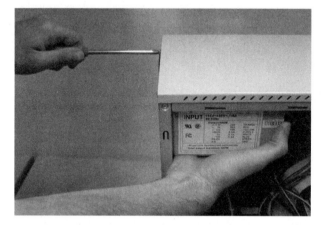

6. Once the power-supply screws have been removed, use the hand supporting the unit to slide it forward, toward the front of the PC case, until the power supply comes completely free.

7. Remove the power supply from the PC case and set it aside.

8. Remove the new power supply from its packaging.

9. Verify that all packaging and other unnecessary items are removed from the power-supply unit and all its connectors.

10. Continuing to observe ESD precautions, carefully insert the power supply in the case, holding it toward the top of the case.

11. Slide the unit toward the back of the case until the screw mounts match those on the PC case and the power-supply electrical socket matches the aperture in the case.

12. Supporting the unit with one hand, replace the mounting screws on the back of the PC case.

13. Once the power supply is securely mounted, replace all of the internal connections between the power supply and the drive units, motherboard, and other components, making sure that each connector is correctly oriented and fitted securely.

Unless the power-supply unit and all of the connectors are exactly identical to the old unit, you may want to consult with the documentation for the replacement power supply to verify how the connections are correctly made.

14. Arrange the internal connector cables, including any unused cables, so that they don't impede airflow on the inside of the PC case.

> **NOTE** Some power supplies use a modular system that lets you remove any unused cables from the unit.

15. Reconnect the power cable to the power supply at the back of the PC case.
16. Before reattaching the PC-case access panel, power up the computer.
17. Watch the monitor for any error messages and listen for any beep signals.
18. Once you've verified that the computer boots and runs normally, replace the PC-case access panel and secure it with the panel's screws.

Criteria for Completion

You will have successfully completed this task when you have replaced the power-supply unit and verified that the computer boots and operates normally. If the original symptom was a periodically rebooting computer, you may have to remain near the computer for 30 minutes or so, to make sure the computer runs consistently. Notify the staff at the branch office to monitor the computer after you leave so you can make sure that it continues to run normally.

Task 2.4: Managing a Swap File

A computer has only so much active memory on board. When you open a program or run a process, that process runs in the computer's active memory. If you have multiple processes running on a computer with insufficient RAM, the responsiveness of the computer will slow, sometimes to a crawl.

> **NOTE** Windows Vista requires quite a bit more RAM than Windows XP and its predecessors. If you have a Vista-compliant computer, you may still have issues with sufficient RAM, depending on the applications you regularly run and how much work you expect out of your computer at any given time.

One way to remedy this is to add more RAM (see Task 1.2, "Installing RAM"). Another method is to increase the size of the computer's swap file. When a computer is running too many processes to keep active in RAM all at once, it will attempt to temporarily store some in the swap file on the computer's hard drive. If that file is too small, this method of preserving active memory won't work.

Windows Vista offers an additional option called ReadyBoost. For details, see www.microsoft.com/whdc/system/sysperf/accelerator.mspx.

You can increase the size of the swap file so that it will be able to augment the computer's memory.

Scenario

One of the accountants in the billing department has complained that his computer runs too slowly when he has multiple applications open. You have been assigned to increase the size of his computer's swap file to improve performance.

Scope of Task

Duration

This task should take about 10 minutes.

Setup

There is no special setup for this task.

Caveat

On Windows computers, the system usually tries to manage the swap-file size, but you can override those settings. Just make sure there is enough space available for the size of your page file. This task was written based on a Windows XP computer, but it applies just as well to Windows Vista.

The terms *swap file* and *page file* are synonymous.

Procedure

This task will teach you how to manually increase the size of a swap file.

Equipment Used

You will need no special equipment for this task.

Details

This task will walk you through the steps necessary to locate and change a computer's swap-file size.

Changing the Size of a Swap File

1. Sitting in front of a Windows XP computer, click Start ≻ Control Panel.

2. Double-click the System applet.

3. When the System Properties dialog box appears, click the Advanced tab.

4. Under Performance, click the Settings button.

5. When the Performance Options box appears, click the Advanced tab.

6. Under Virtual Memory, click the Change button.

7. Verify that the Custom Size radio button is selected.

8. Change the value in the Maximum Size (MB) field to the size you want for the swap file.

Performance Options

Visual Effects | Advanced | Data Execution Prevention

Processor scheduling

By default, the computer is set to use a greater share of processor time to run your programs.

Adjust for best performance of:

⦿ Programs   ◯ Background services

Memory usage

By default, the computer is set to use a greater share of memory to run your programs.

Adjust for best performance of:

⦿ Programs   ◯ System cache

Virtual memory

A paging file is an area on the hard disk that Windows uses as if it were RAM.

Total paging file size for all drives: 1917 MB

Change

OK   Cancel   Apply

9. Click the Set button.

Virtual Memory

Drive [Volume Label]   Paging File Size (MB)

C: 1917 - 1917

Paging file size for selected drive

Drive: C:
Space available: 90697 MB

⦿ Custom size:
Initial size (MB):   1917
Maximum size (MB):   3000

◯ System managed size
◯ No paging file   Set

Total paging file size for all drives

Minimum allowed: 2 MB
Recommended: 1917 MB
Currently allocated: 1917 MB

OK   Cancel

When you click the Set button (step 9), the value in the window at the top of the box will change to reflect the new initial and maximum size of the swap file.

10. Click OK.
11. Click OK in the Performance Options box.
12. Click OK in the Systems Properties box.
13. Close Control Panel.

Criteria for Completion

You will have successfully completed this task when the value for the maximum size of the swap file has been confirmed. Depending on the amount of increase you made in the swap file, you should notice some improvement in performance.

Task 2.5: Imaging a Disk

Imaging is the process of creating an exact duplicate or clone of the original hard drive, including operating system, applications, and data. If you install the image onto another computer, that computer will become a precise copy of the computer you imaged. This is handy if you want to create a collection of computers all configured the same way. You will need to use some specialized software in order to create an image.

Scenario

You have been assigned to create an image of one of the test computers in the IT department. This computer is used to test new software, including Windows updates and beta software. If the computer experiences a problem after testing new software, it can be restored to its original condition with the image.

Scope of Task

Duration

Depending on the tool you use and the size of your hard drive, this task could take an hour or more.

Setup

You will need to have Norton Ghost or some other similar imaging software available to install on your computer.

Caveat

These instructions will apply to Norton Ghost 10.0, so the exact procedure you experience may be slightly different if you are using a different version of Ghost or a different type of imaging software. Also, this task is specific to creating a hard-drive image and does not provide instructions for installing Ghost or any other imaging software. Those instructions should come with your product.

Norton Ghost 14 is currently available as of this writing, but you'll find that many IT departments haven't invested in the "latest and greatest" applications available when what they already have still works fine.

Procedure

This task will show you how to make a duplicate image of your computer's hard drive.

Equipment Used

You will need no special equipment for this task, but you will need to have a copy of some form of imaging software available.

Details

This task will move you through the steps you will need to take to create an image of a computer's hard drive.

Creating and Verifying a Disk Image

USING NORTON GHOST TO CREATE A DISK IMAGE

1. At the computer you want to image, click Start ➤ All Programs ➤ Norton Ghost.
2. In the list that appears, click Norton Ghost.

After you activated Ghost and entered the product key, a wizard should have taken you though the process of configuring a path where you want the image to be stored using the Easy Setup dialog box. You could have also scheduled a backup at that time.

3. When Ghost launches, click Backup to open the Backup panel.

Norton Ghost 10.0 has three main panels: Backup, Recovery, and Status.

4. Click Back Up Now.

5. In the Back Up Now box, click Define New Backup.

6. When the Define Backup wizard launches, click Next.

7. Select the drive you want to back up, which will most likely be your C drive.

8. Click Next.

After you click Next in step 8, you may get a message asking if you want to add this backup to a preexisting backup or if you want to define a new backup. Choose to define a new backup.

9. Select Independent Recovery Point.

10. Click Next.

11. Click Browse.

12. Browse to the directory you want to use to store the recovery point.

The directory referred to in step 12 can be on the same computer or in a separate directory on another computer on the network.

13. Once the directory is selected, click Next.

14. Type the name of the backup in the Name field.

15. In the Compression drop-down menu, select Standard.

16. If you want, you can enter an optional description of the backup in the Description field.

17. For a backup option, select Manually (No Schedule) to run the backup manually.

18. Click Next.

19. Click Create the First Recovery Point Now.

20. Click Finish.

When you click Finish, the backup will run, imaging the computer's hard drive. It may take some time for this process to complete, so you might as well make a sandwich or grab a cup of coffee while you wait.

VERIFYING THAT THE DISK WAS SUCCESSFULLY IMAGED

1. With Norton Ghost still running, click Recovery to open the Recovery panel.

2. Click Recover My Files.

3. Select the recovery point you just made.

In step 3, if you've made more than one recovery point, they will all be listed here.

4. Click Browse Contents.

5. Select the desired drive in the left-hand sidebar menu.

6. Double-click any of the folders to open them.

7. Select a file.

8. Click File ➢ View File.

You can repeat this process for any folders and files you want to verify.

Criteria for Completion

You will have successfully completed this task when you verify that all of the required folders and files exist in the recovery point.

You can burn the image to a CD or DVD for safekeeping. Then, if it becomes necessary, you can use Norton Ghost with the CD or DVD to restore your computer.

Task 2.6: Searching for Drivers

Usually, you can find drivers for a particular device either on the disc that accompanied the device when it was purchased or online at the manufacturer's website. Occasionally, you will encounter an older device that the manufacturer no longer supports or discover that the manufacturer has gone out of business. Now you are stuck trying to find drivers for this machine or unit.

It might be simpler to buy a newer replacement, but sometimes an older device fills exactly the right role and you want to keep it going as long as possible. If you can find an alternate method of locating drivers for it, you can extend the device's life span.

Scenario

One of your company's branch offices uses a Windows 2000 Professional computer as a print server. The drivers for its network interface card (NIC) have become corrupted, so no one has print services at this office. You have been assigned to locate drivers for the NIC and install them.

Different procedures for installing device drivers were covered in Tasks 1.21 and 1.22, so this task will show you only how to locate device drivers.

Scope of Task

Duration

This task should take about 15 minutes, depending on how obscure the drivers you need are.

Setup

No special setup is needed. All you need is a computer with Internet access.

Caveat

This task requires that you create a free account at www.driverguide.com. When you first go to the sign-up page, you'll hear a small audio message promoting the site, assuming you have speakers attached to your computer. Read each page carefully and either check or clear any check boxes or radio buttons that will result in your signing up for a paid membership or for some other undesired benefit. To avoid agreeing to being spammed, you either have to select a lot of No radio buttons or click the Skip button on these pages. Once you click the verification link in the email you're sent after registering, you can log in. Just make sure to click the Skip button wherever you may find it.

Procedure

This task will show you how to search for device drivers in a large driver repository.

Equipment Used

No special equipment will be necessary.

Details

This task will walk you through the steps of searching for drivers for a particular device.

Searching for the Device Drivers for an Older Device

1. At a computer with Internet access, open a web browser.
2. Type the URL **www.driverguide.com** and press Enter.

After you press Enter in step 2, the main page for the site will open in your browser.

3. In the Login field, type the email address you used to create an account.

4. In the Pwd field, type the password.

5. Click Login.

6. Once you are logged in, click Manufacturers in the overhead list.

7. In the Choose Company box, click the first letter of the name of the device's manufacturer.

8. Click the button with the letter of the alphabet that is the first letter of the device manufacturer's name.

This task assumes that you know the name of the vendor that made the device.

9. Scroll through the list that appears and select the manufacturer.

10. Right below the list, click the Select Company button.

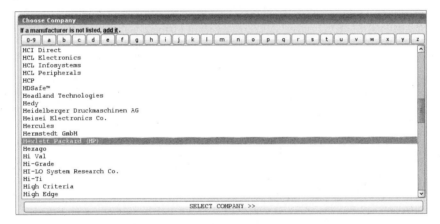

If the page that loads after you click Select Company asks you to input the model name and number of the device, click the List All Company Drivers link.

11. In the list that appears, locate the name of the device.

12. Click the link for that device.

13. Verify that this is the correct device by reading the summary.

14. Click the Download Now link to begin downloading the desired drivers.

Criteria for Completion

You will have successfully completed this task when you have located the required drivers for the device in question.

Task 2.7: Searching for Windows Vista Drivers

This is the opposite problem of the one that Task 2.6 addresses. Instead of needing to find drivers for old devices no longer supported, your task is to find device drivers that are supported by a (relatively) new operating system. Windows Vista has become notorious for what it doesn't support. This is to be expected when an operating system is first released, but after the first service pack was issued, it still continued to be a problem. However, it isn't an insurmountable chore, and this task will illustrate how best to search for and find Vista-compatible drivers.

Scenario

You have received a trouble ticket stating that the HR manager is unable to print from her laser printer. You know that she has just had a new Windows Vista computer installed in her office. You receive instructions from your supervisor to search for and install the drivers that will allow her to print. The instructions include the URL www.radarsync.com/vista/. You proceed to the HR manager's office to respond to her request.

Scope of Task

Duration

This task should take at most about 15 minutes, which includes searching for and downloading the drivers. Tasks 1.21 and 1.22 have already covered how to install drivers.

Setup

There's no special setup for this task beyond Internet access and having a Windows Vista computer.

Caveat

If you are trying this task from a computer with an operating system other than Vista, the site will automatically detect which version of Windows you are running and offer you the latest drivers of the selected hardware for that OS. Since you won't need to actually install the drivers, this won't pose a problem.

Procedure

This task will show you how to locate and download device drivers for Windows Vista computers.

Equipment Used

No special equipment is required.

Details

This task will show you the steps required to locate and download device drivers compatible with a Windows Vista computer.

Locating Device Drivers for a Windows Vista PC

1. At the Windows Vista computer, log in with an account that has administrative privileges.
2. Open a web browser and go to www.radarsync.com/vista/.
3. Scroll down the page until you locate the manufacturer for the device you are seeking.
4. Either click on the name of the device in the manufacturer's box if available, or click More.
5. Scroll until you locate the name of the required device, and then click on its name.

The Add Packs feature on this page requires that you register with RadarSync. You are offered the option to log in or register when you click the Pack It button. It's not necessary to use this feature to complete the task.

6. Click the Download the Latest Version button.

Criteria for Completion

You will have successfully completed this task when you have located and downloaded the Vista-compatible drivers for the desired device.

Task 2.8: Listing All of the Drivers Installed on a Windows Vista PC

You may think that using the Device Manager is the only way to find out what drivers are installed on a Windows computer, but Windows XP and Vista offer another solution. You can use the DeviceQuery command-line utility to show you a comprehensive list.

Most people, except for actual Windows system administrators, don't associate administering Windows with the command line. However, the command line is a powerful tool for performing a large number of helpful tasks. This task shows you only one small sample. If you go on to administer Windows systems, you will be required to learn a great deal more.

Scenario

You have recently installed drivers for a laser printer on the HR manager's Windows Vista computer. The printer now works flawlessly, but the HR manager is concerned about what her new PC does and doesn't support in terms of drivers. Your supervisor has directed you to generate a printable list of the drivers currently installed on her computer using the DriverQuery command-line utility. The other requirements for this assignment are that the list be verbose, showing the filename and the size of each driver, along with being "human-readable." You proceed to the HR manager's office to fulfill the request.

Scope of Task

Duration

This task should just take a few minutes.

Setup

There's no special setup for this task. You can perform this task on both Windows XP and Windows Vista computers.

Caveat

While the task is straightforward, as with many command-line tools, a number of arguments or switches are available to tailor the output of the command. To find out more, go to http://technet.microsoft.com/en-us/library/bb490896.aspx.

Procedure

This task will show you how to generate a printable list of drivers installed on a Windows Vista computer.

Equipment Used

No special equipment is required.

Details

This task will show you the steps required to use the command-line to create a drivers list.

Listing All of the Drivers on a Windows Vista Computer

1. Log in to the Windows Vista computer.
2. Click the Windows Vista button.
3. Click Run, type **cmd** in the Run box, and then click OK to open a command-line window.
4. At the prompt, type **driverquery /v /fo list >drivers.txt** and then press Enter.
5. Use Windows Explorer to navigate to C:\Documents and Settings*username*, where *username* is the name of the account you used to log in to the computer.
6. Locate and open drivers.txt.
7. If you want to print the document, click File ➢ Print. Otherwise, save it to a shared folder on the network or at a location where your supervisor instructed you to store the file.

> **NOTE**   This file can be very large, so don't print it unless you absolutely need to have a hard copy.

Criteria for Completion

You will have successfully completed this task when you have generated a text file containing a list of all the drivers installed on the Windows Vista computer.

Task 2.9: Cleaning Dust Bunnies out of Computers

You might imagine that the inside of a computer is rather clean since it's a sealed box, but plenty of dust gets in through the fan vents. As the months go by, the dust inside the computer's box can become quite thick. Eventually, it will affect airflow in the computer, causing overheating. Also, it's hard to perform maintenance on the inside of a very dusty PC. The process of cleaning out the dust is simple, but it must be performed regularly on all computers.

Scenario

You have been assigned to routinely clear the dust out of all the computers in the various departments of your company. Today, you are starting with your own desktop computer in the IT department.

Scope of Task

Duration

Depending on how dusty the inside of your computer is, this task should take about 5 to 10 minutes.

Setup

There's no special setup for this task. You'll just need to have a computer handy along with a can of compressed air, which can be purchased at any computer or office-supply store.

Caveat

Make sure you perform this task someplace that you don't mind getting dirty. You can take the computer out to the backyard patio or perform this task indoors in an area you can sweep or vacuum afterward.

Procedure

This task will show you how to clear dust out of the inside of a computer.

Equipment Used

You'll need a can of compressed air. Depending on where you perform this task, you may also need a broom or vacuum cleaner to get rid of whatever dust you blow out of your PC's case.

WARNING Do not use any other method of cleaning out the inside of a computer. If you try to use a vacuum cleaner, it will create a large amount of static electricity inside the box, damaging electrical components.

NOTE There are specialty vacuum devices that are safe to use inside a PC's case, but a can of compressed air is less expensive.

Details

This task will show you the steps to go through to clean dust out of a computer case.

Cleaning Out the Inside of a Computer

1. Power down your computer.
2. Locate a screwdriver and remove the screws holding the access panel in place.

WARNING Don't forget to use ESD precautions before putting your hands inside the PC case.

3. Remove the panel.
4. Locate the can of compressed air.

NOTE Usually, a long, thin plastic tube is fitted inside the can's nozzle to direct a focused stream of air.

5. Look inside the computer case and note how much dust is inside.

TIP It might be a good idea to wear protective goggles over your eyes for this procedure.

6. Aim the nozzle of the air can inside the computer case.
7. Depress the trigger to spray air inside the case.
8. Direct the nozzle to hard-to-reach areas inside the case to make sure you blow out any hidden dust and debris.

NOTE Leave the computer case open if you intend to immediately proceed to Tasks 2.10 and 2.11.

Criteria for Completion

You will have successfully completed this task when you have cleaned all of the dust out of the computer case. Don't forget to clean up the mess you made on the floor.

Task 2.10: Cleaning Out Fans

Task 2.9 showed you how to clean dust out of the inside of the computer case. Dust usually enters through the cooling and power-supply fans. These fans can also become dusty and eventually will start to spin more slowly, losing effectiveness. Just as you need to clean out the case, you must regularly clean the fans as well.

Scenario

As part of the process of maintaining the computers in your company, you have been assigned to clean and maintain the cooling fans. You are starting by cleaning the fans in your desktop computer in the IT department.

Scope of Task

Duration

This task should take about 10 minutes or so.

Setup

There is no special setup for this task.

Caveat

This task won't be quite as dusty as Task 2.9, but it's still recommended that you do the task in an area you don't mind making a mess.

Procedure

This task will show you how to clean the dust out of a computer's cooling fan.

Equipment Used

You'll need a can of compressed air (see Task 2.9) and a small brush such as one used for painting watercolors or for cleaning delicate equipment. You can probably find such a brush at any art store or hardware outlet.

Details

This task will show you the steps necessary to clean the cooling fans in a computer.

Cleaning the Computer Fans Using Compressed Air and Brushes

 NOTE   For this task, it is assumed your computer is powered down and the case is already open.

1. Locate the can of compressed air.

 WARNING   Remember to take ESD precautions before touching the inside of the computer case.

2. Direct the long nozzle on the compressed-air can toward the cooling fan.

 NOTE   Using compressed air to clean computer fans in step 2 may or may not be difficult, depending on the design of your computer case and how components are placed.

3. Depress the trigger on the can and direct air at and around the cooling fan.
4. Direct air at and around the chassis of the power supply.
5. From outside the case, spray all visible fans, making sure to clear off as much dust as possible.
6. Check inside the case and see if any additional dust was dislodged.
7. Use the compressed air to clear out any additional dust.
8. Put down the air can and pick up the brush.
9. Reach inside the case and gently brush the fan, including the blades and other components.
10. Repeat step 9 on the outside of the fans, including the power-supply fan.
11. Check one last time to see if any more dust has been dislodged inside the case.
12. Clean out any dust you find with compressed air.

 NOTE   This task shows you how to clean a computer that has a separate external cooling fan; however, some computers do not have this feature.

13. Replace the access panel.
14. Replace the screws holding the access panel in place.

Criteria for Completion

You will have successfully completed this task when the computer's fans are clear of built-up dust.

Task 2.11: Oiling Fans

Along with cleaning fans, you occasionally have to oil them. Fans in a computer have lubrication around their bearings, but eventually that runs dry. When this happens, the noise from the fan becomes louder and quite annoying; this is a sign that the fan bearings are starting to wear out. If you let this go on, the fan will become slower and slower and eventually will stop spinning altogether. That usually means disaster for your power supply and CPU.

I recently received an email from a reader of the first edition of this book. He had a question about oiling a power-supply fan, and said that my instructions conflicted with other documentation he had read about whether he should open the power-supply case. I explained that these instructions are somewhat generic by necessity, since I can't cover every type of power supply made. When in doubt, consult the documentation specific to your PC or device.

Scenario

As part of your regular maintenance duties, you have been assigned to periodically oil the fans in the company's computers. Right now, you are about to perform this task on your own PC in the IT department.

This task picks up where Tasks 2.9 and 2.10 left off.

Scope of Task

Duration

This task should take about 15 or 20 minutes.

Setup

There is no special setup for this task.

Caveat

Although you can use this procedure to oil all the fans in your computer, this task will focus on oiling the bearing in the power-supply fan. Be careful not to use too much oil.

Procedure

This task will teach you how to oil the bearings of fans in a computer.

Equipment Used

You'll need a small can of oil and a screwdriver. Either three-in-one oil (the mineral-based version is better than the vegetable-based product) or sewing-machine oil is acceptable.

Do not use WD-40 for this task. WD-40 and products like it are not lubricants. They are made mainly of kerosene with only a little oil. The kerosene will quickly evaporate and the tiny amount of oil that's left won't last long in rapidly spinning fan bearings.

Details

This task takes you through each of the steps necessary to oil the power supply fan bearings.

Oiling a Power-Supply Fan

ACCESSING THE FAN BEARINGS

1. Locate the power-supply fan at the back of your computer.
2. Locate your screwdriver.
3. Remove the screws holding the finger guard in place over the fan.

There are all kinds of ways the guard can be secured over the power-supply fan. Step 3 refers to only one method. Your computer may be built differently.

4. Remove the finger guard.

The screws also hold the fan in place, but it's unlikely that it will fall out given the lack of space in the fan casing.

5. Locate the adhesive sticker over the center of the fan.
6. Gently pull the sticker aside.

If you accidentally pull the sticker off or rip it, when you are done oiling the bearings, just put a large piece of tape over the area that was covered by the sticker.

7. If there is a rubber or plastic cap covering the bearings, remove it.

Smaller fans typically cover the bearings with just the sticker, but larger fans will likely have the cap as well. When you open the cap (if it has one), you'll see either ball bearings or sleeve bearings inside.

8. Locate the can of oil.

9. Carefully put oil inside the bearing case, but do not overfill.

Excess oil can leak out of the bearing case, no matter what you seal it with.

10. Let the computer sit in position for a few minutes to let the oil permeate the bearings.

11. Soak up any excess oil.

If the back of the fan has any excess oil on it, the sticker will fail to adhere.

12. If the fan came with a cap, replace it.

13. Replace the sticker.

14. Replace the finger guard.

15. Replace the screws holding the guard and the fan in place.

16. Wash your hands.

Chances are you got some oil on your hands during this procedure, and you don't want to get oil all over your keyboard and mouse.

VERIFYING THAT THE FAN FUNCTIONS

1. Power up your computer.

2. Listen to the power-supply fan as the computer powers up.

3. Verify that the fan is spinning smoothly and quietly.

Criteria for Completion

You will have successfully completed this task when you have oiled the bearings and verified that the fan is spinning normally.

Task 2.12: Cleaning and Degaussing CRT Monitors

While flat-screen LCD monitors are ubiquitous these days, you will still encounter the older CRT type (including one sitting on my desk). These monitors get dirty just like any other object and need help. It's not only the dust. People continually touch their monitor screens, putting oily fingerprints on them. If they eat and drink while working on the computer, drops of soda and bits of food are likely to speckle the screen as well. (Imagine someone biting into a nice, juicy apple about 12 inches from their monitor.) Eventually a user will complain of "seeing spots." All computer screens require periodic cleaning.

On top of dirty screens, CRT monitors may sometimes need to be degaussed. You can determine this if you or the user complains of seeing a rainbow effect on the monitor. This is an indication that a nearby magnetic field has affected the monitor. The rainbow effect can be dispelled by a stronger magnetic field. More-recently-made CRT computers come with degaussing equipment built in.

Scenario

One of the sales consultants is complaining that her monitor has a rainbow on it. You take a look and see that her CRT monitor most likely needs to be degaussed. You also notice a lot of dust and specks on the glass. The user goes out to meet a customer, leaving you free to clean and degauss the monitor.

Scope of Task

Duration

This task should take about 10 to 15 minutes.

Setup

There is no special setup for this task.

Caveat

These instructions are for CRT monitors only and do not apply to LCD flat screens.

Although the general cleaning instructions could apply to LCD screens as well, remember that LCD screens are not glass like CRT screens. There are specialty products available to clean an LCD screen, but you would be just as well off using a soft, very lightly moistened cloth to gently wipe the screen down.

Of course, it is not necessary to degauss an LCD monitor.

Procedure

This task will show you how to successfully clean and degauss a CRT monitor.

Equipment Used

You'll need either a spray bottle of water or a mild window cleaner, and a lint-free cloth.

Details

This task will take you step-by-step through the process of degaussing a CRT monitor.

Cleaning and Degaussing a Monitor

CLEANING THE CRT MONITOR

1. Sit in front of the monitor you are going to clean.
2. Spray the water or window cleaner onto the lint-free cloth.

Do not spray any liquid directly on the screen.

3. Wipe the screen to remove any dust, dirt, oils, and other materials.
4. Use the other side of the cloth or another cloth to dry the screen.

DEGAUSSING THE CRT MONITOR

1. Access the monitor's built-in menu.

Usually, you can access the monitor's built-in menu by using the buttons on the front, just below the screen. Depending on the type of monitor you have, the arrangements of the buttons and exactly how the menu is organized will be different than depicted in these instructions.

2. Press the main menu button.

3. Use one of the arrow buttons on the front of the monitor to move to the different selections.

4. Select the degauss option.

5. Press the main menu button again.

 The image will abruptly distort for a moment and then recover. The screen should be degaussed and the rainbow effect should be gone.

Criteria for Completion

You will have successfully completed this task when the screen is clean and there is no rainbow effect present.

Task 2.13: Cleaning Keyboards, Mice, and PCs

Now that you've learned how to clean and maintain the inside of a computer and how to clean a CRT monitor screen (see Tasks 2.9 to 2.12), it's time to learn how to clean the rest of the outside of a computer. Just about everything a person touches needs to be cleaned, and how often do people at work touch their keyboard and mouse? Even the exterior of the PC case gets dusty and scuffed, because users often accidentally kick the PC under their desk many times a day. This is a routine task, but one you'll find yourself doing often.

Scenario

You have been assigned to provide routine maintenance on the PCs in one of the company's branch offices. You've finished servicing the interior of the computers (see Tasks 2.9 through 2.11) and cleaning the CRT monitors (Task 2.12), and now you're beginning the final set of tasks and cleaning the exterior of the PCs, the keyboards, and the mice.

Scope of Task

Duration

Cleaning one PC, keyboard, and mouse should take about 15 minutes.

Setup

There is no special setup for this task.

Caveat

This is a pretty straightforward task without too many "trap doors." However, it is best that the computer you are cleaning be powered down during this process.

Procedure

This task will show you how to clean a PC's case, keyboard, and mouse.

Equipment Used

You'll need a mild solution of rubbing alcohol (isopropyl), some lint-free cloths, a can of compressed air, and a pair of tweezers.

Details

This task will walk you step-by-step through the process of completely cleaning the exterior of a computer and it's peripheral devices.

Cleaning a Keyboard, Mouse, and Computer Case

CLEANING THE KEYBOARD

1. Turn the keyboard upside down over a garbage can (if possible).
2. While holding the keyboard firmly in one hand, strike it sharply on the bottom with the palm of your other hand.

> As you perform step 2, an amazing amount of debris will most likely be loosened and fall from the keyboard.

3. Replace the keyboard in its original position.
4. Locate the can of compressed air.
5. Spray the air between the keys, first in a horizontal pattern and then in a vertical pattern.

> When you spray the compressed air into the keyboard, additional bits should blow loose. Be careful not to drive bits of debris further in between the keys.

6. Dampen a lint-free cloth with your cleaning solution.
7. Rub around each individual key, removing oils and other substances on their surfaces.
8. Rub around the keyboard area.

> You should notice an improvement in the keyboard action when you start typing with it again.

CLEANING A BALL MOUSE

 You may only rarely encounter a ball mouse these days, but they are still used in a few older industrial, office, and home settings.

1. Dampen a lint-free cloth with your cleaning solution.
2. Rub the top of each button and the top of the mouse's surface in general.
3. Turn the mouse over.
4. Turn the ring around the ball (usually counterclockwise) to loosen and remove it.
5. Remove the ball.
6. Rub the cloth over the ball, removing oils and dirt.
7. Rub the ring in the same way.
8. Locate the two rotating wheels inside the ball cage.

 Your ball mouse may have two rollers and one rotating wheel rather than two wheels.

9. Rub the interior of the ball cage and the rotating wheels, removing oils and dirt.

 The two wheels inside the ball cage collect a lot of oils, making them gum up; this is usually the most common problem with a ball mouse.

10. Locate your tweezers and moisten the tips with your cleaning solution.
11. Gently maneuver the tweezers in the ball cage, rotating and cleaning the wheels further.
12. Use a fresh lint-free cloth to wipe away any leftover moisture in the ball cage.
13. Replace the ball.
14. Replace the ring.
15. Return the mouse to its usual position.

CLEANING AN OPTICAL MOUSE

1. Dampen a lint-free cloth with your cleaning solution.
2. Rub the surface of the mouse, including the buttons.
3. Return the mouse to its original position.

 Do not attempt to clean the optical sensor using the cloth with the cleaning solution as in step 2. You'll damage the sensor.

CLEANING THE PC CASE

1. Pull the PC case out from under the desk or otherwise make it easily accessible.
2. Dampen a lint-free cloth with your cleaning solution.
3. Rub the surface areas of the case with the cloth, removing any dust and other substances.
4. Gently rub all buttons, drive-bay covers, and other features on the outside of the case.
5. Gently rub the back areas of the PC, being careful around cables and connectors.

Criteria for Completion

You will have successfully completed this task when all the exterior surfaces of the keyboard, mouse, and PC case have been cleaned.

Task 2.14: Defragging a Hard Drive

Information stored on hard drives using the Windows file systems FAT 32 and NTFS are prone to file fragmentation. As data are added to the drive, they are written sequentially on the drive platters; as information is accessed and edited, however, parts of the files are moved out of sequence. This means that the read/write heads in the drive must zip to and fro locating the different pieces of a single file. Defragmenting the drive improves read performance. This is a regular maintenance task. Desktops should be defragged once every couple of weeks to once a month, depending on how heavily they are used. Servers should be defragged on a weekly basis.

Occasionally, you'll hear the question "Can defragging too frequently damage a hard drive"? While it's true that defragging a drive does involve a certain amount of wear on the drive, it is the general consensus among hardware gurus that allowing your drive to go too long without being defragged is far more damaging than the defrag process.

The Linux ext3 and ext4 file systems only rarely need to be defragmented. They do not write new data sequentially but instead write new data to a new area of the platter not near the other data. In other words, a hard drive with a Linux operating system writes to different points on the platters each time a new file is saved. The data is sufficiently spread out over the drive's geometry, so the drive needs to be defragged only when it becomes nearly full.

Scenario

You have been assigned to defragment the hard drive of a Windows 2000 Server machine being used as a print server for the data-processing department. You are working after regular business hours, so the end users won't need to access print services while you're performing the defrag.

Scope of Task

Duration

Depending on the size of your hard drive, how much data is on board, how badly fragmented the data is, and how full the drive is, this process could take several hours.

Setup

No special setup is required for this task. Although the example uses Windows 2000 Server, you can use any Windows computer to complete the task.

Caveat

This is a pretty straightforward task with very few "gotchas." It just takes some time.

Procedure

This task shows you the steps to take in defragmenting a Windows 2000 Server.

 The steps are the same or substantially similar for other Windows operating systems.

Equipment Used

No equipment is required for this task.

Details

This task will take you through the steps to defragment a hard drive-disk running Windows 2000 Server.

Performing a Disk Defrag on a Windows Computer

1. Sitting at the keyboard of the computer, click Start ➤ My Computer.
2. Right-click the drive you want to defrag, which will most likely be the C drive.
3. Select Properties.

4. The Local Disk (C:) Properties box will open. Click the Tools tab.

5. Under Defragmentation, click the Defragment Now button.

6. Click Analyze.

When the analysis dialog box opens, click Defragment. The defragmentation process will begin. The defragmentation process could take a long time. All you can do is periodically check on its progress until it finishes.

7. A dialog box will open telling you that the process has completed. Click Close.

8. Close the disk-defragmentation utility.

9. Close the Disk Properties box.

10. Close the My Computer box.

11. Log off the server.

Criteria for Completion

You will have successfully completed this task when the disk-defragmentation utility reports the disk has been defragmented.

Task 2.15: Scheduling Automatic Defragging in Windows Vista

One of the things that has always bugged me about the Windows defragging utility is that there wasn't an option to schedule the tool to run automatically. After all, defragging is a task that just begs to be done at two in the morning when you're asleep. I can't believe that Microsoft waited until Windows Vista to implement this option. Fortunately, they finally got around to it.

Scenario

You have received a trouble ticket directing you to report to the support department for your company and schedule each of their Windows Vista computers to automatically run the defragmentation utility every Tuesday starting at 2 a.m. This specific day and time is required since the help desk staff's regular hours are from 6 a.m. to 8 p.m. seven days a week and the other automatic tasks are scheduled to be performed on most of the other available days and times when the help desk is not open.

Scope of Task

Duration

This task should take only a few minutes.

Setup

No special setup is needed for this task, but you will need to have a computer running Windows Vista available.

Although the scenario requires that you perform this task on numerous computers in a support department, to successfully complete the task you need only to set the defragmentation schedule on one Vista computer.

Caveat

While the "good news" is that the Windows defragmenter utility finally has the ability to be scheduled, there are a few points of "bad news." The first point isn't bad news as such, but could potentially pose a problem. By default, the Windows Vista defrag utility is enabled and scheduled to run every Wednesday, starting at 1 a.m. If you are unaware of this fact, you may have other automatic tasks set to run at the same time. It's best to have all of your "after-hours" tasks running at different days and times to prevent any sort of conflict.

Another downside to the Vista defragger is that it runs in the background, providing no visual representation of the defragmentation process. You are not presented with a graphic illustration of the state of the hard drive's fragmentation before and after the utility runs.

Procedure

This task will instruct you on how to schedule the Windows Vista defragmentation tool to run automatically at a specific time and day of the week.

Equipment Used

No special equipment is needed to complete this task.

Details

This task will show you how to set up the Vista defragger to run automatically on a regular schedule.

Scheduling the Windows Vista Defragmentation Tool to Run Automatically

1. Click the Windows Vista button and, in the menu that appears, click Control Panel.
2. Click System and Maintenance, and then click Defragment Your Hard Drive.
3. Click Modify Schedule.
4. When the Disk Defragmenter Modify Schedule dialog box appears, next to How Often use the menu to select Weekly.
5. Next to What Day, use the menu to select Tuesday.
6. Next to What Time, use the menu to select 2:00 AM.
7. Click OK in the dialog box and then click OK again to close the utility.

   The defragmentation utility is now scheduled to start the tool every Tuesday at 2 a.m.

Criteria for Completion

You will have successfully completed this task when you have set the defragmentation tool to run each Tuesday at 2 a.m. and have closed the utility.

Task 2.16: Defragmenting a Single File

As you are likely aware, it can take quite some time to defragment an entire hard drive, depending on the extent of the drive's file fragmentation and the system load on the computer. There may be times when you want to quickly optimize a single file that, due to heavy computer use, has been fragmented extensively across the hard drive. Both Windows XP and Windows Vista offer the option of defragmenting an individual file on the computer's hard drive, but not natively.

This scenario requires that you download and install a utility called Contig, which is free from Microsoft. The utility is ideal for defragging a large, often-used file such as a virtual machine image. While downloading and installing Contig is outside the scope of this task, the process is very easy to do. Go to `http://technet.microsoft.com/en-us/sysinternals/bb897428.aspx` and follow the instructions to install the tool on your Windows XP or Vista computer.

Scenario

You have been tasked with performing a defragmentation on a virtual machine in a file called `vsrv01.vmx` on a test machine in your IT department. The machine is running Windows Vista and has the Contig utility installed and available. You have been given the instructions for using Contig to complete your task. You are in the server room at the keyboard of the Vista computer and are ready to begin.

Scope of Task

Duration

This task should take no more than a few minutes, depending on your degree of comfort in using the command-line utility, and the size of the file you choose to defragment.

Setup

No special setup is needed for this task. Although you can perform this task on either Windows XP or Vista, a Windows Vista machine was used for the purpose of this task.

Caveat

As previously mentioned, the Contig tool requires that you use the command line. Although a third-party utility exists that would allow you to perform this task in a GUI, and honing your command-line skills is always desirable. You will also need to know the exact path for the file to be defragmented as well as the exact location of Contig on your computer's hard drive.

If you're interested, the aforementioned utility is called Power Defragmenter and is available at www.excessive-software.eu.tt/. Most of the content on this site is in English, but some entries are not. When the page loads, click DOWNLOADS under Links on the left side of the web page, then download the PowerDefragmenter zip file to your PC.

Procedure

This task will tell you how to use the Contig utility to defrag a single file on a Windows Vista computer.

Equipment Used

No special equipment is required, but you will need to be working at a Windows XP or Vista computer that has Contig installed.

To use the Open Command Prompt Here option described in this task, you must use a Windows Vista computer, which has this option available by default. You can install this option on a Windows XP computer by following the instructions at www.petri.co.il/add_command_prompt_here_shortcut_to_windows_explorer.htm. Otherwise, you will need to open a command-line window after logging in, and use the cd command to navigate to the directory where you installed Contig.

Details

This task will take you through the process of defragmenting a single file on a Windows Vista computer using Contig.

Using Contig to Defragment a Single File on a Windows Vista Computer

1. Log in to the computer using an account with Administrator privileges.
2. Use Windows Explorer to navigate to the folder where you installed Contig.
3. Press and hold the Shift key, and then right-click the folder where you installed Contig.
4. When the menu appears, select Open Command Prompt Here.

You must press and hold the Shift key in order for the Open Command Prompt Here option to be available. Also, you must click on the folder in the right or main Explorer pane and not in the left menu pane.

5.   At the command prompt, type **Config <*filename*>** where <*filename*> is the path to the file you want to defragment.

> The full path to the file will look something like C:\Documents and Settings\JMPyles\Virtual_Machines\vsrv01.vmx.

6.   Press Enter to begin the defragmentation of the file.

Criteria for Completion

You will have successfully completed the task when you have executed the command and the file has been defragmented.

Task 2.17: Upgrading a Graphics Card

Task 1.13 showed you how to install a basic video card. However, if you want your computer to be able to use high-end graphics utilities or play many of the newer computer games, you may find it necessary to upgrade the card currently installed in your PC. The following task will show you how to install a PCI Express x16 graphics card into a compatible motherboard.

Scenario

You have received a trouble ticket to install an MSI GeForce 8400GS 256MB low-profile graphics card into the computer of one of the designers in your company's graphic-design department. The designer has just installed a new, high-end graphics program on his computer that the on-board graphics card does not support. You will also need to go to the NVIDIA site to download the latest drivers for the card after the new card is installed (www.nvidia.com/page/home.html).

You have been provided with the card and take it and your tools to the designer's cubicle. He is away on his lunch break, so you will be able to work undisturbed. You have an Administrator log in to this computer, so you will be able to log in to the PC after the card is installed to download and install the drivers and to test the card's operation.

> This task will show you how to physically install a graphics-card upgrade, but we won't go through the process of locating and installing drivers from the Internet. Task 1.22 showed you how to locate and install drivers from sites on the Web. Refer to that task if you need a refresher.

Scope of Task

Duration

This task should take about 15 minutes or so.

Setup

No special setup is required beyond having a computer with a PCI Express x16 (PCIe x16)–compatible motherboard, the specified graphics card, and the necessary tools. The computer used for this task was a Dell Dimension C521.

Caveat

As always, make sure to take ESD-precautions when performing this task. Also, prior to beginning it is wise to uninstall the drivers for the on-board graphics card, since having the drivers of two different cards on a single computer can cause unexpected and undesired results. The instructions for uninstalling software using the Windows Add/Remove Programs utility can be found in Task 1.26.

 Many on-board graphics cards are integrated into the motherboard and cannot be physically removed. This task doesn't require that you remove the old graphics card. Uninstalling the on-board card's drivers will be sufficient for the purposes of this task.

Procedure

This task will show you how to upgrade a graphics card on a computer.

Equipment Used

You'll need the required screwdrivers to remove the PC's access panel and the screws attaching the panel for the PCIe x16 motherboard slot, unless clips are used instead. Also, you will need your ESD-prevention equipment to prevent damage to the computer's electronic components while you are working inside the machine.

Details

This task will take you through the steps necessary to install an upgrade card.

Upgrading a PCIe x16 Graphics Card in a Computer

1. Power down the computer.
2. Remove the power cord attached to the PC's power supply.

3. Remove the monitor, keyboard, mouse, and Ethernet cord connections from the PC.

4. Locate the appropriate screwdriver and remove the PC's access panel.

5. Take ESD precautions before proceeding.

6. Locate the on-board graphics card.

7. Remove the monitor DVI/VGA lead from the output connection on the on-board graphics card.

8. Remove the screws or clips attaching the panel for the PCIe x16 slot on the back of the computer.

9. Locate the new PCIe x16 graphics card, and remove it from the antistatic packaging.

10. Locate the PCIe x16 slot on the computer's motherboard.

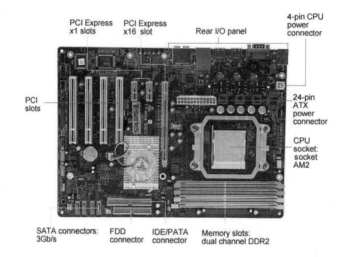

11. Gently insert the new graphics card into the PCIe x16 slot.

12. Secure the card, either with the available clips or screws.

13. Attach the monitor DVI/VGA lead to the output connection on the new card.

14. Replace the PC's access panel and secure it using the screws you previously removed.

15. Reattach the power cord, monitor, mouse, keyboard, and network connections.

16. Power up the computer and wait for the operating system to load.

17. When the computer is completely up and running, open a web browser and go to the website of the new graphics card's manufacturer.

18. Locate the latest drivers for the card you just installed.

Choose the drivers that are compatible with the computer's operating system, such as Windows XP or Vista.

19. Download and install the card's drivers.

20. Once the drivers are installed, set the monitor to the screen resolution desired by the PC's user.

21. Log off the machine when finished.

Criteria for Completion

You will have successfully completed the task when you have installed the card and the correct drivers, and set the monitor to the desired screen resolution.

Task 2.18: Checking and Reseating RAM

Occasionally, because a PC has been moved, nudged, or otherwise jolted over time, certain components may have become unseated. RAM sticks are sometimes slightly jiggled out of their slots. When a RAM stick becomes unseated, the computer can no longer access it and performance may slow or errors will occur. Although you shouldn't have to do this task too often, it is sometimes a good idea to check how internal computer components are seated.

Scenario

After her PC was moved to a new department, a user complains that her computer is responding very slowly. She also says that when she boots the PC, it reports a lower value for memory than she knows she has. You investigate and consider the idea that one of the RAM sticks in her PC may have become unseated. She takes a break, allowing you to open her PC and reseat the RAM.

Scope of Task

Duration

This task should take about 10 minutes.

Setup

No special setup is necessary to complete this task.

Caveat

Make sure to take ESD precautions when performing this task. In this example, the PC is already powered down and ready for you to open.

Procedure

This task will show you how to check and reseat a stick of RAM.

Equipment Used

You'll need a screwdriver to remove the PC-case access panel.

Details

This task will take you through the steps necessary to check and reseat a stick of RAM.

Checking and Reseating a Stick of RAM

CHECKING THE RAM

1. Locate a screwdriver and remove the screws holding the access panel in place.
2. Remove the access panel.

 Use ESD precautions to prevent damaging electronic components inside the computer.

3. Locate the RAM sticks inside the computer.

RESEATING THE RAM

 You may want to read Task 1.2 to refresh your memory on how RAM is installed.

1. Release the clips on the first stick of RAM.

 For this task, it is assumed that there are two sticks of RAM in the PC.

2. Remove the stick of RAM.
3. Reseat the stick of RAM, making sure it is gently but firmly pushed into the RAM slot.
4. Replace the clips holding the RAM stick in place.
5. Repeat steps 1 through 4 with the second RAM stick.
6. Replace the access panel.
7. Replace the screws holding the access panel in place.

VERIFYING THE AMOUNT OF RAM IN THE COMPUTER

1. Power up the computer.
2. Notice on boot if the computer reports a change in on-board memory.

 In step 2, you should see a screen that states that the amount of RAM has changed to the amount of RAM that should be on the computer.

3. After the OS loads, right-click My Computer.

 For this task, it is assumed that as an IT staff member, you are able to log on to the PC as an Administrator.

4. Click Properties.
5. On the General tab, note the amount of RAM registering. It should be the amount of RAM that is installed on the PC.

Criteria for Completion

You will have successfully completed this task if you have reseated the RAM sticks and the computer reports that the amount of RAM on board is what is actually installed on the motherboard.

 In your particular case, if no RAM sticks were unseated, there will be no change in reported memory.

Task 2.19: Checking and Reseating PCI and PCI Express Cards

Just as RAM sticks can become unseated after a move, so can other components, including PCI and PCI Express cards. A number of important components may be provided by these expansion cards, including video, audio, network interface cards (NICs), modems, and other devices. If one of these devices should suddenly not be recognized, checking the positioning of the device in its slot and reseating it might be a good idea.

Scenario

After his PC was moved to a new department, a user complains that he can no longer play audio CDs on his computer. You investigate and suspect that his PCI audio card may have become dislodged during the move. The user has a team meeting scheduled and leaves you alone to check on his computer.

Scope of Task

Duration

This task should take about 10 minutes.

Setup

No special setup is required for this task.

Caveat

Make sure to take ESD precautions when performing these steps. The task assumes that the PC is already powered down and ready for you to open. This task is substantially similar to Task 2.18, "Checking and Reseating RAM."

Procedure

This task will teach you how to check and reseat a PCI or PCI Express card.

 Although PCI and PCI Express represent different standards, physically seating and reseating these types of cards is virtually the same task.

Equipment Used

You will need a screwdriver to remove the screws holding the access panel in place.

Details

This task will take you through the necessary steps to check and reseat a PCI expansion card.

Checking and Reseating a PCI Expansion Card

CHECKING A PCI CARD

1. Locate the screwdriver and remove the screws holding the access panel in place.
2. Remove the access panel.

Remember to take ESD precautions before putting your hands inside the PC case.

3. Locate the PCI sound card.

RESEATING THE PCI CARD

It might be a good idea to review Task 1.3 to refresh your memory on how a PCI card is installed.

1. Use the screwdriver to remove the screws holding the PCI card in place.

2. Carefully remove the PCI card from its slot.

3. Check the small cable connection from the PCI card to the CD player to make sure it is firmly in place.

4. Reseat the PCI card gently but firmly into its slot.

5. Replace the screw holding the PCI card in place.

6. Replace the access panel.

7. Replace the screws that hold the access panel in place.

VERIFYING THAT THE PCI CARD FUNCTIONS

1. Power up the PC.

2. After it boots, log in.

For this task, it is assumed that as an IT staff member, you have the ability to log in as an Administrator.

3. Locate an audio CD from the user's collection.

4. Insert the CD into the CD drive.

If Autoplay is enabled and the speakers are installed and turned on, the CD should begin to play.

Criteria for Completion

You will have successfully completed this task when the PCI card functions normally.

As with Task 2.18, if there was nothing wrong with the selected PCI card in your computer in the first place, reseating it will not change its performance.

Task 2.20: Checking Internal Connectors

There are quite a number of internal connectors inside a computer. Not only can RAM and PCI cards become unseated (see Tasks 2.18 and 2.19), but any other connector inside a computer also can work its way loose. Sometimes you have to do a general inspection of the connectors in a PC's case to make sure they are all linked firmly. Even in a PC that hasn't been moved lately, subtle motions of the box may have caused a connection to separate just enough to cause a problem.

Scenario

A user in the reception area reports that her PC won't start. She's made sure it's plugged in and that the surge protector is turned on, but when she pushes the power button on the PC, nothing happens. You investigate and can find no external cause. You decide to open up the case and see if there is a reason for the problem inside.

Scope of Task

Duration

This task should take about 10 minutes.

Setup

No special setup is required to complete this task.

Caveat

Make sure to take ESD precautions before putting your hands inside the box.

Procedure

This task will show you how to verify that internal connectors inside a PC's case are firmly connected.

Equipment Used

You should need only a screwdriver to successfully complete this task.

Details

This task will walk you through the steps of checking internal connectors in a PC to make sure they are all securely fitted.

Checking Internal Connectors

VERIFYING THAT ALL INTERNAL CONNECTORS IN THE COMPUTER ARE FIRMLY SEATED

1. Unplug the computer's power cord from the surge protector.
2. Locate a screwdriver and remove the screws holding the access panel in place.
3. Remove the access panel.

 Make sure you use ESD precautions before putting your hands inside the computer.

4. Locate the connectors between the power supply and the motherboard.
5. Disconnect the connectors.
6. Firmly reseat the connectors.
7. Locate the hard-drive cable connector on the motherboard.
8. Pull the connector away from the hard-drive controller connector.
9. Carefully reseat the connector to the hard-drive controller.
10. Repeat steps 8 through 10 for the CD/DVD drive.
11. Repeat steps 8 through 10 for the floppy-disk drive if one is present.
12. Locate the CPU.
13. Locate the lever that will release the CPU from its slot.

 Review Task 1.5 to refamiliarize yourself with installing a CPU.

14. Pull the lever up to release the CPU.

 It should not be necessary to remove the CPU fan or thermal paste. You should check the CPU fan's connector, though.

15. Reseat the CPU in its slot.
16. Replace the lever to its original position, securing the CPU in place.
17. Make a general visual survey of the interior of the PC to verify that you didn't miss any connectors.
18. When finished, replace the access panel.
19. Replace the screws holding the panel in place.
20. Plug the PC's power cord back into the surge protector.

VERIFYING THAT THE PC FUNCTIONS NORMALLY

1. Power up the PC.
2. When the PC loads the OS, log on as Administrator.
3. Open various applications and services to verify that the PC is operating normally.

Criteria for Completion

You will have successfully completed this task when you can power up the computer and it behaves normally.

 If there were no loose connections in your computer, this task will not change its performance.

Task 2.21: Speeding Up Windows 2000 Professional

You may be wondering why the name of this task isn't "Speeding Up Windows XP Professional" (see Task 1.33, "Tweaking Windows XP") or "Speeding Up Windows Vista." Believe it or not, there are still many companies that use Windows 2000 for a variety of tasks. This may be due to the company having designated certain routine maintenance functions to be performed by the Windows 2000 computers that are available. For whatever reasons, you won't always be working with Windows XP or Vista workstations as a PC tech.

Just about any computer can be tweaked to work faster and more efficiently; this includes Windows 2000. Here is a collection of tips that can help a Windows 2000 computer run faster; however, as you will see, they are not for every Windows 2000 computer.

Scenario

One of your company's warehouses has three workstations running Windows 2000 Professional. These workstations perform routine tasks relative to inventory accounting. You have been assigned to optimize performance on these computers by disabling certain services or preventing them from being started automatically at boot.

Scope of Task

Duration

This task should take about 20 to 30 minutes.

Setup

It would be ideal if you had a Windows 2000 Professional Desktop to work with, but if not, see how far you can follow along on your XP machine. You may not be able to complete many of the steps in this task if you are using Windows Vista.

Caveat

Disabling unnecessary services is an excellent way to enhance the performance of a computer, but the role the computer plays and the environment it works in will determine what services you should and shouldn't disable. If the computer operates in a corporate environment, however unlikely this may be, you will have fewer options in terms of disabling services.

 Be careful which services you disable. You could cause the computer to fail to function properly or fail to function at all.

Procedure

This task will teach you how to access and disable certain services on Windows 2000 Professional to improve performance.

Equipment Used

No special equipment is needed for this task.

Details

This task will take you through the process of disabling or otherwise making unavailable certain services on Windows 2000 Professional computers to improve their responsiveness.

Disabling Services to Improve Computer Performance

ACCESSING SERVICES IN WINDOWS 2000 PROFESSIONAL

1. Sitting at the keyboard, right-click My Computer.

 For step 1, it is assumed that the My Computer icon is on the Desktop.

2. Click Manage.
3. In the Computer Management dialog box, expand Services and Applications.
4. Select Services.

After you select Services in step 4, all of the services installed on the computer and their status are displayed in the main window of Computer Management.

VERIFYING AND STOPPING SERVICES

1. Scroll to the top of the Services list and locate Alerter.

2. Double-click Alerter.

3. In the Alerter Properties box on the General tab, verify that the Alerter service is stopped.

4. Verify in the Startup Type menu that Manual is selected.

The Alerter service provides administrative alerts to specified computers and users. If this service is not needed by this group of computers, you can leave it stopped and on manual startup.

5. Close the Alerter Properties box.

STOPPING THE MESSENGER SERVICE AND SETTING IT TO MANUAL

> The Messenger service receives administrative alerts and works with the Alerter. If the Alerter is stopped, you can safely stop Messenger.

1. Scroll down the Services list until you locate the Messenger service.

2. Double-click Messenger.

3. Look to see if the service is started or stopped.

4. Look to see if the startup type is Automatic, Manual, or Disabled.

![Messenger Properties (Local Computer) dialog box showing the General tab with Service name: Messenger, Display name: Messenger, Description: Sends and receives messages transmitted by administra, Path to executable: C:\WINNT\System32\services.exe, Startup type: Automatic, Service status: Started]

5. Set the startup type to Manual.

6. Click the Stop button to stop the service.

7. When the service stops, close the Messenger Properties box.

STOPPING THE UNINTERRUPTIBLE POWER SUPPLY (UPS) SERVICE

> If you don't need Windows to control the UPS devices that service these desktops or if they don't use UPS devices, it is safe to turn off this service.

1. Scroll down the Services list to Uninterruptible Power Supply.

2. Perform steps 2 through 5 under "Verifying and Stopping Services," substituting the term *Services* for *Alerter*.

CHECKING AND VERIFYING OTHER SERVICES

 Many services can be stopped by following steps 1 through 7 under "Stopping the Messenger Service and Setting It to Manual."

1. If the workstations have manually assigned IP addresses, you can perform steps 1 through 7 for the DHCP client.

2. If the end users don't need very rapid access to locate files and folders, you can perform the steps for the Indexing Service.

3. If the users don't need to access and remotely manage the Registries on these computers, you can perform the steps for the Remote Registry Service.

4. If these computers don't use any form of removable storage such as USB or tape devices, you can perform the steps for the Removable Storage Manager Service.

5. If these computers don't make use of IPSec security or don't require the use of VPN, you can perform these steps for the IPSec Policy Agent Service.

6. If the users don't run applications under the credentials of another user, you can perform the steps for the RunAs Service.

7. If these computers don't use online voice-connection applications such as NetMeeting, you can perform the steps for the Telephony Service.

 Keep track of which services you are stopping in case they need to be re-enabled. This will be covered in detail in Task 2.34, "Tracking Work Done on a PC."

8. When done, close the Computer Management window.
9. Log off the computer.

Criteria for Completion

You will have successfully completed this task when you have stopped the unnecessary services running on the computer and verified that they can be started only manually.

Task 2.22: Flashing the BIOS

I suppose "flashing" could be taken the wrong way, but this is actually a method of enhancing a computer's basic functioning. BIOS, or basic input/output system, is a very old element in PC engineering. The BIOS is software on a special chip on the motherboard that dictates the boot process, initializes essential hardware, and determines the abilities and capacities of the computer (such as how big a hard drive it can use).

In the "bad old days," you were stuck with whatever BIOS your motherboard came with. If newer versions of the BIOS supported larger hard drives and faster CPUs or fixed particular bugs, you needed to get either a new motherboard or a new computer. Now it's possible to upgrade the BIOS and keep the motherboard; however, it's not the same process as updating a program living on your hard drive.

Flashing BIOS requires special software tools, and if you make a mistake and damage or destroy the BIOS, you will turn your PC into nothing more than a really big paperweight (short of replacing the BIOS chip). Let's take a look at this process.

Scenario

You have been assigned to flash the BIOS of an older PC used in the manufacturing department. This computer has a floppy-disk drive available. A BIOS update has been issued that fixes several bugs and allows the computer to use a faster CPU. You have the computer on your workbench in the IT department. It is powered up and connected to the Internet. You are ready to proceed.

Scope of Task

Duration

This task should take anywhere from 30 to 60 minutes.

Setup

This process will reset the CMOS to the factory configuration. Before initiating this task, record the CMOS BIOS settings (see Task 2.23). You will need this information after the BIOS is flashed so you can restore the settings to where they were prior to this task.

Caveat

As previously mentioned, if this process goes wrong, your computer probably won't even boot. The only remedy is to secure a chip with the appropriate BIOS on board and install it on the motherboard. For this task, you will need to verify ahead of time that your computer's BIOS will look to the A (floppy disk) drive for the boot sector before the C (hard) drive. There are dozens of specific methods of flashing BIOS, depending on the type of motherboard and BIOS you have. The method you'll need to use may not be quite the same as the instructions listed here.

 Most tutorials on flashing BIOS require that a bootable floppy diskette be used, but most modern computers are produced without floppy-disk drives. One answer is to use an external USB floppy drive; however, you can also create and use a bootable USB drive. A good set of instructions for accomplishing this task can be found at www.csd.dficlub.org/forum/showthread.php?t=1136. If this site isn't available, type **bootable USB drive to flash bios** In your favorite search engine.

> See the section "Changing the Boot Order of a Computer" in Task 1.23 to see how to configure the BIOS to look to a particular drive first for the boot sector.

Procedure

This task will teach you how to flash (update) the BIOS chip on a computer's motherboard.

Equipment Used

With some computer motherboards, you can simply download the BIOS upgrade as a zip file into a folder on your hard drive. Older motherboards require that you save the BIOS update on a boot disk, boot the computer into DOS, and flash the BIOS from the command line. The method used in this task will require a floppy disk. Your computer must have a floppy-disk drive.

Details

This task will take you step-by-step through the process of downloading and installing a BIOS update for a computer's motherboard.

Downloading a BIOS Upgrade and Flashing the BIOS

IDENTIFYING THE MOTHERBOARD AND BIOS

> You absolutely must know the specifications of your motherboard and BIOS to make sure you download the correct update.

1. Boot the computer.
2. When the main BIOS screen appears just after the computer powers up, press the Pause/Break key on the keyboard.

> Pressing the Pause/Break key in step 2 will pause the boot process and let you write down the details regarding the computer's BIOS.

3. When finished, press Enter to continue booting the computer.

> See Task 2.1 and follow the steps to find the make and model of your motherboard. You can also use the tool described in that task to identify your BIOS and gather many other details about your computer system.

LOCATING AND DOWNLOADING THE LATEST BIOS

1. Open a web browser.

2. Type in the URL for the motherboard manufacturer's website.

> You can also use a search engine to locate the correct website.

3. Locate the latest update for your motherboard's BIOS.

> Locating an update for your motherboard's BIOS can be difficult, depending on the vendor's website. The most straightforward method would be to search for your specific motherboard and then locate the latest BIOS update on that page. If you have trouble finding it, you can call or email the vendor's technical support and ask for assistance.

4. Download the latest BIOS zip file into a preselected folder on the computer's hard drive.

> There may have been several updates issued for your BIOS, but only download and install the update containing the features and fixes you need. This may not be the latest BIOS update. Only flash your BIOS when you require the specific feature or fix offered.

> While there are many benefits to updating your BIOS, the possibility of a "bad flash" always exists. Only flash your BIOS to fix a bug you are actually experiencing or to add a feature you require.

> Read any installation instructions available on the motherboard vendor's website regarding your particular motherboard and BIOS. There may be steps you need to take that are not included in this task. For example, some motherboards require that you physically set a jumper or switch to a different position prior to flashing the BIOS.

INSTALLING THE BIOS UPDATE ON THE BOOT DISK

> Ideally, a computer's boot disk is already kept in a prearranged spot near the computer, such as a locked desk drawer. If you don't have a boot disk for your computer, you can go to www.bootdisk.com and locate the correct download to create a boot disk.

Newer versions of electronically erasable programmable read-only memory (EEPROM) allow you to run the BIOS update directly from the hard drive so the creation and use of a boot disk is unnecessary. In all likelihood, your computer supports this process. The purpose of this task is to teach you this process using older or legacy equipment.

1. Insert the boot disk while the computer is still running.

2. Use Windows Explorer to navigate to the location of the zip file.

3. When you have located the zip file, right-click it.

4. Click Copy.

5. Navigate to the A drive.

6. Double-click to open it.

7. Right-click in the A window.

8. Click Paste.

9. When the zip file is loaded on the disk, right-click it.

10. Click Extract All.

Some BIOSs require that you download and install a separate flash utility before you begin step 1 in this section. In this example, the utility is integrated with the flash.exe file.

11. Open the README.txt file that was extracted.

12. Read this file and write down any specific steps, commands, and command switches you will need to know to flash the BIOS correctly.

13. Close all open files and folders.

14. Leave the disk in the computer's A drive and reboot the computer.

FLASHING THE BIOS FROM THE COMMAND LINE

The computer will reboot to a command-line prompt.

1. Once the computer boots, at the A:\> prompt, type **dir**.

2. Verify that all required files are present on the diskette.

3. Type the command you located in the README.txt file or at the motherboard vendor's website to initiate the BIOS flash.

The command you wrote down in step 12 of the previous section will include all of the switches or arguments necessary to proceed through the flash process without further intervention from you. The process is very fast and you will be able to see the BIOS being reprogrammed on the screen.

4. Remove the boot disk.
5. Reboot the computer.
6. When the main BIOS screen appears, note the change in the BIOS.
7. Allow the boot process to complete and the operating system to load.

Criteria for Completion

You will have successfully completed this task when you flash the BIOS, reboot the computer, and note on the BIOS screen that the changes show the current BIOS version. You can also enter the CMOS setup itself to verify this and make sure all the configuration settings are correct.

Task 2.23: Changing the CMOS Battery to Correct a Slow PC Clock

The CMOS battery is usually a small lithium-ion battery similar to the ones that power wristwatches. It is located on your motherboard and provides electricity to hold certain configuration settings, including system time, even when the computer is completely powered down. The lifetime of this battery is roughly 10 years, but how long it actually lasts usually depends on how heavily the computer is used.

Most computers in a corporate environment receive their time from a local or Internet time server. This doesn't mean that the local system time is unimportant. If the CMOS battery dies, not only will the system time be lost, so will other configuration settings your computer depends on. A slow system clock is just the first sign of a dying CMOS battery.

Scenario

The shipping department on the main loading dock uses a Windows 2000 Professional computer as a file and print server for its local computers. It is usually powered down on the weekends and powered up again Monday morning. You have received a trouble ticket from shipping saying that the computer prompts them to press the F10 key every time the computer is powered up in order to save the date and time. This is the classic sign of a dying CMOS battery. You look up the system information for this computer and find the correct replacement battery in inventory. You take the battery and your tools and report to the main loading dock.

 As mentioned in previous tasks, Windows 2000 computers are sometimes still used to perform routine tasks that don't require a more recent operating system such as Windows XP or Vista.

Scope of Task

Duration

This task should take about 30 minutes or less.

Setup

There is no special setup for this task.

Caveat

When you remove the CMOS battery, the BIOS chip will lose power and the information will be lost. Make sure you record all of your configuration information prior to removing the battery. Also, make sure you have the correct replacement battery for your motherboard.

 The easiest way to perform this task is to simply remove and immediately replace the same battery.

Procedure

This task will teach you the proper method of replacing a dying CMOS battery.

Equipment Used

You will need a Phillips-head screwdriver to open the access panel and a flat-head screwdriver to remove the CMOS battery. You also will need your ESD equipment so you can reach into the computer case safely.

Details

This task takes you through the process of recording your BIOS settings, replacing a CMOS battery, and restoring computer settings.

Replacing a CMOS Battery

RECORDING THE BIOS SETTINGS

1. Sitting at the keyboard, reboot the computer.

2. When the computer begins to boot, press the correct key to enter into Setup.

The key to enter Setup can be Esc, F1, F12, or some other key or key combination, depending on the BIOS. See Task 1.23, "Reformatting a Hard Drive," for more detailed instructions on entering the BIOS.

3. Use the Tab and Enter keys to navigate to the different screens in the BIOS Setup.

4. Write down all of the configuration information contained on all of the screens.

5. When finished, press the correct key combination to save and exit the BIOS.

Make sure you didn't miss any areas of the setup. You will need this information after you replace the battery.

REPLACING THE CMOS BATTERY

1. Power down the computer.

2. Disconnect the power cable from the power supply.

3. Locate your Phillips-head screwdriver.

Make sure to take ESD precautions before opening the computer case.

4. Remove the screws holding the access panel in place.

5. Remove the access panel.

6. Position the computer so the motherboard is lying flat.

7. Locate the CMOS battery on the motherboard.

8. Locate your flat-head screwdriver.

9. Gently pry the battery up out of the socket on the motherboard.

Be extremely careful when you are performing these steps. You could accidentally puncture the motherboard or battery slot. Also, some CMOS batteries are held in place by small clips. Make sure to move them aside prior to removing the battery.

10. Locate the replacement battery.

11. Gently but firmly insert it in the socket on the motherboard.

12. Verify that it is securely in place.

13. Verify that you did not inadvertently loosen any connections or components while working inside the computer.

14. Put the computer back in its original position.

15. Replace the access panel.

16. Replace the access-panel screws.

17. Plug the power cord back into the power supply.

RESTORING THE BIOS SETTINGS

1. Boot the computer.

2. Using the correct key or key combination, enter the BIOS Setup.

3. Using the Tab and Enter keys, access each page in the BIOS and restore the settings, using the information you wrote down in the section "Recording the BIOS Settings" earlier in this task.

4. Press the correct key combination to save the settings and exit the BIOS.

5. Allow the computer to continue to boot.

6. Instruct the loading-dock staff to periodically monitor the system time to verify that it is accurate.

Criteria for Completion

You will have successfully completed this task when you have replaced the battery and restored the BIOS settings and the computer boots and operates correctly.

Task 2.24: Resetting Passwords

This is one of the most common tasks you will perform as a PC support tech. It seems like end users have a great deal of difficulty remembering their passwords. One reason for this may be that the "strong" passwords typically required in a corporate setting are not always easy to remember.

A strong password is one that is not easily guessed by an intruder or discovered by a dictionary attack. It is usually a combination of letters and numbers but can also contain special characters such as $ and #.

In a Windows Active Directory domain environment, when a user forgets their domain-logon password, resetting it is a simple procedure.

Scenario

You receive a trouble ticket stating that one of the users in the training department has forgotten his password. You agree to reset it and will notify him of his temporary password. You advise him that he will be required to reset the password once he logs on.

> **WARNING** Proper security protocol states that no one besides the end user should know his or her logon password, not even the IT staff. When you reset a password, use the password format provided by your supervisor and then record that this temporary password was used. The end user is responsible for changing the password to one only they know.

Scope of Task

Duration

This task should take about 10 minutes at most.

Setup

This task was created using a Windows Server 2003 domain controller.

> **TIP** You can order a free copy of the Windows Server 2003 Evaluation Kit at http://technet.microsoft.com/en-us/windowsserver/bb430831.aspx. This is a 180-day evaluation copy of the server software. Once you install Windows Server 2003 as a member server, you can promote it to a domain controller for the sake of this task. Once the operating system is installed, open the Run box and type **dcpromo** to promote the server to a domain controller.

> **TIP** You can order a free copy of Windows Server 2008 trial software at www.microsoft.com/windowsserver2008/en/us/trial-software.aspx.

Caveat

Resetting a password on a local Windows XP or Vista computer is a different process than resetting a domain user's password, so unless you have access to a Windows Server domain controller, it will be difficult for you to follow these instructions.

Procedure

This task will show you how to reset a domain user's password.

Equipment Used

You will need no special equipment to complete this task.

Details

This task will take you through the necessary steps to reset a domain user's password in a Windows Active Directory domain.

Resetting a Domain User's Password

ACCESSING THE DOMAIN USER'S ACCOUNT ON A DOMAIN CONTROLLER

1. Sitting at the keyboard of a domain controller, click Start ➢ Programs ➢ Administrative Tools ➢ Active Directory Users and Computers.

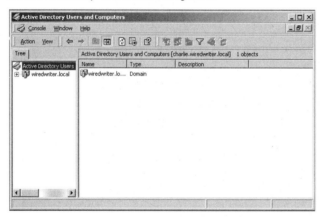

2. Expand the domain.
3. Select the Users folder.
4. Scroll down in the main display pane and locate the user.

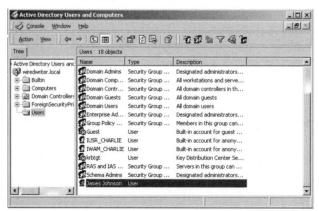

5. Right-click the user's name.

6. Click Reset Password.

7. When the Reset Password box appears, type the temporary password in the New Password field.

8. Type the temporary password again in the Confirm Password field.

9. Check the User Must Change Password at Next Logon check box.

10. Click OK.

Reset Password	? X
New password:	████████
Confirm password:	███████
☑ User must change password at next logon	
	OK Cancel

11. When the confirmation box appears, click OK.

12. When the verification box appears stating that the password for the user has been changed, click OK.

13. Close the Active Directory Users and Computers box.

14. Log off the server.

VERIFYING THAT THE PASSWORD HAS BEEN RESET

1. Telephone the user and tell him the temporary password.

2. Have him log in to the domain with the temporary password.

Step 9 in the section "Accessing the Domain User's Account on a Domain Controller" will result in the user being forced to immediately change his password.

3. Verify that the user has changed his password.

Criteria for Completion

You will have successfully completed this task when you have reset the domain user's password and he is compelled to change the password to one only he knows.

If you want to make the task more interesting, create a client machine using Windows XP Professional, join that machine to the domain, and go through the steps the end user would have to take to log on to the domain and change his password.

Task 2.25: Creating a New Local User in Windows Vista

Multiple Local Group Policy Objects (MLGPO) is a new feature that is included by default in all versions of Windows Vista. It improves upon the Local Group Policy settings used in Windows XP and allows administrators to apply different Local Group Policy levels to local users on stand-alone computers. While such Group Policy settings are applied by domain controllers (DCs) for computers that are domain members, MLGPO is ideally used for computers used in stand-alone settings, such as in publicly accessible Internet kiosks or other shared computer environments like schools and libraries.

This task will show you only how to create a nonadministrative user account on a Windows Vista computer that would be appropriate for one of these settings. For more information on MLGPO, perform a search for this data at http://technet.microsoft.com/en-us/default.aspx.

Scenario

A new Windows Vista computer has been installed in the Internet kiosk in the lobby of your company's main office. You have been assigned to create a nonadministrative user on that computer, so guests in the lobby can use it for accessing the Web without compromising security on the corporate network. It is after business hours, and you are at the keyboard of the computer in the lobby and ready to get to work.

Scope of Task

Duration

The task will take just a few minutes.

Setup

No special setup is required for this task beyond needing access to a Windows Vista computer and having an administrative logon for the computer.

Caveat

There are no particular caveats associated with this task; however, you must have the name you want to use for the new user in this task prepared before proceeding, such as "internet01." Don't forget to record the password you use for this user's account.

Procedure

This task will show you how to create a nonadministrative user for a Windows Vista local computer.

Equipment Used

No special equipment is required.

Details

This task will take you through the steps required to create a nonadministrative user for a local Windows Vista computer.

Creating a Nonadministrative User Account on a Windows Vista Computer

1. Log in to the Windows Vista computer with an account that has administrative privileges.
2. Click the Windows Vista button.
3. In the menu that appears, right-click Computer and then click Manage.
4. Click the arrow next to Local Users and Groups.
5. Right-click Users, and then click New User.
6. In the Username field, type the name of the user, such as **internet01**.
7. In the Full Name field, type the name of the user, such as **internet01**.
8. In the Password field, type the password to be used with this user account.
9. In the Confirm Password field, type the same password that you used in the Password field.
10. Clear the User Must Change Password at Next Logon check box.
11. Select the Password Never Expires check box.
12. Select the User Cannot Change Password check box.
13. Click Create, and then click Close.
14. Click File, and then click Exit to close the dialog box.

Criteria for Completion

You will have successfully completed this task when you have created the new, nonadministrative local user on the Windows Vista machine. You can test the new user account by logging out of your administrative account and logging in as the new user.

Task 2.26: Testing Ports with an Online Scanner

Testing the effectiveness or ineffectiveness of your firewall and other security procedures is vital in order to keep the network safe from outside attack. As an entry-level PC support tech, you will not be expected to configure or monitor network security measures. Depending on the size of your organization, that task will be performed by either a senior staff member or a security specialist.

However, you may occasionally be asked to test an individual computer or server's security with an online port scanner. This is a utility provided for free by various security organizations, and it can be very effective in detecting which ports of a computer are vulnerable from the Internet.

Scenario

A new test server has been set up and you have been asked to use an online port scanner to verify the vulnerability of the port settings on the device and record the results. You are told that the test server has deliberately been left with some vulnerabilities to determine how quickly an attack occurs from the outside.

Scope of Task

Duration

The task will take about 10 to 15 minutes depending on the length of the scan and the speed of your Internet connection.

Setup

No special setup is required for this task.

Caveat

You may be shocked at just how vulnerable your computer is after the scan results are displayed.

Procedure

This task will show you how to use an online port scanner to check a computer's vulnerability.

Equipment Used

No special equipment is required.

Details

This task will take you through the steps required to use an online scanner to scan the security of various ports on a computer or server.

Locating and Using an Online Port Scanner

1. At the computer you intend to scan, open a web browser.
2. Use your favorite search engine to search for "online port scanner" or a similar word string.
3. When the results come in, select Shields Up.

 In step 3, you could select any number of other services, but Shields Up is the tool used in this task.

4. When the initial page loads, scroll down and click Proceed.
5. When the next page loads, scroll down until you see the ShieldsUP!! Services box.
6. Click the Common Ports button.

7. The scan will begin.

8. Scroll down and review the results when the scan is concluded.

9. Compare the results to what the IT staff expected.

Criteria for Completion

You will have successfully completed this task when you can view the results of the port scan. You can perform other specialized scans on this site and obtain a text summary of the results that you can then print.

Task 2.27: Changing Printer Toner

This is another extremely common task you will be performing as a PC tech. It isn't a particularly difficult task, but you'll find yourself doing it on an almost daily basis. The procedure differs somewhat depending on the make, model, and size of the printer. (Some large and specialized printers use separate and rather large cartridges for the colors black, blue, green, yellow, and red.)

Scenario

You receive a trouble ticket stating that the toner is low in the printer used by the software-development department. You look up in your records the type and model of printer they use, locate the correct replacement cartridge in inventory, and report to the department.

Scope of Task

Duration

This task should take about 5 to 10 minutes at most.

Setup

No special setup is required for this task, outside of access to a printer and the correct toner cartridges.

Caveat

There are a number of different printer types and models in existence as well as different types of printer cartridges and procedures for changing them. The steps in this task may not quite match the ones you'll need to take to change your printer cartridge.

Procedure

This task will show you how to change the toner cartridge in a printer type that is typically used in a business environment.

Equipment Used

In addition to having access to a printer, you will need an appropriate toner cartridge to use in this task. For this example, it is advisable to have a drop cloth or two handy to put the cartridges on and to wipe up any toner mess. The simplest way for you to complete this task is to remove the toner cartridge in your printer and then replace it.

Details

This task walks you through the steps necessary to remove an empty printer cartridge and replace it with a fresh unit.

Changing a Printer's Toner Cartridge

OPENING THE PRINTER

1. When you arrive at the printer, put the box containing the new cartridge aside.
2. Look at the printer readout and verify the error message indicating it is low on toner.

 This display will vary depending on the make and model of the printer.

3. Locate the latch securing the main access panel of the printer.
4. Pull the latch, releasing the panel.
5. Open the panel.

REPLACING THE CARTRIDGE

1. Locate the cloth you brought with you.
2. Spread the cloth on the floor below the open access panel.
3. Verify that there is sufficient room on the cloth to hold two toner cartridges and protect the floor from spills.
4. Open the box containing the new cartridge.
5. Remove the cartridge and place it on the cloth.
6. Locate the old cartridge inside the printer.
7. Locate the cartridge-release latch.
8. Pull the latch to release the old cartridge.
9. Carefully pull the cartridge toward you, out of the printer.
10. Place the old cartridge on the cloth to contain any toner spills.
11. Locate the new cartridge and remove any tape or seals covering toner access.

 You may have to shake the cartridge prior to step 11 to ensure that the toner is distributed evenly inside the cartridge.

12. Correctly orient the new cartridge and push it in its container inside the printer.
13. Verify that it is firmly in place.
14. Close the latch securing the cartridge.
15. Close the printer's access door.
16. Close the latch and secure the door.

CLEANING UP AND CONDUCTING A TEST PRINT

1. Put the old cartridge in the box the new cartridge came in.
2. Note any toner spills on the cloth.

 If you used the drop cloth correctly, there should be no spills on the floor.

3. If you have toner on your hands, wipe them thoroughly on a clean section of the cloth.
4. Carefully fold the cloth so all of the spilled toner is inside and cannot spill out.
5. Place the cloth inside the box with the old toner cartridge.
6. Access the printer controls and print a test page.

 The procedure for accessing the printer controls in step 6 is highly variable and no one method can be presented. Alternately, you could have an end user print a test page from a computer.

7. When the test page prints correctly, remove the box containing the spent cartridge and cloth and dispose of it appropriately.

There are programs available that will recycle spent print cartridges. Your IT-department supervisor will be aware of the procedure used in your department.

Criteria for Completion

You will have successfully completed this task when the toner cartridge has been replaced and the printer is printing normally.

Task 2.28: Scanning a Document Using Windows Vista

As you are likely aware, one of the difficulties many people have with Windows Vista is that it doesn't support all of the applications and products people use, both professionally and personally, to be productive. One of the functions Vista may not support on your scanner or HP All-in-One imaging device is scanning documents.

This is the result of the lack of full-featured drivers being available for imaging products and particularly for older imaging products. While the absence of full-featured drivers may not allow you to use the advanced scanning features of your imaging device, the basic printer drivers on board Vista will enable you to use several workaround methods. This task will show you how to use three such methods with an HP imaging device.

An HP OfficeJet 6110 All-in-One printer was used to create this task. The task scenarios should work the same way for other imaging devices, but expect there to be some differences.

Scenario

The chief operations officer (COO) for your company has had a new Windows Vista computer installed in his office, but complains that he is unable to scan documents from Vista using his HP OfficeJet 6110 All-in-One device. You have been assigned the task of instructing the COO as to workaround methods he can use to scan until drivers become available for Vista that support his imaging device, or until he acquires a more Vista-compatible device. You have searched the HP site and have discovered three methods that will work. You schedule a time to meet with the COO in his office to walk through these methods with him. You arrive at the appointed time and begin the tutorial process.

Scope of Task

Duration

It should take about 15 minutes or so to progress through the steps associated with the three workaround methods.

Setup

The only setup that's required is for an imaging device to be directly attached to a Windows Vista machine and for both machines to be powered up and running. The imaging device should also have adequate ink it its print cartridges, an original document to scan must be on hand, and blank paper should be available.

Caveat

The steps in these tasks should work with all HP All-in-One imaging devices, but the results cannot be guaranteed for other HP devices and for non-HP devices.

Procedure

This task will teach you three workaround methods to scan a document using an HP All-in-One imaging device with Windows Vista.

Equipment Used

As previously stated, a computer running Windows Vista and an HP All-in-One printer with scanning abilities are required to get the most out of this set of tasks.

Details

This task will walk you through the various workaround methods for scanning a document from Windows Vista using an HP All-in-One device.

Scanning a Document from an HP All-in-One Device Using Windows Vista

LOADING THE ORIGINAL DOCUMENT

 You will use this same method for loading an original document in the HP imaging device, regardless of the following workaround methods you select.

1. Make sure that both the Windows Vista PC and the HP All-in-One device are connected, powered up, and ready.
2. Raise the top cover of the imaging device.
3. Place the original document, print side down, onto the glass, using the guides around the glass to line up the document.

4. Close the lid.

SCANNING A DOCUMENT USING WINDOWS PHOTO GALLERY

1. Click the Windows Vista button.

2. In the menu that appears, click Programs.

3. Click Windows Photo Gallery.

4. When the program opens in a separate window, click File and then click Import from Camera or Scanner.

5. Click Import.

6. Click Scan.

The document will be scanned.

SCANNING A DOCUMENT USING PAINT

1. Click the Windows Vista button.

2. In the menu that appears, click Programs.

3. Click Accessories.

4. Click Paint.

5. When the program opens in a separate window, click File, and then click From Scanner or Camera.

6. Click Scan.

The document will be scanned.

SCANNING A DOCUMENT USING WINDOWS FAX AND SCANNING

 You can use this method with only Windows Vista Ultimate, Vista Business, and Vista Enterprise versions.

1. Click the Windows Vista button.

2. In the menu that appears, click Programs.

3. Click Windows Scan and Fax.

4. When the program opens in a separate window, click New Scan.

5. Click File, and then click Scan.

The document will be scanned.

Criteria for Completion

You will have successfully completed this task when you have scanned a document using all three methods. Remember, though, that your results may not be the same if you are using an imaging device different from the HP All-in-One series used to create this scenario.

Task 2.29: Managing Windows Startup and Recovery Behavior

By default, when Windows suffers from an extreme failure such as the dreaded Blue Screen of Death (BSOD), it automatically reboots. Unfortunately, there may be valuable information contained in the BSOD that you will not be able to read before the PC restarts. Of course, both XP and Vista are much more stable than Windows 98, so the BSOD appearance is rare, but it's still not completely a thing of the past. You can take control of the reboot process so that it's not automatic, which will allow you to read valuable troubleshooting messages should the BSOD happen to you.

Scenario

You have been assigned to diagnose a computer that has suffered a BSOD. The user reports that she started her computer on Monday morning as usual and, after the operating system had fully loaded, double-clicked on her web-browser icon in the system tray. The browser didn't launch, so she double-clicked again and the system seemed to freeze. The BSOD appeared, but the computer rebooted before she could read any of the information that appeared.

The system seems responsive now and you'd like to try and duplicate the error but be able to read the BSOD message. For that, you will need to disable the automatic reboot under Startup and Recovery.

Scope of Task

Duration

Disabling the automatic reboot feature will just take a few minutes.

Setup

No special setup is required.

Caveat

There are no special issues associated with this task and you do not need a computer that is malfunctioning to successfully change this setting. A Windows XP computer was used to create this scenario.

Procedure

This task will teach you how to disable the automatic reboot feature under Startup and Recovery.

Equipment Used

No special equipment is required. This task should work the same on Windows XP and Vista computers.

Details

This task will walk you through the procedure disabling the automatic reboot feature under Startup and Recovery.

Disabling Automatic Reboot Under Startup and Recovery

1. Click Start.
2. In the menu that appears, right-click My Computer.
3. Click Properties.
4. Click the Advanced tab.
5. Under Startup and Recovery, click Settings.
6. Clear the check box next to Automatically Restart.
7. Click OK.
8. Click OK to close the System Properties box.

Criteria for Completion

You will have successfully completed this task when you have cleared the Automatically Restart check box and saved your changes by clicking OK. This task does not require that your computer suffer a BSOD event or that you solve such an error.

Task 2.30: Performing Asset Management of PCs

There's an old saying that "the job's not over until the paperwork is done." This is as true in IT as in any other profession. Actually, there is quite a bit of record keeping involved in providing PC technician services. This task will focus on performing asset management of newly purchased computers.

Asset management is the labeling of all equipment, software, and other property or assets of a company. Usually a specific serial number is issued to a device or other object, and that number is recorded on a spreadsheet or database along with all relevant data about the asset. In this fashion, it is possible to keep track of the company's property, particularly when transfers or moves occur. Additionally, you can record any changes in the asset, including repairs or upgrades.

Scenario

The training department has just received six new PCs. The computers have already been installed but have not yet been assigned tracking numbers and recorded in the IT department's records. You have been assigned to perform asset management for these new computers.

Scope of Task

Duration

Conducting asset management on a single computer will take only a few minutes.

Setup

No special setup is required. It is assumed that the PCs are powered up.

Caveat

If you are involved in a long asset-management task, you can eventually get a little bored and careless. Make sure you are recording the asset numbers and other information correctly. An error on the books will mean you won't be recording accurate information for at least one computer.

Procedure

This task will teach you the correct method to perform asset management on newly received computers.

Equipment Used

Materials typically used during asset management are a series of small labels sequentially numbered and stating, "Property of *Company Name.*" You will also need a pad or ledger book to record information for each asset item and a pencil or pen.

    Once the procedure is complete, you'll enter the information into a data-tracking utility such as Microsoft Excel or Access.

Details

This task will walk you through the procedure of recording asset information for a set of newly arrived computers.

Conducting Asset Management

RECORDING INFORMATION FOR THE NEWLY ARRIVED PCS

1. When you arrive at the training department, locate the first computer.

2. Locate your asset tags (labels), ledger book, and pen.

3. Select the first tag.

4. Record the asset tag number in the book that is being used.

 Alternatively, the book you are using in step 4 can be prenumbered sequentially with the asset numbers.

5. Place the tag on the appropriate area of the PC case.

 Most companies have a convention of where asset tags are to be placed on a PC case, such as the right side panel in the upper-left corner. Follow whatever conventions your company uses.

6. Log on to the computer.

7. Right-click My Computer.

8. In the Computer Properties box, click the Computer Name tab and record the following in the ledger:
   - Computer name
   - Domain dame
   - Computer location (which department it has been installed in)

9. Click the General tab and record the following in the ledger:
   - Operating system (including version number and service pack)
   - Who it is registered to
   - The OEM number
   - The manufacturer's name
   - The CPU type
   - The RAM information

10. Click the Support Information button and record the following in the ledger:
    - The manufacturer's asset tag number
    - The express service code, if any
    - The URL for the manufacturer's support web page
    - The telephone number to the manufacturer's customer-support office

Not all systems have a Support Information button. You can gain the same information by right-clicking My Computer, selecting Properties, and reading the information from the General tab of the System Properties box.

11. Click OK to close the box.

12. Click OK to close the System Properties box.

13. Record the date the computer was received.

INVENTORYING A MONITOR

1. Locate the next asset tag in sequence and record it in the ledger.

2. Attach the tag to the appropriate location on the monitor.

3. Record the manufacturer's name.

4. Look on the back of the monitor.

5. Record any serial-number information present.

6. Record the monitor's location.

7. Record the asset number of the computer associated with this monitor.

8. Record when the monitor was received.

INVENTORYING A KEYBOARD

1. Locate the next asset tag in sequence and record the number in the ledger.

2. Attach the tag to the appropriate location on the keyboard (usually on the bottom).

3. Record the manufacturer's name.

4. Look on the bottom of the keyboard.

5. Record any serial-number information present.

6. Record the keyboard's location.

7. Record the asset number of the PC associated with this keyboard.

8. Record when the keyboard was received.

After you are done with the first computer, proceed to the next PC and repeat the entire process. Repeat until all of the asset information is recorded.

RECORDING ASSET DATA AND SAVING IT

1. Once you have completed the asset inventory process on the newly arrived equipment, return to your office and open the utility you use to record asset data.

2. Open the particular file used to record PC asset data.

The document used to record PC asset data will be preconfigured to include categories to be used in listing these computers, including asset number, computer name, domain name, computer location, and so on, just as you recorded these data in the ledger.

3. Complete the data-entry process for each PC's asset information.

4. Open the recording document for monitor assets (if separate) and transcribe the information.

5. Open the recording document for keyboard assets (if separate) and transcribe the information.

6. Save all documents and close.

7. Close the application.

8. Return the asset ledger book to its storage area (usually a file cabinet that locks).

Criteria for Completion

You will have successfully completed this task when you have placed asset tags on all relevant equipment (most companies don't inventory mice) and associated those asset numbers with the details for PCs, monitors, and keyboards.

To further duplicate the experience, you could open Excel or Access on your computer and record the data in various documents as outlined in this task.

Task 2.31: Performing Asset Management on Inventory

You have to keep track of not only new PCs, monitors, and keyboards, but also any other type of asset that is the responsibility of the IT department. Although the department can't possibly have every conceivable replacement part and unit you'll need, it is typical to keep commonly required equipment and devices on hand. Naturally, you'll need to record not only newly arrived inventory, but also what you already have on hand (or at least verify that the inventory was previously recorded). Also, whenever someone takes a piece of inventory such as a printer-toner cartridge, they should update the records so the staff will know when that asset was removed and which department needed it.

Conducting asset management on your inventory is how equipment budgeting is managed between departments in a company.

Scenario

You have been assigned to organize and perform asset management on the hardware closet. It has not been inventoried for quite some time and the records need to be updated. You spend some time organizing the equipment types shelf by shelf and then locate the hardware ledger book and start the recording process.

Scope of Task

Duration

Depending on how much equipment you have to inventory, this could take a while, perhaps an hour or more for the IT department of a small to midsized company.

Setup

In a home lab setup, it is unlikely that you have a significant amount of equipment to inventory. To approximate this task, you can locate a closet in your home or storage cabinet in your garage and organize and inventory the contents. (Besides, you've been meaning to clean up that mess for ages, haven't you?)

Caveat

As with asset management of PCs, your data keeping is only as good as your accuracy and organization. For example, make sure that a complete stranger looking at your ledger would be able to tell exactly how many hard drives you have on tap, as well as their type, capacity, and so on.

Procedure

This task will show you how to conduct a standard inventory of equipment in a storage closet.

Equipment Used

All you'll probably need is a notepad or ledger book and a pencil or pen.

Details

This task will go through the motions of recording an IT department's hardware assets contained in a storage closet.

Performing an Equipment Inventory

1. Go to the top shelf of the hardware closet.

 Actually, you could start anywhere, but it makes sense to either start at the top and work your way down or start at the bottom and work your way up.

2. Go to the far left side of the top shelf.

3. Write down the type of devices stored here. (We'll start with hard drives.)

4. Write down the hardware type as *hard drives* and record the following:

- Total number of hard drives
- Total number of hard drives by manufacturer
- The model number, speed, and capacity of each hard drive for each manufacturer
- If possible, when each hard drive was received

5. For the hard drives, create blank listings for the following:

- When a particular hard drive was removed
- Who removed it
- Which department requires the hard drive
- The name and location of the computer that requires the drive
- Who authorized the job requiring the hard drive

 The listings made in step 5 will be used when a tech needs to check out a piece of equipment in response to a trouble ticket.

6. Move to the next set of items on the shelf (let's say optical drives).

7. Record all the information listed in steps 4 and 5 for the optical drives (or as much as applicable).

8. Move to the next item on the shelf or the next shelf.

9. Repeat steps 4 and 5 for each type of hardware asset located on the different shelves in the closet.

10. When finished, close and lock the closet.

11. Go to your computer and open the application used to record inventory data.

12. Transcribe the information you wrote down into the required documents.

13. Save your work and close the documents.

14. Close the application.

15. Place the asset book in an area available to IT staff.

The supervisor for the IT department is responsible for establishing a procedure for IT staff to check in newly arrived hardware and check out hardware required for a job. This information should be recorded in the ledger and then regularly transcribed into asset inventory documents in the application of your choice.

 This procedure can be used for any assets possessed by the IT department, including software, software licenses, tools, office equipment, manuals, and other technical books and documentation.

Criteria for Completion

You will have successfully completed this task when you have organized your storage closet by object type and recorded the relevant information about each type of object and each specific object per type.

Task 2.32: Performing Asset Management of a PC's Hardware

It is helpful to record the hardware installed in a PC so that you know what its capacities are and can keep track of changes when it is serviced. Ideally, this is done when the device is first received or constructed, but in a lot of organizations the data isn't recorded due to lack of time or staff availability. However, having a baseline of the hardware installed makes it easy to determine what equipment is on board and to track any hardware configuration changes you make over time.

Scenario

You have been assigned to record the hardware installed in a group of computers located at one of your company's branch offices. That information is currently not on file in the IT department and you are part of the project to update the records. You take the necessary equipment and report to the branch office. It is after hours and only the office manager is present to give you access to the building and the computers.

Scope of Task

Duration

Inventorying the hardware in a single PC will take about 15 to 30 minutes, depending on how extensive an inventory you conduct.

Setup

No special setup is required.

Caveat

Remember to make every attempt to keep accurate records during the task.

Procedure

This task will teach you what you need to know to inventory the hardware on a computer.

Equipment Used

Except for a ledger book and pen, no special equipment is required.

Details

This task will move you through the steps of inventorying all of the hardware installed on a computer.

Performing an Inventory of a Computer's Hardware

1. At the computer, click Start.
2. Right-click My Computer. The System Properties box appears.

3. Click the Hardware tab.
4. Click Device Manager.

5. When the Device Manager box appears, expand the first item, which should be Computer.

6. Create a category called Computer in your ledger.

7. Write down the information you can see when you expand Computer.

8. Right-click ACPI Multiprocessor PC.

9. Click Properties.

10. Click the Driver tab.

11. Record the information on this tab.

12. Click Driver Details.

13. Record the information in this box.

14. Click OK.

15. Click the Details tab.

16. Record the information on this tab.

17. Click OK.

18. Go to the next item in Device Manager (Disk Drives).

19. Expand it.

20. Repeat steps 8 through 17 and record the relevant information.

This example is erring on the side of caution by showing you how to gain very detailed information about each device installed on the computer. In all likelihood, the most you'll have to record is the type, make, and model of each piece of hardware.

21. When you have finished this process with each installed device, close Device Manager.

22. Close System Properties.

23. Log off the computer.

24. Repeat the entire process with the next computer.

25. Repeat this process until all computers are inventoried.

This information will become part of the baseline and history for each computer in your records. Once the information is entered, any changes to a computer's hardware can be recorded so that a complete record of any work done on any PC is available.

The scenario presented in this task will be continued in Task 2.33, "Performing Asset Management on a PC's Software."

Criteria for Completion

You will have successfully completed this task when you have gone through each device listed in Device Manager and recorded at least the make, model, and type of device in your ledger book.

Task 2.33: Performing Asset Management on a PC's Software

Just as it is helpful to inventory the hardware installed on a computer, you will gain the same benefits when you record all of the applications installed on a PC. It is best to start with a baseline, but as with PC hardware, you may not have that luxury. Once you have a record of the software, you can use this as the basis for recording any changes such as applications being updated, installed, or uninstalled (and to determine if the end user has installed unsupported software on the computer).

Scenario

This task is a continuation of the scenario presented in Task 2.32, "Performing Asset Management of a PC's Hardware."

You are still at the branch office and have completed your inventory of each computer's hardware. Now you are going to inventory the software applications installed on each computer.

In real life, you would have inventoried an individual PC's hardware and software before moving on to the next machine.

Scope of Task

Duration

Taking inventory of the application software on a single computer should take about 15 minutes, depending on how detailed you are.

Setup

No special setup is required.

Caveat

As always, try to make sure that you are accurately recording the information for each computer.

Procedure

This task will teach you how to create a list of all of the application software installed on a computer.

Equipment Used

Except for your writing implement and ledger, you will need no special equipment.

Details

This task will show you the procedure for accessing a list of a computer's application software and recording it for asset management.

Accessing and Recording a List of Software Applications

1. Click Start ➢ Control Panel.

 In this example, Control Panel is in Classic view.

2. Double-click the Add or Remove Programs applet.

Add or Remove Programs			
Currently installed programs:	Show updates	Sort by:	Name
Actiontec Gateway		Size	0.80MB
To change this program or remove it from your computer, click Change/Remove.			Change/Remove
Ad-aware 6 Personal		Size	1.97MB
Adobe Acrobat 7.0.1 and Reader 7.0.1 Update		Size	1.77MB
Adobe Acrobat 7.0.2 and Reader 7.0.2 Update		Size	2.37MB
Adobe Download Manager 1.2 (Remove Only)			
Adobe Reader 7.0		Size	37.07MB
AVG Free Edition		Size	16.80MB
Belarc Advisor 6.0		Size	1.75MB
Camtasia Studio 2		Size	32.77MB
Conexant D850 56K V.9x DFVc Modem		Size	0.51MB
Conexant SmartHSFi V92 56K DF PCI Modem		Size	0.29MB
DAO			
Dell Picture Studio - Dell Image Expert			
Dell Solution Center			
Dell Support 5.0.0 (766)		Size	6.50MB
Digital Line Detect		Size	0.21MB

Change or Remove Programs
Add New Programs
Add/Remove Windows Components
Set Program Access and Defaults

3. Select the name of each piece of software in turn and record the following:

    ▪   The name of the software

    ▪   The size of the software

    ▪   How frequently the software is used

    ▪   When it was last used

 If you want to see a list of all the Windows updates on the computer, check the Show Updates check box at the top of the Add or Remove Programs box.

4. Make a note if you see any unsupported software installed on the computer.

5. Repeat this process for all the computers in the office.

Criteria for Completion

You will have successfully completed this task when you have recorded all the information regarding installed software on the PC.

Task 2.34: Tracking Work Done on a PC

Tasks 2.32 and 2.33 took you through the processes necessary to discover and record all data relevant to a computer. Ideally, this information represents an overall baseline of the device that can be used to assist in tracking any changes in the PC over time. Each time you receive a trouble ticket and provide a service to a particular machine, you will be required to enter the information about those changes in the computer's records at the IT department. This is one way of seeing if there is a pattern of the same problem occurring on a particular computer or if some past repair job may have contributed to a current issue.

Scenario

You receive a trouble ticket from the support desk stating that one of the managers in the accounting department is unable to print to her local printer. As usual, you look up the records for that computer and printer prior to responding. You notice that both devices were only recently installed and there have been no prior trouble tickets for either the PC or the printer.

Scope of Task

Duration

Reviewing the records and then recording new data usually take about 15 minutes, depending on the amount of material and the level of detail.

Setup

You will in all likelihood have to simulate this situation, unless you want to record an actual troubleshooting task you have performed. In lieu of actually recording it in Excel or Access, you can just write the steps you took on a pad of paper.

Caveat

As with all documentation tasks, you must be sure you are recording the data correctly. It is also helpful to record the information as soon as possible after the event rather than trying to remember what happened when you get around to documenting it a few days later.

Procedure

This task will show you how to create and maintain a record of work done on a computer.

Equipment Used

No special equipment is needed except a pen and paper to record how you responded to the trouble ticket.

Details

This task will outline the steps to take when recording the work you've done on a computer and maintaining the overall records for the device.

Documenting Work Performed on a PC

REVIEWING THE RECORDS

1. Open the application where computer asset information is stored.
2. Look up the specific computer involved by asset number or name.
3. Review the documents (if any) regarding past trouble tickets.
4. Look up the specific printer involved by asset number or name.
5. Review the documents (if any) regarding past trouble tickets.
6. Create an entry under the computer's asset number (you may have to change this later if the problem turns out to be the printer), opening a new incident.
7. Include the trouble-ticket number. (The trouble-ticket number and asset number for the computer will be cross-referenced later.)
8. Save the information and close the open documents.
9. Close the application.

 This task won't address the actual troubleshooting methods involved or the nature of the problem. This information will be presented in Task 4.11, "Troubleshooting a PC That Can't Print to a Local Printer," so we'll skip over that part of the story.

RECORDING THE RESOLUTION OF A TROUBLE TICKET

1. After the work is done and the issue is resolved, return to the IT department.

 Sometimes an issue isn't resolved in a single visit. This task takes the point of view of a simple resolution.

2. Open the record-keeping application on your computer.
3. Open the incident you created under the computer's asset number.
4. Record the description of the problem as described to you by the user.
5. Record the steps you took to troubleshoot the problem.
6. Record the problem that you discovered.
7. Record the steps you took to correct the problem.
8. Include any hardware or software assets used to resolve the problem.

 If you used any hardware from the inventory cabinet, for example, you'll need to record that information in the hardware inventory records.

9. Record how you tested that your solution was correct.
10. Date and time-stamp the incident if your software is capable.
11. Mark the incident as closed.
12. Send an email to your supervisor with the incident number for review.
13. Send an email to the support desk notifying them of the resolution and requesting they close the trouble ticket at their end.
14. Close your incident.
15. Save your work.
16. Close the document.
17. Close the application.

Criteria for Completion

You will have successfully completed this assignment when you have recorded all of the information relevant to this repair job and saved it.

Phase

3

Networking
Computer Systems

You may be asking yourself what a PC desktop-support tech is doing performing any sort of networking function. Although trade schools, universities, and certification vendors may segregate IT operations into distinct and separate categories, real life is rarely so neat. Desktop support isn't all hard drives and RAM sticks. There are quite a number of elementary networking tasks you will perform in the course of your duties.

The tasks in this phase map to Domains 1, 3, 4, 5, and 6 for the CompTIA A+ Essentials (220-701) exam objectives, and to Domains 1, 2, 3, and 4 of the CompTIA Practical Application (220-702) exam objectives.

Task 3.1: Mapping Drives

Mapping a network drive is a handy way to give end users access to various file shares by making a share appear as if it were a separate drive on their computer. You can set up a share so that it uses a particular drive letter, and that letter is the one all your users will use to access that share. After it's set up, all the user has to do is open My Computer and open the drive. The information on the share will appear as if it were on a partition on the user's local hard drive.

Scenario

A new employee in accounting needs to get access to the accounting department's share on one of the servers. You've been assigned to map a network drive on her computer to that share and then test to make sure it works.

Scope of Task

Duration

This task should take 5 or 10 minutes at most.

Setup

You will need two computers that are networked together. One will act as the server with a shared folder and the other as the client machine. If you are unsure how to create a shared folder on a computer, see Task 3.2, "Creating File Shares."

Caveat

In a real production environment, be careful which directories you make available for sharing. Make sure that the directory doesn't contain any information that shouldn't be accessed by unauthorized personnel. Also, be careful which drive letters you use. Some devices that you may want to connect to a computer come hard-coded with a particular drive letter. If you use that letter for a share and then try to connect the device, you will be unable to access the device.

> See Task 4.18, "Troubleshooting the Inability to Connect a USB Digital Camera to a PC," for information on diagnosing connection problems involving a mapped drive.

Procedure

This task will teach you what you need to know to map a network drive to a server share on a client computer.

Equipment Used

No special equipment will be needed.

Details

This task will take you through the steps needed to map a network drive.

> This task was written using Windows XP, but the steps should work just as well if you are using Windows Vista.

Mapping a Network Drive

ACCESSING AND MAPPING THE DRIVE FROM A CLIENT PC

1. At the client machine, right-click My Computer.
2. Click Map Network Drive.
3. When the Map Network Drive box appears, use the Drive drop-down menu to select a drive letter.

4. In the Folder field, type the path of the share.

> The share path you enter in step 4 is usually the server name followed by the share name and is expressed as *server_name**share_name*.

> For step 4, you can also use the Browse button to browse for the location of the share.

5. Check the Reconnect at Logon box.

6. Click Finish.

> After you click Finish, Windows will attempt to locate and open the share.

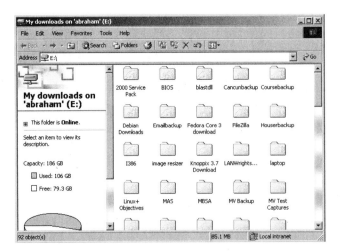

7. Close the window.

TESTING THE MAPPED DRIVE

1. Double-click My Computer to see if the mapped drive appears.

2. Double-click the (E:) drive (or whatever drive letter you assigned to the mapped drive) to open it.

3. Close My Computer.

Criteria for Completion

You will have successfully completed this task when you have verified that you have mapped the correct drive letter to the server share.

Task 3.2: Creating File Shares

As you saw in Task 3.1, very often users need to access file shares on a file and print server in order to locate documents, forms, and other tools of their trade. Rather than have the users download copies of a shared folder's contents to their local drives, it is very common for users to access their tools across the network in a shared folder. (Never share the root of your hard drive; instead, share only those folders on the network that other users must access.) Of course, before the users can locate their tools in the appropriate directory, the directory has to be shared to the network. Here's how to do that.

Scenario

A folder on the Research team's server needs to be shared so the team can use it to save and access work for a new project. The file and data already exist. You have been assigned to create the network share of the folder on the Engineering server.

Scope of Task

Duration

This task should take about 5 to 10 minutes.

Setup

There is no special setup for this task.

Caveat

As was mentioned in Task 3.1, be careful of what you share and to whom. Verify with your supervisor the specific directory to be shared and whatever permissions need to be configured.

Procedure

This task will show you how to set up a simple shared folder on the network.

Equipment Used

No special equipment will be needed for this task.

Details

This task will take you through the steps necessary to locate and share a folder on a server to the network.

 As in Task 3.1, this task was written using Windows XP Professional SP 2. This computer is a domain member and the shared folder is on an NTFS partition. You should be able to perform this task reasonably well with Vista and other Windows operating-system versions, but there will be some differences depending on the exact version of the operating system and partition type (FAT vs. NTFS) as well as the file-sharing type (Simple File Sharing vs. Access Control Lists).

Creating a File Share

1. Sitting at the server's keyboard, right-click the Start button.
2. Click Explore.
3. Navigate to the location of the folder you want to share.
4. Select the desired folder.
5. Right-click the desired folder.

6. Click Sharing.

7. Click the Share This Folder radio button.

8. Verify that the name of the share is correct in the Share Name field.

9. Click the Permissions button.

10. On the Share Permissions tab in the Permissions box, click Add.

11. In the Select Users, Computers, or Groups box, scroll down and select the Engineers group.

 Make sure you select the correct domain in the Look In drop-down menu of the Select Users, Computers, or Groups box.

12. Click Add.

13. Click OK.

The Engineers group will be added to the Share Permissions box after you click OK in step 13.

14. Under Permissions, check the boxes of the permissions you want this group to have.

15. Click OK.

16. In the Research Properties box under User Limit, click the Maximum Allowed radio button.

17. Click OK.

If you were using Simple File Sharing, no Security tab would be present.

Notice in the Local Disk (C:) box that after you click OK in step 17 the Research folder is shared.

18. Close any other open boxes.

Criteria for Completion

You will have successfully completed this task when you have shared the folder on the network. You can further test this by attempting to access the share from another computer on the same network segment.

Task 3.3: Configuring PCs to Use Dynamic Addressing

Each computer on a network requires a unique Internet Protocol (IP) address that is on the correct subnet in order to communicate with the other computers on the network segment. The computer will also need the IP address of the local Domain Name System (DNS) server and the address of the gateway router that provides access to other subnets and the Internet.

In a small workgroup environment, you can manually configure these address settings for a limited number of computers. In a corporate environment, manually setting IP addresses for hundreds of computers would be impractical and a real pain in the neck.

Fortunately, with the use of a Dynamic Host Configuration Protocol (DHCP) server on the network, addressing information can be automatically assigned to a computer when it is first powered up. In order to use dynamic addressing, the computer must be configured to request and accept this information.

Even as I write this second edition, IPv6 is far from being ubiquitous, so it is still quite common to perform such tasks using IPv4.

Scenario

You are setting up a PC for a newly hired member of the accounts receivable department. One of the tasks you must perform is verifying that the computer is configured to accept dynamic IP addressing. The PC is powered up and you are logged in and ready to proceed.

Scope of Task

Duration

This task should take no more than 5 or 10 minutes.

Setup

To verify that the configuration is correct, you must have a DHCP server available on your lab network. Most DSL and cable modems come equipped with a built-in DHCP server, so this service should be readily available to most people.

Caveat

The DHCP server should be directly connected to the network segment it is serving so that dynamic addressing requests and offers do not have to cross a router. Also, the server must be configured to provide the correct addressing information for the network segment and have sufficient DHCP leases to provide addresses for all of the computers on the segment.

Configuring a DHCP server typically is not one of the tasks a beginning PC support tech is assigned. Instructions for configuring a DHCP server are not included in this book. See *Network Administrator Street Smarts: A Real World Guide to CompTIA Network+ Skills* by Toby Skandier (Sybex, 2009) for more information.

Procedure

This task will show you how to configure a Windows XP computer to accept dynamic addressing information.

Equipment Used

You will not need any special equipment to complete this task.

Details

This task will take you through the necessary steps to set up a computer to accept dynamic IP addressing from a local DHCP server.

Configuring a Computer to Accept Dynamic Addressing

SETTING THE LOCAL AREA CONNECTION ON A PC TO ACCEPT DYNAMIC ADDRESSING

1. Sitting in front of the computer, click Start ➢ Connect To ➢ Show All Connections.

 The procedure will be slightly different if you are using a Windows 2000 machine. You will have to Click Start ➢ Settings ➢ Network and Dial-up Connections to get to the Network Connections box.

2. In the Network Connections box, right-click the Local Area Connection icon.
3. Click Properties.
4. When the Local Area Connection Properties box opens, select Internet Protocol [TCP/IP] from the list.

 The Internet Protocol [TCP/IP] check box in the Local Area Connection Properties box should be checked by default.

5. Click Properties.

6. In the Internet Protocol [TCP/IP] Properties box, select the Obtain an IP Address Automatically radio button.

7. Select the Obtain DNS Server Address Automatically radio button.

8. Click OK.

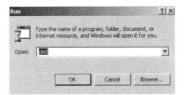

9. Click OK to close the Local Area Connection Properties box.

10. Close the Network Connections box.

VERIFYING THAT THE PC IS RECEIVING DYNAMIC ADDRESS INFORMATION

1. Click Start ➤ Run.

2. In the Run box, type **cmd**.

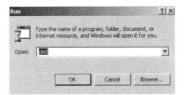

3. Click OK.

4. When the command-line emulator opens, at the prompt type **ipconfig/all**.

5. Press Enter.

 After you press Enter in step 5, the IP addressing information should display in the command-prompt window.

```
C:\WINNT\system32\cmd.exe                                        _|□|
        IP Routing Enabled. . . . . . . . : No
        WINS Proxy Enabled. . . . . . . . : No
        DNS Suffix Search List. . . . . . : test.local
                                            wiredwriter.net

Ethernet adapter Local Area Connection:

        Connection-specific DNS Suffix  . : wiredwriter.net
        Description . . . . . . . . . . . : UMware Accelerated AMD PCNet Adapter
        Physical Address. . . . . . . . . : 00-0C-29-91-96-3A
        DHCP Enabled. . . . . . . . . . . : Yes
        Autoconfiguration Enabled . . . . : Yes
        IP Address. . . . . . . . . . . . : 10.9.8.203
        Subnet Mask . . . . . . . . . . . : 255.255.255.0
        Default Gateway . . . . . . . . . : 10.9.8.7
        DHCP Server . . . . . . . . . . . : 10.9.8.7
        DNS Servers . . . . . . . . . . . : 10.9.8.7
                                            192.168.0.1
        Primary WINS Server . . . . . . . : 10.9.8.7
        Secondary WINS Server . . . . . . : 192.168.0.1
        Lease Obtained. . . . . . . . . . : Monday, July 03, 2006 7:15:44 PM
        Lease Expires . . . . . . . . . . : Tuesday, July 04, 2006 12:03:44 AM

C:\Documents and Settings\Administrator>
```

If an IP address in the 169.254.x.x range (169.254.0.1–192.168.255.254) should be displayed, this indicates that a DHCP server was not available and the address was assigned by Automatic Private IP Addressing (APIPA). The computer will not be able to connect to the rest of the network with this address.

6. At the command prompt, type **exit** to close the command-prompt window.

Criteria for Completion

You will have successfully completed this task when your computer receives automatic IP addressing information from your local DHCP server and is able to communicate with other computers on the network.

Task 3.4: Renewing a Dynamic Address Assignment

This task is somewhat similar to the previous one in that you need to have a computer that dynamically received an IP address assignment from a DHCP server. This time, you will need to understand how to perform a release and renew of a dynamically assigned IP address on a Windows XP or Vista computer. It's a relatively simple task, but one that you will commonly perform as part of troubleshooting a computer that has lost its connection to the network.

Renewing a DHCP address is also useful when APIPA has previously assigned an address to a client computer, due to a DHCP server being unavailable. Once a DHCP server is available, use the renew command to request a DHCP address for the client.

Scenario

You receive a trouble ticket on Monday morning stating that one of the marketing staff cannot connect to the LAN or the Internet. On Friday, he left his computer logged in but locked his desktop, and at that time he had a network connection. You respond to the ticket, go to the marketing person's cubicle, and begin diagnosing the problem. He allows you access to his keyboard and is still logged into the computer.

Scope of Task

Duration

This task will take about 5 minutes.

Setup

There is no special setup for this task and it can be performed on both a Windows XP and a Vista computer.

Caveat

The computer will need to receive a dynamic IP address assignment from a DHCP server. See Task 3.3 for more information on configuring a computer to receive dynamic IP addressing.

Procedure

This task will teach you how to renew a dynamic IP address assignment.

Equipment Used

No special equipment is necessary.

Details

This task will show you how to release and renew a dynamic IP address on a Windows computer.

Releasing and Renewing a Dynamic Address Assignment

1. Open a command-prompt window and verify that the computer has an assigned IP address.

The section "Verifying That the PC Is Receiving Dynamic Address Information" in Task 3.3 will show you how to open the command-prompt window and issue the **ipconfig/all** command, which will tell you if DHCP is enabled and if an IP address is assigned to the computer. Even if an address is apparently assigned, the computer may still not be connected to the network and renewing the address assignment may still be required.

2. At the command prompt, type **ipconfig/release**, press Enter, and wait for the prompt to return.

3. At the prompt, type **ipconfig/renew** and press Enter.

4. After you have received the message stating that the address has been renewed, test the connection by typing **ping www.google.com** and then pressing Enter.

> While Google currently responds to echo requests, this may not be so indefinitely. Firewall settings at either the requestor's or receiver's end may refuse the echo request, even though there is a connection.

5. After the successful ping test, type **exit** at the prompt and press Enter to close the emulator.

> In Windows XP, in the classic view of Control Panel, you can click on Network Connections, Local Area Connection, and then click the Support tab to see the computer's assigned IP address. In Windows Vista, you can find the computer's IP address in the network map. Click Control Panel ≻ Network and Internet ≻ Network and Sharing Center, select View Full Map, and then hover your cursor over the icon representing the computer to see the IP address assigned.

Criteria for Completion

You will have successfully completed this task when you have installed, released, and renewed the IP Address for the computer and it has acquired a valid IP Address for your network.

Task 3.5: Installing a Network Printer

Although it is common to have a print server control the printing processes of several networked printers in a business environment, you can also install printers that have a print server built in. Instead of the printer connecting to a server or computer with a printer or USB cable, it connects directly to the network with its own network interface card (NIC). As a PC support technician, you occasionally may be asked to install and configure a new network printer on a network segment.

Scenario

The research department has hired several new engineers over the past few months and it needs another network printer installed in its area. You have been assigned to install the network printer and make it available on the Research network segment. You have been given all the information you need, including the printer's IP address, subnet mask, and hostname. Another tech has already added the printer's IP address information to the DNS server. All you need to do is install the printer itself.

Scope of Task

Duration

This task will take about 30 to 45 minutes.

Setup

Ideally, you will need a printer with a NIC and built-in print server. There are models available for the home and small-office user; however, it is still more popular for this class of user to have a printer connected to a PC with either a printer cable or a USB cable.

 I continue to mention printer cables, just in case you're working with older equipment, but most printers connected to PCs these days use USB.

Caveat

There is no single procedure for installing a network printer, so for this task I will present a generic set of steps. Most of the installation is done using the printer's configuration buttons and display, but navigating printer menus is as much art as it is technology. If you have a network printer, make sure the instruction manual and any installation discs are handy.

Procedure

This task will teach you how to install a network printer.

Equipment Used

No special equipment is necessary except for a patch cable to connect the printer to the network, and whatever manuals and installation software came with the printer.

Details

This task will walk you step-by-step through the process of installing a network printer so that it can be accessed by computers on the same network segment.

Installing a Network Printer

ACCESSING THE CONTROLS TO CONFIGURE A NETWORK PRINTER

1. Power up the print device.
2. Locate the Ethernet patch cable.
3. Connect one end of the cable to the printer's NIC.
4. Connect the other end to an Ethernet port.
5. Once the power-up and self-test are finished on the printer, locate the control buttons.
6. Locate the display window.
7. Click Menu.
8. Click Configure Device Menu.
9. When the menu appears, use the Down arrow to navigate to Configure Device and select it.
10. When the Configure Device menu appears, use the Down arrow to navigate to Manual and select it.
11. When the hostname appears, use the letter and number buttons on the printer to input the printer's hostname.

 In this scenario, your supervisor will provide you with the appropriate IP address, subnet mask, default gateway, and TCP connection time-out information.

12. Click Next.
13. When either the Secure Web or Web Options menu item appears, use the Down arrow to navigate to HTTP and select it.
14. Click Next.
15. When the IP address fields appear, use the number keys to input the printer's IP address.
16. Click Next.
17. When the subnet mask fields appear, use the number keys to input the subnet mask.
18. Click Next.
19. When the Default Gateway IP address fields appear, use the number keys to input the gateway's IP address.
20. Click Next.
21. When the time-out field appears, use the number keys to set the TCP connection time-out in seconds.
22. Click Next.
23. Click Save.

24. Click Online.

25. Click Exit.

CONFIRMING THE CONFIGURATION SETTINGS ON A NETWORK PRINTER

1. Click Menu.

2. Click Information Menu.

3. Click Network Cfg.

4. Click Print.

After you click Print, the network-configuration page will print with all the network information you configured on the printer, including IP address, subnet mask, and so on.

5. Verify that the information on the page is correct.

VERIFYING THE PRINTER'S NETWORK CONNECTION

1. Go to a computer on the same network segment as the new network printer.

2. Click Start ➢ Run.

3. In the Run box, type **cmd**.

4. Click OK.

5. When the command-prompt window opens, at the prompt, type **ping 192.168.0.2**.

For this task, it is assumed that 192.168.0.2 is the IP address of the printer. The IP address on your network printer may be different.

6. Press Enter.

7. Observe the output of the ping command to confirm the network connection.

```
C:\WINNT\system32\cmd.exe                                          _ |□|
Microsoft Windows 2000 [Version 5.00.2195]
(C) Copyright 1985-2000 Microsoft Corp.

C:\Documents and Settings\Administrator>ping 192.168.0.2

Pinging 192.168.0.2 with 32 bytes of data:

Reply from 192.168.0.2: bytes=32 time=1ms TTL=64
Reply from 192.168.0.2: bytes=32 time=1ms TTL=64
Reply from 192.168.0.2: bytes=32 time<10ms TTL=64
Reply from 192.168.0.2: bytes=32 time=1ms TTL=64

Ping statistics for 192.168.0.2:
    Packets: Sent = 4, Received = 4, Lost = 0 (0% loss),
Approximate round trip times in milli-seconds:
    Minimum = 0ms, Maximum =  1ms, Average =  0ms

C:\Documents and Settings\Administrator>
```

The final test would be to connect a PC on the network segment to the network printer and print a test page. This will be covered in Task 3.17.

Criteria for Completion

You will have successfully completed this task when you have installed and configured the network printer and pinged the printer from a computer.

Task 3.6: Making a Straight-Through Cable

One of the less glamorous jobs you will be assigned is making network cables. Although it is true that an IT department may keep a supply of patch cables handy, sometimes cables of a specific length that aren't easily purchased are needed. You will need to become familiar with the tools necessary to make a network cable and how to pin out different types of cable.

A straight-through cable is one that connects two unlike devices, such as a PC to a switch or a switch to a router. See Task 3.7, "Making a Crossover Cable," to see how to make a cable to connect two like devices.

 Newer network devices may have autosensing Ethernet ports that can detect the cable type and adjust to be able to use the cable.

Scenario

Several new servers are going to be installed in the server room, and your supervisor has assigned you to make the straight-through patch cables that will connect the servers to the patch panel.

 Typically, servers and computers are not directly connected to a switch. Instead, they are connected to a patch panel and then other patch cables connect the specific patch-panel ports to the switch ports.

Scope of Task

Duration

Making a single straight-through cable can take about 10 to 15 minutes; however, if you are not practiced in this task, making a cable successfully the first time can take much longer.

Setup

You will need a supply of Category 5 (Cat 5) or Cat 5e cable and a number of RJ-45 network connectors (get more than you think you'll need).

 This task will also work if you use Cat 6 cable, but you don't need to go out and buy Gigabit-capable cable for the sake of performing this task.

Caveat

Some people learn to make network cables very easily, but it can be a difficult chore for others. Don't be disappointed if the first few cables don't work. It takes practice to become proficient with this task.

Procedure

This task will show you how to successfully make a network straight-through cable.

Equipment Used

You will need the following pieces of equipment to complete this task:

- A wire stripper
- A wire cutter
- A crimp tool
- A cable tester

The cable tester is optional for this task because you can also test whether the cable works by connecting one end to a PC's NIC and the other end to a switch and then attempting to ping another computer on the network. Also, some wire strippers and cutters come as a single tool.

You should be able to find everything you need, including RJ-45 connectors and Ethernet cable, at your local computer-supply store or a large hardware store.

An optional bonus tool would be to have a desk lamp with a built-in magnifying lens. This will help you see the individual pairs of wires as they emerge from the cable jacket.

Details

This task will take you through the process of constructing and testing a straight-through patch cable.

Constructing a Straight-Through Patch Cable

PREPARING TO CONSTRUCT THE CABLE

1. Locate your tools.
2. Arrange your tools on your workbench.

3. Locate the RJ-45 connectors.

4. Arrange two connectors on the workbench.

5. Locate a length of Cat 5 or Cat 5e cable.

In a medium to large IT department, cable will be purchased in spools rather than lengths. You will need to pull out the appropriate length of cable (actually, pull out more than you need) and cut it away from the spooled cable using the wire cutters.

6. Arrange a light so you can see the cable end clearly (an optional magnifying lens comes in very handy about now).

7. Locate a pin-out diagram for a straight-through cable connection.

Four pairs of wires are bound inside the cable jacket. When you untwist the pairs, you'll see that each wire is differently colored. Those wires must be inserted into the RJ-45 connector in the correct color-coded order for the cable to work correctly.

You can use your favorite search engine to locate a pin-out diagram for a straight-through cable, such as the one displayed in the following illustration.

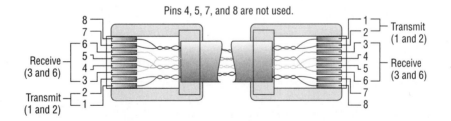

Pin Number	Wire Color		Straight-Through		Pin Number	Wire Color
			Wire	**Becomes**		
Pin 1 →	Orange/White		1 →	1	Pin 1 →	Orange/White
Pin 2 →	Orange		2 →	2	Pin 2 →	Orange
Pin 3 →	Green/White		3 →	3	Pin 3 →	Green/White
Pin 4 →	Blue		6 →	6	Pin 4 →	Blue
Pin 5 →	Blue/White				Pin 5 →	Blue/White
Pin 6 →	Green				Pin 6 →	Green
Pin 7 →	Brown/White				Pin 7 →	Brown/White
Pin 8 →	Brown				Pin 8 →	Brown

MAKING THE CABLE ENDS

1. Locate the wire stripper.

2. Hold out one end of the cable.

3. Use the wire stripper to strip off a length of the cable jacket, leaving the pairs of twisted wires inside intact.

 It is very important to strip off the correct length of the cable jacket. You must expose just enough of the wires so that they'll be able to be completely inserted into the RJ-45 connector and so that a small length of the cable jacket also fits in the connector.

 If you strip off too much of the cable jacket, when you crimp the RJ-45 onto the cable, the tiny wires will extend outside the connector, making them vulnerable to breakage. If you strip off too little of the cable jacket, the wires won't be long enough to make a firm connection to the pins inside the RJ-45.

4. Untwist the exposed twisted pairs.

5. Refer to your pin-out diagram to order the colors of the wires correctly.

 Even after you untwist the wires, they have a tendency to shift position between your fingers. You will have to press your finger and thumb together securely to keep them in the right order.

6. Trim the wires straight across ½ inch from the wire jacket.

7. Locate an RJ-45 connector.

8. Locate pin 1 in the connector.

 Look in the open end of the RJ-45 connector. Orient the connector so that the broad end of the opening is up and the narrow end (with the clip) is down. You will see eight copper connectors inside. They are ordered 1 through 8, left to right.

9. Refer again to the pin-out diagram and orient the correctly colored wires to their pin numbers as follows:

   - Orange/White to Pin 1
   - Orange to Pin 2

- Green/White to Pin 3
- Blue to Pin 4
- White/Blue to Pin 5
- Green to Pin 6
- White/Brown to Pin 7
- Brown to Pin 8

 The pin-out in this task represents the ANSI/TIA/EIA 568A standard. You could also use pin-outs based on the 568B standard as long as both ends of the cable use the same standard.

10. Insert the wires into the open end of the RJ-45 connector, making sure the wires are straight across ½ inch from the wire jacket.
11. Locate the crimp tool.
12. Insert the RJ-45 connector into the crimp tool.

 Step 12 is the most difficult part of the process. You have to hold the wires in the RJ-45 connector in the correct order, making sure the connection remains firm while you hold the connector in the crimp tool and use the grips of the tool to clamp down on the connector.

13. Press the handles of the crimp tool firmly together and hold with the RJ-45 inside the tool.
14. Release the pressure on the handles and remove the connector.
15. Look closely at the RJ-45 connector and verify that the wires are in the correct order and that the pin connectors are making good contact with the wires.

 The connectors are usually clear plastic so you can see through them.

16. Locate the other end of the cable and repeat steps 1 through 15 with this end.

 The pin-out order on both ends of a straight-through cable is identical.

TESTING THE NEWLY MADE CABLE

1. Locate the new cable.

2. Connect one end to the NIC port of a PC.

3. Connect the other end to an active switch.

4. Verify that there is at least one other computer connected to the switch or hub.

 Both computers will have to be configured with IP addresses that are on the same subnet. If you are using a DHCP server on the network, see Task 3.3, "Configuring PCs to Use Dynamic Addressing." Otherwise, you'll need to configure the IP addresses of both PCs manually.

5. Open a command-prompt window on one of the computers.

6. Ping the IP address of the other computer.

 See Task 3.5, "Installing a Network Printer," and review steps 1 through 5 in the section "Verifying the Printer's Network Connection" if you aren't sure how to ping another computer.

Criteria for Completion

You will have successfully made a straight-through cable when you have gone through steps 1 through 6 in the section "Testing the Newly Made Cable" and successfully pinged one computer from the other.

 See Task 3.8, "Testing Network Cables," for more information.

 If the cable you made does not work, the most likely cause is that either the order of wires in one or both connectors is wrong or some of the wires in the connector are not in contact with their corresponding pins. In either event, the way to proceed is to cut off both RJ-45 connectors and repeat the task until you have successfully built a cable. I recommend that you establish a "track record" of successfully building a number of cables to firmly establish that you have acquired this skill.

Task 3.7: Making a Crossover Cable

To make a crossover cable, you use the same skills you use to make a straight-through cable. (See Task 3.6.) However, the purpose of a crossover cable is different. Whereas you use a straight-through cable to connect dissimilar devices in a network directly together, you use a crossover cable to connect two like devices. The simplest form of networking is connecting two PCs together using a crossover cable. As long as both computers have IP addresses on the same subnet, they'll be able to communicate. You won't often have to make a crossover cable as a PC tech, but the occasion does sometimes come up. As mentioned in the previous task, newer networking devices can autosense the cable type and adjust to allow a connection.

Scenario

The folks in the IT department have been trying to connect a new high-speed cable modem to a server using a straight-through cable but they aren't getting a link light. After consulting the documentation for the modem, they discover that the device acts like a server and they'll need to use a crossover cable to make the connection between both devices and begin testing. You have been assigned the task of making the crossover cable.

Scope of Task

Duration

This task should take about 10 to 15 minutes, especially if you've been practicing Task 3.6 sufficiently.

Setup

You can use the same setup you used for Task 3.6.

Caveat

The caveat for this task is the same as for Task 3.6.

Procedure

This task will show you the process of making a crossover cable.

Equipment Used

See Task 3.6. You will need exactly the same equipment to complete this task.

Details

This task will take you through the steps necessary to make and test a crossover patch cable.

Constructing a Crossover Cable

PREPARING TO MAKE THE CROSSOVER CABLE

1. Locate your tools.
2. Arrange your tools on your workbench.
3. Locate the RJ-45 connectors.
4. Arrange two RJ-45 connectors on your workbench.
5. Locate a length of Cat 5 or Cat 5e cable.
6. If using a spool of cable, cut away a length of cable from the spool using the wire-cutting tool.
7. Locate a diagram of the pin-out for a crossover cable.

 The pin-outs for each end of the cable are different. See the subsequent diagram for details.

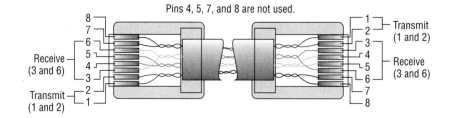

Pins 4, 5, 7, and 8 are not used.

Pin Number		Wire Color		Crossed-Over			Pin Number		Wire Color
Pin 1	→	Orange/White		Wire	Becomes		Pin 1	→	Green/White
Pin 2	→	Orange					Pin 2	→	Green
Pin 3	→	Green/White		1 → 3			Pin 3	→	Orange/White
Pin 4	→	Blue		2 → 6			Pin 4	→	Blue
Pin 5	→	Blue/White		3 → 1			Pin 5	→	Blue/White
Pin 6	→	Green		6 → 2			Pin 6	→	Orange
Pin 7	→	Brown/White					Pin 7	→	Brown/White
Pin 8	→	Brown					Pin 8	→	Brown

MAKING THE CABLE ENDS

1. Locate the wire stripper.
2. Hold out one end of the cable.
3. Use the wire stripper to strip off a length of the cable jacket, leaving the pairs of twisted wires inside intact.

> Remember the necessity of stripping off the correct amount of the cable jacket, as you learned in Task 3.6.

4. Untwist the exposed twisted pairs.

5. Refer to your pin-out diagram to order the colors of the wires correctly.

> Since both ends are pinned out differently, choose one pin-out from the diagram and start with it. Just remember to switch to the other pin-out when constructing the other end of the cable.

6. Trim the wires straight across ½ inch from the wire jacket.

7. Locate an RJ-45 connector.

8. Locate pin 1 in the connector.

> Refer to Task 3.6 to find out how to locate pin 1.

9. If you selected the left-hand pin-out scheme in the previous diagram, orient the correctly colored wires to their pin numbers as follows:

- Orange/White to Pin 1
- Orange to Pin 2
- Green/White to Pin 3
- Blue to Pin 4
- Blue/White to Pin 5
- Green to Pin 6
- Brown/White to Pin 7
- Brown to Pin 8

10. Insert the wires into the open end of the RJ-45 connector, making sure the wires are straight across ½ inch from the wire jacket.

11. Locate the crimp tool.

12. Insert the RJ-45 connector into the crimp tool.

13. Press the handles of the crimp tool firmly together and hold with the RJ-45 inside the tool.

14. Release the pressure on the handles and remove the connector.

15. Look closely at the RJ-45 connector and verify that the wires are in the correct order and that the pin connectors are making good contact with the wires.

16. Locate the other end of the cable and repeat steps 1 through 8.

17. If you pinned out the first end of the cable as described in step 9, orient the correctly colored wires to their pin numbers as follows:

- Green/White to Pin 1
- Green to Pin 2
- Orange/White to Pin 3
- Blue to Pin 4
- Blue/White to Pin 5
- Orange to Pin 6
- Brown/White to Pin 7
- Brown to Pin 8

18. Repeat steps 10 through 15.

The pin-out in step 9 represents the ANSI/TIA/EIA 568B standard.

The pin-out in step 17 represents the ANSI/TIA/EIA 568A standard.

TESTING THE NEWLY MADE CABLE

1. Locate two PCs to use for the test.

2. Verify that they both have been manually configured to have IP addresses on the same subnet.

Since these computers are currently not networked, they will not be able to receive dynamic addressing from a DHCP server.

3. Connect one end of the crossover cable to the first computer's NIC port.

4. Connect the other end of the cable to the second computer's NIC port.

5. At one computer, open a command emulator and ping the other PC's IP address.

See Task 3.5, "Installing a Network Printer," and review steps 1 through 5 in the section "Verifying the Printer's Network Connection" if you aren't sure how to ping another computer.

Criteria for Completion

You will have successfully completed this task when you have completed steps 1 through 5 in the section "Testing the Newly Made Cable" and were able to ping the other computer.

 See Task 3.8, "Testing Network Cables," for more information.

Task 3.8: Testing Network Cables

A wide variety of network-cable testers is available. Depending on how detailed a test you want the equipment to run, they can cost anywhere from $35 to $3,500. The simplest device is a single unit that both ends of the cable connect to and that verifies the point-to-point wiring of all eight wires in the cable. You can also purchase adapters to test crossover cables. This sort of device allows you to test a cable's functioning without having to connect it to a computer or switch.

Scenario

You have made several straight-through cables to be used to connect some new servers to the patch panel in the server room. (See the scenario for Task 3.6.) You now need to test them to make sure they are functional.

Scope of Task

Duration

This task should take you only a few minutes.

Setup

No special setup is needed, except you will need at least one of the cables you constructed in Task 3.6.

Caveat

This task shows the use of a generic cable tester. The device you use may function differently. Refer to the manual for your device for details.

Procedure

This task will teach you how to use a cable tester to test the functioning of a straight-through cable.

Equipment Used

In addition to a straight-through cable, you'll need a cable tester. You can purchase such a device at any computer- or electronics-supply store.

Details

This task will walk you through the process of testing a straight-through patch cable to determine if it functions correctly.

Using a Cable Tester to Test the Straight-Through Cable

1. Locate the cable tester.
2. Power up the unit.

 Most of these devices require a 9-volt battery to operate. The battery has to be purchased separately.

3. Locate the cable you want to test.
4. Insert one end of the cable into an RJ-45 port on the tester.
5. Insert the other end of the cable into the other RJ-45 port on the tester.
6. Review the operation of the eight LED lights on the front of the tester.

 If all eight lights flash continually in sequence, the cable is sound. If a light fails to light up, it indicates that the wire number of that light does not have a connection.

 If one of the LED lights fails to illuminate, the most common cause is that the numbered wire for that light was not secured to the corresponding RJ-45 pin in one of the connectors.

Criteria for Completion

You will have successfully completed this task when you have used the tester to determine whether all eight pins of the cable are connected.

For this task, the cable doesn't have to be functional for you to be successful. You just need to be able to use the tester to determine the cable's status.

Task 3.9: Setting Up a Mail Account

One of the most common duties you'll have as a PC tech is setting up email accounts for new employees. After you do it a number of times it'll become old hat, but the first few times, you'll be carefully following the instructions given to you by your supervisor. This task will show you the procedure for setting up Outlook to use an Exchange server to access email; however, the specifics such as the hostname of the Exchange server will have to be provided by your IT department.

Scenario

A new user in the accounting department needs to have her email account set up for her. You have been assigned to perform this task. You report to her cubicle, have her log on to her computer, and then sit down at the keyboard to begin the process.

Scope of Task

Duration

This task should take about 15 minutes.

Setup

Short of having an Exchange Server handy, it will be difficult for you to comply with all of the steps in this task. If you have Microsoft Outlook installed on your computer, you can follow along with the steps. Because there won't be an Exchange server available, however, the account you create won't be functional.

You may have gone through a similar process using Outlook to set up your email account with your ISP's mail server. Most, but not all, of the steps are the same.

This task was written using Outlook 2003, but you should be able to successfully perform this task using other versions of Outlook. Also, a Windows XP computer was used during the creation of this task.

Caveat

The trapdoors in this task have to do with having the correct information, such as the hostname or IP address of the Exchange Server. If you don't have the correct information or if you input it incorrectly, you will not be able to successfully create the user's account.

Procedure

This task will show you how to use Outlook to create a mail account for a user on an Exchange server.

Equipment Used

You will need no special equipment to complete this task.

Details

This task takes you through the step-by-step process of creating a new user account in Outlook that will create a mail account on an Exchange server.

Creating a User Email Account in Outlook for an Exchange Server

1. Sitting at the user's computer, click Start ≻ Control Panel.
2. Double-click the Mail applet.

You can create an Exchange Server account only by opening the Mail applet in Control Panel.

3. In the Mail Setup box, click E-mail Accounts.
4. Click the Add a New E-mail Account radio button.
5. Click Next.
6. Click the Microsoft Exchange Server radio button.
7. Click Next.

8. Under Exchange Server Settings, type the hostname of the Exchange server in the Microsoft Exchange Server field.

9. Type the user's name in the format *last name, first name* in the User Name box.

In step 9, you can click the Check Name button to verify that there is a domain account for this user.

10. Click Next.

11. Click Yes when you receive the message stating that mail from the Microsoft Exchange Server will be delivered to the Personal Folder on the local computer.

Outlook will make a connection to the Exchange server and verify the account name. When the process is finished, Outlook will start and the user will be prompted to log on.

Criteria for Completion

You will have successfully completed this task when the user can log on to the Exchange server from Outlook and retrieve her mail.

If you were following along with the steps in Outlook without having an Exchange server available, the setup would terminate when Outlook couldn't connect to the Exchange server after step 11.

Task 3.10: Joining a Computer to a Domain

When a new user is assigned to a new computer, the computer will need to become a domain member in order to access all of the resources in the Windows Active Directory domain. This is a pretty straightforward task, but it does require that you have domain administrator rights and the name of the domain for the computer to join. This is a fairly common task along with setting up a mail account (see Task 3.9), so you'll quickly get used to doing this.

Scenario

A new user has been hired in the marketing department. A new computer has been installed for him but it needs to be joined to the Active Directory domain for the company. You have been assigned to perform this task.

Scope of Task

Duration

This task takes around 15 to 20 minutes.

Setup

You'll need Windows Server 2003 or Windows Server 2008 running on your network as a domain controller, and a client computer to successfully finish this task.

You can receive a free trial version of Windows Server 2003 by going to http://technet.microsoft.com/en-us/windowsserver/bb430831.aspx.

You can receive a free trial version of Windows Server 2008 by going to www.microsoft.com/windowsserver2008/en/us/trial-software.aspx.

This task was created using a Windows XP Professional computer and a Windows Server 2003 server.

Caveat

When joining a computer to a domain, you must log in with credentials of someone who has permission to create a computer domain member. Your supervisor will provide you with the correct username and password.

Procedure

This task will show you how to join a client computer to a domain.

Equipment Used

No special equipment will be needed for this task.

Details

This task will show you the steps necessary to join a client computer to a Windows Active Directory domain.

Joining a Computer to a Domain

JOINING A WINDOWS COMPUTER TO THE ACTIVE DIRECTORY DOMAIN

1. Sitting at the computer you want to join to the domain, log on as the local administrator or have the user log on using his account.

2. Right-click My Computer.

3. Click Properties.

4. In the System Properties box, click the Computer Name tab.

5. Click Change.

6. Click the Domain radio button.

7. Type the name of the domain in the Domain field.

8. Click OK.

9. In the User Name field, type the name of an account with rights to join a computer to the domain.

10. In the Password field, type the correct password for that account.

11. Click OK.

12. When the Welcome to the Domain dialog box appears, click OK.

13. When you are prompted to restart your computer, click OK.

14. When the next dialog box appears, asking if you want to restart the computer now, click Yes.

> The computer will reboot when you click Yes in step 14.

VERIFYING THAT THE COMPUTER JOINED THE DOMAIN

1. When the computer reboots, in the Log On to Windows box, click the Log On To drop-down menu and select the domain name.

2. Make sure your username and password are correctly input.

3. Click OK.

4. Once you are logged in, right-click My Computer.

5. Click Properties.

6. In the System Properties box, click the Computer Name tab.

7. Notice that the Full Computer Name field now includes the name of the domain the computer has just joined.

Criteria for Completion

You will have successfully completed this task when you have joined the computer to the domain and have verified it as outlined in the last portion of this task.

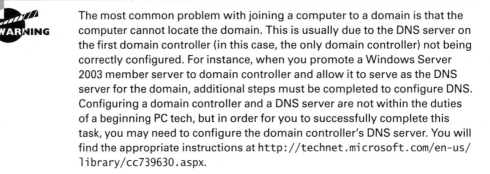

The most common problem with joining a computer to a domain is that the computer cannot locate the domain. This is usually due to the DNS server on the first domain controller (in this case, the only domain controller) not being correctly configured. For instance, when you promote a Windows Server 2003 member server to domain controller and allow it to serve as the DNS server for the domain, additional steps must be completed to configure DNS. Configuring a domain controller and a DNS server are not within the duties of a beginning PC tech, but in order for you to successfully complete this task, you may need to configure the domain controller's DNS server. You will find the appropriate instructions at `http://technet.microsoft.com/en-us/library/cc739630.aspx`.

Task 3.11: Creating a User in Active Directory

All resources in an Active Directory domain are considered objects. This includes computers, printers, groups, organizational units, and users. In order for a user to be identified in the domain (let's say another user wants to locate them using Active Directory), that user must be added to Active Directory on a domain controller (DC). This process can be done using the Remote Desktop Web Connection web interface or locally at any DC in the domain. This is a fairly routine task. On the heels of joining a computer to the domain for a new user, you now add the user to Active Directory.

Scenario

Now that you have joined the new employee's computer to the domain (see Task 3.10), you must add him to Active Directory at a domain controller. You go to the server room and sit at the keyboard of a domain controller. You log on using the domain administrator's credentials and get to work.

Scope of Task

Duration

This task should take about 10 minutes.

Setup

You will need to be working with a domain controller to successfully complete this task. See Task 3.10 for instructions on how to acquire an evaluation copy of Windows Server 2003 or Windows Server 2008.

 This task was created using a Windows XP Professional computer and a Windows Server 2003 server.

Caveat

Assuming you have rights to log on to the DC and you have all of the relevant information regarding the new user, this task should go smoothly.

Procedure

This task will teach you how to add a new user to an Active Directory domain.

Equipment Used

No special equipment is required to complete this task.

Details

You will be shown the proper steps for accessing a domain controller and adding a new user to the domain.

Accessing Active Directory Users and Computers to Add a User

1. Sitting at a domain controller, click Start ➢ Administrative Tools ➢ Active Directory Users and Computers.

2. Expand the domain name.

3. Click on the Users folder.

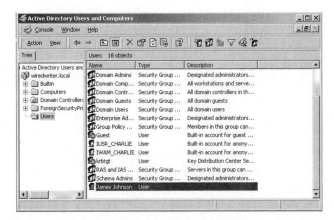

4. Right-click the Users folder.

5. Click New.

6. Click User.

7. In the New Object – User box in the First Name field, type the user's first name.

8. In the Last Name field, type the user's last name.

9. Verify that the user's first and last names are correct in the Full Name field.

10. In the User Logon Name field, type the user's logon name.

 If a user's full name is "Charles Emerson Winchester," for example, his logon name for step 10 could be "cewinchester."

 Notice that the domain name is appended in the field after the User Logon Name field in the System Properties box on the Computer Name tab after the computer has been joined to the domain.

11. Click Next.

12. In the Password field, type the new user's temporary password.

13. In the Confirm Password field, type the password again.

 Make sure the password you enter in step 12 is of sufficient length and complexity to be accepted by the domain controller. If it isn't, you won't be allowed to complete the process of creating the user.

14. Check the User Must Change Password at Next Logon check box.

Checking the check box in step 14 is a security precaution. You must inform the user of his temporary password and that the system will force him to change his password to one no one knows when he first logs in.

 See Task 2.24, "Resetting Passwords," for more details about changing passwords.

15. Click Next.

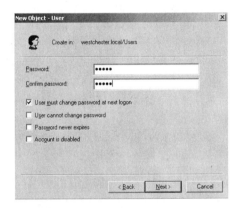

16. When the confirmation box appears, review your selections and click Finish.

17. The user is created and his name is displayed in the Active Directory Users and Computers main pane.

18. Close all open dialog boxes.

19. Log off the domain controller.

Criteria for Completion

You will have successfully completed this task when the domain controller confirms that the new user was added to Active Directory.

Task 3.12: Mapping Network Cables

Tracing and documenting network cables is another of those mundane jobs that try a tech's soul, but it absolutely must be done. If you've ever been in a server room, you probably could describe the experience as visiting a nest of snakes. Ethernet cables are everywhere, and sometimes not particularly well contained. Even when cable-management efforts such as plastic ties and rack-mounted brackets are used, you still often have trouble telling where a cable plugged into a patch panel terminates. Unless you've been keeping records since the network was first built and updating them diligently after every change, you have only one alternative—trace and document the mess all at once.

This process isn't limited to the server room. You also have to know which patch-panel port is used to connect every end-user machine and any other device physically on the network. This means not only crawling around the floor of the server room, but also crawling under users' desks (you have no idea what you may find under there). The alternative, doing nothing, means that if an interruption of network services occurs or a user says they can't connect to the network, you will have one very difficult time locating the single, specific cable that leads from the user's computer to the patch panel and to the switch.

Scenario

There is no current documentation for the network-cable connections from the several patch panels servicing multiple switches and where those cables terminate in the server room. You have been assigned the task of physically tracing each cable, discovering where each one terminates, labeling each cable at both ends, and ultimately documenting the cabling scheme.

Scope of Task

Duration

Depending on the size of your company's network, this project could take weeks (working part-time on it every day...remember, you have other jobs to do as well). In a small setup like a home lab, the project might take 30 minutes to an hour, including labeling and documentation.

Setup

It's difficult to simulate this task in a home or small lab environment, at least in scope. If you have two or three computers linked through a small five-port switch, it shouldn't take much time at all to trace down the cable connections; however, you can still follow the steps by labeling each end of the cable and creating a simple diagram of your cabling scheme.

Caveat

In a small home network, this task should virtually be a piece of cake. In a large corporate IT department, the biggest issue is not getting confused as to which cable goes where. Bad documentation is worse than none at all.

Procedure

This task will teach you the process of tracing network cabling, then labeling the cables and documenting the overall layout.

Equipment Used

You'll need something to label the cable ends with. The easiest and most inexpensive way is to get a roll of masking tape and a marker. In a production environment, you'd be using a label maker for this task. Documenting the overall cable scheme will require no more than a pencil and paper. If you have Microsoft Visio or some other diagramming software available, you can use that as well. In a business environment, you'd use a software tool to create the diagram. You'll probably need a pencil and small notepad to write down information as you are tracing cables.

Details

This task will take you through the process of going from one end of a network cable to the other, identifying where the cable connects at each end, labeling each end with information that will identify the cable, and diagramming the entire layout when finished.

Tracing and Documenting a Network-Cable Scheme

TRACING AND LABELING NETWORK CABLES

1. Locate the first cable connection in the first port of the first patch panel.

 There is most likely sufficient documentation identifying which patch-panel port goes to which switch port.

2. Use your pencil and pad to note the number of the patch panel and the patch-panel port number.

For port number 1 on patch panel A, you could use the designation A01.

3. Grasping the cable, physically trace it through its path in the server room until you locate the other end.

Tracing a cable's path sounds easier than it is. Cables have the annoying habit of getting tangled with many other cables, stuck behind heavy server racks and other equipment, and, unfortunately, being the same battleship-gray color as every other cable in the room. This task will be dusty and noisy (all of the motors and fans in a server room make enough noise to be deafening), and you'll most likely suffer from pinched fingers more than once.

4. Upon locating the other end, make note of the device the cable is connected to and which network interface card (NIC) it is connected to in the event that the device is multihomed.

A multihomed device contains two or more NICs, allowing the device to be connected to more than one network segment.

5. Retrieve your labeling device.

6. Label each end of the cable with an identifier.

The identifier in step 6 could be something like A01-SVR01.

7. Write the information on your pad. This will be the basis for your diagram.

8. Repeat this process for every cable in the room.

Quite a number of cables will be directed upward through a space in the ceiling tile and into the plenum space (where the air ducts and structural framework above the ceiling are located). These cables travel to other parts of the building, ultimately connecting with computers, printers, and other devices in various cubicle and office spaces. This task will not have you trace those cables.

This task can be performed much more quickly using a tone generator and probe, also known as a fox and hound, but explaining how to use that equipment is outside the scope of this task.

TURNING NOTES INTO DOCUMENTATION

1. Sitting at your computer, open your diagramming software.

If you are doing this in a home lab, a pencil and paper will suffice for step 1.

2. Consult your notes.
3. Begin using the diagramming software to create a logical diagram of your network's connections.

A logical diagram represents relationships between devices, not their actual locations relative to each other and to scale.

The following graphic represents a logical diagram created with open-source software called Dia and transformed into a TIF file by another open-source program named GIMP. Both applications are available for free download for Windows and Linux computers. For Windows-compatible programs, you can find Dia at http://dia-for-windows.en.softonic.com/; you can find GIMP at www.gimp.org/windows/.

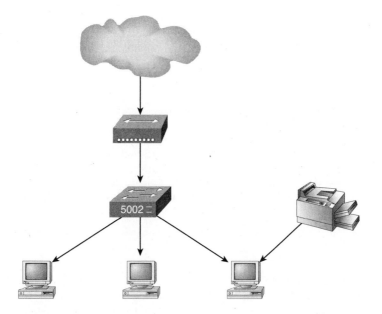

4. After you have the various objects in place, begin to label each port with an identifying label.

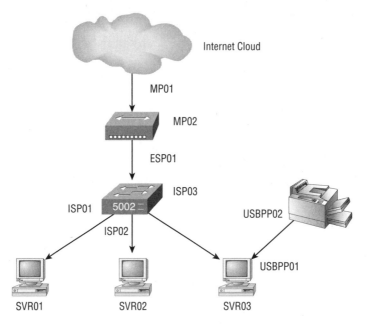

5. Continue to create the diagram until all of the ports and connections are accounted for.

You may have to make more than one diagram to contain the multitude of connections.

In the previous diagram, a particular convention was used to identify ports and connection types. For example, MP01 is Modem Port 01 and indicates the network's gateway port to the Internet. ESP01 is External Switch Port 01 and indicates the switch's outward-pointing port to the modem. You can develop whatever convention you desire, but in a production environment you will be provided with a convention by your supervisor.

Criteria for Completion

You will have successfully completed this task when both ends of each cable in your network are labeled so that anyone reading the labels would be able to identify the termination points. Next, you must have created sufficient and accurate notes with which to make a logical network diagram. Finally, you must have created an accurate diagram that shows all of the network connections, including their identification labels.

This task has presented a simple form of network diagramming. Network diagramming can become very detailed, especially when you are documenting an enterprise-level data center.

Task 3.13: Setting Up a Local User ID

Although it is important to know how to set up a user ID on an Active Directory domain, you must also know how to set up a user account on a local machine. For example, you may need to configure a computer for more than one end user to log on to locally. Alternately, you may need to set up an account for IT staff to be able to log on to the local machine with administrator rights without using the account named Administrator.

This task was created using a Windows XP computer. See Task 2.25, "Creating a New Local User in Windows Vista," for the steps involved using a Windows Vista computer.

Scenario

Two users in the clerical department have a job-share arrangement with a single position. One user accesses the computer to do work in the morning and another user needs a separate logon to do her work in the afternoon. You have been assigned to create the second user's local account ID.

Scope of Task

Duration

This task should take about 10 minutes.

Setup

There is no special setup for this task.

Caveat

In a production environment, it is unusual to create local accounts for users. Typically, all users log on to the domain and receive access to services via Active Directory. You are more likely to create a local administrator account under an innocuous name to allow IT staff access. In a smaller company or branch office, however, users may need access to the local machine to perform specific tasks.

Procedure

This task will show you how to create a local account on a Windows XP computer.

Equipment Used

No special equipment will be necessary for this task.

Details

You will be taken through the necessary steps to create a new local user account on a Windows XP computer.

Creating a Local User ID Account

SETTING UP THE NEW LOCAL USER ACCOUNT ON A COMPUTER

1. Sitting at the computer, click Start ➤ Control Panel.

For this task, it is assumed Control Panel is in Classic view.

2. Double-click the User Accounts applet.
3. In the User Accounts box, click Create a New Account.
4. Type the name of the new account in the available field.
5. Click Next.
6. On the Pick an Account Type page, click the Limited radio button.

This user will not need to be the administrator of the local machine.

7. Click Create Account.

![Screenshot of the User Accounts window showing the "Pick an account type" page with Computer administrator and Limited radio buttons, Limited selected, and a description of limited account capabilities, with Back, Create Account, and Cancel buttons.]

When you click Create Account, the user account is created and displayed in the User Accounts box.

SETTING UP THE NEW ACCOUNT PASSWORD

1. In the User Accounts box, click the new user's icon.

2. Click Create a Password.

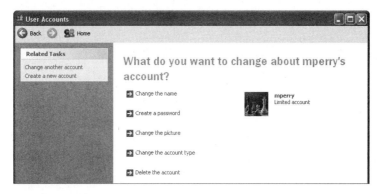

3. Type the user's password in the Type a New Password field.

4. Type the same password again in the Type the New Password Again to Confirm field.

Although it is available, I don't recommend that you use the Password Hint field because the "hint" would be visible to anyone who uses the computer.

5. Click Create Password.

After you click Create Password, the password for the new account is created on the local machine and you are returned to the Change Account page for this user.

6. Close all windows on this machine.

7. Log out.

8. Have the new user log on to the local machine to verify her credentials.

Criteria for Completion

You will have successfully completed this task when you have created the new account and the user can log on using the credentials you have created.

Task 3.14: Adding a Network Peripheral-Port Device to a PC

Although most modern PCs come with ample peripheral ports for average use, sometimes a user needs additional USB or other port types added. Also, older PCs are outfitted with fewer USB ports and a user might need to use additional USB devices. Today, users often have a USB cradle for their handheld, use a local USB printer, have an external USB hard drive for additional storage or backups, and attach additional devices as well. You will occasionally need to install additional peripheral ports on a PC to allow the user the ability to create a larger "local" network, or PAN.

 A PAN, or personal area network, is usually composed of a collection of devices that are connected to a single PC via USB or wireless. A PAN gives an end user the ability to create simultaneous, short-range network connections to a computer for data storage, printing, and other tasks.

Scenario

A manager in accounting needs additional USB ports on her PC to network several personal devices with her computer. Instead of choosing to install a USB hub, your supervisor gives you an internal five-port USB 2.0 adapter PCI card. You are to install the module into an open PCI slot, install the software, and test the unit. You gather your tools and proceed to the manager's office to do the install.

Scope of Task

Duration

This task should take about 30 minutes.

Setup

This task is somewhat similar to Task 1.3, "Installing a PCI Card," so you can review the steps in that task. If you are using the PCI Express bus, see Task 1.4, "Installing a PCI Express Card." However, this task also requires you to install the driver software and test the unit by attaching multiple USB devices to the module's ports.

Caveat

The example in this task uses a USB 2.0 device; although these modules are supposed to be backward-compatible with USB 1.0, it is advisable to test all devices by attaching them to module ports and making sure they function properly before you call it "a job well done."

 USB 3.0 standard devices are expected to be available for consumer purchase in 2010. Windows 7 and Linux drivers for USB 3.0 are currently under development and are expected to be available sometime in 2009 (and may be available by the time this book is in print).

Procedure

This task will teach you how to install the hardware and software for a network port module and how to test the device to make sure it works.

Equipment Used

You'll need one or two screwdrivers and your ESD equipment since you'll be installing the device inside the box. To properly test your success, you'll need a collection of USB devices (ideally) to attach to the PCI card once it's installed and operational.

Details

This task will take you through the steps required to install a multiport network peripheral device, install the drivers and any other required software, attach multiple USB devices to the ports of a multiport USB PCI card, and then test their functioning.

Installing and Testing a Multiport Network PCI Card

INSTALLING THE PCI NETWORK CARD IN A PCI SLOT

1. Verify that the PC is powered down.
2. Unplug the power cord from the PC's power supply.
3. Remove the screws attaching the access panel to the PC.
4. Remove the access panel.

 Take ESD precautions before working inside the machine.

5. Locate an available PCI slot in the PC.

6. Remove the screw or screws attaching the PCI-slot cover to the PC's frame.

7. Remove the PCI-slot cover.

8. Locate the PCI card, which should be stored in an antistatic bag.

9. Carefully remove the module from its packaging.

10. Examine the unit to determine if there is any obvious damage.

11. Assuming there is no damage, slowly guide the module into the PC case.

12. Orient the PCI pins on the module over the PCI slot.

13. Gently but firmly push the module in place.

14. Make sure the USB ports are correctly aligned at the back of the PC.

15. Use the screw you removed with the PCI-slot cover to secure the PCI card in place.

16. Replace the PC's access panel.

17. Replace the screws securing the panel to the PC's frame.

18. Plug the power cord back into the PC's power supply.

INSTALLING THE NETWORK-MODULE SOFTWARE

1. Locate the CD that came with the card.

2. Locate the documentation that came with the card.

3. Read any special instructions on how to install the software.

Some devices require that you use the manufacturer's own installer rather than a Windows wizard to install the software.

4. When the PC powers up, Windows will detect the new hardware and display a message indicating that new hardware has been installed.

5. Open the CD or DVD drive door.

6. Insert the disc.

7. Close the door.

When you close the drive door, the disc should autoplay and launch an installation wizard. For this example, the manufacturer's installer is used, so if Windows opens an installer wizard, close it.

8. Follow the instructions on the manufacturer's installer wizard.

9. When you are finished, you will be prompted to reboot the PC.

TESTING THE NETWORK CARD

1. Once the PC has rebooted, locate the devices the user wants attached to the new card.

> It is best if the user is present when you are attaching devices, because she will have to advise you of the exact setup she wants.

2. Plug in the first device.

3. Verify that it is recognized.

> The process of verifying recognition will be different depending on the devices involved; no one method is used. A digital camera may be recognized differently than a USB printer.

4. Follow steps 2 and 3 with the next device.

5. As you add devices, verify that units previously connected to the module are still being recognized.

> If you have a situation in which a previously connected device becomes unrecognized when you attach a subsequent device, it may indicate a resource conflict. This would most likely occur as you install the PCI card because the USB controller uses one set of system resources (I/O, IRQ, DMA) for all devices controlled on the USB bus.

6. Continue to follow steps 2 through 5 with each device you attach to the network module until finished.

7. Have the end user access the devices and use them the way she normally does and make sure that she can operate them as required.

Criteria for Completion

You will have successfully completed this task when you have installed the module hardware and software and tested the performance of all attached peripheral devices, making sure they work.

Task 3.15: Setting Up VPN on a PC

VPN, or virtual private networking, is a method used by a computer to transmit data securely over a public network such as the Internet. It is often used by traveling business people who need to connect to the home office from remote locations. It is also used by end users to telecommute or work while physically at home by connecting to the work network via VPN.

As a PC tech, you will be required to configure PCs and laptops to use VPN to connect to servers at the home office. From the users' point of view, it will be as if they were connected to the company's internal LAN when in fact, over the Internet, they could be working 10 miles or 1,000 miles away.

Scenario

One of the marketing executives needs to work from home several times a week. You have been assigned to go to his home and set up his PC to connect to the office LAN using VPN. You have been provided with all of the configuration information necessary to complete the task. You arrive at the executive's home and are shown to the computer you will be working on.

Scope of Task

Duration

This task should take about 15 to 20 minutes.

Setup

It would be ideal if you have a server setup that you could actually connect to using VPN, but if not, you'll still be able to follow the steps in this task.

Caveat

To set up a PC to use VPN, you must have the correct server setup at the home office. The server system will need to be configured with a VPN IP-address pool so the connection has access to an address on the local network segment. A VPN "tunnel" will also need to be set up for the specific connection that the user will access using an encryption protocol such as Point-to-Point Tunneling Protocol (PPTP).

 Configuring VPN on the server side is not a task usually assigned to a beginning PC tech, and therefore the procedure is not covered in this book.

Procedure

This task will teach you how to configure a VPN connection on a Windows XP computer.

Equipment Used

No special equipment is required for this task.

Details

This task will take you step-by-step through the process of configuring a Windows XP Professional computer to securely connect to a VPN server over the Internet.

You can use either XP Professional or Home editions to establish a VPN connection; however, XP Home cannot join to a domain.

Configuring a Windows XP Professional Computer to Use VPN

SETTING UP VPN ON A WINDOWS XP PRO PC

1. Sitting at the computer and logged on as the user, click Start ➤ Control Panel.

For this example, Control Panel is set to Classic view.

2. Double-click the Network Connections applet.
3. When the Network Connections box opens, click Create a New Network Connection.

Create a New Network Connection is located in the upper-left corner of the Network Connections box.

4. When the New Connection wizard launches, click Next.

5. Click the Connect to the Network at My Workplace radio button.

6. Click Next.

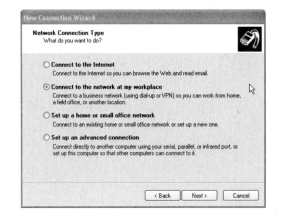

7. Click the Virtual Private Network Connection radio button.

8. Click Next.

9. Type the name of the connection in the Company Name field and click Next.

> The name used in the Company Name field should be unique. It is suggested that you use the same name as the one used to configure the VPN tunnel on the server side.

10. Click the Do Not Dial the Initial Connection radio button on the Public Network screen and click Next.

The choice in step 10 is available only if you already have a VPN configured.

For this task, it is assumed you are using a high-speed Internet connection.

11. When the VPN Server Selection screen appears, type either the hostname or IP address of the VPN server.

In step 11, it is best to type in the IP address of the server.

12. Click Next.

13. When the Completing the New Connection Wizard screen appears, click Finish.

You have the option to add a shortcut to the VPN connection to the Desktop by clicking the appropriate check box on the final page. This option is advisable.

TESTING THE VPN CONNECTION

The Connect to the VPN Connection logon box appears right after the end of the previous step. At this point, it's best to talk the user through this part of the process so he can learn how to make the VPN connection quickly.

1. Have the user type his username in the User Name field.

2. Have the user type his password in the Password field.

The user would have been provided with this information by the IT-department supervisor ahead of time.

3. Have the user click Connect.

4. After the VPN server has verified the user's credentials, he will be connected to all of the shared folders he has rights to on the work network.

Criteria for Completion

You will have successfully completed this task when the PC has been configured to use a VPN connection and is able to successfully connect to the remote server.

If you do not have access to a remote VPN server, the task is considered successfully completed when you are finished with the New Connection wizard.

Task 3.16: Setting Up Dial-Up Networking

In-house, if you lose a connection to a server in the server room, you can usually link to the server via a console session using a serial port. With a remote server at a branch office, this isn't so easy. If you lose the primary connection to the server over the Internet, you usually have no alternative networking route to log in to the server and diagnose the problem.

That's where dial-up redundancy comes in. You can configure the server to use a dial-up connection as a redundant link in the event that the Ethernet connection goes down. Here's how it works.

Scenario

One of the company's branch offices is using a Windows 2000 Server to provide file and print services. Since it continues to perform adequately for the branch office's needs, no upgrade has been considered necessary. Occasionally, the main network link between the main and branch office has gone down and your supervisor has decided that a redundant dial-up connection to the remote server from a main office server is required. You have been assigned to go to the server room and set up a link on one of the servers. You've been provided with all of the configuration information you need to accomplish the task. You sit at the server keyboard and get ready to work.

Although it's rare, you will still sometimes see companies using legacy hardware and operating systems to perform low-level tasks, and they will require periodic maintenance and configuration. Being able to work with legacy hardware and software will be a particular asset on those occasions.

Scope of Task

Duration

This task will take about 20 to 30 minutes.

Setup

You will need access to a Windows 2000 Server, Windows Server 2003, or Windows Server 2008 machine.

    This task uses Windows 2000 Server as an example.

Caveat

It is particularly important to make sure this task is done right. In the event of a network outage, the only way to remotely administer the server is through the dial-up connection. If this fails, the server can be accessed only if someone physically travels to the branch office (a considerable distance from the main office) to resolve the issue.

Procedure

This task will show you how to set up a redundant dial-up connection to a Windows 2000 Server machine.

Equipment Used

No special equipment will be necessary for this task.

Details

This task will walk you through the procedural steps of setting up a redundant dial-up network connection on a Windows 2000 Server machine.

Establishing a Redundant Connection Using Dial-Up Routing

CREATING A REDUNDANT CONNECTION TO THE REMOTE SERVER USING DIAL-UP

1. Using the server's keyboard and mouse, click Start ➢ Programs ➢ Administrative Tools ➢ Routing and Remote Access.

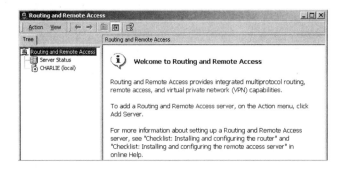

2. Right-click the server name.

3. Click Configure and Enable Routing and Remote Access.

4. When the Routing and Remote Access Server Setup wizard launches, click Next.

5. On the Common Configurations screen, click the Manually Configured Server radio button.

6. Click Next.

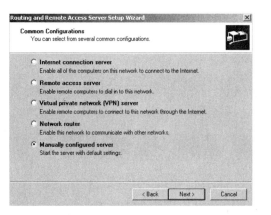

7. When the Completing the Routing and Remote Access Server Setup Wizard screen appears, click Finish.

8. On the Routing and Remote Access screen, click Yes.

 After you complete the steps, the service will take a few moments to start.

CONFIGURING THE DEMAND DIAL INTERFACE

1. Under the server name, right-click Routing Interfaces.

2. Click New Demand-Dial Interface.

3.   When the Demand Dial Interface wizard launches, click Next.

4.   On the Interface Name screen, type the name of the demand-dial interface.

5.   Click Next.

Demand Dial Interface Wizard	☒
Interface Name Select the name by which this new interface will be known.	
Select a name for this demand dial interface. A common practice is to name interfaces after the network or router to which they connect.	
Interface name:	
SRVInt01	
< Back Next > Cancel	

6.   On the Connection Type screen, click the Connect Using a Modem, ISDN Adapter, or Other Physical Device radio button.

7.   Click Next.

Demand Dial Interface Wizard	☒
Connection Type Select the type of demand dial interface you want to create.	
⦿ Connect using a modem, ISDN adapter, or other physical device.	
○ Connect using virtual private networking (VPN)	
< Back Next > Cancel	

8.   On the Protocols and Security screen, check the Route IP Packets on This Interface and the Send a Plain-Text Password if That Is the Only Way to Connect radio buttons.

NOTE   Although it is true that sending a plain-text password is a security risk, it maximizes your ability to quickly log on to this server over a dial-up connection in an emergency.

9.   Click Next.

10. When the Dial Out Credentials screen appears, type the username, domain name, and password (and confirm the password) to this account in the displayed fields.

11. Click Next.

12. When the Completing the Demand Dial Interface Wizard screen appears, click Finish.

 When you have finished, the new demand-dial connection appears in the Routing and Remote Access screen's main pane.

 Unless the dial-in router has a compatible configuration, you will not be able to make a connection between the servers.

Criteria for Completion

You will have successfully completed this task when you have finished setting up the server for demand-dial routing.

Task 3.17: Connecting a PC to a Network Printer

Task 3.5 showed you how to set up a network printer but stopped short of making the connection between a PC and the printer. This task will take up where Task 3.5 left off. As you recall, a network printer is equipped with its own network interface card (NIC) and a built-in print server. Once the printer is installed on the desired network segment, all that's left to do is to set up the PCs to connect to and print from the network printer.

Scenario

You have just finished successfully installing a new network printer in the research department. Now you must verify that the PCs on the local network segment can connect to the printer and print from the device. You go to the first PC and begin the process.

Scope of Task

Duration

This task should take about 10 to 15 minutes.

Setup

Ideally, you'll have a PC on the same network segment as a network printer.

Caveat

With Windows XP and Vista machines, it should be relatively simple to connect to a network printer. You will need to have the hostname or IP address of the print device. If you don't have that information or can't browse to the printer, you won't be successful at this task.

Procedure

This task will show you how to connect a PC to a network printer.

Equipment Used

No special equipment will be needed for this task.

Details

This task will guide you through the steps of connecting a Windows computer to a printer directly connected to the network.

Connecting a Computer to a Network Printer

CREATING A CONNECTION BETWEEN A PC AND THE NETWORK COMPUTER

1. Sitting at the computer, click Start ➤ Printers and Faxes.

Remember, this is a Windows XP Professional computer.

2. Click Add Printer.
3. When the Add Printer wizard launches, click Next.
4. On the Local or Network Printer screen, click the "A network printer, or a printer attached to another computer" radio button.

You could also select Connect to This Printer and enter the hostname or IP address of the printer in the available field.

5. Click Next.

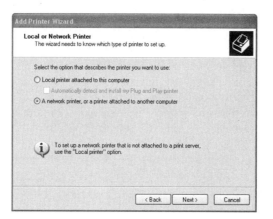

6. Click the Browse for a Printer radio button.

7. Select the name of the desired network printer from the list.

8. Click Next.

9. On the Default Printers screen, select Yes.

10. Click Next.

11. When the Completing the Add Printer screen appears, click Finish.

TESTING THE CONNECTION TO THE NETWORK PRINTER

1. In the Printers box, right-click the newly installed printer.

2. Click Properties.

3. Click Print a Test Page.

4. The Print a Test Page box appears. If the test page prints correctly, click OK.

5. Close the Printers window.

Criteria for Completion

You will have successfully completed this task when you can print a test page from your computer to the network printer.

Task 3.18: Managing Windows Vista Outbound Firewall Settings

One of the issues with the Windows XP firewall is that it could only monitor activity going into your computer. If your computer was already potentially compromised, and an unauthorized application was trying to connect to the Internet, you would have no way of knowing this by using XP's onboard firewall. Third-party firewall applications would be your only way to discover this from within XP. Windows Vista corrects this but presents another problem. By default, all outbound settings are allowed and setting outbound filtering to block specific applications, port numbers, or IP-address ranges requires that they be set manually. This task shows you a simple example of this process.

Scenario

One of your company's branch offices uses six new Windows Vista computers. In addition to the firewall appliance used in the network closet at that office, the office's manager wants each computer's on-board firewall to block outbound traffic for all applications, allowing them to make connections using only specific port numbers. You will perform this task by creating a single new rule in the outbound firewall filter for each Vista computer.

It is possible to create numerous outbound filter rules, but the process is exceptionally detailed and beyond the scope of this book and the A+ certification requirements. This task shows you the level of complexity by describing the configuration of one simple rule.

You have been assigned to configure the outbound firewall filters of the Vista computers and have arrived at the branch office with the necessary instructions, including the specific list of port numbers to be used by the applications on the Vista computers to make outbound connections.

Although the scenario requires that you perform this task on six Vista computers, the requirements of this task are satisfied if you perform the steps on just one such computer.

Scope of Task

Duration

This task should take about 10 to 15 minutes per computer.

Setup

All you'll need is a computer running Windows Vista.

Caveat

There are extreme limitations to configuring the outbound firewall filters for Vista's on-board firewall. The configuration doesn't allow you to create an all-purpose rule that will block all potential malware connections. You can create a series of outbound filter rules, but you need to set up your filters for each specific type of malware, including name, port number, IP-address range, and so on. The process of manually configuring these filters for every possible known threat would take an enormous amount of time.

A good free third-party firewall application that will allow you to set up specific outbound firewall filtering is provided by ZoneAlarm. Find out more at www.zonealarm.com/security/en-us/anti-virus-spyware-free-download.htm.

Procedure

This task will show you how to access the Advanced Security dialog box for the Windows Vista firewall.

Equipment Used

No special equipment will be needed for this task.

Details

This task will guide you through the steps of accessing the outbound filters for Windows Vista's on-board firewall and configuring a new rule.

Configuring the Outbound Filter for the Windows Vista Firewall

VERIFYING THAT THE WINDOWS FIREWALL IS TURNED ON

1. At the computer, click the Windows Vista button.
2. Click Control Panel.
3. Click Security.

4. Click Turn Windows Firewall On or Off.

5. In the Windows Firewall Settings dialog box, on the General tab click the On (Recommended) radio button.

6. Click OK.

ENABLING OUTBOUND FIREWALL FILTERING

1. Click the Windows Vista button.

2. Click Control Panel.

3. Click System and Maintenance.

4. Click Administrative Tools.

5. Double-click Windows Firewall with Advanced Security.

6. In the left-hand menu, click Windows Firewall and Advanced Security.

7. In the main pane, select Windows Firewall Properties.

8. Click the Private Profile tab.

9. Under Firewall State, select Block from the Outbound Connections menu.

10. Click OK.

ALLOWING APPLICATIONS TO MAKE OUTBOUND CONNECTIONS USING SPECIFIC PORTS

1. In the Windows Firewall with Advanced Security dialog box, right-click Outbound Rules in the left-hand pane and then select New Rule.

2. In the Rule Type pane, select Custom and then click Next.

3. In the Program pane, click All Programs and then click Next.

4. In the Protocol and Ports pane, select either TCP or UDP from the Protocol Type menu.

5. Select Specific Ports from the Local Port menu.

6. In the available field, enter the port numbers you were provided with, separated by commas.

7. When finished, click Next.

8. In the Scope pane, accept the default selection, Any IP Address, for both Local IPs and Remote IPs, and then click Next.

9. In the Action pane, accept the default selection of Allow the Connection, and then click Next.

10. In the Profile pane, select the options that are available for the Domain, Private, and Public selections, and then click Next.

11. In the Name pane, enter a name for your new rule in the Name field and enter an optional description of the new rule in the Description field.

12. Click Finish.

13. When the new rule appears in the main pane of the Windows Firewall with Advanced Security dialog box, close all of the dialog boxes you opened.

14. Repeat the process for the other five Vista computers in the office.

Criteria for Completion

You will have successfully completed this task when you have created a new outbound firewall filter rule and it has appeared in the main pane of the Windows Firewall with Advanced Security dialog box.

As you can see by performing these steps, there are many more options available in the configuration of Windows Vista's outbound firewall rule settings, but your duties as a PC tech aren't likely to require that you know how to configure this utility in great detail.

Task 3.19: Monitoring Network Activity with the Windows Vista Firewall

One of the advantages of using the Windows firewall in Vista is that the firewall lets you monitor activity on the network. This allows you to detect potential threats and respond to them before an incident occurs that compromises your PCs (or at least soon afterward). This task involves enabling and then periodically reviewing the Windows Firewall log file. It is a manual rather than an automated process.

Scenario

One of your company's branch offices uses six new Windows Vista computers. You recently completed an assignment, at the request of that office's manager, to configure the Windows firewall on each PC to block all outbound traffic on the computers except for a few specific applications. You receive a second request to enable the log file for the Windows firewall on each computer and demonstrate how to access and view the log files to the manager. In addition to the security applications that are functioning in that office's network closet, the manager wants to make sure that each computer is secure. Your supervisor verifies that this is a proper request and provides you with the information necessary to complete this task.

You make an appointment with the branch-office manager and meet him at the office. Seated at a Windows Vista computer and logged in as a local administrator on the machine, you begin the demonstration.

Scope of Task

Duration

This task should take about 10 to 15 minutes per computer.

Although the scenario requires that you perform this task on six machines, for the purpose of this task you need only complete the steps on one Vista PC.

Setup

All you'll need is a computer running Windows Vista.

The User Account Control (UAC) feature is turned off on the Windows Vista machine used to perform this task.

Caveat

Although enabling and viewing the log files for the Windows firewall isn't a complicated task, it may be difficult to successfully communicate how to properly view the log file, unless the individual has a basic familiarity with the contents of these files and some understanding of network security. While it may be more appropriate for IT staff to perform monitoring functions, you will sometimes see a request from nontechnical managers to be allowed such access as well.

You must be logged into the Windows Vista computer as a local administrator to have the authority to manage the firewall settings. Also, some settings may be unavailable if they are managed by Group Policy.

Procedure

This task will show you how to enable logging for the Windows firewall and how to view the log files.

Equipment Used

No special equipment will be needed for this task.

Details

This task will guide you through the steps of enabling and viewing the log files for the Windows Vista firewall.

Enabling Logging on the Windows Vista Firewall

1. Click the Windows Vista button.

2. Select All Programs.

3. Select Administrative Tools.

4. Select Windows Firewall with Advanced Security.

5. Right-click Windows Firewall with Advanced Security in the console tree.

6. Select Properties.

7. Select the desired tab, such as Domain Profile, Private Profile, or Public Profile.

8. Under Logging, click Customize.

9. Either accept the default path for the log or click Browse and navigate to the desired location.

10. Either accept the default maximum file size for the log of 4096KB or use the up or down arrow to change this value.

11. Perform one of the following:

    ▪ Create a log entry when Windows Firewall drops an incoming network packet by changing Log Dropped Packets to Yes.

    ▪ Create a log entry when Windows Firewall allows an inbound connection by changing Log Successful Connections to Yes.

12. Click OK.

13. Click OK again.

Viewing the Windows Firewall Log File

1. Verify that you are still on the Advanced tab, Security Logging, and in Settings.

2. Under Log Settings, click Save As and save the current log with a name that uniquely identifies the log file.

3. Right-click the name of the log file you just created and then click Open.

4. View the log file in Notepad and when finished, close the text file.

5. Close all of the dialog boxes you opened to accomplish this task.

Criteria for Completion

You will have successfully completed this task when you have enabled logging in the Windows firewall and have successfully demonstrated how to view the log file.

 Viewing the log file right after you enable logging will not show much in the way of information, since the firewall has not been able to collect much data. Waiting a few minutes or an hour will produce more results, depending on the level of network activity.

Phase

4

Troubleshooting and Restoring Computer Systems

Nothing will turn your hair gray faster than troubleshooting problems. Most textbooks serve up a canned set of problems that a five-year-old could solve in their sleep. Real-world problems are quite different, and some of them are unique, with no known cause. Nevertheless, when a cry such as, "I can't print!" or, "Where are my emails?" rings out, you will be expected to investigate and solve the problem.

Each of the tasks that follow is based on trouble tickets from an actual IT department. They are real problems that you could face at any time. This section not only presents the problems and their solutions; it also documents how the solutions were discovered. Computer-system problems come and go, but your problem-solving skills will be a constant in every situation you encounter. Pay close attention to what follows. These tasks could help save you a lot of time and frustration.

The tasks in this phase map to Domains 1, 2, 3, 4, 5, and 6 for the CompTIA A+ Essentials (220-701) exam objectives, and Domains 1, 2, 3, and 4 of the CompTIA Practical Application (220-702) exam objectives.

Task 4.1: Scanning for and Removing Viruses

Despite the best efforts of network-security engineers, occasionally a virus will invade the system and infect at least some of the computers on your network. Although medium- and enterprise-level antivirus and scanning products have the ability to limit network communications to and from a machine suspected of being compromised, once even one computer has been infected, that PC has to be scanned and the invader isolated.

One major difference between home-based and business-based antivirus systems is that an antivirus gateway scans all traffic coming into and going out of the corporate network, attempting to detect malicious software. Each individual business desktop also has the capacity to scan the local system for viruses. Also, although an individual home PC connects to the antivirus vendor's server to download virus definitions, in a business-based system you will have a server set up to download the definitions and then push them out to all of the desktops.

Scenario

The main office network has been attacked by a virus. Although the threat was contained to just a few departments, numerous PCs were compromised. You have been assigned to the design department to perform local virus scans on the desktops and have the detected virus quarantined.

> Advanced antivirus solutions will send the virus to a quarantine folder on the local machine and then send a copy of the virus to a secure folder on the quarantine server.

Scope of Task

Duration

If you are running a scan on the entire hard drive, it could take quite some time. Once the scan is complete and the virus is detected, having it quarantined takes very little time.

Setup

You can easily follow these steps by using your personal computer's antivirus tool; however, you will not have the opportunity to detect and isolate a threat unless your computer has already been compromised.

Caveat

Regardless of the computing environment you are using, it is vital to keep your virus definitions completely current and to have your machines routinely scanned for possible threats.

> The computer you will use for this task must have an antivirus program installed and the program must be configured to download the latest virus definitions and scan the computer on a daily basis.

> If you are not currently running an antivirus program on your computer (and shame on you if you aren't), you can access a free copy of Grisoft's AVG antivirus solution at this URL: http://free.grisoft.com/doc/avg-anti-virus-free/lng/us/tpl/v5.

Procedure

This task will show you how to run a virus scan and how to quarantine any detected threats.

Equipment Used

No special equipment is required for this task.

Details

You will be taken through the steps of scanning a networked PC for threats and isolating any viruses that are detected.

Scanning for and Isolating a Virus

PERFORMING THE SCAN

1. Log on to the computer as an administrator.
2. Double-click the antivirus product icon on the Desktop to open it.
3. Click the Scan for Viruses button.
4. Select the drive or partition you want to scan.
5. Click Scan.

Even if the virus is detected early in the scanning process, allow the scan to run to completion in the event that there is more than one intruder on board.

DETECTING AND QUARANTINING A VIRUS

1. When the scan is complete, review the list of detected threats provided by the antivirus program.
2. Select all of the viruses detected. There may be a Select All button or you can hold down the Ctrl key and use your mouse to click on each threat until they are all highlighted.
3. When offered the option, click Quarantine All.

It's best to quarantine a virus rather than immediately deleting it. The virus may be "living" in a location that contains vital program files for the PC, and deleting the virus can also delete these files. The worst-case scenario is that you will be unable to reboot the computer and load the operating system if you delete the virus and associated files.

4. When offered the option to send a copy of the virus to the quarantine server, click Yes. You will receive a message stating that the virus was successfully quarantined.

5. Verify that the antivirus program is configured to contact the antivirus server and download any available definitions on a daily basis.

6. Verify that the antivirus program is configured to scan the computer on a daily basis.

Criteria for Completion

You will have successfully completed this task when you have completely scanned your computer's hard drive and, if any viruses were detected, you were able to quarantine them.

Task 4.2: Scanning for and Removing Malware

Malicious software, or *malware*, is more than just viruses, Trojan horses, and worms. It also includes keyloggers, spyware, zombies, web-browser hijackers, and any other software types that are designed to be installed on your computer without your knowledge and permission. This software is intended to damage or disrupt as many computers as it can access. The process of scanning for and quarantining malware is substantially similar to the process for using an antivirus program (see Task 4.1). You can use a malware scanner from the same vendor that produces your antivirus solution or you can use a completely different vendor's product.

Scenario

You receive a trouble ticket from a user complaining that the web browser on his laptop is "going crazy." You discover that the home page for his browser has been mysteriously changed to an adult-content website and the browser resists all efforts to change it back to the corporation's main web page. Also, multiple web-browser windows pop up every few seconds without end, filling the screen and making it impossible to work.

The user had his laptop with him on a business trip he recently returned from and you suspect he may have downloaded some software that included a web-browser hijacker. You are able to gain control of the web browser's behavior only when the laptop is not connected to the network.

 At this point, you should advise the IT department that a compromised machine had temporarily been connected to the network so they can determine if any other devices have been affected.

You proceed to log on to the laptop and access the antimalware program. To update the definitions, you access the antimalware server from a separate computer, download the latest definitions to a prepared folder, and then transfer those files to a USB thumb drive.

Scope of Task

Duration

Just as in Task 4.1, the scanning process can be lengthy if you are scanning the entire hard drive, but once the scan is done, any detected threats can be quickly selected and isolated from the rest of the system.

Setup

You will need to have some sort of malware scanner installed on your computer. Here's a list of websites where you can download free versions of the vendors' malware scanner:

- AVG Anti-Virus and Anti-Spyware: `http://free.avg.com/download?prd=afe`
- Spybot Search and Destroy: `www.safer-networking.org/en/download/index.html`
- Ad-Aware SE Personal: `www.pcworld.com/downloads/file/fid,7423-order,1-page,1-c,antispywaretools/description.html`

 If you have Grisoft's free AVG antivirus solution already installed, the anti-spyware software is also present. There is no need to download and install AVG's software a second time.

Caveat

At least for home use, no malware scanner is 100 percent effective. What one scanner will miss, another will find. It's prudent to run two or three of the previously listed pieces of software to verify that you have cleared all the threats off your system.

Procedure

This task will teach you how to scan for malware on a computer and how to quarantine it if found.

Equipment Used

No special equipment is necessary to complete this task.

Details

This task will walk you through the steps of scanning for and quarantining any malware found on a computer.

Scanning for and Quarantining Malware

MANUALLY UPDATING MALWARE DEFINITIONS

1. Sitting at the computer, double-click the antimalware program's icon on the Desktop.

2. Click Control Center.

3. Select Update Manager.

4. Click the Settings button.

5. When the Settings box opens, click the URL tab.

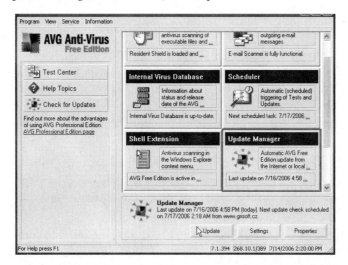

6. Plug the USB thumb drive into a USB port on the computer.

7. Wait for the drive to be recognized by the computer. (In this example, the drive will be assigned drive letter E.)

8. In an empty row below the URL of the program's usual update page, type the path to the malware-definitions update on the thumb drive.

9. Click OK.

10. Select the path to the USB drive.

11. Click the Move Up button.

12. Click OK.

13. With the Update Manager still selected, click Update.

14. Allow the program to update its definitions from the USB drive.

15. Click OK when the update is complete.

16. Click Settings.

17. Click URL.

18. Select the server path for the USB drive.

19. Click Delete.

20. Click OK.

21. Click Test Center.

SCANNING FOR MALWARE

1. Click Scan Computer. The scan will begin.

![AVG Free Edition Test Center screenshot showing scan results]

Just as in Task 4.1, allow the scan to complete even if malware is detected early in the process. You want to make sure that all threats on your computer are detected.

2. When the scan is complete, if any threats were detected, select all of those displayed in the list. In your program, there may be a Select All button, or you can select multiple names in the list by holding down the Ctrl key and clicking on each item with your mouse.

3. Click Next.

4. When offered the option, click Quarantine.

5. Click Next.

6. When offered the option, click Send Copy to Quarantine Server.

7. Click Next.

8. Click Finish.

TESTING THE MALWARE REMOVAL

1. Notify the IT department that you want to test the laptop by connecting it to the network and the Internet.

2. Reconnect the laptop to the LAN.

3. Open a web browser.

4. Set the default home page for the browser to the corporate website.

5. Close the web browser.

6. Open the browser again and note which site opens in the window.

7. Note if any other windows open without being specifically opened by you.

Criteria for Completion

You will have successfully completed this task when you have scanned for malware, quarantined any discovered threats, and tested the computer to verify that the aberrant behavior has been neutralized.

Task 4.3: Scanning for Rootkits

A rootkit is more than a single malicious program designed to compromise your computer. It's a tool or collection of tools that are created and covertly installed on your PC for the purpose of gathering your private information and even taking complete control of your machine, turning it into a spam-transmitting zombie. Your standard antivirus and antimalware solution may not detect the presence of a rootkit on your Windows XP or Vista computer, but there are other ways to find and remove this menace.

Scenario

You receive a trouble ticket stating that a user's laptop, which he often takes on business trips, has been frequently accessing the Internet and transferring data across the network for long periods of time when the computer was supposed to be idle. The user has run all of the usual antivirus scans and his machine appears to be clean. You consult with your supervisor and she suspects that a rootkit may have been installed on the user's laptop. She advises you to attach the laptop to a test network that's isolated from the company's production network but that has Internet access. You're to download and install Microsoft's RootkitRevealer tool and scan the computer using it, to see if her suspicions can be confirmed. Once you have run the scan, you are to contact your supervisor again so she can evaluate the results and take further action.

She provides you with the necessary URL and instructions on how to use RootkitRevealer. You take possession of the laptop, take it to your workbench, and connect it to the test network. You then go to the URL you have been provided, download the tool, unzip the compressed file, and get ready to work.

Go to www.microsoft.com/technet/sysinternals/utilities/Rootkit Revealer.mspx to download this tool onto your Windows XP or Windows Vista computer.

Scope of Task

Duration

The RootkitRevealer scan can take some time, depending on the number of files that need to be scanned.

Setup

No special setup is necessary. Just download the zip file from the previously referenced URL, unzip the file, open the folder, and launch the utility.

Caveat

RootkitRevealer doesn't provide the same type of results that your antivirus program does when it detects a virus. According to Microsoft, the tool's output presents a list of API and Registry anomalies, which may or may not indicate the presence of the rootkit. While the utility's results aren't precise, in many cases it will disclose the presence of AFX, HackerDefender, and Vanquish rootkits that cloak their operating files or Registry keys on your system.

Microsoft recommends that you close all files and applications prior to running the RootkitRevealer to avoid "false positives." The tool has no pause function, so once the scan is started, you must either allow it to complete, or click Abort to cancel the scan.

The process of removing a rootkit is beyond the scope of this task and book. The removal process can vary widely depending on the type and nature of the rootkit located.

Procedure

This task will show you how to launch RootkitRevealer and read the results.

Equipment Used

No special equipment is required.

Details

This task will take you through the steps of launching Microsoft's RootkitRevealer and observing the results. The task assumes you have already downloaded the RootkitRevealer tool onto your computer and unzipped the downloaded file.

For more detailed information about RootkitRevealer, read the information available at the previously referenced URL or read the RootkitRevealer. chm file in the RootkitRevealer folder you downloaded from Microsoft.

Scanning a Windows PC for Rootkits

1. Navigate to the location where you downloaded and unzipped the RootkitDefender folder, and then open the folder.

2. Double-click the RootkitDefender executable file to launch the tool.

3. When the dialog box appears, click Run.

4. When the License Agreement dialog box appears, click Agree.

5. When the RootkitRevealer dialog box appears, click Scan.

6. Allow the scan to progress while at least periodically observing the results as they occur.

7. When the scan is completed, note the number of discrepancies found in the lower-left corner of the RootkitRevealer dialog box.

In the described scenario, you would summon your supervisor at this point, allow her to examine the results, and then take whatever further action she advises. In our task, you can either close the tool now, or follow the optional suggestion in the subsequent section of this task.

Grisoft used to produce a free rootkit-removal tool, but it has since been integrated into their commercial Internet Security product. To find out more, go to: www.avg.com/us.90821.

Criteria for Completion

You will have successfully completed this task when you have used RootkitRevealer to scan for rootkits on your Windows XP or Windows Vista computer. You are not required to verify the presence of rootkits or to remove any you may find.

If you choose, you can use Google or another search engine to search for the results the RootkitRevealer produces and see if any of them indicate the presence of a rootkit. If you find a rootkit is on your PC, use a search engine again to locate the correct removal instructions, and then remove the rootkit.

Task 4.4: Changing Backup Tapes on a Server

Changing a backup tape on a server is a bit more involved than changing a cassette tape or a CD. Although changing tapes sounds like an entirely physical process, there is a software side of it, too.

Tapes must be changed every day so that you always have the server's latest information changes available in case you have to do a restore. This is an activity that will become a constant for you. However, a backup tape isn't going to do you much good if the backup process itself failed or if the data on the tape has become corrupted. You have to check on the status of the previous night's backup before swapping tapes.

Scenario

You have been given the daily responsibility of changing the backup tape on a server located at one of your company's branch offices. You'll need to verify that the backup was successful, report to your supervisor when a backup was not successful, remove and label last night's tape, and insert a fresh tape for tonight's backup.

You travel to the branch office and the manager shows you to the server room. You take the fresh tape out of your pocket and place it next to the keyboard. Then you start to work.

Scope of Task

Duration

This task should take about 15 minutes.

Setup

You will need access to tape backup hardware, including the recording unit and at least two tapes. You also will need to have compatible backup software installed on the computer you will be using for this task.

Caveat

Most people don't have a tape backup unit attached to their home computer, so you may not have access to the equipment required to complete this task. Nevertheless, this is an extremely common activity for a PC tech and you'll need to know how to run this procedure in a work environment.

Since backup units and software are so variable, the instructions for this task are quite generic. Your experience will no doubt differ.

Procedure

This task will show you how to change backup tapes on a server.

Equipment Used

This task requires that a backup tape unit be attached to a computer or server.

Details

This task will take you through the steps required to verify that the prior backup was successful, to safely eject the tape, to label the prior tape, and to insert the fresh tape.

Changing a Backup Tape on a Server

VERIFYING LAST NIGHT'S BACKUP

1. Sitting at the server's keyboard, log on to the server as an administrator.

 You can also log into the server with a regular user account and use elevated privileges to perform administrative tasks.

2. Double-click the icon for the server's backup application on the Desktop.
3. After the program opens, click Backup Schedule in the menu.
4. Double-click the date and time link for last night's backup.
5. Verify that the message shown indicates that the backup was successful.
6. Open the collapsible menu for that backup and verify that all of the selected drives and partitions were successfully backed up and that none were skipped.
7. Close the collapsible menu.
8. Click Return to Menu.

REMOVING A BACKUP TAPE

1. At the main menu, click Service ➤ Hardware ➤ Tape Cartridge Unit ➤ Unlock.
2. Locate the tape recording unit for the server.
3. Check the status lights on the unit.

 In this example, the unit has three status lights. The first is the Ready light, indicating whether a tape is present and ready for recording. The second is the Activity light, which indicates whether there is tape activity (such as recording or restoring). The third is a Fault light, which indicates a worn or damaged tape in the unit.

4. Verify that the first light is a solid green, indicating that there is a tape present.

5. Verify that the other two lights are off, indicating that there is no tape activity and that there are no tape faults.

6. Press the eject button on the unit.

 When ejecting the tape, you'll notice the first green light flashing, indicating that the tape is in the process of being removed.

7. Remove the tape from the unit.

8. Locate a pen or marker.

9. Label the tape with the server's hostname and the date of the backup.

10. Remove the new tape from its case and place the tape by the keyboard.

11. Place last night's tape in the case and place the case in your pocket.

 You'll give last night's tape to your supervisor when you return to the main office, and your supervisor will make sure the tape is stored safely offsite.

INSERTING A BACKUP TAPE

1. Pick up the new tape and gently insert it into the tape unit's cassette slot. The motorized unit will accept the tape automatically. The first green light will start flashing again, indicating that a tape is being inserted.

2. Verify that the first light returns to a solid green, indicating that the tape is present and ready.

3. Verify that the second and third lights are still off.

 If the third light glows amber, it indicates that the tape is worn or damaged.

4. After you turn back to the keyboard, verify that the menu for the Tape Cartridge Unit is still displayed.

5. Click Lock.

6. Click Return to Menu.

VERIFYING THE SCHEDULED BACKUP

1. At the main menu, click Backup Schedule.

2. Double-click the date and time for tonight's backup.

3. Verify that the status for this backup is active.

4. Back out to the main menu.

5. Click Exit to close the program.

6. Log off the server.

7. Verify that last night's tape is in your pocket.

8. Return to the main office and give the tape to your supervisor.

Criteria for Completion

You will have successfully completed this task when you have verified the success of the previous backup, removed the old tape, inserted a fresh tape, and verified that the coming night's backup is scheduled.

Task 4.5: Changing the Backup Schedule on a Server

Although this task isn't performed often, the backup schedule on a server will occasionally need to be changed. If you are assigned this task by your supervisor, you will be supplied with detailed instructions on the proper procedure for changing the schedule.

Scenario

You have recently been made responsible for changing the backup tapes on a server at a branch office. (See Task 4.4.) After studying the amount of time backups have been taking on this server, your supervisor has determined that due to an increase in data storage, backups need to be scheduled to start two hours earlier. This will give the backup unit more time to record all of the information that needs to be saved to tape. The tape's capacity is sufficient for the increase in data.

You are provided with a detailed list of instructions that you will follow to change the backup schedule. You drive to the branch office with a fresh tape and your instructions. Once you arrive, you go to the server room, sit down at the keyboard, and start working.

Scope of Task

Duration

Including changing tapes, this task should take about 30 minutes.

Setup

You will need access to tape backup hardware, including the recording unit. Backup software that's compatible with the recording device should be installed on the computer you will be using for this task.

Caveat

You must follow the instructions for changing the backup schedule to the letter. If you make a mistake and allow too little time for the backup, it won't be finished before the beginning of the workday. If you schedule it too soon, some of the data may be in use when the backup starts.

Procedure

This task will teach you how to change the scheduling for backups on a server.

Equipment Used

You will need a backup unit attached to the computer you will use for this task unless you can use software that will simulate a change in schedule without the actual hardware being present.

Details

This task will show you the steps you need to follow to locate the scheduling menu for your backup software and change it to required specifications.

Changing the Scheduled Backup Time on a Server

ACCESSING THE BACKUP SCHEDULING CONTROLS

1. Sitting at the keyboard, log on to the server as an administrator.
2. Double-click the icon for the backup application on the Desktop.
3. When the application opens, click Backup Schedule.
4. Click Scheduling.
5. Click Change.

 There are a number of elements you can change, including how often the backup occurs; however, you want all of the settings to remain the same except for the start time.

CHANGING THE SCHEDULE TIME

1. Click the Start Time drop-down menu.
2. Select the time written in the instructions given to you by your supervisor.
3. Click Save. A dialog box will appear, notifying you that the scheduling change was made successfully.

4. Double-click the date and new time for tonight's backup.

5. Verify that the status for this backup is active.

6. Click Return to Menu.

7. Follow the steps outlined in Task 4.4 to change the tape and end the task.

Criteria for Completion

You will have successfully completed this task when you have changed the scheduled time for the backup to start and verified the change.

Task 4.6: Backing Up Outlook

In corporate environments that use Microsoft Exchange Server to manage mail, when you back up the Exchange Server, you back up the mail. However, if your company is small or administers small branch offices with no connection to the main office's mail server, it may be necessary to back up mail from individual computers at these offices.

This task is one you should rarely perform in an enterprise networking environment, but on the odd occasion when a request such as this comes in, you'll be glad you know what you're doing.

Scenario

You are at a small office and have been assigned to back up mail information from Microsoft Outlook mail clients. The data is stored on the local hard drives of each computer. You review the instructions for backing up Outlook files, log on to the computer, and get ready to work.

Scope of Task

Duration

Depending on the amount of information being backed up, this task should take about 20 to 30 minutes.

Setup

You will need access to a computer with Microsoft Outlook installed.

Caveat

This should be a fairly straightforward procedure; however, make sure you remember the location where you stored the backup in case you need to restore the mail to Outlook.

Procedure

This task shows you how to back up Microsoft Outlook data from the local hard drive.

Equipment Used

No special equipment is needed to complete this task besides an external USB storage device.

Details

This task walks you through the steps of accessing and copying Outlook PST files from the hard drive of the local computer to an external USB drive.

Backing Up Mail Files from Outlook

ATTACHING EXTERNAL STORAGE TO THE COMPUTER

1. Locate the external USB drive you brought with you.
2. After logging on, attach the drive's USB cable to a USB port on the computer.
3. Verify that the other end of the cable is attached to the drive and that the drive is attached to a power source and is active.
4. Click Start ➤ My Computer.
5. Verify that the external USB drive is recognized and assigned a drive letter. An information balloon should appear from the Taskbar stating that a new hardware device has been recognized.
6. Close the balloon.
7. Close My Computer.

COPYING PST FILES FROM OUTLOOK TO AN EXTERNAL DRIVE

1. Right-click the Microsoft Outlook icon on the Desktop.
2. Click Properties.
3. In the Mail Setup box, click Data Files.

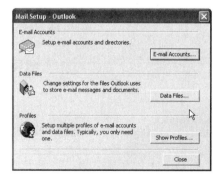

4. In the Outlook Data Files box, select the folder or folders you want to copy. The usual choices are Personal Folders and Archived Folders.

5. Click Open Folder.

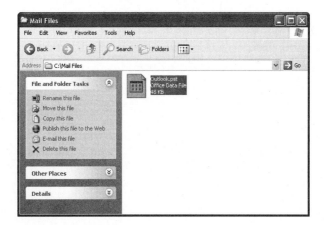

6. Click Edit ➢ Select All and then choose Edit ➢ Copy.

7. Click Start ➢ My Computer.

8. Double-click the icon for the USB storage device.

9. When you have selected the correct folder for the desired user/computer on the drive, right-click inside of it.

10. Click Paste.

11. Close the USB-drive window.

12. In Outlook, click Close.

13. In the Mail Setup box, click Close.

14. Disconnect the USB drive from the computer.

15. Log off the computer.

Criteria for Completion

You will have successfully completed this task when you have copied Outlook PST files from the local computer to the external drive.

Task 4.7: Quickly Diagnosing Windows Vista Problems

Windows Vista comes with a utility that lets you quickly scan the system for problems and provides an easy-to-read report of any problems found on the computer. It's not a substitute for experience and keen problem-solving skills, but it does take a lot of the footwork out of tracking down whatever may be ailing a Vista PC.

Scenario

The HR manager calls you stating that her new Windows Vista computer doesn't seem to "work right." She isn't able to completely articulate what the issue seems to be, but wants you to come to her office and check her computer. You contact your supervisor and she assigns you this task, suggesting you use Vista's Reliability and Performance Monitor to do a quick scan of the PC to see what sort of problems the computer may be experiencing. You are provided the instructions on how to locate and run the utility.

After arranging a time to meet with the HR manager in her office, you arrive, sit at the computer's keyboard, log in as an administrator, and begin your work.

Scope of Task

Duration

This task should take only a few minutes to complete, since the Reliability and Performance Monitor's scan of the system is very quick.

Setup

No special setup is required.

Caveat

Use this tool only as a necessary first step to locate or rule out potential problems. You will still need to use a wide variety of troubleshooting skills to successfully find and repair problems on Windows Vista computers.

Procedure

This task will show you how to use Vista's Reliability and Performance Monitor to scan a computer for problems.

Equipment Used

No special equipment is required except, of course, a Windows Vista computer.

Details

This task will take you through the steps of launching and reading the Windows Vista Reliability and Performance Monitor to discover potential problems on a computer.

Using the Windows Vista Reliability and Performance Monitor to Diagnose Problems

1. Click the Windows Vista button and then click Control Panel.

2. In the Control Panel, click System and Maintenance, Performance Information and Tools, and then click Advanced Tools.

3. Click Generate a System Health Report.

4. When the report is generated, review the list of errors, indicated by red Xs in the Reliability and Performance Monitor dialog box.

5. Make a note of the information presented in the Cause, Details, and Resolution fields for each error.

Criteria for Completion

You will have successfully completed this task when you have read the list of errors produced by the utility and noted the information related to each problem, including the potential solution. You can then use this information to devise a plan to investigate each error in more detail and repair the problems.

Task 4.8: Troubleshooting a Randomly Rebooting PC

So far, many of the tasks that have been presented have been unambiguous in terms of a solution. From this point on, you will be required to respond to issues with a cause and solution that aren't always apparent. As you gain experience, you will become more confident in troubleshooting computer and network issues, but when confronted with a problem you can't successfully diagnose, you can always rely on other IT staff to lend a hand.

A randomly rebooting computer is a classic troubleshooting problem. You will encounter this problem only occasionally; however, being able to diagnose such an issue is a handy skill to possess.

Scenario

You receive a trouble ticket saying that for the past several days, one of the computers in accounts receivable has been spontaneously rebooting. You are assigned to investigate.

Scope of Task

Duration

The amount of time required to accomplish this task will vary depending on the cause and solution. Under ideal circumstances, it should take an hour or so.

Setup

As you will see when you progress through the steps, this issue is difficult to simulate and would require that you be presented with a PC that is actually experiencing this symptom.

Caveat

Troubleshooting any computer problem involves both drawing on your experience and a certain amount of trial and error. As you gain experience, you will be able to assess a particular problem in terms of the most likely cause. You can then test to see whether your assumption is correct. If so, you can implement the solution and resolve the issue. If not, you can move on to the next most likely cause and test for that. Sometimes, however, the cause ends up being something unexpected.

Procedure

This task will show you how to diagnose the cause of spontaneous reboots on a computer.

Equipment Used

Often when you begin a troubleshooting task, you don't immediately know what tools or equipment will be needed. In this case, in order to successfully resolve the issue, you'll need a screwdriver and ESD protection.

Details

This task will take you through the steps of diagnosing the cause of a computer spontaneously rebooting, determining the solution, and repairing the computer.

Diagnosing and Repairing a Spontaneously Rebooting Computer

INITIALLY INVESTIGATING A SPONTANEOUSLY REBOOTING COMPUTER

1. Locate the user of the computer.

2. Have the user explain in detail the nature of the problem. Before even touching the computer, it is important to get as many details about the issue as possible from the user. The following list includes some of the questions to ask in this situation:

   - When did the problem begin?

   - Were any changes made to the hardware, software, or configuration settings of the computer just prior to the problem occurring the first time?

   - How often does the computer spontaneously reboot?

   - What tasks is the user performing just prior to a reboot?

   - Is there anything that the user does on the computer that decreases or increases the frequency of the reboots?

> In this case, there seems to be no particular pattern to the reboot incidents. They occur at random, regardless of what the user is doing at the computer and even when she is away from the PC. No recent changes have been made to the computer, although the user has considered requesting a newer model since her PC is quite old.

3. Locate the PC.

4. Check all of the external power connections, including the connection on the PC's power supply, the connection of the power cord to the surge protector, and the surge protector's connection to the wall plug.

5. Perform a visual inspection of the power button on the outside of the PC.

> Occasionally, the power button will stick after being pressed and will create a partial connection that can cause the PC to reboot if the case is nudged or bumped.

DIAGNOSING THE PROBLEM AT YOUR WORKBENCH

1. After powering down the PC, disconnect all of its connections at the user's work area and take the computer to your workbench in the IT department.

> In this example, the problem cannot be resolved at the user's work area.

2. Place the PC on your workbench.

Do not connect any power cords or peripherals to the PC.

3. Locate your tools and your ESD protection.
4. Using the appropriate screwdriver, remove the screws holding the access panel in place.
5. Remove the access panel.
6. Use ESD precautions.
7. Check the internal connectors from the power supply to the motherboard, all drives, and any other available connections to make sure they are secure.
8. Check to make sure the RAM sticks are seated properly, and reseat if necessary.
9. Check to make sure the CPU is seated properly, and reseat if necessary.
10. Check to make sure all expansion cards are seated properly, and reseat if necessary.

See Task 2.18 for details about seating RAM sticks. See Task 2.19 for details about seating expansion cards.

11. Check the connections to the power button.
12. Secure any loose connections and replace the access panel.
13. Replace the screws holding the access panel in place.

It's possible that a connection may have become just loose enough to cause an intermittent problem, even if it didn't feel particularly loose.

14. Check the play of the power button to make sure it can be fully depressed.
15. Verify that the power button is in the off position (that is, the button is not pressed in so that it causes the computer to boot the moment power is applied to the power supply).

TESTING YOUR FIRST ASSUMPTION

1. Connect the PC to a monitor, keyboard, and mouse.
2. Verify that the monitor has power and is turned on.
3. Plug a power cord into the back of the PC's power supply and verify that the other end of the cord is plugged into a wall plug or surge protector that is powered.
4. Press the PC's power button.

5. Allow the PC to boot.

6. Observe the PC's behavior once the operating system has loaded.

The only way to test your solution is to leave the PC powered up for an extended period of time until you determine that it is not exhibiting its symptomatic behavior. You'll need to be present but can occupy your time with paperwork or other tasks that still let you pay attention to the computer.

At this point, you should consider testing the power supply. See Task 2.3, "Testing and Replacing a Power Supply," for details.

CONTINUING TO DIAGNOSE THE PROBLEM

In this example, your initial assumption was not correct and the computer still exhibits symptomatic behavior.

1. Power down the computer.

2. Disconnect the power cord from the power supply.

3. Locate an appropriate replacement power supply and place it on your workbench.

4. Remove the screws holding the access panel in place.

5. Remove the access panel.

6. Take ESD precautions and prepare to replace the power supply with a new unit.

Refer to Task 1.6 for the procedure involved in installing a power supply.

7. Once you have replaced the power supply, replace the access panel and the screws that hold it to the PC case.

TESTING YOUR SECOND ASSUMPTION

1. Reconnect the power cord to the power supply.

2. Power up the computer.

3. Continue to observe the PC's behavior once the operating system has loaded.

A spontaneously rebooting computer is often the sign of a dying power supply. Recall that the user mentioned that her PC was an older model.

Criteria for Completion

You will have successfully completed this task when the PC remains powered for an extended period of time and the symptom does not reoccur.

Task 4.9: Troubleshooting an Intermittent Boot Failure of a PC

On the surface, this problem seems fairly similar to Task 4.8, but in fact it could be caused by a wide variety of circumstances. Problems that occur intermittently are some of the most maddening. It's like driving a car that has an intermittent knock in the engine. When you take it to the garage, the knock won't manifest itself. After you drive away again, the knock reappears. Under these circumstances, your job is to work with the computer and attempt to replicate the problem so you can observe and, hopefully, repair it.

Scenario

You receive a trouble ticket Monday morning stating that one of the users in the administrative office can't seem to power up his computer. The ticket states that when the user presses the power button, sometimes the unit powers up, but there's no image on the screen. On other occasions, when the user presses the power button the unit does not power up at all.

You suspect that the PC's power supply is failing, but your supervisor suggests that there could be a number of other causes, including a failing motherboard capacitor. You take your toolkit, including your multimeter, with you to the user's computer and prepare to begin the diagnostic process.

Scope of Task

Duration

The duration of this task depends on how quickly you are able to find the cause of the problem based on your diagnostic methods and the complexity of the problem.

Setup

As in the previous task, this issue is difficult to simulate and would require a PC that is actually experiencing this symptom.

Caveat

As previously stated, troubleshooting any computer problem involves both drawing on your experience and a certain amount of trial and error. The first step is to gather as much information as possible about the problem from the user, then logically proceed through several testing steps, eliminating possible causes until the actual cause of the problem is determined. This might take some time, but as you become more experienced with similar problems, you can more quickly hone in on the solution.

Procedure

This task will show you the process of diagnosing a computer with intermittent boot problems.

Equipment Used

Since the scenario begins by suspecting a failing power supply, you'll need a multimeter for part of this task.

Details

This task shows you the steps in diagnosing a computer that only intermittently powers up but never receives an image on the monitor.

Diagnosing a PC That Only Intermittently Powers Up

INITIALLY INVESTIGATING A COMPUTER BOOT PROBLEM

1. You contact the computer's user and begin the investigation by asking him questions regarding the problem.

    - When did the problem first occur?

    - Have there been any recent configuration changes to the settings on the PC?

    - Were any changes made to the hardware or software of the computer just prior to the problem occurring for the first time?

    The user says he normally powers down his computer on Friday before leaving work for the weekend, then powers up his computer on Monday morning and leaves the computer powered all week. At the end of each workday during the week, he logs off his PC but leaves it in a running condition. When he came into work today, Monday morning, he discovered the problem described in the trouble ticket.

2. You sit at the computer and press the power button, but nothing happens.

3. After waiting a few minutes, you press the power button again and hear the computer powering up, but see no images on the monitor.

4. You press the power button on the monitor several times and determine it is on.

5. You check the power-cord connections between the monitor and the power strip, but the connections are firm.

6. You check the connection between the monitor and the PC, but the connections are firm.

7. You check the power-cord connections between the PC and the power strip, but the connections are firm.

8. You power down the PC.

TESTING YOUR FIRST ASSUMPTION

1. You decide to test your first assumption that the power supply of the computer is failing, remove the multimeter from your toolkit, and prepare to open the access panel to the PC.

See Task 2.2 to determine the specific type of a power supply and Task 2.3 to go through the steps of testing a power supply.

2. Based on your testing of the power supply, you determine that it is not the cause of the problem, though you are still convinced it is a power-related issue.

TESTING YOUR SECOND ASSUMPTION

1. Telling the user that you will return shortly, you go back to the IT department and find a spare power strip.

Although your supervisor suggests testing the power connection to the motherboard next, you suspect another cause, and it will only take a few minutes to test.

2. Returning to the user's cubicle with the spare power strip, you look under his desk at the existing power strip and verify that the power button on the strip is lit and that the strip is actively receiving power.

3. You ask the user to power down all devices that are connected to the power strip under his desk.

4. After the user has powered down all relevant devices, you go under his desk and disconnect all of the power cords connected to the power strip.

5. You disconnect the power strip from the wall power socket and plug in the replacement power strip.

6. You plug all of the power cords you removed from the old power strip into the replacement power strip, and verify that the power button on the strip is in the on position with the strip receiving power from the wall outlet.

7. You tell the user to power up all of the devices he powered down before you removed the old power strip.

8. You tell the user to power up the computer monitor and the PC.

9. You verify that the PC powers up and that the expected images appear on the computer screen.

10. After the computer successfully boots and the operating system loads, you have the user power down and then power up his PC a few times to make sure it operates normally.

Criteria for Completion

You will have successfully completed this task when the computer can be powered down normally and then powered up and operated normally.

 Although this problem could have many different causes, in this situation, a failing power strip providing intermittent power to the PC and monitor was the culprit. Testing the causes that can be accessed most easily and quickly can solve the problem or at least swiftly eliminate a potential cause.

Task 4.10: Troubleshooting a Failed RAM Upgrade

As you read in Task 1.2 and Task 2.18, installing and upgrading RAM is a very common task for a PC technician. Most of the time, it is a very routine operation, but occasionally things don't go as planned. In that event, you will need to troubleshoot why a RAM installation or upgrade doesn't work. Sometimes it's as simple as a bad stick of RAM, but occasionally, the cause is more complex.

Scenario

You receive a trouble ticket to upgrade the RAM on two identical PCs in the accounts receivable department to 2GB. Both PCs currently possess insufficient memory, resulting in significant work slowdowns by their users. Your supervisor provides you with four identical sticks of 1GB PC3200 RAM. You check the current specifications on the two computers in the IT department's records and you find that the first computer has two sticks of 256MB RAM, while the other computer has two sticks of 128MB RAM.

You take your toolkit and the replacement RAM sticks to the accounts-receivable department and locate the two PCs. The users are out to lunch, so you won't be disturbing their work while you do the upgrade. You plan to open each computer, remove the old sticks of RAM and replace them with the new sticks of RAM, then boot up each computer to verify the memory upgrade is successful.

See Task 1.2 for the specific instructions on opening a PC case and replacing RAM sticks. Also see Task 2.18 for the specific instructions on replacing and reseating RAM sticks in a PC.

You replace the two sticks of 256MB RAM with the two sticks of 1GB RAM in the first computer, power up the PC, and verify the new RAM is recognized and that the machine boots normally. You replace the two sticks of 128MB RAM in the second computer with the two sticks of 1GB RAM, power up the computer, and discover that the beep codes indicate the RAM is not recognized. The computer does not boot successfully. The two computers and four sticks of 1GB RAM are all supposed to be identical. You need to find out what went wrong and successfully upgrade the RAM in the second computer so that it will be able to run normally and not experience performance slowdowns.

Scope of Task

Duration

This task could take 30 to 60 minutes or possibly longer, depending on the number of steps taken to diagnose the problem and the extent of the research required to find the solution.

Setup

The problem being described is very specific and you will not likely be able to duplicate it unless you are presented with a PC that is experiencing the same symptoms as the one presented in this scenario.

Caveat

While a RAM problem may seem to have a limited number of causes and solutions, occasionally the information initially presented about the computers you are working on may not be correct, resulting in a problem with an unlikely cause. It's important to recheck all of your records about machines you are working on to make sure your information is accurate.

Procedure

This task will show you the process of diagnosing a failed RAM upgrade.

Equipment Used

The equipment required includes a standard PC toolkit, including ESD-prevention gear and the RAM sticks necessary to perform the upgrade.

Details

This task shows you the steps in diagnosing a failure in upgrading the RAM in a computer.

Diagnosing a Failed RAM Upgrade

TESTING TO VERIFY THE COMPUTER WILL BOOT WITH THE ORIGINAL RAM

1. With the PC case of the second computer open, take ESD precautions and remove the two sticks of 1GB RAM, placing them in their antistatic bags.

2. Remove the two original sticks of 128MB RAM from their antistatic bags and replace them in the PC, making sure they are correctly seated.

3. Leaving the computer access panel off and verifying that the PC and monitor are connected to an active power strip, power up the PC.

4. Verify that the beep codes indicate that the original RAM is recognized and that the PC powers up normally.

5. After the operating system loads and you've verified the computer behaves normally, power down the computer.

TESTING YOUR FIRST ASSUMPTION

1. Take the two sticks of 1GB RAM back to the IT department, believing one or both sticks are defective, and replace them with two other identical sticks.

2. Return to the accounts-receivable department and to the PC you are attempting to upgrade.

3. Using ESD precautions, remove the two sticks of 128MB RAM and replace them with the two new sticks of 1GB RAM, making sure they are properly seated.

4. Verify that the computer and monitor are plugged into the active power strip, and then power up the computer.

5. The computer powers up, but the beep codes and monitor message indicate that the RAM is not recognized, so the original upgrade RAM sticks were not defective.

NOTE   At this point, the user should be back from lunch and you'll need to replace the original sticks of RAM so that he can do his work. You arrange to return to his computer after normal working hours to perform the upgrade, assuming you are able to discover why the RAM upgrade was unsuccessful and solve the dilemma. You instruct the user to power down his computer when he leaves work for the day.

RESEARCHING YOUR SECOND ASSUMPTION

1. Returning to the IT department, you check your records to verify that both of the computers you are upgrading are actually identical.

2. You find out that both computers are the same make and model, but the second PC is older than the first PC.

3. You discover that the first PC supports 128MB, 256MB, 512MB, and 1GB non-ECC RAM up to 4GB.

4. You discover that the second, older PC supports only 128MB, 256MB, and 512MB non-ECC RAM but up to 2GB.

TESTING YOUR SECOND ASSUMPTION

1. You acquire four sticks of 512MB RAM of the appropriate type for the computer you are attempting to upgrade.

2. You take the RAM sticks and your toolkit to the accounts-receivable department after normal working hours and access the computer requiring the upgrade.

3. Making sure the PC is powered down, you open the computer's access panel.

4. Using ESD precautions, you remove the two sticks of 128MB RAM from the PC and install the four sticks of 512MB RAM.

5. Verifying that the computer and monitor are plugged into an active power strip, you turn on the monitor and power up the PC.

6. You verify that the normal beep codes sound and that the message on the monitor indicates the amount of RAM has increased by the desired amount.

7. Pressing Enter to continue, you watch as the PC boots normally and the operating system loads.

8. You replace the access panel on the PC and power it down, then leave a note for the user that the RAM in his computer has been successfully upgraded.

Criteria for Completion

You will have successfully completed this task when you have upgraded the RAM in the computer with the desired amount of memory.

Task 4.11: Troubleshooting a PC That Can't Print to a Local Printer

Diagnosing printing problems is an extremely common task. If the problem ends up being the printer's hardware, the problem will probably be turned over to the printer vendor's repair person since companies often have support contracts with a printer's manufacturer.

The sort of print problems you'll be asked to investigate involve faulty connections, configuration settings, and driver issues.

Scenario

You receive a trouble ticket stating that the manager of the finance department can't print to his new local printer. You pack up your toolkit and report to the manager's office. The manager isn't in but his executive assistant shows you to his computer and printer. You notice that there is one printer connected to the PC via a USB cable. The PC is powered.

Scope of Task

Duration

Ideally, this task should take about 15 minutes.

Setup

You can simulate this task with a computer that is connected to a local printer.

 This task was written using Windows XP, so all of the instructions will be consistent with that operating system.

Caveat

There are an almost endless number of causes of a complaint such as "I can't print." It is important to gather all of the information available about the problem to try to narrow down the likely causes.

Procedure

This task will show you the process of diagnosing local printer problems.

Equipment Used

No special equipment is necessary for this task.

Details

This task shows you the steps in diagnosing a complaint of a user who prints to a local printer.

Diagnosing a PC That Can't Print to a Locally Connected Printer

INITIALLY INVESTIGATING A LOCAL PRINT PROBLEM

1. Ask the executive assistant what she knows about the print problem. Here is a list of some appropriate questions to ask in this situation:

    - When did the problem first occur?

    - Has the user ever successfully printed to the printer?

    - Have there been any recent configuration changes to the printer settings on the PC?

    - Were any changes made to the hardware, software, or configuration settings of the computer just prior to the problem occurring for the first time?

    - Do any error messages display when the user attempts to print?

The executive assistant has limited information. She tells you that the manager changed out his original local printer for a new one late yesterday right before he left work for the day. This morning, he complained that he couldn't print to the new printer and asked that she call the help desk with a request for assistance.

2. Sit down at the keyboard and log on as Administrator.

3. Click Start ➤ Printers and Faxes.

4. When the Printers and Faxes box opens, verify that the new printer is available. You see that the currently attached local printer is not set as the default printer; the default printer is indicated by a white check mark in a black circle.

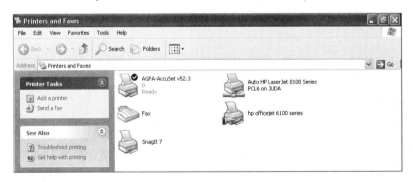

5. Ask the executive assistant the make and model of the user's previous printer.

6. Verify that it is the previous printer that is set as the default printer.

TESTING YOUR FIRST ASSUMPTION

1. Right-click the icon for the currently attached printer.

2. Click Set as Default Printer.

3. Verify that the check mark now appears next to the current printer.

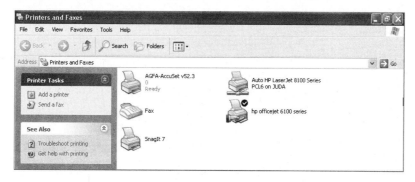

4. Log off the PC.

5. Have the executive assistant log on to the computer as the user.

6. Once the logon is complete, click Start ➢ Printers and Faxes.

7. Verify that the currently attached printer is set as the default printer.

8. Right-click on the default printer.

9. Click Properties.

10. When the Properties box opens, click Print Test Page. A dialog box will appear asking you to click OK if the test page prints properly.

11. Remove the test page and verify that it printed properly.

12. Click OK in the dialog box.

13. Click OK in the printer Properties box.

14. Close the Printers and Faxes box.

15. Click Start ➢ All Programs ➢ Microsoft Word.

You will want to verify that applications can also print correctly.

16. When a blank Word document opens, type a line of text.

17. Click File ➢ Print.

18. When the Print box opens, verify that the local printer appears in the Name field.

19. Click OK.

20. If the Word document prints successfully, close the Word document without saving it.

21. Log off the computer.

Criteria for Completion

You will have successfully completed this task when you can print from the locally attached printer.

Task 4.12: Troubleshooting a PC That Can't Print to a Network Printer

As mentioned in the introduction to Task 4.11, print problems are among the most common tasks you'll be called on to diagnose, and there are a large number of causes. Problems connecting to network printers can be even more difficult to troubleshoot than local printer problems because you need to factor in any problems on the local area network (LAN) as well as typical print-problem issues.

Scenario

You receive a trouble ticket stating that a user in the newly established software-systems department can't print to the network printer. You gather your toolkit and the network-configuration information for that department and report to the user.

Scope of Task

Duration

Ideally, this task should take about 15 or 20 minutes.

Setup

You can simulate this task using a computer that is connected to either a local or a network printer.

Caveat

As always, gather as much information about the problem as possible to reduce the potential number of likely causes and solutions.

Procedure

This task will show you how to diagnose network printing problems.

Equipment Used

No special equipment is required for this task.

Details

This task will take you through the steps of diagnosing the cause of network printing problems.

Diagnosing Problems Printing to a Network Printer

INITIALLY INVESTIGATING A NETWORK PRINTING PROBLEM

1. You approach the user and ask him some questions regarding the issue. The following list includes some appropriate questions to ask in this situation:

   - When did the problem first occur?

   - Has the user ever successfully printed to the printer?

   - Have there been any recent configuration changes to the printer settings on the PC?

   - Were any changes made to the hardware, software, or configuration settings of the computer just prior to the problem occurring for the first time?

   - Do any error messages display when the user attempts to print?

   - Has the user experienced other networking problems?

   - Does anyone else in the department have problems printing to the network printer?

   - Does anyone else in the department have any networking problems?

 You discover that the network printer was installed late last Friday after everyone had gone for the day. This morning, everyone was able to print to the network printer except this user. He says he gets no error messages and that the print job just hangs.

2. You log on to the user's computer as a domain administrator and access the IT-department intranet site.

3. You navigate to the IT work logs for last Friday and find the work record for the network printer install.

4. You read the entire record and notice that access to the printer for this department is limited to standard business hours.

5. The user explains that the projects developed by the software-systems department are highly confidential and printing is limited to normal work hours as part of the security measures applied to this department.

6. You close the IT intranet site and log off.

TESTING YOUR FIRST ASSUMPTION

1. Locate the PC.

2. Locate the patch cable attaching the PC to the Ethernet port.

3. Verify that the connection is secure at both ends.

4. Verify that the link light on the NIC is on.

5. Sit at the computer's keyboard again and log on as Administrator.

6. Click Start ➤ Run.

7. In the Run box, type **cmd**.

8. Press Enter.

9. When the command-prompt window opens, type **ipconfig/all**.

10. Verify that the PC has an IP address and that the correct configuration settings are present.

 Although the user states that he is having no other network-related problems, it's still a good idea to make sure the network configuration is correct.

```
C:\WINDOWS\system32\cmd.exe                                    _ □ ×
        Connection-specific DNS Suffix  . :
        Description . . . . . . . . . . . : VMware Virtual Ethernet Adapter for
VMnet1
        Physical Address. . . . . . . . . : 00-50-56-C0-00-01
        Dhcp Enabled. . . . . . . . . . . : No
        IP Address. . . . . . . . . . . . : 192.168.150.1
        Subnet Mask . . . . . . . . . . . : 255.255.255.0
        Default Gateway . . . . . . . . . :

Ethernet adapter Local Area Connection:

        Connection-specific DNS Suffix  . :
        Description . . . . . . . . . . . : Intel(R) PRO/100 VE Network Connecti
on
        Physical Address. . . . . . . . . : 00-07-E9-55-51-5F
        Dhcp Enabled. . . . . . . . . . . : No
        IP Address. . . . . . . . . . . . : 10.9.8.219
        Subnet Mask . . . . . . . . . . . : 255.255.255.0
        Default Gateway . . . . . . . . . : 10.9.8.7
        DNS Servers . . . . . . . . . . . : 10.9.8.7
                                            192.168.0.1
        Primary WINS Server . . . . . . . : 10.9.8.7
        Secondary WINS Server . . . . . . : 192.168.0.1

C:\Documents and Settings\JMPyles>_
```

11. Refer to your information sheet for this network segment and compare the user's network settings to the data sheet.

12. Look up the IP address of the network printer.

13. Ping that IP address from the user's computer.

```
C:\WINDOWS\system32\cmd.exe                                    _ □ x
          Physical Address. . . . . . . . : 00-07-E9-55-51-5F
          Dhcp Enabled. . . . . . . . . . : No
          IP Address. . . . . . . . . . . : 10.9.8.219
          Subnet Mask . . . . . . . . . . : 255.255.255.0
          Default Gateway . . . . . . . . : 10.9.8.7
          DNS Servers . . . . . . . . . . : 10.9.8.7
                                            192.168.0.1
          Primary WINS Server . . . . . . : 10.9.8.7
          Secondary WINS Server . . . . . : 192.168.0.1

C:\Documents and Settings\JMPyles>ping 10.9.8.200

Pinging 10.9.8.200 with 32 bytes of data:

Reply from 10.9.8.200: bytes=32 time=107ms ITL=128
Reply from 10.9.8.200: bytes=32 time=4ms ITL=128
Reply from 10.9.8.200: bytes=32 time=2ms ITL=128
Reply from 10.9.8.200: bytes=32 time=1ms ITL=128

Ping statistics for 10.9.8.200:
    Packets: Sent = 4, Received = 4, Lost = 0 (0% loss),
Approximate round trip times in milli-seconds:
    Minimum = 1ms, Maximum = 107ms, Average = 28ms

C:\Documents and Settings\JMPyles>_
```

14. Type **exit** and press Enter to close the command-prompt window.

TESTING YOUR SECOND ASSUMPTION

1. Click Start ➢ Printers and Faxes.

2. Verify that the network printer is the default printer by looking for the white check mark in the black circle.

3. Right-click the printer.

4. Click Properties.

5. Click Print Test Page. A dialog box opens indicating that the test page has been sent to the printer.

6. Look for any error messages.

7. No error messages appear. You notice that the print-job icon appears in the right-hand corner of the system tray but the job doesn't print.

8. Double-click the print-job icon. You see the print job in the queue but there is no activity.

```
hp officejet 6100 series                                    _ □ x
Printer  Document  View  Help
Document Name          Status      Owner      Pages   Size      Subr
Test Page                          JMPyles    1       213 KB    1:11:
1 document(s) in queue
```

9. Select the document by clicking on it.

10. Click Document ➢ Restart.

11. When the document still doesn't print, click Document ➢ Properties.

12. Review the Test Page Properties box. You notice in the Schedule area that the time the user is allowed to access the printer is misconfigured with a start time of 8:00 PM and an end time of 5:00 AM.

13. Click OK to close the Properties box.

14. Verify that the document is still selected.

15. Click Document ➤ Cancel. A dialog box appears asking if you want to cancel the print job.

16. Click Yes. The print job disappears from the printer window.

17. Close the printer window.

18. Right-click the printer.

19. Click Properties.

20. In the Properties box, click the Advanced tab. Notice that the time the printer is available is misconfigured with a start time of 8:00 PM and an end time of 5:00 AM.

21. Click the PM next to 8:00 to select it.

22. Type **A**. PM will change to AM.

23. Click the AM next to 5:00 to select it.

24. Type **P**. AM will change to PM.

25. Click OK.

26. Right-click the network printer.

27. Click Properties.

28. Click Print Test Page.

29. After the test page prints, click OK to close the dialog box that opened in Step 5.

30. Click OK to close the Properties box.

31. Close the Printers and Faxes box.

32. Log off the computer.

You are able to perform these tasks on the user's computer because you are logged in as a Domain Administrator. The user's normal login will not give him sufficient rights to make these changes independently.

VERIFYING THAT THE USER CAN PRINT FROM AN APPLICATION

1. Have the user log on to the computer.

2. Have the user open Microsoft Word.

3. Have the user type some text in the document.

4. Have the user print the document.

5. Verify that the document prints to the network printer.

Criteria for Completion

You will have successfully completed this task when the user can print to the network printer.

Task 4.13: Troubleshooting the Error Message "The Specified Domain Either Does Not Exist or Could Not Be Contacted"

Periodically, issues come up when trying to join a Windows PC to a Windows Active Directory domain. Virtually all medium and large companies use Active Directory Services to manage computers and resources on the network. If a computer can't join a domain, it can't be used effectively to do work in the business.

Scenario

You've been assigned to join a computer to the company's domain. A new user has been hired in the design department and will be arriving tomorrow. You report to the design department and are directed to the computer. You sit down at the keyboard and log on as Administrator.

Scope of Task

Duration

This task should take about 30 minutes.

Setup

Ideally, you will need a client computer networked with a Windows 2003 Server or higher domain controller. The PC used for this task was Windows 2000 Professional. While you can use Windows XP Professional or Windows Vista, the task steps will be somewhat different.

 See Task 3.10, "Joining a Computer to a Domain," for more information.

Caveat

This sort of problem can be especially frustrating because any number of different computer-, server-, or network-related problems can be contributing factors.

Procedure

This task will teach you how to troubleshoot problems joining a computer to an Active Directory domain.

Equipment Used

No special equipment is needed for this task.

Details

This task will walk you through the steps in troubleshooting a problem of joining a computer to a Windows Active Directory domain.

Diagnosing a Problem Joining a Computer to a Domain

DISCOVERING THE PROBLEM

In most of the previous troubleshooting tasks, you already knew the outstanding problem when you received the trouble ticket. In this scenario, you are the one who discovers the problem.

1. Click Start ➢ Run.
2. In the Run box, type **cmd**.
3. At the command prompt, ping the IP address of the nearest domain controller and verify the connection.
4. Once it is verified, type **exit** and press Enter to close the command-prompt window.
5. Right-click My Computer.
6. Click Properties.
7. In the Properties box, click the Network Identification tab.

8. Click Properties.

9. Click the Domain radio button.

10. In the Domain field, type the correct name for the domain.

11. Click OK. An error message will appear.

12. Click OK.

TESTING YOUR FIRST ASSUMPTION

You notice that, in the Identification Changes box under the Computer Name field, the full computer name is displayed with the DNS suffix `network.local`. This may be interfering with the computer joining the domain.

1. Click More. Notice the Primary DNS suffix displays here as `network.local` too.

2. Delete the entry in the Primary DNS Suffix of This Computer field.

3. Verify that the check box Change Primary DNS Suffix When Domain Membership Changes is selected.

4. Click OK.

5. You are prompted to reboot the computer.

6. Click OK.

7. When the second prompt appears, click Yes.

8. After the machine reboots, log on as Administrator.

9. Repeat steps 2 through 7 in the "Discovering the Problem" section.

10. Verify that the full computer name contains no DNS suffix.

11. Verify that the Domain radio button is still selected and that the domain name is still in the Domain field.

12. Click OK. The same error message as before will appear.

13. Click Cancel to close the Identification Changes box.

14. Click Cancel to close the System Properties box.

TESTING YOUR SECOND ASSUMPTION

1. Open a command-prompt window.

> See the first three steps in the section "Discovering the Problem" earlier in this task if necessary, for details about opening a command-prompt window.

2. Ping the domain controller's IP address.

3. Ping the domain controller by hostname.

4. Ping the domain controller by name and DNS suffix.

```
C:\WINNT\system32\cmd.exe                                    _ □ X
Reply from 10.0.0.1: bytes=32 time=3ms TTL=128

Ping statistics for 10.0.0.1:
    Packets: Sent = 4, Received = 4, Lost = 0 (0% loss),
Approximate round trip times in milli-seconds:
    Minimum = 0ms, Maximum =   22ms, Average =   6ms

C:\Documents and Settings\Administrator>ping charlie

Pinging charlie [10.0.0.1] with 32 bytes of data:

Reply from 10.0.0.1: bytes=32 time<10ms TTL=128
Reply from 10.0.0.1: bytes=32 time<10ms TTL=128
Reply from 10.0.0.1: bytes=32 time<10ms TTL=128
Reply from 10.0.0.1: bytes=32 time=11ms TTL=128

Ping statistics for 10.0.0.1:
    Packets: Sent = 4, Received = 4, Lost = 0 (0% loss),
Approximate round trip times in milli-seconds:
    Minimum = 0ms, Maximum =   11ms, Average =   2ms

C:\Documents and Settings\Administrator>ping charlie.wiredwriter.local
Unknown host charlie.wiredwriter.local.

C:\Documents and Settings\Administrator>_
```

5. Look at the datasheet for this job and verify the domain name for this task.

6. Call the help desk and verify that the domain name is correct.

7. Have the help desk verify that the domain controller and local DNS server are operating. The help desk reports that both servers are operating normally and that they have received no calls from anyone else on that network segment stating that they could not connect to the domain.

> Although the PC could use any DC to join the domain, it is better to use one on the same network segment since the process doesn't have to cross one or more routers.

TESTING YOUR THIRD ASSUMPTION

1. Click Start ➢ Settings ➢ Control Panel.

2. Double-click Administrative Tools.

3. Double-click Event Viewer.

4. When the Event Viewer opens, select System Log.

Type	Date	Time	Source	Cat
Warning	7/23/2006	2:55:45 PM	Dnsapi	Noi
Information	7/23/2006	2:55:45 PM	Dnsapi	Noi
Warning	7/13/2006	10:25:19 PM	Print	Noi
Warning	7/13/2006	10:21:06 PM	Print	Noi
Warning	7/13/2006	10:21:05 PM	Print	Noi
Warning	7/13/2006	10:04:29 PM	Dnsapi	Noi
Information	7/13/2006	10:04:29 PM	Dnsapi	Noi
Information	7/13/2006	9:49:01 PM	Browser	Noi
Warning	7/9/2006	8:51:37 PM	Dnsapi	Noi
Information	7/9/2006	8:51:37 PM	Dnsapi	Noi
Information	7/9/2006	8:34:29 PM	Browser	Noi
Information	7/9/2006	8:31:34 PM	eventlog	Noi
Information	7/9/2006	8:31:34 PM	eventlog	Noi
Information	7/9/2006	8:30:50 PM	eventlog	Noi
Warning	7/9/2006	8:29:46 PM	Browser	Noi
Warning	7/9/2006	8:28:41 PM	MrxSmb	Noi
Warning	7/9/2006	8:28:28 PM	W32Time	Noi
Error	7/9/2006	8:27:56 PM	Netlogon	Noi
Error	7/9/2006	8:27:55 PM	Netlogon	Noi

Event Viewer - System Log   110 event(s)

5. Double-click on the most recent warning to read it.

6. Review all of the information available.

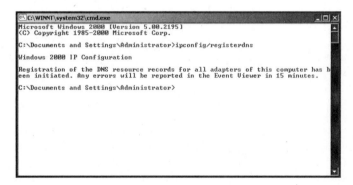

7. Click OK to close the Event Properties box.

8. Close Event Viewer.

9. Close Administrative Tools.

10. Open a command-prompt window.

11. Type **ipconfig/registerdns**.

12. Press Enter.

13. After the appropriate period of time passes, check the System Event Logs in the Event Viewer for errors.

Follow steps 1 through 3 in this section to open the Event Viewer.

14. Close the Event Viewer.

15. Close Administrative Tools.

16. Open a command-prompt window.

17. Ping the domain controller by its hostname and DNS suffix.

18. Close the command-prompt window.

> Follow the steps in Task 3.10, "Joining a Computer to the Domain," to join this computer to the domain.

Criteria for Completion

You will have successfully completed this task when you discover the cause of the error, correct it, and join the computer to the domain.

> If the issue had been with the domain controller, DNS server, or other high-level server or network problem, you would have handed off the task to a network technician or administrator to resolve before you attempted to join the computer to the domain.

Task 4.14: Troubleshooting Long Load and Print Times for Microsoft Word and Excel

As mentioned previously (see Tasks 4.11 and 4.12), much of your time as a PC technician will be spent trying to solve printing issues. Sometimes the print problem will come disguised as an application problem and careful questioning and investigation will be required to discover the true cause. On other occasions, the primary issue is with the application—and more often than most techs would like to admit, the true cause is sometimes a mystery.

Scenario

You receive a trouble ticket stating that a user in the HR department is having trouble loading Microsoft Word and Excel documents on her PC and that print times to the printer are also long. The printer is a shared device, attached to another PC in the same department. The user was able to load Microsoft Office documents and print normally prior to today. You report to HR and locate the user.

Scope of Task

Duration

This task should ideally take about 15 minutes.

Setup

You should be able to follow the steps in this task using a computer with either a local or a network printer. This task was written using Windows 2000 Professional. While you can use Windows XP Professional or Windows Vista to perform the proecdure, some of the specific steps will be slightly different.

Procedure

This task will show you how to diagnose issues related to printing from Microsoft Office products.

Equipment Used

No special equipment is needed for this task.

Caveat

Some problems you will be asked to resolve seem almost unique and you may find yourself trying to figure out exactly where to start.

Diagnosing Microsoft Office and Printer Problems

INITIALLY INVESTIGATING THE PROBLEM

1. Locate the user and ask her a few questions about the problem. Here are some relevant questions you could ask in this situation:

    -   When did the problem first occur?

    -   Have there been any recent configuration changes to the printer settings on the PC?

    -   Were any changes made to the hardware, software, or configuration settings of the computer just prior to the problem occurring for the first time?

    -   Do any error messages display when the user attempts to print?

    -   Do any error messages appear when she is loading a Word document or Excel spreadsheet?

    -   Are any other applications exhibiting similar behavior?

    -   Are there any issues with the PC that is directly connected to the printer?

You discover that the problems first started this morning after the user logged onto her computer. She says there have been no changes made to her computer or printer in months. No error messages appear when she tries to load documents or print. The only applications involved are Microsoft Office products.

2. Verify that the user is logged onto the computer.

3. Click Start ➢ Settings ➢ Printers, and right-click the network printer.

4. Click Properties.

5. Click Print Test Page.

6. After the test page prints, click OK to close the verify test page printing box.

7. Click OK to close the Properties box.

8. Click Start ➢ All Programs ➢ Microsoft Word. You notice that Word takes an exceedingly long time to open.

9. When Word does open, open a new document. This process also takes quite a bit of time.

10. Type a line of text in the new document.

11. Click File ➢ Print.

12. When the Print box opens, verify that the desired printer is selected.

13. Click Print. Printing takes much longer than usual but is finally accomplished.

14. Take the document out of the printer and look at it to verify that it has printed correctly.

TESTING YOUR FIRST ASSUMPTION

1. With the Printers box still open, right-click the printer.

2. Click Delete.

3. When the verification box appears, click Yes. A warning message appears stating that the default printer has been deleted.

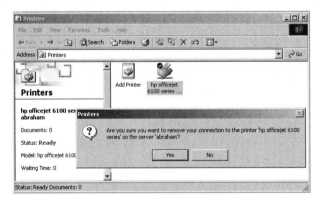

4. Click OK.

5. Double-click the Add Printer icon.

See Task 3.17 and follow the steps to add the network printer again.

6. Once the printer is reinstalled, print a test page.

7. Once the test page prints, open Word. In this case, Word opens normally.

8. Open a new document and type in a line of text.

9. Click File ➤ Print.

10. When the Print box opens, click Print. The test document prints normally.

11. Repeat steps 7 through 10 with Microsoft Excel.

Criteria for Completion

You will have successfully completed this task when the computer opens and prints Microsoft Office applications normally.

This is one of those troubleshooting tasks with no apparent cause, at least not one that you can discern. Occasionally, certain applications will "interact" with a printer and cause both the application and the printer to experience problems. If reinstalling the printer was not successful, your next step would have been to uninstall and reinstall Microsoft Office.

Task 4.15: Troubleshooting a CD Player Not Recognizing Audio CDs

You will often be assigned to resolve an issue having to do with a device used by a PC. In this case, you will need to know how to diagnose problems with optical devices. There can be both configuration and hardware issues involved, so if this problem cannot be solved while the PC is at the user's work area, you will have to take the computer to your workbench and attempt to resolve it there.

Scenario

You receive a trouble ticket stating that a user's optical drive has stopped recognizing audio CDs but is still able to open data CDs. You review the ticket and see the user works in the marketing department. You go to marketing and locate the user.

Scope of Task

Duration

This task should take about 15 minutes.

Setup

No special setup is required except access to a computer with an internal optical drive.

Caveat

The nature of this problem limits the possible causes since the drive can access one type of information but not another. Still, there are multiple possible causes.

Procedure

This task will teach you how to diagnose problems with optical drives.

Equipment Used

You will need no special equipment for this task.

Details

This task will guide you through the steps of diagnosing a problem with an optical drive.

Troubleshooting a Problem with an Optical Drive

INITIALLY INVESTIGATING THE OPTICAL DRIVE PROBLEM

1. Locate the user and ask him a few questions about the problem he's having. Here are some appropriate questions to ask in this situation:
    -   When did the problem first occur?
    -   Have there been any recent configuration changes to the optical drive?
    -   Were any changes made to the hardware, software, or configuration settings of the computer just prior to the problem occurring for the first time?
    -   Do any error messages display when the user attempts to play an audio CD?
    -   When the user opens a data CD, does he note any unusual behavior?
    -   Has the user tested the drive with more than one audio CD?

In this case, the user denies any recent changes to the PC or to the optical drive. He admits that he has only tried playing one audio CD, a recording of a training seminar he needs to review. No unusual behavior occurs when he opens data CDs, but when he puts in an audio CD, the drive either doesn't recognize there is a disc present or it indicates that the file type is unknown.

2. Sitting in front of the keyboard, ask the user to show you the collection of training CDs.

3. Ask the user to give you the disc he tried to play earlier.

4. Open the optical drive.

5. Put the disc in.

6. Close the drive.

7. Double-click My Computer.

8. Pay attention to the optical drive icon and listen for the sound of the disc spinning up. In this case, the drive is completely ignoring the disc.

9. Remove the disc from the drive.

10. Select another disc from the same collection and put it in the drive.

11. Observe the drive icon in the My Computer box. This time the drive seems to recognize that a disc is present, but you receive an error message stating the data type is unknown.

12. Remove the disc from the drive.

13. Ask the user or any of his coworkers if they have any other audio discs.

14. When one is located, put it in the optical drive.

15. If the symptomatic behavior persists, remove the disc.

16. Ask the user for a data disc.

17. Insert the data disc into the optical drive.

18. Notice if the disc is recognized and if you can open the disc to access the data files.

19. After the disc is recognized and you can access the data, remove the disc from the drive.

20. Close the My Computer box.

TESTING YOUR FIRST ASSUMPTION

1. Right-click My Computer.

2. Click Properties.

3. In the Properties box, click the Hardware tab.

4. Click Device Manager.

5. When Device Manager opens, expand the DVD/CD-ROM drives.

6. Select the optical drive.

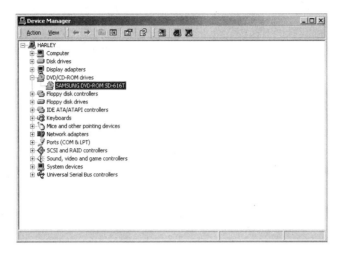

7. Right-click the drive name.

8. Click Properties.

9. On the General tab, see if any error messages appear.

10. Click the Properties tab.

11. Notice that the Enable Digital CD Audio for This CD-ROM Device check box is checked.

12. As this is not the default setting for optical devices used by your organization, ask the user for an explanation. The user remembers that he changed the setting a week ago, right before he left for vacation. The problems with audio CDs began to occur after he came back.

13. Deselect the check box.

14. Click OK.

15. Close Device Manager.

16. Click OK to close the System Properties box.

17. Locate the first CD you used to test the drive.

18. Open the drive and put the disc in.

19. Close the drive. You hear the disc spin up and a dialog box opens asking you what application you want to use to play the CD.

20. Select a player.

21. After the disc starts playing correctly, stop the playback.

22. Remove the disc from the drive.

23. Close any open dialog boxes.

Criteria for Completion

You will have successfully completed this task when the optical drive can recognize and play both data and audio CDs.

The Enable Digital CD Audio feature in Windows does not always interact well with all optical drive hardware. The permanent solution in this case is to disable the feature. If the user absolutely must play digital audio CDs, you will have to install a unit that is compatible with this feature.

Task 4.16: Troubleshooting the Error Message "Print Processor Unknown"

Here is yet another in a series of print-related problems. This one is characterized by a specific error message, which is a good thing because you can usually go to www.support. microsoft.com and search the Support Knowledge Base for the specific error and then discover the solution. No one can be expected to remember every single error message that a computer can deliver (with the exception of folks who write certification exams), so you will find yourself on the computer using your favorite search engine quite a lot.

Scenario

You have received a trouble ticket stating that several users in the Sales department have been receiving errors when they tried to print documents. The error reads as follows:

```
Event ID: 61
Event Type: Error
Event Source: Print
Description: The document document_name owned by username failed to
    print. Win32 error code returned by the print processor: 63(0x3f)
```

The sales-department staff had been printing normally until this morning. Instead of reporting to the sales department, you decide to first research the error message to see if you can narrow down the possible causes of the problem.

Scope of Task

Duration

Determining the cause of the problem should take less than 15 minutes. Correcting the problem could take a bit longer.

Setup

Ideally, you will need a Windows 2000 or higher server machine acting as a print server for one or more printers on a network. The network should have at least one client computer that you can print from.

Caveat

When interpreting an error message issued by Windows, you are better off searching the Microsoft support site than using a search engine such as Google. Google or any other search engine can cast too wide a net in its search, and you may end up spending a lot more time than necessary chasing down the answer to the problem.

Procedure

This task will show you how to research a printer error message and discover the solution to the printing problem.

Equipment Used

No special equipment is necessary to complete this task.

Details

This task will teach you the steps necessary to search for a specific error message, investigate your computing environment to determine how this error applies, and resolve the error.

Searching for and Discovering the Solution to an Error Message

SEARCHING FOR THE ERROR MESSAGE

1. Sitting at a computer connected to the Internet, open a web browser.
2. Type **www.support.microsoft.com** into the address field.

Be sure to bookmark all of the links you frequently use to research problems.

3. When the Microsoft support page loads, locate the search field in the upper-right corner of the web page.
4. Type **Win32 error code returned by the print processor** into the search field.
5. Press Enter.
6. Scroll through the results and select the one most likely to answer your query.

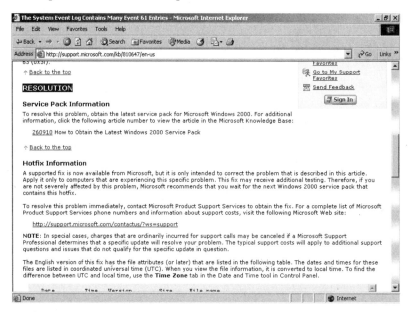

7. Click the link to open it.

8. Review the page to see if the information relates to your current issue.

9. Locate the specific resolution to the problem.

DISCOVERING HOW THE ERROR MESSAGE APPLIES TO YOUR SITUATION

1. Open another web-browser window or tab.

2. Go to the IT department's intranet site.

3. Look up the records regarding work orders for the sales department for the past few days. Specifically look for any work related to printers and print servers.

> **NOTE** You discover that the usual print server for the sales department suffered a catastrophic failure just after the close of business last night. The on-call tech contacted the IT-department manager by phone and received instructions on performing an emergency replacement of the print server with an older unit that has been in storage. The tech replaced the server with the older model and managed to get it up and running. The newer print server is being repaired today and should be back in service by tomorrow or the next day.

4. Review the records to see if there is a notation of what operating system and version the older print server is running. You discover that the print server is running Windows 2000 Server but you can't tell what the latest service pack is on the server. You find the hostname of the server in the records.

5. Open the Remote Desktop Web Connection web page.

6. Log on to the Windows 2000 Server print server as Administrator.

7. Right-click My Computer.

8. Click Properties.

9. On the General tab under System, look for the service pack number. You discover that this Windows 2000 Server machine is running Service Pack 3.

10. Click OK to close the Systems Properties box.

RESOLVING THE PROBLEM

1. Contact your supervisor and advise her of the situation. You are directed to update Windows 2000 Server to Service Pack 4 using a support disc stored in the IT department. This will allow the sales department to print pending the repair of the newer print server.

2. You acquire the support disc from where it is stored and use it to apply Service Pack 4 to the print server.

3. After the print server has been updated, phone the manager of the sales department.

4. Ask if he is one of the users who has had print issues. If he has been having printing problems, he can serve as your informant. If not, have him locate a user who has been experiencing the Event Type 61 error.

5. Have the informant print a document.

6. Verify that the document printed correctly and no errors were displayed.

7. Verify that several users who previously had printing problems can now print without errors.

Criteria for Completion

You will have successfully completed this task when you have correctly found the resolution to the error message and have applied it to your network, resolving the problem.

Task 4.17: Troubleshooting a "New Hardware Found" Message Appearing Repeatedly After Installing a New Scanner

Although some problems seem to almost continuously repeat themselves (such as "I can't print" problems), others seem like they are totally one of a kind. These sorts of problems can be difficult to diagnose because there is little or no support information on them. They may be puzzles to even the more experienced staff in your department. When you lack a solid framework for figuring out a problem, sometimes you have to just try changing things to see what happens.

Scenario

You receive a trouble ticket stating that a user's computer gives her a "New Hardware Found" message every time she reboots. Last week you installed a SCSI scanner on her PC and you recall you initially had that problem when logged on as Administrator, but the problem disappeared when you were logged on as the user. Now apparently the issue has resurfaced. You have been assigned to investigate and resolve the issue. You pack up your toolkit and report to the user at her branch office.

Scope of Task

Duration

Discovering what the problem is should take you about 30 minutes.

Setup

Ideally, in order to successfully complete this task, you would need to have a SCSI scanner (or printer or other peripheral device) attached to a PC with a SCSI controller installed as a PCI card.

Caveat

SCSI problems can be notoriously difficult to resolve—or at least to resolve easily. The most likely candidates for causes are issues with termination and device ID numbers.

See Task 1.9, "Installing a SCSI Drive," for a refresher on how SCSI devices are installed and set up.

Procedure

This task will teach you how to investigate and resolve a problem with a SCSI peripheral device.

Equipment Used

You will need no special equipment to complete this task.

Details

This task will take you through the steps required to investigate and resolve a problem with a SCSI device attached to a computer.

Diagnosing and Repairing a Problem with a SCSI Device

INITIALLY INVESTIGATING AN ISSUE WITH A SCSI DEVICE

1. Sitting at the computer, click Start ➤ Shut Down.
2. When the Shut Down Windows box appears, use the arrow to select Restart.
3. Click OK and allow the computer to reboot.
4. Observe the computer monitor as the operating system loads.

You notice that the New Hardware Detected balloon appears from the system tray after Windows XP has loaded. The user tells you that this happens every time she reboots or starts the computer after it has been shut down the previous night. She tells you that the problem started after you installed the SCSI scanner device late last week.

TESTING YOUR FIRST ASSUMPTION

1. Locate the SCSI cable connection on the back of the PC.
2. Unplug the cable.
3. Reboot the PC.

4. Observe the monitor as the operating system loads. You notice that the "New Hardware Found" message does not appear.

5. Plug the SCSI cable into the connector on the PC.

6. Reboot the computer.

7. Observe the monitor for messages as the operating system loads. You see a message that identifies the "new device" as "SCSI Devices 0-6."

8. Go over to the SCSI device.

9. Locate the dip switches on the back of the SCSI scanner.

Sometimes, the terminator settings and SCSI ID settings for the device are controlled by dip switches.

10. Locate the first dip switch that controls the SCSI terminator.

11. Change its setting from the down position to the up position.

Terminator dip switches have only two settings: on and off; however, it's possible to mistake one for the other.

12. Return to the PC and reboot it. When the OS loads, the "Found New Hardware" message is displayed.

TESTING YOUR SECOND ASSUMPTION

1. Return to the SCSI scanner.

2. Return the terminator dip switch to its original position.

When you had originally set up this scanner, you gave it the SCSI ID of 1. The SCSI controller itself is usually set at ID 0.

3. Change the dip switches to change the SCSI ID from 1 to 6. Changing the SCSI ID can be accomplished by different dip-switch configurations, depending on the make and model of SCSI device you are using.

4. Return to the computer and reboot it.

5. As the operating system loads, look for any messages. You notice that no "New Hardware Found" message occurs.

6. After a few minutes, reboot the computer again. After the second reboot, no "New Hardware Found" message occurs.

7. You ask the user to scan a document with the scanner to test its functioning. The scanner and computer behave normally.

Criteria for Completion

You will have successfully completed this task when you can reboot the computer without a "New Hardware Found" message occurring and when the computer and scanner behave normally.

Task 4.18: Troubleshooting the Inability to Connect a USB Digital Camera to a PC

This is another one of those problems that seems simple on the surface but turns into quite an adventure. Often a user will report one problem and possible solution and when you investigate, you find that the root problem and cause are something completely different. Sometimes you can't resolve the issue on your first attempt, and need to revisit it at least one more time to figure out the solution.

Scenario

You receive a trouble ticket stating that the manager of the finance department suddenly can't upload pictures from his USB digital camera or print via his USB printer. The ticket further states that the problems started happening after another technician installed a four-port USB switch recently. You have been assigned to investigate the problem. You pack up your toolkit and report to the finance manager's office.

Scope of Task

Duration

In a real-life situation, this problem would take days to track down, as you'll see when you begin to follow the steps. Your mileage may vary.

Setup

You will need a computer, a USB hub, and at least one or two USB devices to connect to the PC through the hub.

Caveat

This task will be difficult to simulate in your home or small lab due to the odd combination of circumstances that originally brought this problem about.

Procedure

This task will teach you how to troubleshoot multiple problems with USB devices.

Equipment Used

To follow the steps of this task properly, you'll need to acquire a USB PCI card, Phillips-head and flathead screwdrivers, and ESD protection.

Details

This task will take you step-by-step through the process of diagnosing multiple problems related to USB devices connecting to a PC.

Tracking Down and Resolving Problems with USB Devices

PERFORMING THE INITIAL INVESTIGATION AND TESTING

1. Locate the user and ask him some initial questions regarding the problem. Here is a list of some typical questions to ask regarding this sort of problem:

   - When did the problem begin?
   - Is the problem intermittent or constant?
   - What changed right before the problem started?
   - Was any new hardware or software installed recently?
   - Have any configuration changes been made recently?
   - Has the user tried to do anything to solve the problem?
   - When is the last time the user connected the camera to the PC?

The user explains that the problems began when another PC tech installed a USB hub on the PC. He uses an older PC with just two USB ports, but he has multiple USB devices he needs to connect to his computer. The original solution was to install the USB hub. The only changes made to the computer were the ones made by the other technician. Besides installing the hub, she mapped a new network drive for him so he could connect to files on the new management server. The user says when he connected the camera to the PC three months ago, it worked fine. He tried late yesterday and it wouldn't connect. His printer is still hooked up to the hub attached to his PC, but he disconnected the camera.

2. The user is currently logged on, so you sit at the computer and start to work.
3. Click Start ➤ Settings ➤ Control Panel and double-click Printers and Faxes.
4. Right-click the locally connected USB printer.
5. Click Properties.

6. Click Print Test Page. The test page prints normally.

7. Ask the user for permission to open one of his Word documents so you can try to print it.

8. Navigate to the location of the chosen document.

9. Right-click the document.

10. Click Print. The Word document prints normally.

11. Locate the USB camera and power it on.

12. Locate the USB cable for the camera and use it to connect the camera to the USB hub.

13. At the computer, click Start ➢ My Computer.

14. When My Computer opens, look for the USB camera. It should be recognized as a USB mass storage device and have a drive letter assigned.

15. There is no sign of the USB camera in My Computer. Unplug the camera's cable from the hub but leave the other end connected to the camera.

16. Connect the cable directly to one of the PC's USB ports. Since the computer has only two USB ports and the USB hub is attached to one of them, you have only one option for attaching the camera to the computer directly.

17. Once the camera is connected, verify that it is still powered up.

18. Return to the computer, and in the My Computer window, click View ➢ Refresh. Look again for the USB camera in the My Computer window.

19. There is still no sign of the camera. Disconnect the camera cable from the PC's USB port and power down the camera.

TESTING YOUR FIRST ASSUMPTION

1. Locate and review the documentation that came with the camera.

2. Locate the installation disc that came with the camera.

3. Click Start ➢ Settings ➢ Control Panel.

4. Double-click Add or Remove Programs.

5. When Add or Remove Programs opens, scroll until you locate the camera's software.

6. Select the camera's software in the list and click Remove.

7. If a dialog box opens asking if you want to remove all of the camera's software components, click Yes.

8. Review the camera's documentation about installing the camera's software.

9. Follow the steps in the documentation and reinstall the software. The process for reinstalling this software can be highly variable depending on the make and model of the camera. A generic set of steps is presented here.

10. Open the PC's optical drive and insert the camera's installation disc.

11. Close the drive door.

12. Open My Computer.

13. Right-click the optical drive and click Autoplay. The software installer wizard launches.

14. Proceed through the wizard until the camera's software is successfully reinstalled.

15. Consult the camera's documentation again and make sure there are no more steps to take before connecting the camera to the computer.

16. Power up the camera.

17. Connect the camera to the USB hub.

18. With My Computer still open, refresh the view.

19. The camera is still not recognized. Switch the connections of the camera with the printer to rule out a dead port.

20. Refresh the view in My Computer.

21. The camera is still not recognized. Proceed through the steps to print another test page from the computer to the USB printer. The test page prints normally.

TESTING YOUR SECOND ASSUMPTION

You return to the user's office the next day after having consulted with your supervisor. You have been directed to install a PCI card with multiple USB ports into the PC to see if this will solve the problem. When you arrive, the user says that the printer has stopped printing again.

1. Sitting at the computer, access Printers and Faxes.

2. Attempt to print a test page to the local USB printer. The attempt fails.

3. Check the printer's cable connection to the USB hub and verify that it's secure.

4. Check the printer's cable connection to the printer. You notice that the connection is loose.

5. Secure the cable connection to the printer.

6. Print a test page. The test page prints successfully.

7. Follow the steps in Task 1.3 to install the USB PCI card in the user's computer.

8. Once the card is installed and the PC case closed, power up the computer.

9. Click Start.

10. Right-click My Computer.

11. Click Properties.

12. On the System Properties box, click the Hardware tab.

13. Click Device Manager.

14. Expand Universal Serial Bus Controllers and verify that the card you just installed is recognized.

15. Close Device Manager and System Properties.

16. Disconnect the USB hub from the computer.

17. Switch the printer's cable from the hub to one of the USB ports on the newly installed card.

18. Attempt to print another test page. The attempt to print a test page fails.

19. Verify that the printer's USB cable is securely connected to the port on the computer.

20. Check the cable's connection to the printer. You notice that the cable is disconnected. You touch the printer and notice it rocks in position.

21. Lift the printer and move it aside. You see that the printer has been placed on a small stack of papers and booklets that is not level. You surmise that the printing problem may have been caused by the printer being periodically jostled, resulting in the cable becoming loose or disconnected.

22. Move objects around on the desk so that the printer is level on the desktop.

23. Reattach the cable to the printer.

24. Attempt to print another test page. The test page prints normally.

25. Power up the USB camera and attach it to a USB port on the newly installed card.

26. Open My Computer and look for an indication that the camera is recognized. The camera is not recognized.

27. Switch the USB ports for the printer and camera and retest. The camera is still not recognized; however, the printer successfully prints another test page.

28. Disconnect the camera's cable from the port on the PC.

29. Telephone the IT department and consult with one of the other techs. The tech has a suggestion but says that it is unlikely to work. You decide to try it anyway.

TESTING YOUR THIRD ASSUMPTION

1. Click Start ➤ My Computer.

2. Look for mapped network drives in the My Computer window under Network Drives. You recognize all of the drive mappings, including the one to the new server that has been assigned drive letter G.

3. Right-click the G drive and click Disconnect. The drive vanishes from the My Computer box.

4. Verify that the USB camera is still powered up and reconnect the camera's cable to the USB port.

5. In My Computer, click View ➤ Refresh. The camera appears in the My Computer box and is assigned drive letter G.

It is somewhat rare, but occasionally you will encounter a USB device that can connect to a computer only by using a precoded drive letter. When drive letter G was recently assigned to a new mapped drive, the camera could not connect using that drive letter, which resulted in the problem.

6. Test the connection by uploading photos from the camera to a folder on the PC.

7. Disconnect the camera from the computer.

8. Power down the camera.

9. Power up the camera.

10. Reconnect it to the PC and verify that it is again recognized and can exchange data.

11. Inform the user of the solution.

12. Telephone the IT department and verify that it is acceptable to use a different drive letter to connect the user to the new server.

13. Right-click My Computer and select Map Network Drive.

14. Select drive letter H from the list.

15. Type the path to the server in the Folder field.

16. Verify that the Reconnect at Login box is checked.

17. Click Finish to map the network drive.

18. Open My Computer and verify that the camera is recognized and the mapped drive is present.

19. Close all windows.

Criteria for Completion

You will have successfully completed this task when all USB devices can successfully connect to the PC and data can be transferred over those connections.

Task 4.19: Troubleshooting an Empty Outlook Contacts Folder

Troubleshooting email problems in the enterprise involves not only the email client (in this case, Outlook), but also the email server (Exchange). As a new PC tech, you will most likely need the assistance of your supervisor or a more seasoned technician. Troubleshooting and maintaining email is as much art as science, at least to the uninitiated. This is the sort of problem that seems mysterious at first but has a solution that's well known to techs and admins who've had to face it before.

Scenario

You receive a trouble ticket that a user at another building in your company's campus tried to open his Microsoft Outlook Contacts folder to address an email and found that it was empty. The help desk informs you that several other users in the same department have recently made similar complaints. You have been assigned to investigate the problem and attempt to resolve it.

One of the senior techs tells you that the only way to solve this problem is to uninstall and reinstall Outlook. Your supervisor advises you to take a look at the problem and to call her once you've made your evaluation rather than taking such an extreme approach to the problem.

You report to the department in question, locate the user who first reported the problem, and begin to question him.

Scope of Task

Duration

In a real-life situation, this could take anywhere from 30 minutes to several hours. In this particular scenario, the task should take about 15 minutes or less.

Setup

The ideal setup is to have a computer with Microsoft Outlook using Exchange Server as its mail server. That is most likely impractical for many readers; however, following along using your Outlook client software will be instructive.

Caveat

Part of a medical doctor's Hippocratic oath reads, "First, do no harm." The idea is to not make a bad situation worse. Blindly stumbling around, trying this setting and that in the hopes of chancing upon the solution, could compound the problem and erase vital clues as to the original source of the dilemma. If you feel like you are in over your head, you probably are. If your supervisor tells you to call her (or him) after taking certain steps, don't assume that you can exceed your directive and try to solve the problem on your own. One of the ways people learn is by paying attention to an educated and experienced tutor. We learn by listening, then doing.

Procedure

This task will show you how to investigate and resolve Microsoft Outlook problems.

Equipment Used

No special equipment will be necessary for this task.

Details

This task will show you step-by-step how to investigate and resolve a specific Microsoft Outlook issue.

Resolving an Issue with an Empty Outlook Contacts Folder

CONDUCTING THE INITIAL INVESTIGATION

1. Here are some common questions you can ask the end user:

    - When did the problem begin?

    - What changes were made to the computer's hardware and software just prior to the user noticing the problem?

    - Do any other users have the same problem?

    - Does this user's computer have any issues in common with other affected computers?

    - Has the user done anything to try to resolve the problem?

    - If so, what has he done and what was the result?

 The user states that the problem began a few days ago. He learned that three other users in the same department have the same problem. As far as the user knows, no changes have been made to his computer or any other affected computer.

2. Sitting at the user's computer, double-click the Outlook icon on the desktop to open Outlook.

3. Click Tools ➢ Address Book in the top toolbar.

4. Click the drop-down menu arrow for the Show Names from The field and choose Contacts. The Contacts folder is completely empty.

5. Use the drop-down menu arrow to open the list again.

6. Click another selection, such as All Contacts. Your selection is populated normally.

7. Make other selections from the list. All other menu selections are normally populated. Only the Contacts folder is empty.

CONSULTING WITH YOUR SUPERVISOR

1. Call your supervisor as directed and report your situation.

2. As your supervisor gives you specific instructions, write them down on a pad.

TESTING THE FIRST ASSUMPTION

1. Following your supervisor's instructions, right-click the Outlook icon.

2. Click Properties.

3. Click the E-mail Accounts button.

4. Under Directory, select the View or Change Existing Directories or Address Books radio button.

5. Click Next.

6. Select the Outlook Address Book radio button.

7. Click Remove.

8. Click Finish.

9. Click Add.

10. Click Add Additional Address Book.

11. Click Next.

12. Select the name of the Exchange mail server from the list.

13. Click Next.

14. When the Add E-mail Account dialog box prompts you to exit Outlook and restart it, click OK.

15. Click Finish.

16. Click Close in the Mail Setup – Outlook box.

TESTING YOUR FIRST SOLUTION

1. Double-click the Outlook icon on the desktop to open it.

2. Click Tools ➢ Address Book.

3. Click the drop-down menu arrow for the Show Names from The field.

4. Click Contacts. The Contacts folder is populated. The user examines the folder and reports that all of the expected addresses are present.

Criteria for Completion

You will have successfully completed this task when you have recovered the contents of the Outlook Contacts folder.

Task 4.20: Troubleshooting No Restart of UPS Device Service After Being Connected

A UPS, or uninterruptible power supply, is a device that stands between your servers and the primary power outlet. The idea is that if there is an interruption of main power, the battery inside the UPS will keep the servers going until you can perform a graceful shutdown on all of them. This avoids unpleasant events like data loss or corruption. UPS devices also "treat" the power as it goes through the device so that any small sags or spikes in the current are "smoothed out."

Although the power doesn't go out every day (hopefully), it is still a big concern if your UPS device goes out on you. It means that until it is repaired or replaced, your valuable server data are at risk of a power outage. Power can go out for a wide variety of reasons, ranging from a thunderstorm to a car accident. You never know when an outage will occur, so keeping your UPS going is a must.

Scenario

You receive a trouble ticket stating that the folks at one of the branch offices can't restart the UPS device service after moving their small server. They powered down the server and UPS unit for about half an hour for the move yesterday. The server rebooted properly but the office manager who was in charge of the move received an error message stating that the UPS service is stopped. The manager says she configured the Power Options setting in Windows to control the device right after powering the computer up but the UPS service didn't start.

You've been assigned to visit the branch office and attempt to resolve the problem. You report to the branch office, contact the office manager, and begin asking her questions about the specifics of the problem.

Scope of Task

Duration

This task should take no more than 30 minutes.

Setup

The ideal setup would be to have a UPS device attached to a PC.

 You can probably pick up a UPS device from your local computer store for $40 to $80 and can probably find one even cheaper on eBay.

Caveat

UPS devices can range in size from smaller than a shoebox to larger than a commercial freezer, depending on how much power they are expected to deliver. Depending on the make and model, their configuration settings and requirements can be radically different. The exact steps you take with your own UPS device may vary from the ones outlined here.

Procedure

This task will teach you the skills necessary to diagnose and resolve a problem with a UPS device.

Equipment Used

Except for what was described in the Setup section, no special equipment is required.

Details

This task will show you the steps to take to investigate and resolve an issue when the UPS service fails to restart.

Diagnosing and Resolving Problems with a UPS Device

INITIALLY INVESTIGATING THE PROBLEM

1. Some reasonable questions to ask the user are as follows:

   - What events occurred prior to the start of the problem?
   - What have you done to try to resolve the issue?
   - What changes to the hardware and software have been made recently?
   - Have there been any prior issues with the UPS unit?

> If you were diligent, you would have checked the repair records for this office to determine the service history of the server and UPS device.

> The office manager explains that the server and networking devices are kept in a utility area just off the main floor. They also use the room for their printer, copier, and fax machines. When they replaced the copier with a larger unit, the manager decided that everything would have to be moved around so the new copier would fit. The office staff correctly powered down the server and moved it and the UPS device to another area in the room. When they powered up the server and UPS device, the server seemed unchanged but the UPS device was not working, even though there was no other indication of a problem, such as a warning message. If the manager attaches the server to the UPS device and then unplugs the device, instead of the battery taking over and the alarm sounding, the server shuts down.

> After further questioning and a brief search, the manager tells you that she cannot locate the UPS device's manual or any other information or software related to the device.

2. Sitting at the server (actually, they are using a Windows XP Professional machine as their "server"), click Start ➢ Control Panel.
3. Double-click Power Options.
4. Select the UPS tab. You see a notice stating, "The UPS service has lost contact with the UPS device."

TESTING YOUR FIRST ASSUMPTION

1. On the UPS tab, click Select. You notice that the computer is configured to communicate with the UPS device on COM1.
2. Check the connection of the cable attached to the serial port on the computer.

3. Check the connection of the other end of the cable attached to the UPS device.

4. Use the On Port drop-down menu to switch from COM1 to COM3.

5. Verify that American Power Conversion is selected in the Select Manufacturer menu.

> The UPS device used in this example is manufactured by American Power Conversion (APC).

6. Verify that the correct model of the device is selected in the Select Model field.

7. Click Finish. You see a notice stating, "To commit the new settings, choose OK or Apply."

8. Click Apply. After a pause, the message "UPS Service Has Lost Contact with the UPS Device" appears.

9. Click Select and return the port setting to COM1.

> It is good troubleshooting practice to return the setting to the original configuration if a change has not produced results. If you start making too many changes, you won't be able to tell what is or isn't having an effect on the computer.

10. Click Cancel to close the Power Options box.

TESTING YOUR SECOND ASSUMPTION

1. While still in Control Panel, double-click Administrative Tools.

2. Double-click Event Viewer.

3. When the Event Viewer opens, click System.

4. Double-click the most recent error message. You see a message stating, "The Uninterruptible Power Supply service terminated with the following error: The UPS service is not configured correctly."

5. Click on messages subsequent to the error message. On the series of information events that follow, you read these messages:

   - "The Uninterruptible Power Supply service was successfully sent a start control."
   - "The Uninterruptible Power Supply service entered the running state."
   - "The Uninterruptible Power Supply service was successfully sent a stop control."
   - "The Uninterruptible Power Supply service entered the stopped state."

6. Close all open events.

7. Close the Event Viewer.

8. While still in Administrative Tools, double-click Services.

9. Scroll down until you see the Uninterruptible Power Supply service.

10. If it is not selected, click the Extended tab near the bottom of the Services box.

11. Click the link in Restart the Service.

12. When the service restarts, close the Services box.

13. Close Administrative Tools.

14. Open Power Options in Control Panel.

15. Click the UPS tab and check the status of the UPS device. You continue to see that the UPS service has lost contact with the UPS device message.

16. Close Power Options.

DOING FURTHER RESEARCH AND TESTING YOUR THIRD ASSUMPTION

1. Open a web browser on the computer.

2. Use a search engine to locate the UPS manufacturer's website.

3. Navigate to that website.

4. On the main page in the top navigation menu, click Support.

5. Locate and then click the Phone Support link.

6. Locate the toll-free number for technical support.

7. Call technical support. After you navigate through a voicemail system and wait for a period of time, a support representative answers your call. You explain the situation to the rep and he looks up possible resolutions to the problem.

An alternative set of steps to perform prior to calling tech support is to search the vendor's online knowledge base to see if it records this problem and its solution.

8. After finishing the call with the vendor's tech-support rep, open Power Options.

9. Select the UPS tab and then click Select.

10. Click the drop-down menu arrow under Select Manufacturer and choose (None).

11. Click Finish.

12. Click OK.

13. Close Control Panel.

14. Verify that the UPS device is powered and running.

15. Make sure the server is not in active use and ask users to close all files they are accessing and disconnect from the server.

16. Unplug the UPS device from the wall electrical socket.

You would never want to unplug the UPS device on a machine providing active services such as DHCP or DNS to the network. Before performing such a task, you want to make absolutely sure that there will be no loss of services or data as a result of the server losing power. If necessary, provide another server as a substitute while you are performing this test.

17. The UPS device issues an alarm and the server continues to operate from power in the UPS unit's battery. Plug the UPS device back into the main electrical socket.

This particular UPS device model was initially configured to be controlled not by Windows but rather by its own on-board process.

Criteria for Completion

You will have successfully completed this task when you have restored the UPS device to proper functioning and it provides battery power to the computer when the main power terminates.

Task 4.21: Troubleshooting a System Conflict with a Hidden Device

It's difficult to imagine that there may be "hidden" devices attached to your computer, but in this case, "hidden" means a device that is not reported by your Windows XP or Windows Vista Device Manager. Devices are not reported by the Device Manager if they are not Plug and Play devices. Since modern devices are Plug and Play, you should only encounter such a problem if older, legacy machines are connected to your computer. These older devices can cause problems if they result in device conflicts with other machines attached to a PC. Ironically, you normally use Device Manager to diagnose device conflicts. How can you perform such a conflict diagnosis if the device is invisible to Device Manager?

Scenario

You receive a trouble ticket from a user in the accounting department that states the speakers on his computer aren't working. He can't use anything that plays music or other sound at all. You check the maintenance records for this computer and discover that a new sound card was installed just yesterday. You suspect that the sound card is defective and decide to replace it with an identical unit. Taking your toolkit and the sound card, you go to the user's cubicle and prepare to swap out the cards.

Scope of Task

Duration

Once the actual reason for the sound-card failure is discovered, it should take only a few minutes to resolve the issue.

Setup

No special setup is required.

Caveat

This is another example of assuming a problem has a specific cause when, in fact, the cause is very different.

Procedure

This task will teach you how to diagnose problems related to hidden-device conflicts.

Equipment Used

Despite the initial assumption that the sound card is at fault, for the purpose of this task, you do not need to remove and replace a PCI or PCI Express card on your test computer.

Details

This task walks you through the process of discovering a hidden-device conflict on a Windows XP or Windows Vista computer.

Investigating and Resolving a Device Conflict

TESTING YOUR INITIAL ASSUMPTION

1. You report to the user's work area with your toolkit and the new sound card and advise the user that you believe his current card is faulty and plan to install a working card.

 See Task 1.3, "Installing a PCI Card," and Task 1.4, "Installing a PCI Express Card," for specific instructions on how to replace one extension card with another.

2. After having replaced the sound card and powering up the computer, you discover that the PC still cannot play sound from any application or from an audio disc in the optical drive.

3. You verify that the speakers are plugged into the correct port and that the connection is secure.

4. You verify that the speakers are turned to a sufficient volume for sound to be heard.

5. You go to Control Panel, double-click Sounds and Audio Devices, confirm that the volume slider is set to the High position, and confirm that the Mute check box is clear.

6. You reinstall the card you had earlier removed and verify that sounds still cannot be played.

7. You call the IT department and discuss the situation with your supervisor, receiving additional troubleshooting instructions.

TESTING YOUR SECOND ASSUMPTION

1. You click Start, right-click My Computer, and then click Properties.

2. In the System Properties box, you click the Hardware tab and then click Device Manager.

3. When Device Manager opens, you look but are unable to find any device conflicts.

4. Click View and then click Show Hidden Devices.

5. Verify that there is a device conflict present between a legacy scanner and the sound card.

6. With the user's permission, you right-click on the scanner in Device Manager, which the user hasn't needed for quite some time, and click Uninstall.

7. Close the Device Manager.

8. Physically disconnect the scanner from the computer.

9. Ask the user to open an application he expects to play sound.

10. Verify that the user's application plays sound appropriately.

Criteria for Completion

You will have successfully completed this task when you have resolved the hidden-device conflict and the user's computer can play sounds normally.

Task 4.22: Troubleshooting Excel Locking Up

Sometimes different applications don't work and play well together. On top of that, a seemingly random event could further alter the situation and cause yet another problem that seems to have no origin and no solution. Troubleshooting is rarely a "by-the-book" recipe (with the possible exception of the solutions in this book). Often, when you respond to a trouble ticket, you have no idea what you're really walking into.

Scenario

You receive a trouble ticket stating that one of the managers at the mechanical operations plant is having trouble accessing an Excel document. Every time she opens it and tries to work with it, another application spontaneously launches and Excel freezes. This has been happening for a week. You have been assigned to investigate and resolve the issue.

You report to the plant and locate the manager in question. She takes you to her office and directs you to the computer. She mentions that she thinks another one of her staff tried to access and copy an Excel file a few days ago, right before the problem started.

Scope of Task

Duration

In a real-world scenario, this task could take hours or even days, depending on how much time you have to work on it on any given day (remember, you have other duties to perform) and how well your problem-solving skills have been honed.

Setup

All you'll need is a Windows computer that has Microsoft Excel installed.

Caveat

Exactly duplicating this situation is difficult because of the unusual combination of events that caused the problem.

Procedure

This task will teach you how to diagnose problems with Excel and other applications.

Equipment Used

You will need no special equipment for this task.

Details

This task walks you step-by-step through the process of investigating and resolving a problem with Microsoft Excel.

Investigating and Resolving an Issue with Excel

PERFORMING THE INITIAL INVESTIGATION

1. Sitting at the computer, open Excel.

2. The end user directs you to the specific file that has been having problems and you open it. Another application opens and tries to load microphone dictating software. Both programs lock up.

3. Press Ctrl+Alt+Del.

4. When the Windows Security box opens, click Task Manager.

5. Click the Applications tab.

6. Select Microsoft Excel and click End Task.

7. When Excel closes, select the other application and click End Task.

8. When both applications are closed, close Task Manager.

The user informs you that she doesn't use the dictation program. It was installed on the computer by her predecessor. You call the IT department and discuss the matter with your supervisor. Your supervisor informs you that the dictation software is not supported by IT and was likely installed by the previous user without permission. You are given permission to remove the dictation program. Your supervisor informs you of how to perform this task.

If at all possible, do not allow end users to install unsupported applications on company computers. The end result could most likely be problems such as the one presented here.

TESTING YOUR FIRST ASSUMPTION

1. Click Start ≻ Control Panel.

2. Double-click Regional and Language Options.

3. Click the Languages tab.

4. Click Details.

5. In the Installed Services pane, select the dictation program.

6. Click Remove.

7. Click OK.

8. Click OK to close Regional and Language Options.

9. Close Control Panel.

10. Open Excel.

11. Open the Excel file that has been locking up.

12. Attempt to make a change to the document.

13. Try to save your changes. You receive an error message stating that your changes cannot be saved.

14. Close the file.

15. Open another Excel file.

16. Make changes to that file.

17. Attempt to save that file. You can successfully save the file.

TESTING YOUR SECOND ASSUMPTION

1. Open the file that has been having problems.

2. Click Help ➢ Detect and Repair in the top toolbar. The Detect and Repair dialog box appears, stating that the service will automatically find and fix errors in all Office files.

3. If it's not already checked, check the Restore My Shortcuts While Repairing check box.

4. Click Start. Windows Installer appears and prepares to repair the file. This process may take some time. When the setup is finished, a dialog box appears stating that Microsoft Office Setup has completed successfully.

5. Click OK.

6. Close the document and Excel.

7. Open Excel and open the document.

8. Make a change to the Excel document.

9. Attempt to save your changes. You can successfully save your changes.

10. Close the file and close Excel.

11. Direct the user to open Excel and the file, make the appropriate changes to the document, and save them. The end user is successful.

 There may be times when you'll solve a problem without completely understanding the cause at the level of the program.

Criteria for Completion

You will have successfully completed this task when the end user can access Excel and her other applications normally.

Task 4.23: Troubleshooting No Monitor Image When the PC Is Powered Up

Some problems seem very basic in terms of causes and solutions, but the occasional "head scratcher" can still make an appearance. However, there are still only so many reasons for a PC to be on and operating but have no image displaying on the monitor.

Scenario

You receive a trouble ticket stating that a user in research says she powered up her PC this morning but no image appears on her monitor. Yesterday, the monitor was working fine. The user states that she's tried "everything" to fix the problem but with no success. You report to research and locate the user at her computer.

Scope of Task

Duration

This task should take about 10 to 15 minutes.

Setup

No special setup is required.

Caveat

You can complete this task using either a CRT or an LCD monitor (not including laptops).

 In the case of CRT monitors, *do not* open up the monitor case and attempt to probe inside. The risk of a dangerous and even fatal electrical shock is high *even if the monitor is unplugged!* This task only requires that you follow the subsequent steps, and none of them includes opening up a CRT monitor.

Procedure

This task will teach you how to diagnose basic monitor and video issues.

Equipment Used

No special equipment is needed for this task.

Details

This task will go through the steps of diagnosing a nonresponsive monitor and providing a solution.

Troubleshooting a Problem with a Blank Computer Monitor

YOUR INITIAL INVESTIGATION AND TESTING YOUR FIRST ASSUMPTION

1. Push the power button on the monitor.
2. If no image appears, push it again.

3. Crawl under the desk, locate the monitor's power cord, and make sure it is securely connected to a power source.

4. Go to the back of the monitor and verify that the power cord is securely connected to the monitor.

5. Sitting at the computer, locate the brightness and contrast controls, adjusting them and seeing if an image appears.

> The five steps in the first section represent the three most common causes of this complaint: the monitor is turned off, it has no power, and the brightness and contrast controls are not correctly adjusted.

6. Get permission from the user to take the PC to your workbench for further tests.

TESTING YOUR SECOND ASSUMPTION

1. Take the PC to your workbench.

> Most IT-tech workstations include a working monitor, keyboard, and mouse to be used for testing computer problems.

2. Connect the PC to a keyboard, mouse, monitor, and power supply.

3. Verify that the monitor is connected to a power supply.

4. Turn on the monitor.

5. Power up the PC. A correct image appears on the monitor. You observe the monitor through the boot process and the loading of the operating system. There continues to be no problem with the image.

6. Return the PC to the user along with a monitor that is known to be in good working order.

> Only superheroes carry heavy objects over long distances. Get a cart to take any heavy equipment from and to the user.

7. Reconnect the PC, monitor, input devices, and power connections.

8. Power up the PC and monitor. A good image appears on the monitor.

9. Remove the old monitor from the user's work area.

> Monitors get old and finally give out. If the issue had not been the monitor, the next most likely suspects would have been corrupted video drivers, an unseated video card, or a damaged video card.

Criteria for Completion

You will have successfully completed this assignment when the user can get a viable image on the computer's monitor.

Task 4.24: Troubleshooting the Inability to Connect to a Mapped Drive

One way to make it easier for users to access resources on servers is to map a network drive to the shared folder on the server. (See Task 3.1, "Mapping Drives.") Although the user could type the path in the Run box, it is easier for most people to open up My Computer, click on a drive, and have it open. If you tell a user that her accounts-payable template is on her J drive, you don't have to explain that it's actually on the "such-and-such" server and can be accessed by entering the path \\server_name\share_name.

Occasionally, a user will complain that he or she can't access a mapped network drive, and it will be your job to find out why and to resolve the issue.

Scenario

You receive a trouble ticket stating that a user in the payroll department can't access her J drive to retrieve her most recent accounting data. You check the work records for her computer and the server the J drive is mapped to and see no recent problems recorded. You access the relevant server using the remote web connection interface and are able to connect to the server and the share. You report to payroll and locate the user. She is already logged on, so you sit down at the computer and start to work.

Scope of Task

Duration

This task should take you about 10 minutes.

Setup

Ideally, the computer you use for this task will have a mapped network drive that connects to a local or network shared folder.

Caveat

Sometimes a problem is relatively simple to solve. The only reason you might have a difficult time is if you overlook the obvious.

Procedure

This task will help you learn to solve problems with mapped drives.

Equipment Used

No special equipment is required for this task.

Details

This task will take you through the process of investigating a mapped drive issue and determining the solution.

Discovering and Resolving a Mapped Drive Problem

BEGINNING THE INVESTIGATION

1. Click Start ➢ My Computer. You notice that the J drive is missing from the Network Drives area but see the drive letters for the hard drive, floppy drive, and optical drive.

2. Close My Computer.

3. Click Start.

4. Right-click My Computer.

5. Click Map Network Drive.

6. Use the drop-down arrow to expand the Drive menu and look for the J drive mapping. You noticed that no drive letters are mapped, including the J drive.

7. Select the J drive.

8. Click the Browse button by the Folder field and browse to the required server share.

9. In the Browse for Folder window, select the network share.

10. Click OK.

11. Select the Reconnect at Logon check box.

12. Click Finish. The J drive window opens, showing you the contents of the shared folder.

13. Close the J drive window.

TESTING YOUR FIRST ASSUMPTION

1. Click Start ➢ Log Off.

2. When the Log Off Windows dialog box appears, click Log Off.

3. When the user is logged off and the Log On box appears, have the user log on.

4. Once the user is logged on, click Start ➢ My Computer.

5. In the Network Drives area, the J drive appears.

6. Double-click the J drive to open it.

7. Close the J drive.

The most likely explanation for this issue is that somehow, the Reconnect at Logon check box had been cleared and when the user logged off the computer, the drive mapping was lost.

Criteria for Completion

You will have successfully completed this task when the drive mapping is restored and the user can log off and log back on and still connect to the mapped drive.

Task 4.25: Troubleshooting the Inability to Access a Shared Folder on a Remote Computer

This task is similar to Task 4.24, "Troubleshooting the Inability to Connect to a Mapped Drive;" however, it is a bit more complicated. Although both tasks involve a user being unable to access a shared folder on the network, there are a wide variety of causes for such an event. It's a good idea to become familiar with this sort of problem because you'll encounter it often.

Scenario

You receive a trouble ticket stating that a user in the chemical lab located at a branch office can't access a shared folder on the local server. Recently, all of his data has been added to a single shared folder on a new server so he and his team members can share their work. Unfortunately, he and his coworkers can't get to those files in the shared folder.

You access the work record for that office and see that a new server was installed over the weekend. Data from several PC hard drives were consolidated into one shared folder on that server. There is no indication that there were problems with the installation and setup.

You report to the chem lab and locate the user.

Scope of Task

Duration

This task should take about 15 minutes.

Setup

For this task, you will need to have two computers networked together. One of the computers will need to have a folder shared on the network.

Caveat

Network access problems can be many and varied. This is one of those situations where asking the user a few well-worded questions will help narrow down your search.

Procedure

This task will teach you how to diagnose and resolve problems accessing network shares.

Equipment Used

No special equipment is required for this task.

Details

In this task, you will go through the steps necessary to investigate and resolve a problem accessing shared network folders.

Diagnosing and Resolving an Inability to Access a Network Share

PERFORMING YOUR INITIAL INVESTIGATION

1. These are some relevant questions to ask the user who first discovered the problem:
   - When did you discover the problem?
   - Do all users on your team have the same access problem?
   - Has there ever been a time when you were able to access the shares?
   - Are you able to access other shared folders and devices?
   - What exactly can you access and not access?

 You discover that everyone in the office can open the shared folder and open documents but that no one can modify the documents, not even the document owners. This started after their data was moved off their local hard drives and into the shared folder on their office server. Everyone is able to access all of the shared folders and devices that were not moved during last weekend's server installation.

2. Sitting at the user's computer, click Start ≻ Run.
3. Ask the user for the path to the shared folder and type the path in the Run box.
4. Click OK. The shared folder opens and you can see the documents the folder contains.

5. Double-click one of the documents to open it. You notice in the blue title bar over the Word toolbar that the name of the document and Microsoft Word are displayed along with (Read Only).

6. Close the document and open others to see if they're all Read Only. The user confirms that all documents in the folder are Read Only for everyone in the office.

7. Close all documents and the network share.

TESTING YOUR FIRST ASSUMPTION

1. Have the user show you where the server is located.

2. Sitting at the server's keyboard, log on as Administrator.

 In a large networked environment, specific administrator accounts are created on servers so IT staff can log on regardless of where in the network the servers are located and which departments they serve.

3. Navigate to the shared folder.

4. Right-click the folder.

5. Click Sharing and Security. In Network Sharing and Security on the Sharing tab, you notice that the Share This Folder on the Network check box is checked but the Allow Network Users to Change My Files check box is cleared.

6. Check the Allow Network Users to Change My Files check box.

7. Click OK. The Setting Share Permissions box appears, showing the progress of changing the share configuration. This process may take a few moments.

8. When the process is finished, click OK to close the shared folder.

9. Return to the user's computer and access the remote share.

10. Open a document in the shared folder. When the document opens, it is no longer tagged as Read Only.

11. Make some minor change to the document and save it.

12. Close the document.

13. Open the document again and notice if the modification is still present.

 There were two signs that the problem is resolved: when you attempted to save the changes and did not receive a message stating that the document is read only and when the document closed after accepting the saved modifications.

14. Have the user make changes to other files and save them.

15. Verify that all users in the office can access, modify, and save documents.

Criteria for Completion

You will have successfully completed this task when all users can open, read, modify, and save their own files and other shared files in the folder.

Task 4.26: Troubleshooting the Inability to Connect to the Network

In previous tasks, you've investigated problems with users having difficulty accessing some resource on the network. There are times when you will need to diagnose a situation in which the user can't connect to the network at all. If all users on a network segment lose connectivity, you can be reasonably assured that the problem lies with an internetworking device in the server room. When a single user has a connection problem, there can be any number of causes.

Scenario

You receive a trouble ticket stating that a user in the data-entry section of the administrative department has lost her connection to the network this morning. She had a connection when she first logged on but lost it after working about an hour. You check the service logs and see that no one else from her department has reported any networking problems. You check the switch that serves Admin's network segment and use the cabling documentation (see Task 3.12, "Mapping Network Cables") to locate the switch port assigned to the user's computer. The link light on that port is dark.

Your supervisor enters the server room and you explain the problem. She tells you to report to the user and investigate the problem at that end while she consoles into the switch to see if there is a problem with the switch port.

Scope of Task

Duration

Once you access the user's computer, this task will take about 10 minutes.

Setup

For this task, you will need two computers that are networked together through a hub or switch.

Caveat

Since network-connection problems have many causes, this is another situation in which your investigation should begin by questioning the user.

Procedure

This task will illustrate how to diagnose a general network-connection problem.

Equipment Used

You will need no special equipment to complete this task.

Details

This task will walk you step-by-step through the process of investigating a general network-connection problem experienced by a single user.

Diagnosing a Network-Connection Problem

BEGINNING YOUR INITIAL INVESTIGATION

1. Here are some questions to ask the user:

   - When did the problem occur?

   - What were you doing right before you lost connectivity?

   - Are you experiencing a total loss of connectivity or is it intermittent?

   - Have you ever had this problem before?

   - Have any changes been made to your computer's hardware or software recently?

   - Have you made any changes to the computer or immediate networking environment recently?

 The user reports that she logged onto the domain at 8 a.m. as usual and experienced no problems. An hour later, she was attempting to access a remote file share when she lost her network connection. She cannot access any network resource at all. She said that no changes have been made to her computer recently but she needed a second network connection at her desk to accommodate her manager's laptop. At her manager's request, she is copying some files to the laptop in preparation for the manager's upcoming trip to a conference. She brought in a small five-port switch from home to split her connection. You discover that she installed it a few days ago under her desk.

2. Go under the user's desk and locate the switch.

3. Verify the network-patch-cable and power-cable connections. You notice that the patch-cable connections are secure and the cables are configured correctly but the power cable for the switch is disconnected from the switch. It's possible that the user accidentally kicked the switch or snagged her foot in the power cable, causing the cable to disconnect.

4. Reconnect the power cable and verify that the switch's power and link lights come on.

TESTING YOUR FIRST ASSUMPTION

1. Sitting at the computer, click Start ➢ Run.

2. Type **cmd** in the Run box.

3. Click OK.

4. When the command-prompt window opens, type **ipconfig/all**.

5. Press Enter.

 The IP address for the computer is listed at 169.254.69.8 with a subnet mask of 255.255.0.0. You recognize this address range as belonging to Automatic Private IP Addressing (APIPA), which is usually assigned to a computer when it cannot connect to a DHCP server.

6. Type **ipconfig/release** and press Enter.

7. Type **ipconfig/renew** and press Enter. The computer receives an IP address from the DHCP server in the range assigned to the administrative network segment.

8. Type **ping** and then the hostname of a file server and press Enter. You receive a reply from the server.

9. Type **ping** and then the domain name of an Internet host such as www.google.com.

 Some Internet hosts turn off echo replies for security reasons, so this test isn't always reliable. As of this writing, Google allows echo replies.

10. Press Enter. You receive a reply from the Internet host.

11. Close the command-prompt window.

 When you return to the IT department, you will be obligated to report that an end user installed a piece of networking equipment without consulting with the IT department. Since this was done at the request of her manager, your supervisor will need to make appropriate contact with the manager and discuss proper use policy involving the installation of unsupported hardware.

Criteria for Completion

You will have successfully completed this task when the user is once again able to connect to the network.

Task 4.27: Troubleshooting Connection Problems with an External USB Hard Drive

USB devices are ubiquitous in today's computing environment. We quickly and easily attach all kinds of devices to our desktops and laptops via USB and the vast majority of time, the device "just works." Should a USB device ever fail to operate as we expect, I'm sure most people would be at least puzzled. As a PC technician, in this unlikely eventuality, you'll be expected to do something about it.

Scenario

You receive a trouble ticket from a user in sales. He has been using an external USB hard-disk drive (HDD) to connect to his PC and temporarily store data from customer responses to a product demo that his department is using. Today, he plugged the device into his computer and immediately received the message "You may now safely remove hardware." He is unable to access the device at all.

You report to the salesperson's cubicle with your toolkit, sit at the keyboard, and open My Computer. You see the USB device listed as UNKNOWN, UNREADABLE. You double-click the drive icon and receive no response. You suspect a connection problem is the cause.

Scope of Task

Duration

This task should just take a few minutes.

Setup

For this task, you will need an appropriate USB hard-disk drive. A thumb drive will not be sufficient.

Caveat

The only concern you should keep in mind is to maintain standard precautions whenever opening up any device.

Procedure

This task will show you how to diagnose a connection problem between a computer and a USB hard drive.

Equipment Used

You should need only a screwdriver and a second USB device, such as a thumb drive.

Details

This task will take you through the steps of diagnosing a connection problem between a computer and a USB hard-disk drive (HDD).

Diagnosing a Connection Problem Between a PC and a USB HDD

1. Unplug the USB device from the computer, wait a few moments, and then firmly plug the device back into the PC.

2. Experiencing the same problem as the customer described, you unplug the device.

3. Take a thumb drive you brought with you, which you know to be good, and plug it into the PC.

4. When the thumb drive is appropriately recognized by the PC, safely remove the device.

5. Use an appropriate screwdriver from your toolkit to open up the USB HDD, taking all necessary precautions.

6. You visually examine the interior of the device and discover that the drive's IDE pins are not making firm contact with the USB plug head.

7. Press the IDE pins firmly but gently into the USB plug head, verifying that the contact is complete.

8. Reassemble the USB hard-drive device.

9. Plug the device into the USB port of the user's PC and verify that it is appropriately recognized.

Criteria for Completion

You will have successfully completed this task when the USB HDD is recognized by the PC and when the user can access and use the USB storage device normally.

Task 4.28: Troubleshooting a 691 Error Connection Problem

While being a PC tech does not mean you have to be an expert in networking, you still need to know some of the basics. It also means that, regardless of your relative comfort or experience with networking issues, as the local technician you'll be asked to take a look at some of the more basic connection issues and attempt to resolve them. Fortunately, some solutions are easily discovered with just a little online research.

Scenario

You receive a trouble ticket stating that a user in sales is receiving a specific error message when attempting to use her Windows Vista laptop's on-board modem to connect to her ISP via dial-up while on a business trip. You phone the user at her hotel room and ask her to specify the error message. She states that the message is "Error 691, 'The port was disconnected.'" You decide to do some research on this error message and tell the user you will call her back in a few minutes.

Scope of Task

Duration

Once you find the proper answer, this task should take just a few minutes.

Setup

No special setup is required.

Caveat

This task has no significant concerns.

Procedure

This task will show you how to diagnose a specific network-connection error in Windows Vista.

Equipment Used

No special equipment is required.

Details

This task will take you through the steps of investigating a specific network-connection error message as related to Windows Vista. Since the vast majority of steps involve performing an Internet search, you will not be involved in physically working at the "problem" computer.

Diagnosing a 691 Network-Connection Error

1. Open a web browser on your computer and then open your favorite search engine.
2. Search for "error 691 vista."
3. Review the various search results.
4. You discover that this error isn't necessarily specific to Vista and indicates "Access denied because username and/or password is invalid on the domain."
5. Phone the user and ask her if she could be attempting to connect to her ISP using an incorrect username or password.

6.   The user insists that the username is correct but that she may have forgotten her password. Advise the user to contact her ISP and ask them to reset her password, then call you back with the results. The user subsequently calls back and confirms that she was using the wrong password.

Criteria for Completion

You will have successfully completed this task when the user calls you back and reports that her ISP reset her password and, with the new password, she is able to successfully make a dial-up connection.

   Sometimes the solution to an error message is as simple as searching for the error and implementing the results.

Task 4.29: Troubleshooting a Scanner Problem

This task is an example of a problem that seems unique or idiosyncratic. Sometimes the "oddness" of a problem can throw off a PC tech and make locating the solution seem more difficult than it really is. Even with problems you've never encountered before, standard problem-solving steps are still the best way to resolve most issues.

Scenario

You receive a trouble ticket from a user in the graphics department with an unusual problem. Normally the scanner in his department is attached to a Windows XP laptop and all scans are managed from that laptop. The user wanted to scan materials from his MacBook and so installed the drivers for the HP scanner onto his MacBook, disconnected the scanner from the Windows laptop, and attached it to his MacBook. He then successfully scanned materials to his MacBook.

Subsequently, the user reconnected the Windows laptop to the scanner, but now when he tries to use the laptop to initiate a scan, the Windows laptop isn't recognized by the scanner. When the user presses the Scan To button on the scanner, the options that appear are specifically for his MacBook, such as Scan to Adobe Photoshop and Scan to Mac Mail—and no options for the Windows laptop appear.

Other symptoms include being unable to initiate a scan from within a Microsoft Office application using the Scanning Wizard, and being unable to open HP Director from the Windows laptop.

You report to the Graphics department and locate the scanner, which is connected to the Windows XP laptop as the user described.

Scope of Task

Duration

This task should take 15 or 20 minutes.

Setup

To exactly duplicate the situation described, you'll need an HP scanner or All-in-One imaging device, a Windows XP laptop, and a Macbook.

Caveat

Since the circumstances surrounding this problem are unique, you may not be able to duplicate the original issue; however, the solution is standard enough that you'll be able to implement it on a Windows XP computer.

Procedure

This task will show you how to diagnose and correct a scanner connection problem.

Equipment Used

No special equipment is required. You most likely won't be able to re-create the problem as described, so acquiring a MacBook (assuming you don't have one) isn't necessary. Having a scanner or printer will be handy when implementing the solution.

Details

This task will take you through the steps involved in diagnosing and solving a connection problem with a Windows computer and a scanner.

Diagnosing a Scanner Connection Problem

TESTING YOUR FIRST SOLUTION

1. Power down both the laptop and the HP scanner and wait a few minutes.
2. Power up the Windows laptop and then power up the HP scanner.
3. Place some media on the scanner bed and close the lid.
4. Use the laptop to start a scan.
5. The scanner continues to fail to recognize the laptop.

TESTING YOUR SECOND SOLUTION

1. On the laptop, click Start ➤ Control Panel.
2. Double-click Add or Remove Programs.
3. Locate the drivers for the HP scanner in the list and uninstall them and all related software.

4. Open a web browser and go to www.hp.com.

5. On the HP site, click Support & Drivers.

6. Select the Download Drivers and Software (and Firmware) radio button.

7. In the For Product field, enter the name and number of the scanner, such as Officejet 6110, and then click Go.

8. If necessary, select the exact name and model number of the product.

9. Select Microsoft Windows XP.

10. Select the latest drivers for the HP device and download them onto the laptop.

11. Once downloaded, install the drivers and reboot the computer.

12. Once the laptop has rebooted, attempt to initiate a scan from the laptop.

13. Have the user perform all the usual scan functions with the Windows laptop attached and verify that they all perform as expected.

Criteria for Completion

You will have successfully completed this task when the Windows laptop can be used to completely manage the HP scanner as expected.

Although you may not know exactly what caused the problem, sometimes reinstalling the drivers and other relevant software for a device will return it to working order.

Task 4.30: Troubleshooting a Persistent "Align Print Cartridges" Message After Cartridges Have Been Replaced and Aligned

This task is another example of a problem that seems more complicated than it really is and that standard problem-solving steps adequately address. Remember, try the most likely and the simplest solutions first. Often they will provide the answer you are looking for.

Scenario

You receive a trouble ticket from a user in reception stating that after he replaced the black and color ink cartridges in his printer and completed the alignment procedure, he still is getting an "align print cartridges" message. He also states that when he tries to print a color document, the only color that prints is red and the ink on the document fades at about a quarter of the way down the page.

After determining the make and model of the printer being used, you locate the proper replacement ink cartridges and take them with you when you go to reception. You suspect that one or both cartridges are defective, but will try a simpler solution before replacing them.

Scope of Task

Duration

This task should just take a few minutes.

Setup

No special setup is required.

Caveat

When working with printer ink cartridges, be careful to avoid creating any ink stains. Also, do not touch the contacts on the ink cartridges or printer carriage directly.

Procedure

This task will show you how to solve an unusual printing problem with a usual cause.

Equipment Used

No special equipment is required, except for access to a printer.

Details

This task will walk you through the steps required to diagnose a printing problem.

Diagnosing a Color Printing Problem

1. Open the panel on the printer to access the ink cartridges.
2. Carefully reach inside and unlatch the black ink cartridge.
3. Reseat the black ink cartridge and re-engage the latch.
4. Unlatch the color ink cartridge, reseat it, and then re-engage the latch.
5. Close the access panel.
6. Follow any instructions on the printer's control panel for aligning the printheads if required.
7. Have the user print the original document and verify that the printout is as expected.

Criteria for Completion

You will have successfully completed this task when the printer produces normal color printouts.

Although the problem could have been created by defective ink cartridges or by dirty or damaged contacts on the cartridges or the print carriage, the cause, in this case, was a poorly seated color ink cartridge.

Index

Note to the Reader: Throughout this index **boldfaced** page numbers indicate primary discussions of a topic. *Italicized* page numbers indicate illustrations.

A

Access (Microsoft), 224
access control lists, 244. *See also* shared folders
access panel, ESD precautions and, **2-4**
access points, 138
access problems. *See also* network access problems
external USB hard drive, **400-401**
scanner, **403-405**
USB digital camera, **371-376**
ACPI Multiprocessor, 232, *232*
activation, 90, 100, 101, 106
Active Directory domain, 272
joining computers to, **272-276**
problems in, **350-356**
"specified domain either does not exist or could not be contacted," **350-356**
user added to, **276-280**
Active Directory Group Policy objects, 128, 212, 307
Active Directory Users and Computers, 277, *277, 279*
adaptive frequency hopping (AFH) spread spectrum signaling, 138
Ad-Aware SE Personal, **314**. *See also* AVG antivirus
Add a Printer Driver Wizard, 135-136
Add or Remove Programs, 105, *235*, **235-236**, 373, 404
Add Printer wizard, 130, 132, 133, 134, 301, 302, *302*, 359
adding. *See* installing
Administrative Tools, 210, 277, 297, 305, 308, 354, 355, 356, 382, 383
Advanced tab, 126, 128, 155, 223
AFH (adaptive frequency hopping) spread spectrum signaling, 138
AFX rootkit, 318
AGP (Accelerated Graphics Port) cards
installing, **50-54**
PCIe cards *v.*, 14
AIDA32 - Personal System Information, *145, 146*
aida32.exe file, 145
Alerter service, 198, *198*
"align print cartridges" message, 132, **405-407**
American Power Conversion (APC), 382
ANSI/TIA/EIA 568A/568B standards, 261, 266
anti-malware programs, 85, 313, 314, 317. *See also* AVG antivirus

antistatic bags
CD-ROM drive in, 38
CPU in, 17, 19
DVD drive in, 43
electronic components in, 3, 4, 12
ESD precautions and, 2-4
keyboard in, 57
laptop hard drive in, 63
laptop optical drive in, 66
multiport USB PCI card in, 290
PCI card in, 12
PCIe card in, 16
PCIe x16 graphics card in, 188
RAM in, 9, 339
SO-DIMM module in, 60
video card in, 52
antivirus programs, 85, 112, 116, 117, 118, 310, 311, 312, 313, 314, 317, 318. See also AVG antivirus
APC (American Power Conversion), 382
APIPA (Automatic Private IP Addressing), 13, 78, 251, 399
Applications tab, 123, 124, 388
asset management
inventorying
computer rollout, 76
computers, 223-227
equipment in storage closet, 227-230
hard drives, 229
hardware (on individual PCs), 230-234
optical drives, 229
software (on individual PCs), 234-236
labels/tags, 224, 225
ledger book, 224, 225, 226, 227, 228, 230, 231, 232, 234, 235
recording/saving asset data, 226-227
AT form factor, 151
ATA drives, 26
ATX form factor, 151
audio cable, 37, 39, 43, 44
audio cards. See sound cards
audio CDs not recognized by optical drive, 359-364
automatic defragmentation utility (Vista), 182-184
Automatic Private IP Addressing. See APIPA
automatic reboot, disabling, 222-223
Autoplay, 41, 45, 66, 107, 110, 193, 290, 374
autosensing Ethernet ports, 257, 263
AVG antivirus (Grisoft), 315, 316
free download, 311, 314
scanning/quarantining malware, 314-317
AVG Internet Security (Grisoft), 319

B

backups
  data
    importance of, 62, 111
    restoration of, 25, 160
  Outlook, 325-328
  tape backup unit
    backup scheduling on, 323-325
    tape replacement on, 320-323
ball mouse. See mice
"bare bones" computer, 22
baselines, 230, 233, 234, 236
battery
  CMOS, replacing, 205-208
  Inspiron, 56, 57, 60, 61, 63, 64, 65, 66
  lithium-ion, 205
  9-volt, 268
  UPS, 379, 381, 384
  wristwatch, 205
beep codes, 9
BIOS (basic input/output system). See also CMOS
  beep codes, 9
  boot order, 87
  bootable USB drive to flash BIOS, 201
  CMOS battery and, 205-208
  CPU's and
    configuring, 21
    specifications, 17
  flashing, 200-205
  motherboards and, 200-201
  online information, 9
  SATA hard drive installation and, 31
  Setup, 207
blank monitor screen, 389-392
blocking issue, 113. See also compatibility issues
blue screen of death (BSOD)
  automatic reboot and, 222-223
  laptop failure and, 62
Bluetooth devices
  discoverable, 137, 138, 139
  installation on Vista, 137-139
  passkeys and, 137
boot disk, 203-204
bootable USB drive to flash BIOS, 201
booting. See also rebooting
  failure, intermittent, 334-337
  order, changing, 87
browser hijackers, 313
BSOD. See blue screen of death
BTX form factor, 151

C

cable jacket, stripping off, 260, 264, 265
cable select, 27, 29, 38
cable tester, 267-269

camera, access problems and, 371-376
cases (PC cases)
  access panel, ESD precautions and, 2-4
  cleaning, 176, 179
  front panel wires, 48-49
  metal corners/edges and, 47
  preparing, motherboard and, 47-49
Cat 5/5e cable, 258, 259, 264
Cat 6 cable, 258
CD-ROM drives. See also optical drives
  drivers and, 36-37, 40
  Enable Digital CD Audio feature, 362, 363, 364
  installing, 35-41
CD-RW, 35, 41
central processing units. See CPUs
chains, SCSI, 32, 33, 34
changing. See replacing; resetting passwords
checking. See also reseating
  internal connectors, 194-196
  PCI/PCIe cards, 191-196
  RAM, 189-191
cleaning
  case, 176, 179
  CRT monitors, 174-176
  dust bunnies, 167-169
  fans, 169-171
  keyboards, 176, 177
  mice, 176, 178
CLI. See command-line interface
client computers
  APIPA and, 13, 78, 251, 399
  DHCP address renewal and, 251-253
  joining, to domain, 272-276
  mapping network drive from, 240-243
  "specified domain either does not exist or could
    not be contacted," 350-356
clock, CMOS battery and, 205-208
cmd, 13, 78, 166, 250, 256, 346, 351, 399
CMOS (complementary metal oxide
  semiconductor), 45
  battery, replacing, 205-208
  restoring settings, 201
color-coded wires, 259, 260-261, 264, 265
COM1, 381, 382
COM2, 382
COM3, 382
command-line interface (CLI), 78, 184, 185
  flashing BIOS from, 204-205
commands
  cmd, 13, 78, 166, 250, 256, 346, 351, 399
  config ‹filename›, 186
  dcpromo, 209
  dir, 204
  driverquery /v /fo ›list drivers.txt, 166
  exit, 88, 251, 253, 347, 351
  format C: /fs:ntfs, 88
  ipconfig/all, 13, 78, 250, 252, 346, 399
  ipconfig/registerdns, 355
  ipconfig/release, 13, 253, 399

ipconfig/renew, 13, 253, 399
map, 88
ping 192.168.0.1, 78
ping 192.168.0.2, 256
ping www.google.com, 78, 253, 399
compatibility issues, 113, 114, 115, 117, 118, 119
complementary metal oxide semiconductor.
    See CMOS
compressed air, 4, 167, 168, 169, 170, 177
Computer Management window, 197, 198, 198, 200
Computer Name tab, 274, 275, 278
computers (PC computers). See also cases; client
    computers; CPUs; hard drives; keyboards;
    laptops; legacy equipment; malware; memory;
    mice; monitors; motherboards; optical drives;
    OS; power supplies; sound cards; virtual
    machines; viruses
    asset management of, 223-227
    "bare bones," 22
    clock, CMOS and, 205-208
    Dell Dimension C521, 186-189
    joining to domain, 272-276
    KVM switch and, 73
    network printer connection with, 300-303
    /OS rollout, 74-79
    speakers, 40, 42, 44, 95, 161, 193, 384,
        385, 386
    work completion, tracking, 236-238
    zombies, 313, 317
config ‹filename›, 186
connection problems. See access problems; network
    access problems
connectors
    IDE, 26
    internal, checking, 194-196
    P1, 151
    P4/P5, 150
    P8/P9, 150, 151
    power supply, 24
    RJ-45, 258, 259, 260, 261, 262, 264, 265, 268
contacts folder problem (Outlook), 376-379
Contig utility, 184-185
cooling solution, CPUs and, 19
CPUs (central processing units)
    BIOS and
        configuring, 21
        specifications, 17
    cooling solution and, 19
    heat-sink fan and, 17, 20
    holes and, 19
    installing, 17-21
    Intel Socket 775, 19
    motherboard support for, 18
    pins and, 19
    protective plate and, 19
    specifications, BIOS and, 17
    testing, after installation, 20-21
    thermal compound and, 18, 19, 20
crimp tool, 258, 260, 261, 265

cross-over cables. See also network cables
    making, 263-267
    testing, 267-269
CRT monitors. See also monitors
    cleaning/degaussing, 174-176
    opening, 390
Crucial Memory Advisor tool, 6-8, 7, 8
CSIC icon, 79
Ctrl+Alt+Del, 87, 124, 388
customizing
    Start Menu, 127
    virtual memory, 128-129

D

data. See also files
    asset. See asset management
    backups. See backups
    loss. See reformatting hard drives
    restoration, 25, 160. See also Norton Ghost
Date and Time Settings box, 93, 93
dcpromo, 209
DCs. See domain controllers
decompression, MPEG-2 compression and, 42
defragmentation
    automatic, 182-184
    Contig utility, 184-185
    hard drive, 112, 179-182
    individual file (virtual machine), 184-186
    Power Defragmenter, 185
    Vista defragmentation utility, 182-184
degaussing CRT monitors, 174-176
Dell Dimension C521, 186-189
Dell Inspiron 8200 laptop. See also laptops
    battery, 56, 57, 60, 61, 63, 64, 65, 66
    hard drive installation on, 62-64
    keyboard installation on, 54-58
    optical drive installation on, 64-67
    SO-DIMM installation on, 58-61
Demand Dial Interface Wizard, 299, 299
demand-dial routing, 296-300
Detect and Repair, 389
device drivers. See drivers
Device Manager, 232, 232
    audio CDs not recognized and, 361-363
    computer hardware inventory and, 231-234
    DeviceQuery command-line utility v., 165
    driver installation and, 80-82
    hidden devices and, 384, 386
    USB digital camera and, 374
device timing, independent, 38
DHCP address, renewing, 251-253
DHCP client service, 200
DHCP (Dynamic Host Configuration
    Protocol) server
    configuring, 248
    dynamic addressing and, 247-251
    NICs and, 11

Dia software, 283, 283
dial-up connection, redundant, 296-300
digital camera, access problems and, 371-376
Dimension C521. See Dell Dimension C521
DIMM A/DIMM B slots, 60. See also SO-DIMM
dip switches, 370
dir, 204
disabling
    automatic reboot, 222-223
    Enable Digital CD Audio feature, 364
    indexing service, 127, 200
    services (Windows 2000 Professional), 197-200
    system sounds, 129
    wallpaper, 127-128
discoverable Bluetooth device, 137, 138, 139
Disk Defragmenter window, 181, 181
DMA, 291
DNS (Domain Name System) server
    configuration, 276
    IP address, 247
    Primary DNS Suffix, 352
docking stations
    installing, 67-71
    peripherals on, 69-70
    purpose of, 55, 67
domain controllers (DCs), 209, 210, 211, 212,
        273, 276, 277, 278, 279, 280, 350, 351, 353,
        354, 356
domain logon password, 209-211
Domain Name System server. See DNS server
domains. See also Active Directory domain
    joining computers to, 272-276
    "specified domain either does not exist or could
        not be contacted," 350-356
DOS, 202
dot-matrix printers, 129
DPI settings, 53
DRAM (dynamic random access memory), 58.
        See also memory
drive bays
    rails and, 38
    tabs and, 38
drive letter, precoded, 375
www.driverguide.com, 161-163, 162, 163
driverquery /v /fo ›list drivers.txt, 166
drivers
    CD-ROM drive and, 36-37, 40
    DVD drive, 44
    installing
        from CD, 80-82
        from Internet, 82-85
        printer drivers, 134-136
    legacy equipment, 82
    for NICs, 160-163
    PCIe card, 16-17
    searching for, 160-163
    sound card, 80-82
    video card

    installing, 53-54
    uninstalling, 51-52
    Vista-compatible, 36, 163-165
    XP, listing, 165-166
drives. See CD-ROM drives; DVD drives;
        hard drives; network drives; optical drives;
        SCSI drives
dust bunnies, 167-169
DVD drives. See also optical drives
    default/standard, 36, 41
    drivers, 44
    installing, 36, 41-45
        on laptop, 64-67
DVI/VGA lead, 14, 188
dynamic addressing, 247-253. See also
        IP addressing
Dynamic Host Configuration Protocol server. See
        DHCP server
dynamic random access memory. See DRAM

E

eBay, 381
echo requests, 253, 399
EEPROM (erasable programmable read-only
        memory), 204
EIA/TIA 568A/568B standards, 261, 266
electronic components, ESD and. See antistatic bags
electrostatic discharge precautions. See
        ESD precautions
email accounts. See also Outlook
    on Exchange server, **269-272**
    Mac Mail, 403
empty Outlook contacts folder, **376-379**
emptying garbage, 76, 79
Enable Digital CD Audio feature, 362, 363, 364
Engineers group, 245, 246
equipment storage closet, inventorying, **227-230**
erasable programmable read-only memory
        (EEPROM), 204
ESD (electrostatic discharge) precautions, **2-4**. See
        also antistatic bags
ESD vacuums, 4
Ethernet cables. See network cables
Ethernet ports, autosensing, 257, 263
Event Type 61 error, **364, 367**
Event Viewer, 354, 354, 355, 356, 382
Excel
    Detect and Repair, 389
    loading/opening problems, **356-359**
    lock up problems, **386-389**
    printing problems, 134, **356-359**
    shutting down, **122-124**
Exchange Server (Microsoft)
    email account on, **269-272**
    empty contacts folder and, **376-379**
    IP address, 270

exit, 88, 251, 253, 347, 351
expansion bus cards. *See* PCI cards; PCIe
    graphics cards
Explorer. *See* Internet Explorer; Windows Explorer

F

failing
    motherboard capacitor, 334
    power strip, **337**
    power supply, 146, 147, 148, 149, 334, 335, 336
failure
    blue screen of death
        automatic reboot and, **222-223**
        laptop failure and, 62
    booting, intermittent, 334-337
    RAM upgrade, **337-340**
    UPS service, **379-384**
fans. *See also* heat-sink fans
    cleaning, **169-171**
    oiling, **171-174**
    PCIe cards and, 14
    video cards and, 53
FAT32, 129, 179, 244. *See also* NTFS
Fax and Scanning, Windows, 221
file sharing permissions, 244, 245, 246, 396. *See
    also* shared folders
files. *See also* data; Excel; Word
    defragmenting, **184-186**
    PST, **326-328**
    sharing. *See* shared folders
    swap, 128, 129, **153-157**
firewalls
    third-party, 303, 304
    Vista
        log files, **306-308**
        outbound filter rules, **303-306**
    XP, 303
    ZoneAlarm, **304**
"First, do no harm," **377**
568A/568B standards, 261, 266
flash drives. *See* thumb drives
flashing BIOS, **200-205**. *See also* BIOS
floppy-disk drive, 195, 201, 202
folders, shared. *See* shared folders
form factors
    AT, ATX, BTX, NLX, micro ATX, 151
    motherboard, 46, 151
format C: /fs:ntfs, 88
40-pin ribbon cables, 38
Found New Hardware message, 290, 326, 368,
    369, 370, 371
freeing system resources, 126
freeware, 109
fresh install
    Windows Vista, **98-103**
    Windows XP, **89-97**
front panel wires (computer case), **48-49**

G

gaming PCIe cards, 15
garbage
    emptying, 76, 79
    printing, 134
gateway, 247, 255, 284, 310
General tab, 10, 61, 226, 362
ghosted hard drives, 25, 28, 75, **157-160**. *See also*
    Norton Ghost
Gigabit-capable cable, 258
GIMP software, *283*, **283**
Google
    echo requests and, 253, 399
    Microsoft support site *v.*, **365**
    ping www.google.com, 78, 253, 399
    RootkitRevealer results and, 319
GPOs (Group Policy objects), 128, 212, 307
graphics cards. *See* video cards
Grisoft AVG antivirus. *See* AVG antivirus
Group Policy objects (GPOs), 128, 212, 307

H

HackerDefender rootkit, 318
hacking. *See* tweaking
hard drives. *See also* jumpers/switches; network
    drives; SCSI drives
    ATA, 26
    defragging, 112, **179-182**
    ghosted, 25, 28, 75, **157-160**
    IDE
        IDE-to-SATA drive power cable adapter,
            24, 30
        installing, **25-28**
    imaging, **157-160**
    indexing service, 127, 200
    inventorying, 229
    laptop, installing, **62-64**
    PATA, 26
    reformatting, **85-88**
    SATA
        BIOS configuration and, 31
        IDE-to-SATA drive power cable adapter,
            24, 30
        installing, **28-32**
        jumper block and, 29
        PCI SATA host adapter, 31
    USB external, access problems and,
        400-401
    virtual memory on, **128-129**
hardware. *See* computers; software; *specific
    hardware*
Hardware Compatibility List (HCL), **115, 116**
hardware storage closet, inventorying, **227-230**
Hardware tab, 231, 374, 386
HCL (Hardware Compatibility List), **115, 116**

heat-sink fans
    CPUs and, 17, 20
    PCIe cards and, 14
    thermal compound and, 18, 19, 20
Help and Support Center Page, **133, 136**. *See also*
    Microsoft support site; TechNet
hidden device conflict, **384-386**
hijackers, web-browser, 313
holes, CPUs and, 19
Home Edition (XP). *See* Windows XP
"hosing" the paging file, 129. *See also* swap files
hostname, 93, 103, 118, 254, 255, 269, 270, 271,
    295, 301, 322, 353, 356, 367, 399
HP All-in-One device
    connection problem, **403-405**
    scanning problem, **219-221**
HTML Tidy, **109-110**
HTTP, 255

I

IDE (integrated drive electronics), 26
IDE connectors, 26
IDE hard drives
    IDE-to-SATA drive power cable adapter, 24, 30
    installing, **25-28**
IDE ribbon cables, 25, 26, 27, 38, 39, 43
identifying
    motherboards, 18, **142-146**
    power supplies, **146-148**
IDE-to-SATA drive power cable adapter, 24, 30
"if it ain't broke, don't fix it," 37. *See also* Windows
    2000 Professional
imaging devices. *See* scanners
imaging hard drives, **157-160**. *See also* ghosted
    hard drives
independent device timing, 38
indexing service, hard drive's, **127**, 200
Industry Standard Architecture (ISA), 10
ink cartridges. *See* toner cartridges
Inspiron 8200 laptop. *See* Dell Inspiron 8200
    laptop
installing
    AGP video card, **50-54**
    Bluetooth devices, on Vista, **137-139**
    CD-ROM drives, **35-41**
    CMOS battery, **205-208**
    computer/OS rollout, **74-79**
    CPUs, **17-21**
    Dell Inspiron parts. *See* Dell Inspiron 8200
        laptop
    docking stations, **67-71**
    drivers
        from CD, **80-82**
        from Internet, **82-85**
        printer drivers, **134-136**

DVD drives, 36, **41-45**
    on laptops, **64-67**
hard drives
    IDE, **25-28**
    laptop, **62-64**
    SATA, **28-32**
heat-sink fan, 20
KVM switches, **71-74**
laptop components
    keyboards, **54-58**
    optical drives, **64-67**
    SO-DIMM, **58-61**
motherboards, **45-50**
network printer, **253-257**
NICs, **10-13**
PCI cards, **10-13**, 385
    five port USB 2.0 adapter, **288-291**
PCIe cards, **14-17**, 385
power supplies, **22-24**, **148-153**, *152*
printers, **129-134**
    network printer, **253-257**
    toner cartridge, **216-219**
RAM, **5-10**
SCSI drives, **32-35**, 369
SO-DIMM, on laptop, **58-61**
software
    HTML Tidy, **109-110**
    Microsoft Office, **105-108**
    non-Microsoft applications, **108-110**
    uninstalling software, **103-105**
    Vista (fresh install), **98-103**
    XP (fresh install), **89-97**
USB 2.0 five-port adapter PCI card, **288-291**
video cards, **50-54**
    PCIe x16, **186-189**
Installing Windows screen, 102, *102*
integrated drive electronics. *See* IDE
integrated video cards, 50, 187
Intel Socket 775, 19
intermittent boot failure, **334-337**
internal connectors, **194-196**
Internet Explorer, 108, 114, 119, 122
Internet Protocol addressing. *See* IP addressing
Internet Protocol [TCP/IP] Properties box,
    250, *250*
internet01, 212, 213
http://www.intertronics.co.uk/products/
    csmdvac.htm., 4
inventorying. *See also* asset management
    computer rollout, 76
    computers, **223-227**
    equipment in storage closet, **227-230**
    hard drives, 229
    hardware (on individual PCs), **230-234**
    keyboards, 226
    monitors, 226
    optical drives, 229
    software (on individual PCs), **234-236**

I/O. *See also* BIOS
  channel, 34
  monitor cable, 69
  slots, 47
  system resources, 11, 291
IP (Internet Protocol) addressing, 247
  APIPA and, 13, 78, 251, 399
  assigned, in Vista/XP, 253
  dynamic, **247-251**
    renewing, **251-253**
  Exchange Server, 270
  IPv4, 248
  IPv6, 248
  printer, 254, 255, 256
  TCP/IP, 249, 250, 255, 305
  VPN, 292, 295
ipconfig/all, 13, 78, 250, 252, 346, 399
ipconfig/registerdns, 355
ipconfig/release, 13, 253, 399
ipconfig/renew, 13, 253, 399
IPSec Policy Agent service, 200
IRQ, 11, 291
ISA (Industry Standard Architecture), 10.
    See also PCI

J

jumpers/switches, **26-27**
  cable select position, 27, 29, 38
  diagram, 27, 38, 43
  master position, 25, 27, 29, 38, 43, 64
  SATA drives and, 29
  SCSI drives, **33-34**
  slave position, 27, 29, 38, 43, 64

K

keyboards, 54
  Bluetooth, **137-139**
  cleaning, 176, 177
  on docking stations, 69
  inventorying, 226
  KVM switches and, **71-74**
  laptop, installing, **54-58**
  ribbon cable, 57
keyboard-video-mouse switches. *See* KVM switches
keyloggers, 313
KVM (keyboard-video-mouse) switches, **71-74**

L

labeling
  asset management, 224, 225
  network cables, **280-285**

LAN (local area network). *See also* network access
    problems; network printers
  DHCP address renewal and, **251-253**
  docking station port for, 70
  NIC installation and, **10-13**
  VPN and, **292-296**
lanes (point-to-point serial links), 15
Language Options box, Regional and, 92, 100, 388
laptops. *See also* Dell Inspiron 8200 laptop
  blue screen and, 62
  docking station
    installing, **67-71**
    purpose of, 55
  installing
    docking station, **67-71**
    DVD drive, **64-67**
    hard drive, **62-64**
    keyboard, **54-58**
    SO-DIMM, **58-61**
  MacBook, 403, 404
Last Known Good Configuration, 85
LCD monitors, 174, 175, 390. *See also* monitors
ledger book, 224, 225, 226, 227, 228, 230, 231,
    232, 234, 235
legacy equipment
  BIOS update and, 204
  dial-up networking and, **296-300**
  drivers for, 82
  scanners, **384-386**
  system conflict with hidden device, **384-386**
Linux, 179, 283, 289
lithium-ion batteries, 205
loading/opening problems, Word/Excel documents
    and, **356-359**
Local Area Connection Properties box, 249, *249*,
    250, 253
local area network. *See* LAN
Local Disk (C:) Properties box, 127, 181, *181*, 246
Local Group Policy, 212. *See also* Group Policy
    objects
local user accounts. *See also* user accounts
  Vista, **212-213**
  XP, **285-287**
log files (Vista firewall), **306-308**
logon password, domain, **209-211**
LPT1, 132

M

MacBook, 403, 404
mail accounts. *See* email accounts
Mail Setup box, 326, *326*
www.majorgeeks.com/download181.html, **18**,
    143, *144*
malware, **313-317**. *See also* AVG antivirus; viruses
  anti-malware programs, 85, 313, 314, 317
  quarantines, 311, 312, 313, 314, 316, 317

reformatting hard drive and, **85-88**
rootkits, **317-319**
spyware, 304, 313, 314
System Restore and, 85, 120
zombies and, 313, 317
map, 88
Map Network Drive, 241, *242*, 376, 393
mapping
    network cables, **280-285**, *283*, *284*
    network drives, **240-243**
master position, 25, 27, 29, 38, 43, 64
memory
    Crucial Memory Advisor Tool, **6-8**, *7*, *8*
    DRAM, *58*
    EEPROM, 204
    RAM
        antistatic bags and, 9, 339
        checking, **189-191**
        correct type, **6-8**
        Crucial Memory Advisor Tool, **6-8**, *7*, *8*
        failed, troubleshooting, **337-340**
        installing, **5-10**
        non-ECC, 340
        reseating, **189-191**
        testing, **9-10**
        verifying, 10, 191
        Vista and, 153
    selecting, **6-8**, *58*
    SO-DIMM
        DRAM *v.*, 58
        installing, on laptop, **58-61**
    vendor websites, 6
    virtual
        customizing, **128-129**
        swap files and, 128, 129, **153-157**
Messenger service, 199, *199*
metallic screws, 47, 49
mice
    cleaning, 176, 178
    on docking stations, 69
    KVM switches *v.*, **71-74**
micro ATX form factor, 151
Microsoft Access, 224
Microsoft Exchange Server. *See* Exchange Server
Microsoft Office. *See* Office suites
Microsoft support site, 365, 366
Microsoft TechNet. *See* TechNet
Millennium (Windows Me), 52
MLGPO (Multiple Local Group Policy
    Objects), 212
monitoring network activity (Vista firewall),
    306-308
monitors
    blank, troubleshooting, **389-392**
    CRT
        cleaning/degaussing, **174-176**
        opening, 390
    on docking station, 69

DVI/VGA lead, 14, 188
inventorying, 226
I/O cable, 69
KVM switches and, **71-74**
LCD, 174, 175, 390
rainbow effect, 174, 176
screen resolution, 17, *53*, 95, 189
motherboards. *See also* BIOS
    BIOS and, **200-201**
    capacitor, failing, 334
    CPU installation on, **17-21**
    CPUs supported by, 18
    form factors, 46, 151
    IDE connectors, 26
    identifying, 18, **142-146**
    installing, **45-50**
    positioning, 46, 48
    system:querying utility and, 18, **143-146**
MPEG PCI card, 42, 43, 44
MPEG-2 compression, 42
MSHOME, 94
MSI GeForce 8400GS graphics card, 186
multimeter, 149, 150, 151, 334, 335, 336
Multiple Local Group Policy Objects
    (MLGPO), 212
multiport network PCI card, **288-291**
Multiprocessor, ACPI, 232
Mute check box, 386
My Computer, *243*

N

narrow SCSI IDs, 34
NCR (No Carbon Required) documents, 130
NetMeeting, 200
network access problems (network connection
    problems). *See also* access problems; LAN
    network drives, **392-394**
    shared folder on remote computer, **394-397**
    single user connection problem, **397-399**
    691 network-connection error, **401-403**
network activity, Vista firewall and, **306-308**
Network Administrator Street Smarts: A Real
    World Guide to CompTIA Network+ Skills
    (Skandier), 248
network cables
    Cat 5/5e, 258, 259, 264
    Cat 6, 258
    crimp tool and, 258, 260, 261, 265
    Gigabit-capable, 258
    making
        cross-over, **263-267**
        straight-through, **257-262**
    mapping, **280-285**, *283*, *284*
    pin-out diagram, *259*, *260*, *264*, *265*, *265*

RJ-45 connectors and, 258, 259, 260, 261, 262, 264, 265, 268
stripping off cable jacket, 260, 264, 265
testing, **267-269**
wires
color-coded, 259, 260-261, 264, 265
twisted, 259, 260, 264, 265
network drives. *See also* client computers
access problems and, **392-394**
Map Network Drive, 241, 376, 393
mapping, **240-243**
Reconnect at Logon box, 242, 376, 393, 394
Network Identification tab, 351, *351*
network interface cards. *See* NICs
network peripheral port device. *See* USB 2.0 five-port adapter PCI card
network printers
connecting computers to, **300-303**
installing, **253-257**
printing problems, **344-349**
Network Settings box, 94, *94*
network shares. *See* shared folders
www.neuber.com/taskmanager/process, **123**
New Connection Wizard, 293, *293*, 294, *294*
New Hardware Found message, 290, 326, 368, 369, 370, 371
NICs (network interface cards), 10. *See also* network printers
DHCP server and, 11
drivers for, **160-163**
installing, **10-13**
9-volt battery, 268
NLX form factor, 151
No Carbon Required (NCR) documents, 130
non-ECC RAM, 340
non-metallic screws, 47, 49
Norton Ghost, **157-160**
NTFS, 86, 88, 92, 129, 179, 244
NVIDIA site, 186

O

Office suites (Microsoft Office). *See also* Excel; Outlook; Word
installing, **105-108**
Office 2003, 106, 107, 108, 270
Office 2007, 106
product key, 107
uninstalling/reinstalling, 359
updates, 108
oil
sewing-machine, 172
three-in-one, 172
WD-40, 172
oiling fans, **171-174**
onboard video cards, 50, 187

online port scanner, **214-216**
Open Command Prompt Here option, 185
opening CRT monitors, **390**
open-source software, 283
operating system. *See* OS
optical drives. *See also* CD-ROM drives; DVD drives
audio CDs not recognized by, **359-364**
installing on laptops, **64-67**
inventorying, 229
optical mouse. *See* mice
OS (operating system). *See also* Windows 2000 Professional; Windows Vista; Windows XP
/computer rollout, **74-79**
Linux, 179, 283, 289
Windows 7, 98, 289
Windows 98, 52, 123, 222
Windows 2000 Server, 180, 296, 297, 367
Windows Me, 52
Windows Server 2003, 209, 273, 276, 277, 297
Windows Server 2008, 209, 273, 277, 297
outbound firewall filters (Vista), **303-306**
Outlook (Microsoft Outlook)
backing up, **325-328**
contacts folder problem, **376-379**
email account, on Exchange server, **269-272**
PST files, **326-328**
Outlook Data Files box, 327, *327*

P

P1 connector, 151
P4/P5 connectors, 150
P8/P9 connectors, 150, 151
paging files. *See* swap files
Paint (program), 221
PANs (personal area network), 137, 288
paperless society, 142
parallel ATA (PATA) drives, 26
passcodes, 137
passkeys, 137
passwords
dial-up connection, 299, 300
domain logon, **209-211**
resetting, **208-211**, 279
strong, 208
user account
Vista, 213
XP, 287
VPN connection, 295
PATA (parallel ATA) drives, 26
patch cables. *See* network cables
Pause/Break key, 202
PC cases. *See* cases
PC computers. *See* computers

PCI (Peripheral Component Interconnect) cards
    checking/reseating, **191-196**, 332
    installing, **10-13**, 385
        five port USB 2.0 adapter, **288-291**
    MPEG, 42, 43, 44
    NICs and, 10
    PCI standard, 10, 14
        AGP cards and, 14
        ISA *v.*, 10
        outdated, 10, 14
        PCI Express *v.*, 10
    sound card, hidden device conflict and, **384-386**
    testing, 13
    USB devices *v.*, 10
PCI Express graphics cards. *See* PCIe graphics cards
PCI SATA host adapter, 31
PCIe (PCI Express) graphics cards
    AGP cards *v.*, 14
    checking/reseating, **191-196**, 332
    drivers, **16-17**
    fans and, 14
    gaming, 15
    heat sink and, 14
    installing, **14-17**, 385
        PCIe x16 graphics card, **186-189**
    PCIe standard (online information), 10, 14
    sound card, hidden device conflict and, **384-386**
www.pcpower.com/products/power_supplies/
    selector/, **147**
Performance Options box, 128, 155, *156*, 157
Peripheral Component Interconnect cards. *See*
    PCI cards
permissions, file sharing, 244, 245, 246, 396
personal area networks (PANs), 137, 288
Photo Gallery (Windows), 221
ping commands
    ping 192.168.0.1, 78
    ping 192.168.0.2, 256
    ping www.google.com, 78, 253, 399
    pinging another computer, 262
pin-out diagram, 259, *259*, 260, *264*, 265
pins, CPUs and, 19
pirated software, 90, 99
plastic scribe, 55, *56*, 57
Plug and Play (PnP) technology, 11, 32, 132, 384
PnP technology. *See* Plug and Play technology
point-to-point serial links (lanes), 15
Point-to-Point Tunneling Protocol (PPTP), 292
port replicators. *See* docking stations
port scanner, online, **214-216**
power connectors, 24
Power Defragmenter, **185**
power strip failure, **337**
power supplies. *See also* UPS
    failing, 146, 147, 148, 149, 334, 335, 336
    fans, oiling, **171-174**
    form factors, 151

identifying, **146-148**
    installing, **22-24**, **148-153**, *152*
    multimeter and, 149, 150, 151, 334, 335, 336
    www.pcpower.com/products/power_supplies/
        selector/, **147**
    power connectors and, 24
    testing, 24, **148-153**, 333
    upgrading, 23
PPTP (Point-to-Point Tunneling Protocol), 292
precoded drive letter, 375
Primary DNS Suffix, 352
"print processor unknown," **364-368**
Printer and Faxes box, *342*, *343*
printers. *See also* HP All-in-One device
    Add Printer wizard, 130, 132, 133, 134, 301,
        302, 359
    "align print cartridges" message, 132,
        405-407
    dot-matrix, 129
    drivers, installing, **134-136**
    Excel documents and, 134
    garbage from, 134
    IP address, 254, *255*, 256
    local, installing, **129-134**
    network
        connecting to computers, **300-303**
        installing, **253-257**
        printing problems, **350-354**
    printing problems
        Excel documents and, 134, **356-359**
        local printers, **340-344**
        network printers, **350-354**
        "print processor unknown," **364-368**
        Win32 error code returned by the print
            processor, 364, 365, 366, *366*
        Word documents and, 134, 343, **356-359**
    test print, **218-219**
    testing, **133-134**
    toner cartridges
        "align print cartridges" message, 132,
            405-407
        recycling, 219
        replacing, 131, **216-219**
        reseating, 406, 407
    USB cables, 130, 131
problems. *See* troubleshooting
Processes tab, 123, 124
processors. *See* CPUs
product activation, 90, 100, 101, 106
product key
    Office, 107
    Vista, 98, 99, 100
    XP, 89, 90, 93
protective plate, CPUs and, 19
Protocols and Security Screen, 299
PST files (Outlook), **326-328**

Q

quarantines, 311, 312, 313, 314, 316, 317. *See also* AVG antivirus

R

www.radarsync.com/vista, **163**, **164**, **165**
rails, drive bays and, 38
rainbow effect, 174, 176
RAM (random access memory). *See also* memory
    antistatic bags and, 9, 339
    checking, **189-191**
    correct type, **6-8**
    Crucial Memory Advisor Tool, **6-8**, *7*, *8*
    failed, troubleshooting, **337-340**
    installing, **5-10**
    non-ECC, 340
    reseating, **189-191**, 332
    testing, **9-10**
    verifying, 10, 191
    Vista and, 153
random access memory. *See* RAM
read only setting (Word documents), 396
Ready to Register with Microsoft? screen, 96, *96*
ReadyBoost, 154
rebooting. *See also* booting
    automatic, disabling, **222-223**
    spontaneous, **148-149**, **329-334**
Reconnect at Logon box, 242, 376, 393, 394
Recovery Console (Windows XP), 85, 86, 87, 88
recovery-disc tools, 86, 87, 120
recycling printer cartridges, 219
redundant dial-up connection, **296-300**
reformatting hard drives, **85-88**
refresh rate, 53
Regional and Language Options box, 92, 100, 388
Reliability and Performance Monitor (Vista), **328-329**
remote registry service, 200
removable storage manager service, 200
removing. *See* Add or Remove Programs; scanning/removing; uninstalling
renewing dynamic addressing, **251-253**
replacing. *See also* installing
    backup tapes (on server), **320-323**
    CMOS battery, **205-208**
    power supplies, **22-24**, **148-153**
    printer toner cartridges, **216-219**
reseating
    internal connectors, **194-196**
    PCI/PCIe cards, **191-196**, 332
    printer ink cartridges, **406**, **407**
    RAM, **189-191**, 332
    sound cards, **191-193**
resetting passwords, **208-211**, 279

resolution (screen resolution), 17, 53, 95, 189
restarting. *See* rebooting
restoration of data, **25**, **160**. *See also* Norton Ghost
restore points (in XP), **119-122**
retention mechanism, 52
ribbon cables
    40-pin, 38
    IDE, 25, 26, 27, 38, 39, 43
    keyboard, 57
riser pins, 46, 47, 48, 49, 50
RJ-45 connectors, 258, 259, 260, 261, 262, 264, 265, 268
road warrior, 55
RootkitRevealer, **317-319**
rootkits, **317-319**
routine tasks, Windows 2000 Professional and, 37, 206
Routing and Remote Access Server Setup wizard, 298, *298*, 300
RunAs service, 200

S

SATA hard drives
    BIOS configuration and, 31
    IDE-to-SATA drive power cable adapter, 24, 30
    installing, **28-32**
    jumper block and, 29
    PCI SATA host adapter, 31
scanners
    HP All-in-One device
        connection problem, **403-405**
        scanning problem, **219-221**
    legacy, **384-386**
    "new hardware found" problem and, **368-371**
    online port scanner utility, **214-216**
    programs
        Paint, 221
        Windows Fax and Scanning, 221
        Windows Photo Gallery, 221
    SCSI, problems with, **368-371**
scanning/removing
    malware, **313-317**
    rootkits, **317-319**
    viruses, **310-313**
screen resolution, 17, 53, 95, 189
scribe, 55, 56, 57
SCSI drives
    chains, 32, 33, 34
    installing, **32-35**, 369
    jumpers/switches, **33-34**
    terminating, 32, 33, 34
SCSI IDs, 34, 370
SCSI scanner problems, **368-371**
seating/reseating. *See* reseating
Select Users, Computers, or Groups box, 245, *245*

serial ATA drives. *See* SATA hard drives
servers. *See also specific servers*
  backup unit
    changing schedule, **323-325**
    tape replacement, **320-323**
  Exchange Server
    email account on, **269-272**
    empty contacts folder and, **376-379**
    IP address, 270
services
  Alerter service, 198, *198*
  DHCP client service, 200
  indexing service, 127, 200
  IPSec Policy Agent service, 200
  Messenger service, 199, *199*
  remote registry service, 200
  removable storage manager service, 200
  RunAs service, 200
  Telephony, 200
  UPS service
    disabling, 199
    restart failure, **379-384**
  Windows 2000 Professional services, **197-200**
Setup (BIOS), 207
sewing-machine oil, 172
shared folders (file shares/network shares)
  access problems with, **394-397**
  creating, **243-247**
  mapping network drives and, **240-243**
  permissions, 244, 245, 246, 396
ShieldsUP!! Services box, *215*, **215-216**, *216*
shutting down software programs, **122-124**
single user network connection problem, **397-399**
691 network-connection error, **401-403**
Skandier, T., 248
slave position, 27, 29, 38, 43, 64
small-outline dual inline memory-module.
  See SO-DIMM
SO-DIMM (small-outline dual inline
  memory-module). *See also* memory
  DRAM *v.*, 58
  installing, on laptop, **58-61**
software. *See also* malware; OS
  Ad-Aware SE Personal, **314**
  Add or Remove Programs, 105, **235-236**,
    373, 404
  anti-malware, 85, 313, 314, 317
  antivirus, 85, 112, 116, 117, 118, 310, 311, 312,
    313, 314, 317, 318
  AVG antivirus (Grisoft), *315*, *316*
    free download, 311, 314
    scanning/quarantining malware, **314-317**
  Dia, *283*, **283**
  freeware, 109
  GIMP, *283*, **283**
  HTML Tidy, **109-110**
  inventorying, on individual PCs, **234-236**
  Norton Ghost, **157-160**

open-source, 283
Paint, 221
pirated, 90, 99
shutting down, **122-124**
Spybot Search and Destroy, **314**
uninstalling, **103-105**
Windows Fax and Scanning, 221
Windows Photo Gallery, 221
ZoneAlarm, **304**
sound cards. *See also* speakers
  checking/reseating, **191-193**
  drivers, **80-82**
  hidden device conflict and, **384-386**
speakers, 40, 42, 44, 95, 161, 193, 384, 385, 386.
  See also sound cards
"specified domain either does not exist or could not
  be contacted," **350-356**
speeding up. *See* tweaking
spontaneous rebooting, **148-149**, **329-334**
Spybot Search and Destroy, **314**. *See also* AVG
  antivirus
spyware, 304, 313, 314
Standard Display Adapter, 52
Start Menu, customizing, 127
Startup and Recovery (Windows), **222-223**
static. *See* antistatic bags; ESD precautions
storage closet, inventorying, **227-230**
straight-through cables. *See also* network cables
  making, **257-262**
  testing, **267-269**
stripping off cable jacket, 260, 264, 265
strong passwords, 208
subnet mask, 13, 78, 247, 254, 255, 256, 262, 263,
  266, 399
Support Center Page, Help and, **133**, **136**. *See also*
  TechNet
support site, Microsoft, **365**, *366*
surge protectors, 21, 22, 24, 131, 194, 195,
  331, 332
swap files (paging files), 128, 129, **153-157**
switches. *See* jumpers/switches
system boards. *See* motherboards
system clock, CMOS battery and, **205-208**
system conflict, with hidden device, **384-386**
System Health Report, 329
System Properties box, 231, *231*. *See also*
  Device Manager
  Advanced tab, 126, 128, 155, 223
  Computer Name tab, 274, 275, 278
  General tab, 10, 61, 226, 362
  Hardware tab, 231, 374, 386
  Network Identification tab, 351, *351*
  System Restore tab, 121
system resources, freeing, 126
System Restore
  restore points and, **119-122**
  viruses/malware and, 85, 120
System Restore tab, 121

system sounds, disabling, 129
system:querying utility, 18, **143-146**

T

tabs
    Applications, 123, 124, 388
    on drive bay cover, 38
    Processes, 123, 124
    System Properties box
        Advanced tab, 126, 128, 155, 223
        Computer Name tab, 274, 275, 278
        General tab, 10, 61, 226, 362
        Hardware tab, 231, 374, 386
        Network Identification tab, 351, *351*
        System Restore tab, 121
tags, asset management, 224, 225
tape backup unit
    backup scheduling on, **323-325**
    tape replacement on, **320-323**
Task Manager, 123, 124, 388
TCP/IP, 249, 250, 255, 305
TechNet (http://technet.microsoft.com)
    Contig (http://technet.microsoft.com/en-us/
        sysinternals/bb897428.aspx), **184**
    DNS Server configuration (http://technet.
        microsoft.com/en-us/library/cc739630.
        aspx.), **276**
    driverquery (http://technet.microsoft.com/en-us/
        library/bb490896.aspx), **166**
    MLGPO (http://technet.microsoft.com/en-us/
        default.aspx.), **212**
    RootkitRevealer (http://technet.microsoft.com/
        en-us/sysinternals/bb897445.aspx), **318**
    Windows Server 2003 (http://technet.microsoft.
        com/en-us/windowsserver/bb430831.
        aspx), **209, 273**
Telephony service, 200
terminating
    processes, 124
    SCSI drives, 32, 33, 34
    SCSI scanner, 369, 370
testing
    CD drive installation, **40-41**
    CPU installation, **20-21**
    cross-over cables, **267-269**
    docking station, **70**
    DVD drive installation, **45**
    hard drive installation, **28**
    KVM installation, **73-74**
    network cables, **267-269**
    PCI card, **13**
    power supplies, **24, 148-153, 333**
    printer driver installation, **136**
    printers, **133-134**
    RAM, **9-10**

SCSI drive installation, **35**
straight-through cables, **267-269**
toner cartridges (test print), **218-219**
thermal compound, 18, 19, 20
third-party firewalls, 303, 304
three-in-one oil, 172
three-wire audio cable, 37, 39, 43, 44
thumb drives (USB), 313, 315, 400, 401
TIA/EIA 568A/568B standards, 261, 266
toner cartridges
    "align print cartridges" message, 132, **405-407**
    recycling, 219
    replacing, 131, **216-219**
    reseating, 406, 407
tracking work completion, on computers, **236-238**
Trojan horses, 313
troubleshooting
    access problems
        external USB hard drive, **400-401**
        scanner connection problem, **403-405**
        USB digital camera, **371-376**
    "align print cartridges" message, **405-407**
    audio CDs not recognized by optical drive,
        359-364
    digital camera connection, **371-376**
    Excel
        loading/printing problems, **356-359**
        lock up problems, **386-389**
    external USB hard drive access, **400-401**
    hidden device conflict, **384-386**
    intermittent boot failure, **334-337**
    monitor image problem, **389-392**
    network access problems
        network drives, **392-394**
        shared folder on remote computer, **394-397**
        single user connection problem, **397-399**
        691 network-connection error, **401-403**
    "new hardware found"/SCSI scanner,
        368-371
    Outlook contacts folder, **376-379**
    printing problems
        Excel/Word documents, **356-359**
        local printer, **340-344**
        network printer, **344-349**
    RAM upgrade failure, **337-340**
    scanners
        connection problem, **403-405**
        SCSI, **368-371**
        workaround scanning, **219-221**
    691 network-connection error, **401-403**
    "specified domain either does not exist or could
        not be contacted," **350-356**
    spontaneous reboots, **329-334**
    UPS service restart failure, **379-384**
    USB digital camera, **371-376**
    Vista, Reliability and Performance Monitor,
        328-329
tunnel, VPN, 292, 294

tweaking
    Windows 2000 Professional, **196-200**
    XP, **125-129**
twisted wires, 259, 260, 264, 265
Type Your Product Key for Activation screen,
    100, *100*

U

UAC (User Account Control), 307
UDP, 305. *See also* TCP/IP
uninstalling
    Microsoft Office, 359
    old video card, 52
    software, **103-105**
    video card drivers, **51-52**
unplugging
    /opening CRT monitor, **390**
    UPS, 384
updates
    BIOS, **200-205**
    Microsoft Office, 108
    Windows Update, 97, 108, 113, 114, 116, 135,
        157, 236
Upgrade Advisor (Windows XP), 112, 113, 114
upgrading. *See also* installing; replacing
    power supplies, 23
    RAM, failure in, **337-340**
    Windows 2000 to XP, **110-115**
        computer rollout and, **74-79**
    XP to Vista, **115-119**
UPS (uninterruptible power supply), **379-384**
    APC, 382
    service
        disabling, 199
        restart failure, **379-384**
    unplugging, 384
USB
    1.0 standard, 289
    2.0 standard, 289
    3.0 standard, 289
    bootable USB drive to flash BIOS, 201
    device, precoded drive letter and, 375
    digital camera, access problems and, **371-376**
    external hard drive, access problems and,
        400-401
    five-port adapter PCI card, **288-291**
    hub, problems and, **371-376**
    PCI cards *v.*, 10
    printer cables, 130, 131
    thumb drive, 313, 315, 400, 401
USB 2.0 five-port adapter PCI card, **288-291**
User Account Control (UAC), 307
user accounts
    Active Directory domain, **276-280**
    Vista, **212-213**
    XP, **285-287**
User Accounts box, 286, *286*, 287, *287*

V

vacuums, ESD, 4
Vanquish rootkit, 318
verifying RAM, 10, 191
video cards (graphics cards). *See also* AGP cards;
    PCIe graphics cards
    drivers
        installing, **53-54**
        uninstalling, **51-52**
    fans, 53
    installing, **50-54**
        PCIe x16, **186-189**
    integrated, 50, 187
    MSI GeForce 8400GS, 186
    onboard, 50, 187
    retention mechanism, 52
virtual machines
    defragmenting, **184-186**
    KVMs *v.*, 71
virtual memory
    customizing, **128-129**
    swap files and, 128, 129, **153-157**
Virtual Memory box, 155, *156*
virtual private networking. *See* VPN
viruses. *See also* AVG antivirus
    antivirus software, 85, 112, 116, 117, 118, 310,
        311, 312, 313, 314, 317, 318
    quarantines, 311, 312, 313, 314, 316, 317
    reformatting hard drive and, **85-88**
    scanning/removing, **310-313**
    System Restore and, 85, 120
Vista. *See* Windows Vista
VPN (virtual private networking), **292-296**
    IP address, 292, 295
    password, 295
    tunnel, 292, 294

W

wallpaper, disabling, **127-128**
WD-40, 172
web-browser hijackers, 313
Welcome Screen (XP), 95, *95*
Which Type of Installation Do You Want? screen,
    101, *101*
Who Will Use This Computer? screen, 96, 97
Wi-Fi, 137, 138
Wikipedia, 14
Win32 error code returned by the print processor,
    364, 365, 366, *366*
Windows 7, 98, 289
Windows 98, 52, 123, 222
Windows 2000 Professional
    "if it ain't broke, don't fix it," 37
    routine tasks and, 37, 206
    services in, **197-200**

speeding up, **196-200**
upgrading to XP, **110-115**
    computer rollout and, **74-79**
Windows 2000 Server, 180, 296, 297, 367
Windows Active Directory Domain. *See* Active
    Directory Domain
Windows Explorer, 119, 136, 166, 185, 204
Windows Fax and Scanning, 221
Windows Me, 52
Windows Photo Gallery, 221
Windows Server 2003, 209, 273, 276, 277, 297
Windows Server 2008, 209, 273, 277, 297
Windows Startup and Recovery, **222-223**
Windows Task Manager, 123, 124, 388
Windows Update, 97, 108, 113, 114, 116, 135,
    157, 236
Windows Vista
    Bluetooth device installation on, **137-139**
    defragmentation utility, **182-184**
    drivers, searching for, 36, **163-165**
    firewall
        log files, **306-308**
        outbound settings, **303-306**
    HCL, 115, 116
    installation (fresh install), **98-103**
    IP address assignment in, 253
    RAM and, 153
    ReadyBoost, 154
    Reliability and Performance Monitor, **328-329**
    scanning document, HP All-in-One device and,
        219-221
    691 network-connection error, **401-403**
    Startup and Recovery, **222-223**
    UAC, 307
    user account, creation of, **212-213**
    XP to Vista upgrade, **115-119**
Windows XP
    configuring, **95-97**
    drivers, listing, **165-166**
    firewall, 303
    Home edition, 89, 94, 96, 111, 115, 116,
        117, 293
    installation (fresh install), **89-97**
    IP address assignment in, 253
    Licensing Agreement, 91, *91*
    Recovery Console, 85, 86, 87, 88
    restore points, **119-122**
    Setup Window, 91, *91*, 92

Startup and Recovery, **222-223**
System Restore
    restore points and, **119-122**
    viruses/malware and, 85
tweaking, **125-129**
Upgrade Advisor, 112, 113, 114
user accounts, creation of, **285-287**
Welcome Screen, 95, *95*
Windows 2000 to XP upgrade, **110-115**
workstation rollout and, **74-79**
XP to Vista upgrade, **115-119**
wire stripper, 258, 260, 264
wireless network
    Bluetooth device, **137-139**
    PANs and, 137, 288
    Wi-Fi, 137, 138
wires
    front panel (computer case), **48-49**
    in network cables
        color-coded, 259, 260-261, 264, 265
        twisted, 259, 260, 264, 265
    three-wire audio cable, 37, 39, 43, 44
"wizard-like" framework, 108
Word (Microsoft Word)
    loading/opening problems and, **356-359**
    printing problems and, 134, 343, **356-359**
    read only setting and, 396
    shutting down, 122
work completion (computer), tracking, **236-238**
WORKGROUP, 94
workstation rollout, **74-79**. *See also* computers
worms, 313
wrist strap, ESD precautions and, **2-4**
wristwatch battery, 205

X

XP. *See* Windows XP

Z

zero insertion force (ZIF) sockets, 18
ZIF (zero insertion force) sockets, 18
zombies, 313, 317. *See also* malware
ZoneAlarm (firewall application), **304**

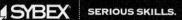

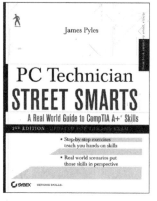